# Theorizing Power

*Also by Jonathan Hearn*
RETHINKING NATIONALISM: A CRITICAL INTRODUCTION
CLAIMING SCOTLAND: NATIONAL IDENTITY AND LIBERAL CULTURE

# Theorizing Power

## Jonathan Hearn

*Senior Lecturer in Sociology,*
*University of Edinburgh, UK*

First published 2012 by
PALGRAVE MACMILLAN
Palgrave Macmillan in the UK is an imprint of Macmillan Publishers Limited,
registered in England, company number 785998, of Houndmills, Basingstoke,
Hampshire RG21 6XS.
Palgrave Macmillan in the US is a division of St Martin's Press LLC,
175 Fifth Avenue, New York, NY 10010.

Palgrave Macmillan is the global academic imprint of the above companies
and has companies and representatives throughout the world.
Palgrave® and Macmillan® are registered trademarks in the United States,
the United Kingdom, Europe and other countries

ISBN: 978–0–230–24656–0 hardback
ISBN: 978–0–230–24657–7 paperback

This book is printed on paper suitable for recycling and made from fully
managed and sustained forest sources. Logging, pulping and manufacturing
processes are expected to conform to the environmental regulations of the
country of origin.

A catalogue record for this book is available from the British Library.
A catalog record for this book is available from the Library of Congress.

10   9   8   7   6   5   4   3   2   1
21  20  19  18  17  16  15  14  13  12

Printed and bound in Great Britain by
CPI Antony Rowe, Chippenham and Eastbourne

# Contents

*List of Figures and Tables*                                        viii
*Preface and Acknowledgements*                                       ix

PART I    CONCEPTUALIZING POWER                                       1

1  Introducing Key Issues                                             3
   Introduction                                                       3
   Physical versus social power                                       4
   Power 'to' versus power 'over'                                     6
   Asymmetrical versus balanced power                                 7
   Power as structures versus agents                                  9
   Actual versus potential power                                     13
   Conclusion                                                        15

2  Meet the Family – Domination, Authority and Legitimacy            18
   Introduction                                                      18
   The 'dominant' academic discourse on power                        18
   Bringing authority and legitimacy back in                         22
   Max Weber's complicated legacy                                    28
   Recapitulation                                                    30
   Power, modernity and ambivalence                                  32

PART II   THEORIZING POWER                                           37

3  European Sources                                                  41
   Introduction                                                      41
   Early modern harbingers: Machiavelli and Hobbes                   42
   Theorists of modernity: Marx, Durkheim and Weber                  48
   Return to Italy: classical elitism and Gramsci                    57
   Conclusion                                                        63

4  American Debates                                                  66
   Introduction                                                      66
   Power: community structures and national elites                   68
   The power of positive function                                    76
   Power hides its face                                              78
   Conclusion                                                        81

5  Epistemological Approaches                                                83
   Introduction                                                             83
   Barnes: self-fulfilling prophecies                                       86
   Foucault: power/knowledge                                                87
   Actor-networks, '*realrationalität*' and the ghost of Machiavelli        92
   Bourdieu: the practice of power                                          97
   On language and culture                                                 100
   Conclusion                                                             103

6  Evolutionary Approaches                                                 106
   Introduction                                                            106
   Energy, technology and evolution                                        107
   Two philosophic histories                                               114
   Modes, forms and sources of power                                       121
   Conclusion                                                             130

PART III  INVESTIGATING POWER                                             133

7  Domination, Authority and Legitimacy in Liberal Society                135
   Introduction                                                            135
   State, economy, and the 'memorable alliance'                            135
   Civil society                                                           139
   Public and private                                                      142
   Competition as legitimation                                             147
   Conclusion                                                             150

8  Religion and Morality                                                   152
   Introduction                                                            152
   Human limits and explanations of religion                               153
   Religion as reflecting the social constitution of power relations       156
   Religion as a medium of power struggles                                 159
   Meaning eclipses power                                                  163
   Power and morality                                                      166
   Conclusion                                                             170

9  Gender, Power and Patriarchy                                            172
   Introduction                                                            172
   Comparative perspectives                                                173
   Public, private and patriarchy                                          178
   Feminism and power                                                      185
   Conclusion                                                             189

10 Identity and Personhood                                                 190
   Introduction                                                            190
   Shifting discourses of power and social identity                        191

A problem of knowledge? 196
An ecological model of identity 200
Conclusion 207

**11 Conclusion: To and Over, Is and Ought** 209
Introduction 209
A useful concept 209
Stories about power 212
A qualified 'ought' 215

*Glossary* 218
*References* 226
*Index* 245

# List of Figures
# and Tables

*Figures*

| | | |
|---|---|---|
| II.1 | A genealogy of theories of power | 39 |
| 6.1 | Hall's model of history | 119 |
| 7.1 | Images of state, economy and citizenry | 136 |

*Tables*

| | | |
|---|---|---|
| 6.1 | Continua of organizational reach | 127 |
| 8.1 | Number of sovereign groups and presence of high god | 157 |

# Preface and Acknowledgements

This book offers a perspective on questions of power by critically surveying the literature on power, and exploring issues of power in relation to several themes. It emerges out of an accumulation of old and new intellectual debts. When I was an undergraduate and then a postgraduate studying anthropology in the late 1980s and early 1990s, power had become a 'hot topic'. Eric Wolf, one of my professors at the CUNY Graduate Center, was a leading figure in this trend, deeply influencing my thinking (he figures prominently in Chapter 6). In recent years I have taught an undergraduate course on theories of power, an experience that, thanks to the keen questions of students, compelled me to further clarify my own position on many points. With this book I turn, after long contemplation, to a topic that I regard as foundational to social science, and one that underlies all my other work.

Although trained as an anthropologist, I now work in sociology as a political and historical sociologist. This background is apparent in how I approach the subject, with a strong emphasis on historical and cultural analysis, and a conception of power as a pervasive aspect of social relations, both intimate and grand, not as something specifically located in political institutions. My approach is shamelessly generalist and synthetic. Whatever the hazards, I defend the necessity of such approaches that combine big theoretical questions with various forays into empirical detail. Too much social science these days operates only at the level of high-flown theory, or within a narrow empirical province. To keep the practice alive we must bring these together, however speculatively.

It may be helpful if I briefly outline how I view social inquiry in order to provide some context for how I approach the subject of power, and evaluate the approaches we will be exploring. I expand on three terms that summarize my position: *realism, naturalism* and *nominalism*. By *realism* I simply mean that I assume the existence of an objective reality beyond our experience, about which it is possible to have knowledge, however imperfect. Although there are some profound disagreements between people about the nature of that reality, nonetheless it is difficult to explain the considerable congruence in individual and cultural understandings of the world without some assumption of an objective reality binding human experiences together. Although we do live, to some degree, within the confines of our 'mental maps' of reality, these are not hermetically sealed or unchanging, and differences between various mental or cultural maps are nonetheless constrained by a fairly robust human-wide common sense about the objective world.

The term *naturalism* frequently refers to the position that social science should be modelled on the natural sciences. I have some sympathy for this view, but I would add that some natural sciences are closer to social science and more suitable as models. While 'hard' sciences such as physics and chemistry can offer some highly abstract research models, social science has much more in common with the life sciences and natural history. Human beings are rather different from atoms and molecules, but rather more like other animals in some respects, having a biological and organic existence that evolves over time. It is good not to forget that we are members of the animal kingdom. However there is another, contrasting sense of nature that should not get lost here. We talk about things having 'natures', that is certain qualities that are specific to them, and define them. We are distinguished from the rest of the natural world by our human nature. I would simply emphasize two obvious and interrelated aspects of being human. First, that we alone have language in the full sense of the capacity to generate highly abstract representations of the world through signs and symbols, in seemingly endless variations. And second, this capacity is linked to our extreme abilities to manipulate and transform the natural, physical world. We cocoon ourselves in artificial worlds of our own making, both mental and physical, like no other creature. Many have emphasized that this makes studying humans and their social relations unique, a separate enterprise from the other sciences. I agree only up to a point, and not to the point that I would reject the possibility of insight based precisely on situating ourselves within the wider natural world and its processes.

Finally, *nominalism* is a word with a long and complex philosophical history. I use it only to flag up the fact that language relates to reality in an often loose and inexact way. This follows on from what's already been said – nominalism in this sense implies realism. It is a call to be vigilant about the fact that the language and concepts through which we do social science, which must generalize and abstract from particulars, is ever prone to misrepresenting reality. This presents a bit of a paradox. On the one hand it implies that we need to constantly scrutinize and refine our conceptual tools, test them against the real world they are meant to describe and explain, and not complacently accept the conceptual paradigms we inherit, whether narrowly from social science traditions or more widely from culture and society. But on the other hand, the hazards of language also come in the form of novelty and innovation. Newness is no guarantee that a conceptual schema maps onto reality more effectively than an older one. I take the view that social science concepts are ultimately best evaluated by their enduring utility, by their continuing usefulness in handling and making sense of real world phenomena. I also think that language more generally is shaped by our day-to-day practical needs for apprehending reality, and encodes a great deal of practical collective wisdom about understanding reality. This means that I am more inclined to have confidence in social scientific language that does not stray too far from normal everyday usage. The novel ideas of a few scholars need to work hard to prove themselves against the experienced wisdom of the human crowd.

Hopefully this quick sketch of my perspective on doing social science, which for me is a broad term that includes more humanistic and interpretive approaches, will help the reader to understand where I'm coming from as they read this book. This is not to say that one must agree with me to benefit from reading it. Much good scholarship, and intellectual enjoyment, is to be had by engaging with those with whom we disagree, and figuring out why. Having said this, admitting my own perspective and biases, I have tried to be fair to those I discuss, and to write in a way that will be informative and at points provocative for any reader, no matter what their theoretical inclination. Moreover, particularly in the middle chapters (5 and 6), I have sought to bring together and compare strains of theorizing about social power that have tended to proceed at a distance from one another, in separate intellectual universes. Minimally, I think it is worth at least facilitating reflection and debate about why such divergence exists, and the comparability and relative merits of such divergent approaches.

The book comprises three main parts. The first part examines problems and debates in regard to the definition and conceptualization of power. The second part offers a long historical sketch of the western tradition of theorizing about power, from the early modern period to the present. The third part explores power more substantively under four thematic headings: liberal society, religion and morality, gender and patriarchy, and identity and personhood. I have provided a glossary at the end to help the reader keep track of the numerous terms and concepts that arise.

I began with debts and end with thanks. The general support of colleagues and administration at the University of Edinburgh, in the School of Social Political Science, and more particularly in Sociology, has been invaluable. The sabbatical that allowed me to concentrate on and complete the book would not have been possible without this support. Many students taking my Theories of Power course, and in other contexts, have pushed me to think harder about what I was saying. I thank them collectively. Mark Haugaard has been a congenial general interlocutor on questions of power over the past several years. In regard to the text itself, David McCrone generously read the whole manuscript, offering useful critical feedback that has improved it. The three anonymous reviewers for Palgrave gave many helpful suggestions, and although I have not felt able to follow all of these, those I have followed make real improvements to the text. Michael Rosie, Hugo Gorringe and Magnus Course pointed me to helpful sources. The ideas in Chapter 7 were originally developed in papers presented at the British Sociological Association's Annual Conference at Glasgow Caledonian University and the Conference on Nationalism and Legitimacy at Nancy-Université, France, both in 2010. I offer my thanks to the various commentators and event organizers. At Palgrave, my editor Anna Reeve has provided strong support and good advice, Esther Croom has kept the project moving, and Ann Edmondson has provided assiduous copy-editing. Of course all responsibility for any shortcomings in the book now before you lies with me. Finally, my wife, Gale Macleod, and children Iskra and Lovel, showed great patience, love and understanding as my thoughts kept wandering off into fields of power. In my first book I managed to include some pets in the acknowledgments. This time it's The Chilli Dogs, whose mutual musicianship on Thursday nights at the Royal Oak has been rejuvenating, and a steady reminder that there's a lot more to life than thinking.

The author and publishers wish to thank the following publishers for granting permission to reproduce copyright material: University of California Press for Figure 6.1, originally from *Powers and Liberties: The Causes and Consequences of the Rise of the West*, by John Hall (University of California Press, 1986); and University of Michigan Press for Table 8.1, originally from *The Birth of the Gods: The Origin of Primitive Beliefs* by Guy E. Swanson (The University of Michigan Press, 1960).
Every effort has been made to trace all the copyright holders, but if any have been inadvertently overlooked the publishers will be pleased to make the necessary arrangements at the first opportunity.

# PART I

# Conceptualizing Power

There is always a question of whether it is best to work from the concrete to the abstract, or *vice versa*. The first part of this book begins with the more abstract – with an exploration of basic concepts and debates around those concepts – for a few reasons. First, it seems unwise to engage a theoretical subject without some initial definition of terms to orient the reader. Moreover, because a basic contention of the book is that power is implicated in all aspects of social life, it would be difficult to decide where to begin in more concrete, substantive terms. I have anchored things at the outset in a set of overarching concepts. Having said this, I do try to illustrate various points as they are being made, and encourage the reader to actively supply their own illustrations of the conceptual points being discussed, as a way of fleshing out the abstract as we go along. Chapter 1 considers a series of key distinctions that recur in debates about power: between power as a physical versus social phenomenon; between power over others versus the power to do things; between power as asymmetrical versus balanced in its distribution; between power as a property of social structures versus agents; and between power as something that actually exists versus potential existence. In Chapter 2 we look at how a rather sprawling notion of power, in practice, often boils down to the more specified ideas of domination, authority and legitimacy, and argue for the enduring utility of these more specified concepts. The chapter concludes by suggesting that the modern era, with its values of individualism and autonomy amid mushrooming systemic social power, evinces deep ambivalences about power, and that these in turn have shaped the ways we theorize about power.

CHAPTER 1

# Introducing Key Issues

## Introduction

The philosopher Bertrand Russell once declared that 'the fundamental concept in social science is Power, in the same sense in which Energy is the fundamental concept in physics' (2004: 4). I agree with Russell on this basic point: power is not just one of the things that social scientists study, but the central thing. This book aims to convince the reader of that. This might appear to be a bold claim. We assume that fields such as politics or international relations are centrally concerned with power – but all social sciences? The argument is simple. The social sciences, understood broadly as having strong affinities with much of the humanities, seek to understand causation in human affairs. Almost all definitions of power fundamentally link it to the ability to have an effect on the world, to make a difference, to cause things to happen. (Russell called it simply 'the production of intended effects' (2004: 23).) If we are interested in why society develops in the way it does, if we want to have an effect on the direction of social change, then we are interested in the nature and scope of human power. This does not deny that some or even much of what happens occurs for causal reasons that are beyond human control. But our long history has been one of bringing more of the world, including each other, under our control – enhancing our causal capacities. Of course, 'the harder they come, the harder they fall'. The more we have control of, the more we have to lose control of, and the more we become aware of the limits of our powers. And while there are rich philosophical traditions of meditation on this paradox, and social experiments seeking to 'opt out' of the power-chase, these do not appear to be altering the general course of human history, or to be diverting the restless search for power. We find ourselves in a permanent situation of power-seeking, which we must address.

Some might object that this statement of the problem, emphasizing causation, reflects a preoccupation with 'explanation'. But, to the extent that we are concerned with 'understanding' our fellow human beings, sympathetically sharing in their experiences rather than accounting for their actions and behaviour, then the argument might be considered to lose force. I don't think so. It seems to me that all human experience is inextricably tied to feelings of power and control over one's life, which in turn are connected to actual circumstances. Power is not just an omnipresent condition of being, it is at the core of who and what we are, as a species and as individual persons. If our aim is a sympathetic understanding of others, then again, we must train our attention on questions of power. That which we cannot escape, we must embrace.

This chapter begins the book's discussion of power and our relationship to it with an exposition of the concept itself, in abstract, apart from its social context and the history of its development. I do this by exploring opposing, or at least contrasting, pairs of terms that have tended to define discussions of power and what it is. These are:

- Physical versus social power
- Power 'to' versus power 'over'
- Asymmetrical versus balanced power
- Power as structures versus agents
- Actual versus potential power.

This series of pairs provides a conceptual 'reference grid' to aid in situating and comparing the specific theories, ideas and arguments we will encounter as we go along. These explorations will be more complex and nuanced than these conceptual antinomies suggest at first. The point is not to be able to place arguments into categorical boxes, but to be able to relate the particular to more general recurring patterns in the discussion of power. As we move through these pairs in this chapter, the emphasis shifts from the problem of 'what do we mean by power?' to that of 'what do we have to bear in mind when studying power?'

Before proceeding, I make one more crucial point. In the eighteenth century the Scottish philosopher David Hume observed that causation is a somewhat mysterious idea. It is natural for us to understand the world as governed by causation, indeed, impossible not to. But causation itself is something that cannot be directly observed, only inferred by observing regularities in the relations between things and events. This leads us to misleadingly imagine some mysterious unified quality or substance called 'causation' that is out there, holding things together. But this is beyond what we can know. As it is with causation, so it is with power. Too easily, we slide from our observations about the specific patterns of human events and relations into a reified, omnibus notion of power (Hume 1978: 165–72). We have to perform a balancing act in which we recognize and look for the constant role of power in social life, while also being modest about our capacity to grasp it, about our power to know power.

## Physical versus social power

Russell's assertion on power as the fundamental concept in social sciences implies an analogy between power in the physical sense of stored energy that is released and transformed under the right conditions (oil burns, volcanoes erupt, lightning strikes) and the kind of power human beings deploy when they act on the world. The analogy is deep, ubiquitous, and sometimes more than an analogy. We do engage in contests of physical strength, whether it's boxers in the ring or firepower on the battlefield. And those who prevail don't just win the contest, but gain more enduring advantages – the boxer gains prestige and higher earnings, the nation-state through war gains territory, access to natural resources and the client-ship of the defeated state. However we commonly describe social encounters involving power, and those who appear to 'hold' power, by means of physical metaphors that facilitate talk, but can also mislead. We talk as though the ability of one person or group to get others to do what they want involves the application of some invisible force – 'she forced me to do it', 'they were held to account', 'the full weight of the law' and so on. While it's easy to become aware that these are metaphors, it is less easy to let go of the habits of thought that these metaphors encourage.

Some have seen this as a key problem in the conceptualization of social power. Bruno Latour has argued that we suffer from an image of power as force, diffusing through a series of physical bodies:

> When it is used as a cause to explain collective action, the notion of power is considered in terms of the diffusion model: what counts is the initial force of those who *have* power; this force is then transmitted in its entirety; finally, the medium through which power is exerted may diminish the power because of frictions and resistances (1986: 267, emphasis in original).

Latour sees this model as crude, and argues that we should instead use a model of 'translation', in which power travels and disperses through a sequence of relatively independent actions, as when a message is passed on through a series of linguistic translators. Latour's argument here owes a debt to Michel Foucault, who had previously argued that

> Power in the substantive sense, '*le*' *pouvoir*, doesn't exist ... The idea that there is either located at – or emanating from – a given point something which is 'power' seems to me to be based on a misguided analysis ... In reality power means relations, a more-or-less organized, hierarchical, coordinated cluster of relations (1980: 198).

These criticisms have force (note the word!). We need to be able to distinguish clearly between power in the physical sense of energy embedded in substances and power in the social sense of the coordination and mobilization of human feelings, thoughts and actions towards ends. The former involves an alternation between the fixing and releasing of potential for change, the latter involves a more constant readiness for action, and a system of relations in which messages affecting those actions can flow in multiple directions. At the same time, if we are too stringent in this distinction, we lose track of underlying connections, and miss something important. Although physical metaphors may misrepresent complex social processes by which we make decisions and direct our actions, often these are oriented towards the physical world and its embedded energies in highly consequential ways. Consider the ways in which nation-states compete to monopolize energy resources, especially oil and nuclear power, and to enable the highest possible levels of energy consumption (including calories) by their populations (Rosa *et al.* 1988). Current struggles between the most economically advanced countries of Europe and North America and rapidly developing economies, such as China, India and Brazil, over who should make sacrifices to reduce global energy consumption, and thus help counteract global warming, drive this point home. The wider context of these conflicts is the entire modern era in which industrialization and economic and military competition have meant the steady pursuit of ever greater energy capture from the natural environment, and ever more effective ways of harnessing and deploying that energy (Nolan and Lenski 2006: 187–212).

In short, our main concern in this book is with the social constitution of power, but we must appreciate that social power is perennially oriented to physical power. The analogies may be dubious, but the connections are real.

## Power 'to' versus power 'over'

This phrase conveniently sums up one of the most basic distinctions in the study of social power, between power as the capacity to realize ends, whether individually or collectively, and power as the control of one agent over others (Ball 1993; Morriss 2002: 32–5). In distinguishing physical from social power we were using it generally in the first sense, as 'power to'. However very often when people think of power, they first think of it in the second sense of 'power over', as what we often call 'domination' (see Chapter 2). This is because we tend to only notice something when it's a problem. We are generally happy to have the power to do things, and think this is as it should be. But 'power over' constantly raises the question, who should have power, and how much, over whom? 'Power over' easily leads to social conflict, and thus becomes the context in which we normally recognize and worry about the phenomenon.

Corresponding to this distinction we can identify two classical kinds of error in regard to our attitudes towards power: conservative and radical. The conservative tends to see whatever 'power to' there is at society's disposal as a premier achievement, as an affirmation of the given social order, and evidence that it is for the best and should be accepted. The radical tends to focus on 'power over', concentrating on its oppressiveness and injustice, and advocating its abolition or transcendence. Conservatives 'uphold authority', radicals 'fight the power'. The conservative downplays power's oppressiveness, the radical fantasizes about a world unsullied by power. Neither extreme is tenable.

In the spirit of the radical, one might want to argue, if it is only 'power over' that really troubles us, can't we simply limit our attention to this aspect, and let 'power to' take care of itself? The problem with this is not just that 'power to' can serve as a bulwark for conservative interests and, therefore, needs to be scrutinized. More deeply, it is that power to and power over are inextricably bound together. In the long train of human evolution, it is the increase in power over, in ever more extensive and complex forms of hierarchic social organization, which has yielded massive increases in our power to. Larger, more complex societies, mobilizing more complexly coordinated social action, and capturing greater proportions of resources, have tended to squeeze out the smaller, less hierarchic forms. Certainly complex systems can become too complicated and inflexible, and subject to collapse. But these failures have not abated the general trend. It is this 'sting in the tail' that makes social power such a difficult subject to grapple with – the part that we want, power to, comes hand in hand with the part that we despise, power over.

## Asymmetrical versus balanced power

The distinction between 'power to' and 'power over' sums up something fundamental about the human problematic of power, but it also glosses over a lot of essential detail. When we investigate actual social power, we find complex combinations of asymmetry and balance in the distribution of power (Kaufman *et al.* 2007; Polanyi 1957: 259–64). As Wrong has observed, some have tried to maintain that when power is equally distributed – is balanced – it disappears; that power to be such must be asymmetrical (Wrong 2002: 10). But this is unsustainable. Many a contest for supremacy plays out through a relative balance of contending powers, as accounts of stagnating trench warfare in the First World War gruesomely attest. Attempts to bring stability to societies that are 'deeply divided' by ethnicity and religion have generally sought workable ways of sharing power between mutually distrustful and competing groups (Smooha and Hanf 1992). More promisingly, the whole idea of 'checks and balances' that has informed modern democratic constitution-making, is premised on the idea of institutionalizing balances of power, between divisions of government (executive, legislature, judiciary), between political factions and parties in society, between the demos and its government. Democracies are highly imperfect, and also prone to imbalances as interests pursue power on an uneven playing field. But the point is that the concept of balance helps us understand how power does or does not work in these cases. The task of concrete description and analysis of power requires us to distinguish between relative symmetry and relative asymmetry, between balance and imbalance. The ability to make these distinctions is essential both for the social scientist trying to understand social causation, and the political actor making strategic decisions.

The error of thinking that power must, by its nature, be uneven is connected to the idea that power is like a zero-sum game, in which by definition, if one party wins, the other loses. This view was roundly critiqued by Talcott Parsons (1963), who argued that complex social systems can generate increasing levels of aggregate power as capacity (power to), even if power accrues to members of the system at differential rates. This may be unbalanced, and may lead to increasingly unbalanced distributions of power, but even so, a 'winner takes all' conception of power is of limited use in analyzing such complex social power dynamics. But the habit of thinking about power in zero-sum terms runs deep, and we should wonder why. It may be partly due to the physical metaphors discussed above, a tendency to see power as a unified and indivisible thing. But it may also be a result of living in the kind of society where power is routinely managed through social institutions that frequently have zero-sum effects. I have in mind two reasons. First, while there are many kinds of public and shared property, private property is a central device for allocating resources in capitalist societies, and basic to private ownership is the idea that the owner gains full control over the disposal of the property in question (barring infringements over the basic rights of others). It is very easy to think of power as being like a commodity that one gains or loses in its entirety. Second, capitalist societies rely heavily on rule-governed processes of competition – for resources, jobs, political office, places at university and so on. Frequently these are designed to have zero-sum outcomes – 'the other guy got the job', 'I didn't get the grant', 'the other couple outbid us for the house'. We manifestly experience power much of the time as a sequence of zero-sum contests, so it is not surprising that this becomes a folk metaphor for thinking about how power works.

All this is not to deny that very often in studying power we are interested in its asymmetries. Power is routinely concentrated in particular centre-points, whether persons, groups, agencies or organizations, and this raises questions about how these centres of power relate to that which they have power over. A classic and helpful orienting statement was provided by Bertrand de Jouvenel:

> Power or authority ... has three dimensions: it is *extensive* if the complying Bs [the power subjects] are many; it is *comprehensive* if the variety of actions to which A [the power holder] can move the Bs is considerable; finally it is *intensive* if the bidding of A can be pushed far without loss of compliance (quoted in Wrong 2002: 14, emphasis in original).

Attention to these three dimensions – extension, comprehension, intensity – will facilitate any initial mapping of power relations. Very roughly, there tends to be an inverse correlation between the first and the second two dimensions. A religious or political cult leader usually has a limited number of followers (extension), but may control many aspects of their behaviour (comprehension), and be able to move them to extreme, even self-threatening behaviour (intensity). A civil aviation authority may be able to ground planes, affecting a multitude of air travellers (extension), with little power over other decisions these people make (comprehension) nor capacity to do much more than prevent them from flying (intensity). Of course the modern stable state has the potential to score quite highly in all three dimensions, with sovereignty over vast populations, the capacity to regulate multiple dimensions of people's lives (employment, consumption, sexual reproduction, retirement) and even to compel people to kill in war, and forbid them to assist loved ones in suicide without penalties. But even here there are significant differences in comprehension and intensity (or at least efforts at these) between more liberal and more authoritarian states. We should also appreciate that states themselves are not monolithic, but rather complex ensembles of organized and institutionalized agencies, with varying scopes and capacities, sometimes working together and sometimes at odds with each other. And each state exists within an international arena of states with varying powers, and an array of para-state, non-governmental, and transnational bodies, all of which condition its powers to varying degrees (cf. Dahl 1968).

Ultimately, it is not an either/or question in regard to asymmetry and balance. What we normally encounter in social life, beginning with local social settings and all the way up to international relations, is a variegated multiplicity of centres of power, with their powers waxing and waning, in a web of relations with shifting combinations and alliances. Specific relationships may be characterizable as either asymmetrical or relatively balanced, but larger fields of power relations will involve relations of both kinds, to varying degrees.

## Power as structures versus agents

In recent decades there has been much discussion among social theorists about the 'problem' of 'structure versus agency' (Barnes 2003; Layder 2006; Sewell 1992). There have been far ranging debates about the degree to which we need to take into account 'social structures' versus 'agency' in our explanations of social processes. By 'structure' we normally mean relatively stable patterns of social relations, such as gender roles and the division of labour, and by 'agency' we mean the intentions and actions of individuals and groups in pursuing their goals. Some garden-variety examples of the problem: Do revolutions come about because of the strategies of revolutionary cadres, or the collapse of economic and class structures? Do people become 'criminals' because of poverty and lack of 'legitimate' opportunities for employment, or because of personal choices? Do I vote for a certain political party as a way of acting on my interests, or in conformity with my class position? Obviously, it's a bit of both. As a problem of explanation, it can be a bit arid, because both structural and agentic accounts can shed light on human events, and even when brought to bear on the same events need not come into conflict as explanations. At worst the problem is one of seeming possibly to have a surplus of adequate explanations (although 'adequacy' is extremely difficult to judge in regard to complex social processes). The reason we need to address it here is that raises not just a question of how we make explanations, but of how we conceptualize social power.

Let's take agency first. There have been attempts in recent years to argue that agency should be understood simply as any action by an element in a network of relations – a person, an organization, but more controversially, a computer, a microbe, a mathematical formula, a volcano – anything that can alter the course of events in a larger process (see Callon 1986; Clegg 1989). More narrowly, Giddens (1984) treats agency as human actions, but of any kind. For example, in speaking our actions serve to reproduce language, even though that general effect is not a part of our intentions in speaking. We will consider these approaches more closely in Chapter 5. Clearly they are at odds with common sense understandings of agency as the ability of people to do things on purpose, deliberately. And many theorists of power take intentionality to be basic to the definition of power. Wrong for example, following Russell, defines power as: 'the capacity of some persons to produce intended and foreseen affects on others' (2002: 2). Thus agency, including intention, is built into the concept. Others, wanting to treat power more as a general property of a system of social relations, while maintaining a link between intention and agency, regard agency as only an aspect of power. In very different ways, both Parsons (1963) and Lukes (2005) exemplify this view, the former emphasizing a society's general 'power to' achieve ends, the latter emphasizing the power, even unwitting, of some members of society 'over' others, by virtue of their position in a system of relations. Peter Morriss (2002) has intervened in the debate, arguing that we tend to confuse influence and power. Though there is a range of overlap in meanings, drawing on OED definitions, he observes 'that "power" always refers to a capacity to do things, whilst "influence" sometimes (and typically) does not' (2002: 12). 'To influence, then, is to affect in some hidden, unclear or unknown way' (2002: 11). Morriss drives this point home by looking at the difference between 'affect' and 'effect':

> The verbs 'affect' and 'effect' take very different objects: you can affect something if you can alter it in some way; you can 'effect' something if you accomplish it. Hence you can affect, but not effect, a person; and you can effect, but not affect, a state of affairs that does not now exist (2002: 30).

To be sure, those that have the power to effect, normally also have the influence to affect, but this doesn't work both ways. If a man walks into a bar, talking to himself in an agitated state, he may affect people, causing them to move to the opposite side of the room, but this is hardly an exercise of power, or a realization of intentions. This distinction doesn't resolve all debate, but it does tend to suggest that the capacity to have intended effects is closely tied to what we normally mean by power in everyday speech.

Accepting this for the sake of argument, there is the further question of what qualifies as 'an agent' with 'intentions'. We think first of individual persons, as the paradigm of willing and acting entities. But we also routinely talk about social groups and formal bodies as collectivities with the power to take decisions and act on them, and we normally understand this to mean that there is some sort of process, formal or informal, fair or unfair, by which a plurality of wills are aggregated, and the larger group or body acts 'as if it were one'. This is reasonable, but becomes more problematic, and needs to be treated more circumspectly as a model of will aggregation, as we increase in scale, and the method of agreement becomes more narrow, vague, and even non-existent. The Board of Directors may have reached a consensus on an issue, but the chances are that the employees of the corporation have had much less say in the matter. (Indeed, shareholders may have greater influence on decisions.) But the headlines will say 'Company X decides to...'. When Americans elect a new president, headlines may say 'Americans choose X as their new leader', when we know in fact many of them didn't, but instead, accepted the aggregate decision of the collectivity. With a modicum of sensitivity, we can keep a critical eye on the use of generalized 'agent-language', aware that it can both help to describe, and to obscure processes of power. In regard to the latter, we need to be particularly sensitive to the ways that, in the pursuit of power, smaller, more compact agents, individuals, political parties, corporations, media groups and so on, will discursively attribute a single will or intentions to large collectivities (Germans, women, Catholics, the middle class, consumers, the people, and so on) that have little means of actually formulating any collective agency. Genuine agency on a smaller scale tends to fade into putative agency on the grand social scale.

Turning to the term 'structure', there are again questions about what this covers. As suggested above, it generally refers to the macro-patterning of social relationships that allows us to describe how a society works in broad strokes. Thus in many traditional pre-industrial societies, social relations have been structured by elaborate images of kinship which guide the distribution of social roles and material resources. In more modern industrial and 'post-industrial' society, kinship structuring gives way to a complex of legal and economic institutions, such as constitutions, laws, markets and currencies, which tend to structure people into 'social classes' with varying life chances and prospects for social mobility. Structures can be both highly material, such as the actual distribution of land ownership in a given country, and highly ideational, such as a system of religious beliefs, or even common sense knowledge. And of course this opposition can be misleading: the ownership of land ultimately rests on people believing in and accepting a set of legal ideas, religious beliefs rest on a clergy with incomes and property-owning religious organizations. We can make analytic distinctions between various types of 'structures' in society – economic, political, cultural – but ultimately, causally, these blend into a complex whole that is not easily pulled apart. Nonetheless, used judiciously, the concept has utility, helping us to model large scale social processes.

Again, our question is, can structures have 'power'? If one person is born into intergenerational poverty and unemployment, and another inherits a trust fund and gets a world-class education, are they both equally subject to the power of the class structure they are born into? Does the latter have a kind of highly indirect power over the former? Or does it even make sense to try to locate power at this macro-level of analysis? (Don't be fooled by my micro illustrations!) If we accept a strong link between power and intention, then we will have reservations about attributing powers to social structures, which cannot have intentions. But we can deny that they 'have' power, while also believing that they 'have a lot to do' with power, in various ways. For example, the economy of the ancient Romans was based on the institution of slavery, which was a basic social structure for that society. Here the structure was constitutive of the power of one social group over another in a very explicit way: slave-owners intended to own slaves. Our hypothetical poor and rich persons in a modern society, find themselves, through accidents of birth, in relatively disadvantageous and advantageous positions in life, and this affects their power over their own lives, and potentially over each other should they come into a more direct relationship. The economic structures they find themselves in are like a battlefield, with better and worse situations on the terrain. And of course those with greater degrees of 'power to' at their disposal, such as the high-consuming citizens of the most advanced capitalist economies in relation to the working poor in less economically developed countries, are able, quite unconsciously, to have a malign influence on the working conditions of the poor. Many remain ignorant of that influence, where they could, in principle at least, become more aware and use their powers to change matters. They may have an interest in their own affluence, be disinclined toward knowing the wider effects of how they occupy their structural position, or may even be quite aware of all this, but feel impotent to change vast structural processes that work to their advantage (Hearn 2008: 47–8).

My point here is that our interest in social power begins with a concern for how we relate to one another, and our responsibility for, and ability to affect, those relations. Social structures shape and are shaped by our power relations, and thus are an important part of the analysis of social power. But the puzzle is precisely to better understand how our real, intentional powers add up to complex social structures over which we have limited control, and which appear to control us much of the time. To work on this puzzle we need to make clear distinctions between agents, whether individuals or collectivities, that have power and structures that affect the dispositions of our powers. I very much agree with Derek Layder (2006) on two points. First, we should resist the temptation to collapse agency and structure into one thing. The dichotomy is useful and does not need overcoming. However at the same time, in order to better model the reality we want to understand, we need to get away from the simple dualism of structures versus agents. As Layder says, our social world is experienced as 'layered' (2006: 271–301). We experience a paradigm of agency in our own persons, which can be 'geared up' by degrees, through participation in ever larger and more complex forms of social organization, into which we channel our wills, successfully or unsuccessfully. We make our way in life through myriad social structures which, at the most macro level, seem very abstract, but which are connected to other sub-structures, such as local government and laws, the ethos of the bureaucracy we work in and so on, that by degrees become less remote, and more susceptible to our powers, especially when these have been 'geared up' a bit. It is not a matter of agency on one side, pitted against structures on the other, but rather a complex interaction of agencies, working through, while at the same time creating, layers of structure. This is a better, more natural image, of the situation we find ourselves in.

## Actual versus potential power

Our discussions of asymmetry and balance and of structure and agency move us towards more methodological questions about how we translate these concepts into social processes we might actually investigate. Our last opposed pair – actual versus potential power – brings us to some fundamentally methodological questions that have stimulated much debate, particularly in the American academy in the 1950s and 1960s, as we will see in Chapter 4 (Wrong 2002: 6–10). The nub of these debates has been this: how do we know power is there when it's not being enacted? Social researchers, or members of a community, may claim that certain persons, groups and organizations hold power because of their wealth, control over means of force, occupation of strategic decision-making positions and so on, but unless we actually observe them using their power, and have a clear definition of what kind of outcomes in a social interaction warrant us in attributing power, then how can we really know if they do have power? In its more extreme, 'behaviouralist' forms this worry has led some researchers to try to define power narrowly as the overt manifestation of power (for example prevailing in a legislative vote, or getting a union to back down on its threat to strike), treating the less observable idea of 'having power' with great distrust (see Dahl 1968; Polsby 1963). If we allow power to be 'in the eye of the beholder', then we may end up learning more about the beholder's view of the world, than about power itself. But this attempt at accuracy can fly in the face of what we actually know. It is an imprudent person that doesn't take into account the potential actions of the powerful, that doesn't look for other signs of power besides just the immediate demonstration of its exercise. Moreover, the actualization of power, especially as a repeating tendency, implies some underlying potential embodied in some entity, which is probabilistically realized under certain conditions. Here, perhaps surprisingly, the physical analogies for power with which we began are more apt. Water has the capacity to corrode iron, that is an aspect of what it is. Successful democratic politicians have the power to win elections, that is what it takes to be one.

Once again Morriss (2002: 14–19) offers helpful clarification, identifying what he calls the 'vehicle fallacy' and the 'exercise fallacy'. The vehicle fallacy is the mistaken idea that if we say someone has power, we must mean that they have some distinct property – powerfulness – that specifically enables them to prevail in a contest of power. A variant on this is the idea that power can ultimately be reduced to some key resource – wealth, weapons, knowledge – that the powerful possess. In either case, the resource or the abstracted property of powerfulness operates as the carrier or 'vehicle' of power that accounts for its presence. This error tries to turn a tendency in events into a substance or a thing. The exercise fallacy is in many ways an attempt to avoid the vehicle fallacy. Here the claim is 'that the power to do something is nothing more than the doing of it: that talking of your *having* power is simply a metaphysically illegitimate way of saying you are *exercising* that power' (*Ibid.*: 15, emphasis in original). Warming to his prey, Morris goes on:

> It is, of course, true that one cannot tell whether an actor is powerful unless *some* set of observations 'attests to' his power. But there is no reason whatsoever why these observations should be of the actualization of that power. When I go to a zoo, I can see that a lion is powerful enough to eat me up by observing its jaws, teeth and muscles, and combining these observations with my general knowledge of animals' masticatory performances. If I am still in doubt, I can observe what the lion does to a hunk of meat, and induce. Not even the most dogmatic positivist would declare that he couldn't know if the lion could eat him up until it had actually done so (*Ibid.*: 16, emphasis in original).

The problem here in Morriss' view, and I agree, is a failure to appreciate that power is a 'dispositional concept', meaning that it refers to a 'relatively enduring capacity of an object' (*Ibid.*: 14), not an event or an episode. With social power, the objects are normally persons, groups, organizations and so on. This view entails that we attribute some 'unseen' but ongoing capacity to the powerful, but this is simply a recognition of the tendencies and regularities in our observations and experiences, not the invention of a mysterious property housed inside the powerful. (Remember Hume's warnings about causation.) This point also indicates that 'power to' (capacity, ability) is, conceptually at least, more fundamental than 'power over'. The former is a precondition for the latter, the latter a possible, perhaps probable, manifestation of the former. Finally, because power is located in 'objects' and can be socially distributed, much like health or a good sense of humour, we normally talk about people 'having' it (but rather more like these than say, blood types, it is something that waxes and wanes, can be gained or lost). This easily leads to the confusion that we can 'have it' in the same way as we have portable possessions, as an object that can be transferred. This linguistic slippage is part of what leads to the problems of confusing physical metaphors discussed above. While one with power can invest it in others, this is not really the transference of a property, but more a matter of making more complex and extending the scope of the object with the capacity, by bringing others into a relationship of power over. I give Morriss the last word on this subject:

> Whilst it is possible to devise a vocabulary which does not contain dispositional concepts, it would be a very impoverished one ... For if we ignore its dispositional properties, the world must appear just a buzzing, bewildering confusion of haphazard events: indeed it is unlikely that anybody could view the world in that way for very long without going mad (2002: 17).

## Conclusion

The idea of power explored above and in the rest of this book is unavoidably embedded in a particular tradition of thought, in 'western culture' broadly understood, and grasped through the English language in particular. We should acknowledge at the outset that power, or its closest cognate, might be understood quite differently from other cultural and linguistic vantage points. In a fascinating essay Benedict Anderson (1990: 17–77) has argued that power is conceived very differently in traditional Javanese culture as compared with the western Anglophone tradition. He sees the western concept as presenting power as an abstract idea, as something that can have heterogeneous sources (wealth, status, means of force and so on), as unlimited in its potential for growth and accumulation, and as something morally ambiguous and in need of legitimation. By contrast, the Javanese concept of power is of something very concrete, tangible and present, a single homogenous thing with a common source, of which there is a limited quantity in the universe, and which stands outside of questions of legitimacy. It just is. It may be that this contrast between Java and 'the West' is standing in for a more general contrast between more 'traditional' and more 'modern' conceptions of power. Be that as it may, just this small glimpse should remind us that we inevitably begin from within a particular stream of meanings and understandings.

But lest we take this to imply that people are trapped in various cultural universes of understanding, we need to also remind ourselves of the unstable and evolving nature of culture. Olivia Smith (1984) offers a striking illustration of this point in her study of the politics of language in Britain between 1791 and 1819. She shows how, through their innovative, educational and populist use of written and spoken language in politicized contexts, figures such as Thomas Paine, William Hone and William Cobbett disrupted conventional distinctions between the 'proper' use of language by the elite and the 'vulgar' use of language by the common people. Such distinctions had served to demarcate a cultural boundary between those who were qualified to participate in public political life and those who, because of their linguistic incompetence, were not. In effect, by challenging linguistic norms, these figures were altering British culture from within, and creating the conditions for greater entry into the political process by the masses. So, we should be aware of the cultural embedding of our ideas, but also alert to the open-endedness of culture.

Dennis Wrong once began an essay by recounting a famous scene:

> Gertrude Stein, bed-ridden with a fatal illness, is reported to have suddenly muttered, 'What, then, is the answer?' Pausing, she raised her head, murmured, 'But what is the question?' and died. Miss Stein presumably was pondering the ultimate meaning of human life, but her brief final soliloquy has a broader and humbler relevance. Its point is that answers are meaningless apart from questions. If we forget the questions, even while remembering the answers, our knowledge of them will subtly deteriorate, becoming rigid, formal, and catechistic, as the sense of indeterminacy, of rival possibilities, implied by the very putting of a question is lost (1961: 183).

What is our question? There are at least two: How do we want to define power? and, perhaps more subtly, What should our attitude towards power be?

I am sympathetic to the definition by Wrong that we have already encountered – power is 'the capacity of some persons to achieve intended and foreseen effects on others' – although I would want to stress that these relations between persons are normally acted out through various organizational forms that exhibit degrees of agency, that we needn't reduce matters to interpersonal relations in order to talk sensibly about power. Thus I might prefer something more like: the capacity of some agents (broadly defined) to achieve intended and foreseen effects on other agents and the world more generally.

In this chapter I have argued that power is a social process, but one that seizes upon the physical world, which in turn can provide analogies that are both useful and misleading for understanding social power. Power involves a complex dialectic of the power to do things, and the power of some people over others. Like it or not, these tend to increase in tandem. The distribution of power is never perfectly asymmetrical nor perfectly balanced, but these terms are useful for the description and analysis of power processes. The distinction between agents and structures is also useful for studying power: it's sensible to talk about agents 'having' power and intentions, and structures shaping, and being shaped by, power. But dichotomous talk can be misleading. Agency and structure are mediated by myriad intervening layers and forms of social organization. Finally, power is a dispositional concept, which means that it is used to characterize tendencies in the relationships between social entities, and should not be construed either solely as observable events, or as some substance or quality found in the powerful.

As for attitude, I have already implied that we need to look for a middle path, between the complacency of the conservative, and the utopianism of the radical. The view espoused here is largely reformist, believing that we find ourselves amid power relations that cannot be transcended altogether, but that can be usefully criticized and changed. I will leave a further discussion of what this might entail to the concluding chapter. But I will reiterate, before we go on, that we must resist the temptation to reduce power to its unappealing forms of 'power over', and always appreciate the indissoluble connection between 'power over' and 'power to.' I will be arguing that this constant temptation towards reduction is not just a conceptual mistake, but a fundamental symptom of modernity and an impediment to understanding our present situation.

# CHAPTER 2

# Meet the Family – Domination, Authority and Legitimacy

## Introduction

In Chapter 1 we outlined some of the main dimensions of the concept of power that bear on how people understand it and help differentiate theories about it. Here we take three terms – domination, authority and legitimacy – that have been central to discussions of power, articulating their differences and relationships to one another. The word 'power' is frequently invoked but, as we have already seen, is extremely broad in its scope, connotations and usages. Ideas of domination, authority and legitimacy operate closer to the ground and, taken together, capture much of what concerns us about power more generally. Much of the time research on power is really concerned with these more specific modes of power, and I argue that we can get more analytic purchase with this more diversified conceptual 'tool kit' than we can with all-embracing applications of the term 'power'. However, in contrast to this assertion, much influential social theory in recent decades has worked with an expansive concept of power, construed mainly as a process of domination, with authority and legitimacy falling by the wayside. This chapter explores each of these concepts, and makes the case for why we need to bring these concepts back into balance with one another. The domination-authority-legitimacy tool kit is part of the intellectual legacy of Max Weber, and we will examine his somewhat idiosyncratic use of these terms and the puzzles that have arisen out of those usages for later theory. This chapter is also the beginning of an argument that runs through the whole book: that the tendency toward monolithic, domination-oriented conceptions of power in recent social theory is symptomatic of a profound ambivalence about power in modern liberal society, which has trouble articulating positive conceptions of power and principled arguments for authority and legitimacy. I develop this wider point at the end of the chapter.

## The 'dominant' academic discourse on power

The word 'power' is fashionable in academia these days, and has been for some time. It turns up ubiquitously in the titles of books and articles, even when these are not directly concerned with the theorization or conceptualization of power. This is partly because just about any topic involves issues of human power relations. But it is also a matter of discursive trends. What in the past might have been presented by linking it to catch-all rubrics such as 'social order', 'social change' or 'conformity and conflict' today, gets linked to 'power'. It is a wonderful, magical, engrossing word that opens up vistas of possibility – a term that covers everything.

Consider a somewhat random sample of titles from my university's catalogue:

- Power and economic change: the response to emancipation in Jamaica and British Guiana 1840–1865. McLewin, Philip J. (1987)
- Power and eros: crossdressing in dramatic representation and theatrical practice. Howard, Jean E. (2001)
- Power and eroticism in Imperial Rome. Vout, Caroline (2007)
- Power and everyday life: the lives of working women in nineteenth-century Brazil. Dias, Maria Odila Leite da Silva (1995)
- Power and faction in Louis XIV's France. Mettam, Roger (1988)
- Power and global sport: zones of prestige, emulation and resistance. Maguire, Joseph A. (2005)
- Power and glory: Jacobean England and the making of the King James Bible. Nicolson, Adam (2003)
- Power and human destiny. Rosinski, Herbert (1965)
- Power and identity in the global church: six contemporary cases. (2009)
- Power and identity in the Middle Ages: essays in memory of Rees Davies. (2007)
- Power and ideology in American sport: a critical perspective. Sage, George H. (1998)

These appear in series when simply searching for 'power' in the title (I have omitted four religious pamphlets from the seventeenth and eighteenth centuries). I am not objecting to the titles, simply illustrating the elastic nature of the term, which is applicable to almost any topic. Only Rosinski's *Power and Human Destiny* represents a general theory of power as opposed to a subject-specific invocation of the idea. It is also the only entry that predates the late 1980s, further suggesting the recent popularity of the term. So why is this? I think it is partly down to the influence of key social theorists, who have made 'power' a term of choice for the social sciences and humanities. But it is power understood in a particular way, through one of its aspects – domination – that has been the real star of the show. I will define the concept of domination generally, before trying to illustrate what I mean by a domination-centric understanding of power, focusing briefly on the three exemplary figures of Michel Foucault, Pierre Bourdieu, and Steven Lukes. Each of these theorists will be considered more closely in their historical context in later chapters.

As I've put it elsewhere:

> When we talk about 'power', often what we mean more specifically is domination. *Domination* refers to a situation where an agent exercises relatively stable, ongoing control over the actions of other agents ('agents' taken broadly to mean anything from individual persons, to social groups, to organizations and institutions). Domination is not episodic. Relations of domination are, by definition, firmly established, and often naturalized and taken for granted (Hearn 2011a: 203).

In the previous chapter I argued that power is best understood in its most fundamental sense, as 'the enduring capacity of an object' normally indicated by agency and the realization of intentions. Domination is not a capacity but a kind of relationship between those with more and less power. Relationships cannot have intentions. For those who tend to equate the concept of power to that of domination, this will make the assertion that intention is central to power (to) unpalatable, because manifestly we can identify relations of domination where the role of intention is only episodic and diffuse (cf. Lukes and Haglund 2005). I would argue that this is a reason for making a clear distinction between 'power to' and domination (mindful that 'power over' sits as a kind of intermediate concept between the two).

We will have frequent occasion to think about domination later in this book when exploring themes of state, economy, religion, gender and interpersonal relations. But first, let's discuss our three key theorists.

Michel Foucault (1926–1984) tended to assimilate concepts of power, knowledge and truth to one another. As he put it in an oft-cited lecture: 'We are subjected to the production of truth through power and we cannot exercise power except through the production of truth' (1980: 93). He argued that our very subjectivity, our sense of having an inner self that we can 'know', is an historical creation, shaped by wider societal patterns of the production of power and truth. For him the modern period was particularly characterized by the rise of institutions and practices (for example criminology, medicine, psychiatry) that make enforceable claims to superior knowledge, to truth, thereby compelling subjects to participate in self-understandings (such as being deviant or ill) suited to their domination by these institutions and practices.

Pierre Bourdieu (1930–2002) was particularly concerned to show that class domination is not just a matter of instrumental economic power, but of the shaping of knowledge, experience and understanding of class relations in such a way that these become natural and common sense for all concerned. Thus for him, '[t]he theory of knowledge is a dimension of political theory because the specifically symbolic power to impose the principles of the construction of reality – in particular, social reality – is a major dimension of political power' (Bourdieu 1994: 161). On this basis he formulated and used concepts such as '*doxa*', those areas of shared knowledge that are taken for granted and uncontested, and '*habitus*', the internalization of power-defined social roles through sensibilities, aesthetic preferences and bodily deportment. Both these ideas served as key analytical tools in his work.

Steven Lukes (b. 1941), in a celebrated critique of political analysis, asserted that: 'A exercises power over B, when A affects B in a manner contrary to B's interests' (1974: 27). Moreover, he argued that power is most effective for A when it operates 'behind the back' of B, when B's true interests have been obscured or distorted. Against contemporaries that preferred to treat power as the public process of settling manifest conflicts of interest (Dahl 1961; Polsby 1963), he presented power as also, and more importantly, a matter of how and why conflicts of interest remain latent and unarticulated, and how the very desires, preferences and motives of the less powerful get formed in the first instance to suit the interests of the dominant. He characterized his approach as a search for an often hidden, 'third dimension' of power, lying behind more public processes of decision-making ('first dimension') and political agenda-setting ('second dimension').

Revisiting this argument thirty years later, Lukes concedes that the term 'power' had been too broad, and that he was really concerned with domination (2005: 12). Like Lukes, Foucault and Bourdieu tended to talk broadly about power, when in fact domination was their central concern. Of course they all used both terms, but often as if they were synonymous. But even their take on domination is rather skewed. Our general definition above does not imply that domination is necessarily beyond the awareness of those dominated. Slaves, prisoners and illegal immigrants all experience the ongoing control of their actions by others, in ways that are quite explicit. And less extreme forms of domination, of parents over children, employers over employees, men over women, are often quite obvious to those involved. But it is as if with this intense focus on 'hidden' forms of domination, more 'apparent' forms of domination fall from view. Yet these may be as illuminating and worthy of research as the more cryptic processes of power. How people understand their own domination may be as important as how they are fooled by it.

There is a further problem. We are frequently subject to the control, not of dominant agents, but of society itself. Some of the regulation of our ideas, feelings and behaviour emerges systemically through the inculcation of various social norms, which are an unavoidable aspect of society. Should we call this 'domination' if there is no identifiable dominating agent apart from society in general? If we observe a taboo on incest, is this evidence that we are being dominated, or just well adjusted? This would seem to stretch the term beyond its utility. Society is indeed full of relations of domination, which we need to understand and be able to critique, but part of doing this involves being able to discern where domination ends, or at least shades into other forms of social control.

Finally, it is important to note, that these three theorists primarily have in mind how power works in modern, western, capitalist, liberal-democratic contexts. Although they range beyond this in the cases they consider, the ultimate purpose is to understand the occult operations of power relations in 'our' kind of society. Their writings, in varying ways that we will explore more closely later on, give a strong sense that there is something peculiarly obscure about the workings of power that we are subject to, that the core social problem is to somehow reveal these workings to us. Theirs are not just theories of power, but ultimately theories of modern power.

The work of these theorists has been highly influential, insightful and provocative for the study of power. I am not questioning the worth of their work, but rather trying to place it in context, and identify limitations. For large portions of academic practice, this understanding of power as cryptic domination has itself become a kind of 'truth', or '*doxa*', which in turn marginalizes other dimensions of power that need to be addressed. On that note, I turn now to domination's siblings – authority and legitimacy – who have been standing a bit behind, out of the limelight.

## Bringing authority and legitimacy back in

These siblings are also twins of a sort. They have a very close, mutually defining relationship because authority is normally understood as power that enjoys legitimacy, and legitimacy as a way of regarding authority. Acknowledging this conceptual interdependence, let us take them in turn.

The definitions of authority and legitimacy provided by the *Oxford Dictionaries Online* are a good starting point, showing both the usual specificity and spread of these terms:

**Authority...**
1 ...the power or right to give orders, make decisions, and enforce obedience...
  • ...the right to act in a specified way, delegated from one person or organization to another...
  • official permission; sanction...
2 (often **authorities**) a person or organization having political or administrative power and control...
3 ...the power to influence others, especially because of one's commanding manner or one's recognized knowledge about something...
  • the confidence resulting from personal expertise
  • ...a person with extensive or specialized knowledge about a subject; an expert...
  • ...a book or other source able to supply reliable information or evidence... (*Oxford Dictionaries Online* 2011a, entry 'authority').

**Legitimate**
1 conforming to the law or to rules...
  • (of a child) born of parents lawfully married to each other.
  • (of a sovereign) having a title based on strict hereditary right.
2 able to be defended with logic or justification; valid... (*Oxford Dictionaries Online* 2011c, entry 'legitimate').

Authority is not just any power, but more specifically the power to make commands and have them obeyed. It implies a communicative relationship, however broadly defined, between the givers and receivers of orders. The source of commands can be a person or an organization, or often a person or group of people in an organization ('the head', 'the committee', 'the board'). And as we know, organizations vary, from the tiny to the vast, from small businesses to states. Some persons and organizations have only authority, others have means of inducement, coercion and force waiting in the wings, casting a shadow over their authority. Just as it is manifested through communication, authority can be, figuratively at least, off-loaded onto the vehicles of communication or texts, classically books and law codes. But for a text to be authoritative, that authority needs to be traceable back to original issuers of commands, to a team of lexicographers, to legislators, to a prophet or a god.

Contained in these definitions of authority are words that point to the question of legitimacy – 'right', 'official', 'recognized' – all of which imply some wider social sanctioning of authority's power. Authority cannot be entirely self-constituting. Without a degree of acknowledgment and acceptance from those receiving and following commands, it cannot exist. Authority needs legitimacy.

The key term for social science is 'legitimacy' but in just about any dictionary this word will simply be defined indirectly as 'the quality or fact of being legitimate'. Similarly, 'legitimation' is simply defined as the 'act of making something legitimate'. (As I write this, my authoritative spell-checker underlines the word 'legitimation' in red!) Right away this gives us clues about a divergence between social scientific and standard usage. In everyday life people are more often concerned with whether or not something is legitimate than with whether it partakes of some more general quality of legitimacy or reflects some process of legitimation. So let us accept this and begin with 'legitimate'. Something is legitimate if it is arrived at in accordance with rules, or at least can be justified according to accepted principles of reasoning. In regard to authority, there is a two-way street. Actions carried out in defiance of authority, at variance with authority's commands, may be illegitimate. However, authority itself is also rule-bound, in need of justification, and potentially can lose its legitimacy. The commands themselves must be legitimate. The definitions quoted above, somewhat archaically, also offer a glaring reminder of central concerns with hereditary claims, to parentage and offices. Legitimacy matters because it affects our claims to valued goods that might be inherited. In current usage, especially in its social scientific guise, there has been a shift in emphasis from 'can x lay claim to y' to 'can x rule over y', from 'is the claim legitimate' to 'does rulership have legitimacy'.

Notions of authority and legitimacy have evolved together, and together they frame much of what we pragmatically want to know about power. If one believes that the true processes of power are largely hidden, as in the conception of domination outlined above, then this will tend to suggest that authority and legitimacy are illusory, just window dressing behind which lies the uncomfortable truth. Then the real task becomes avoiding the deceptions of authority and legitimacy, and revealing the reality of domination. But there is something about this view that is at odds with experience. Because when we survey the myriad power struggles that compose human history, rarely, if ever, do they play out in terms of hidden power relations being exposed, leading straight to social transformation. Rather, the process of changes in power relations normally takes the form of challenges to authority and legitimacy (they can only be challenged together). Major social change usually arises out of changing judgments about existing patterns of authority and legitimacy, not out of the recognition of previously unrecognized domination.

Consider four brief examples:

1   The American Revolution happened partly because the outcome of the French and Indian Wars (a.k.a. the Seven Years War) removed the threat of French territorial claims on North America, thereby making the British colonists less dependent on the protection of Great Britain. This in effect provided the opportunity. But the actual revolution, with all its ideological fervour (Bailyn 1992), arose out of conflict between the colonists and the British parliament over the extent and legitimacy of the latter's authority in the colonies (Hearn 2009a), famously over issues of taxation to pay for the recent war. And as the conflict reached a peak, the colonists' challenge to the regime's legitimacy spread from the British government and governing classes (viewed as a rather effete lot of aristocrats), to the King himself and his fair governance, and thus the Declaration of Independence is written as a set of grievances against George III, resolvable only through separation.

2   The US civil rights movements of the 1950s–1970s began with growing mobilization by African-Americans to oppose racism, to end racial discrimination in housing, employment, education and policing, and to remove obstacles to full voting rights and political participation. The movement used a combination of civil disobedience, legal challenges, legislative pressure, and public demonstration and debate to advance its cause. In the long run, the movement made substantial achievements in all these areas, even if the goal of racial and ethnic equality is still unrealized. It also provided a model for similar challenges to the political status quo by other excluded groups such as Chicanas/Chicanos, Native Americans, women, and lesbians and gays. And the model in many ways spread beyond the US, or at least resonated with similar struggles coming to a head in the late 1960s, most notably in Northern Ireland among the Catholic community, but also in what were often student-led movements in Quebec, Mexico, Germany, France and Czechoslovakia. The US civil rights movement, acutely in the case of African-Americans, was spurred by the manifest contradictions between a society and political system that claimed to be founded on principles of equality, fairness and opportunity, while systematically denying these to various populations. These contradictions tended to weaken the authority of government and other major social institutions.

3  In recent years the UK has been marked by significant political change in the form of devolution, creating a parliament for Scotland and assemblies for Wales and Northern Ireland. The greatest devolution of powers, to the Scottish Parliament in 1999, arose out of growing pressure for more self-determination in Scotland from the 1960s, but growing in intensity, and expanding in terms of a Scottish consensus, from about 1980. Central to this shift was the severe decline in the perception of the legitimacy of the UK government, when it was captured by a Conservative Party whose support in Labour-dominated Scotland was small and declining. Thus the Conservative Party (admittedly contentiously) was often construed as ruling in Scotland without a proper democratic mandate. The political mathematics were exacerbated by matters of policy, the Thatcher and Major governments aggressively advancing neoliberal and deindustrializing policies that appeared to weaken the Scottish economy and contradict prevalent, somewhat more social democratic, views in Scotland. In order to shore up authority and legitimacy in the political system, it became necessary to redistribute these to devolved bodies, and promising to do this was part of the Labour Party's strategy for its return to government in 1997 (Hearn 2000).

4  This book is being written in the wake of the global banking and credit crisis of 2008–2009, which left the world economy in a weakened state and its various paths to recovery still uncertain at the time of writing. In the heartlands of the financial crisis, the US and the UK, a major effect of these events was to place the authority and legitimacy of bankers and the banking regimes in which they operate more fully into public view, and to make them objects of interrogation. The agenda for discussion includes the justifiability of large bonuses for bankers, the adequacy of light touch (often self-) regulation of banking practices and the wisdom of having fewer, large complex banks as opposed to more smaller, specialized banks. More generally, doubt has been cast over the authority and competence of a whole body of economic theory that supported and did not adequately question an overextended system of sub-prime mortgage lending. In a more populist mode, public figures such as Fred Goodwin, the former head of the Royal Bank of Scotland, and Bernie Madoff, the Wall Street investor who ran an elaborate 'ponzie scheme' under the cover of widespread investment-based prosperity, provide a human face of disreputability, an object for public anger. Given the enormous reliance of these two economies on the powers of their financial sectors, in the end there may be limits to calls from government and the public for reform of practices. But the naturalized authority of the market and economic experts has been shaken, forcing the role of public authority in controlling private economic activity onto the agenda.

In all these examples, there are real limits to what analytic purchase on events will be yielded by conceptions of cryptic domination. It is studying the dynamics of authority and legitimacy that most helps to explain the course of events. Admittedly, in each case there is a movement of issues onto the agenda, a politicization of what was formerly normally taken for granted. But this movement is triggered by troubles and conflicts that develop around existing patterns of authority and legitimation that are commonly recognized as such. If one wants to have an effect on the world, one must consider what is centrally at stake when social and political changes do happen, and the answer is – authority and legitimacy.

Before going further, let us consider some interesting and counter-intuitive discussions of authority and legitimacy from the literature on power, to further sharpen our understanding of these terms.

Talcott Parsons (2002[1963]) defined power as the

> generalized capacity to secure the performance of binding obligations by units in a system of collective organization when the obligations are legitimized with reference to their bearing on collective goals and where in case of recalcitrance there is a presumption of enforcement by negative situational sanctions – whatever the actual agency of that enforcement (2002: 78).

In other words (often helpful in the case of Parsons), authority and legitimacy are hard-wired into Parsons' very conception of social power. Although he allows that force and coercion ('negative situational sanctions') may provide insurance for the smooth running of the system, he is quite explicit that power itself is constituted through the acceptance of authority by those subject to it. This conception rests on an elaborate double analogy between money and power, and property and authority. For Parsons, just as money represents the abstraction of specific values into a generalized, exchangeable value, power represents the abstraction of concrete capacities 'to get things done' into a generalized, collective capacity. Correspondingly, just as property is constituted by shared recognitions of bundles of rights in 'things' of value (even ideas), including the capacity to 'alienate' (that is, give or trade away) those rights, so authority arises out of our mutual willingness to alienate our power over things and invest these in a collectively constituted hierarchy of legitimate authorities. Just as money makes no sense apart from there being diverse forms of property, the generalized exchange of which it serves to facilitate, so power only makes sense to Parsons as the by-product of pooling authority. And just as stable money greatly enhances the dynamism and capacity for wealth creation in an economy, so power, in Parsons' sense of symbolically constituted, overarching authority, greatly increases the systemic capacity 'to get things done'. Thus, where we often think of power as ultimate force that lies behind authority, as its true underwriter, for Parsons, power is the effect of authority that has been collectivized and maximized. For him, society as such is almost unimaginable apart from an overarching system of legitimate authority that regulates behaviour.

In an intriguing and mischievous argument, Barnes maintains that we have misunderstood the relationship of authority to power (1986). Arguing almost antithetically to Parsons, he maintains that the 'received view' of authority is as power with something added: consent, legitimacy, institutionalization. But, he counters, 'authority should be thought of as power minus' (*Ibid.*: 190), as a passive form of power that lacks discretion or the capacity to initiate action, and instead is bound and prescribed by that which makes it an authority. He emphasizes the idea that authorities are 'authorities on' something (the rules of the game, the works of an author, the application of scientific techniques and so on), and their powers are dependent on being true to those sources of their authority. Authorities, for Barnes, enforce routine understandings; powers establish them, without being held accountable. Authority is weak, unlike power which is, for want of an alternative, powerful. Now this reading rather reduces authority to the definition of offices and the interpretation of texts, minimizing the degree to which interpretation can be creative, and reducing legitimacy to a definitional aspect of authority instead of a condition that has to be met to create authority in the first place. We should note that Barnes' approach to the idea of authority follows the same path as those who argue for the cryptic nature of domination. Authority, the publicly recognized face of power, is rendered thin and insubstantial. True power lies off stage in the hands of those who write the scripts and establish the routines that we follow, under the guidance of authorities.

In another interpretation of authority, Wrong (2002: 35–64) uses the term in a disconcertingly broad way. He argues that authority is what happens whenever there is an effective command–obedience relationship, and that the reasons for obedience need not rest on autonomous, un-coerced reason. Thus he identifies five different bases of authority:

1 *Coercion,* where commands are obeyed in order to avoid physical or psychological harm.
2 *Inducement,* where commands are obeyed to obtain certain rewards, not because of belief in the validity of the command itself.
3 *Legitimacy,* where there is a recognition of a general right to command, and an obligation to obey, apart from the specific content of orders.
4 *Competence,* where there is recognition of expertise or specialized knowledge that underlies commands (as in the sense that Barnes emphasizes).
5 *Personhood,* where particular concrete commitment to an individual person motivates one to follow the other's will as if it were their own.

Wrong sees these as ideal types, which in reality are often complexly mixed. But, whereas most would argue that authority always rests on legitimacy, for Wrong, this is just one form of authority. To understand Wrong's approach here, it helps to know that he is also known for arguing that sociology (his field) suffers from an 'oversocialized' view of human beings (1961), a criticism directed especially at Parsons. By this he meant a tendency to reduce individual persons to their socially defined roles and statuses, with little room for recalcitrant individual psychology. By weakening the link between authority and legitimacy, in effect he carves out space for a range of less socialized, more individualized motives for obeying commands. He avoids an analysis where compliance with authority becomes, almost by definition, an endorsement of the existing power relations in society.

## Max Weber's complicated legacy

Wrong's broad conception of authority brings us to a curious point that you may have noted by now. Although we often talk about domination and authority as though they were logically opposed, as we have defined them above, they are not mutually exclusive categories. What I described as the 'skewed' use of domination by Foucault, Bourdieu and Lukes is also, by and large, the common sense view. If authority is defined by the presence of legitimacy, domination is defined by the lack of legitimacy. If authority at least has the potential to be regarded as morally right and justified, domination is precisely power that is unjustified. Furthermore, we normally use the term to imply that the condition of domination is somehow harmful to those who are subject to it – it is inherently wrong. And finally, if authority, in order to be legitimate, requires conscious approval and consent by those subject to it, domination, in its cryptic forms, by definition cannot be the object of conscious approval and consent. But, as we noted above, not all domination is cryptic. Moreover, if we accept an authority, then it will be able to *exercise relatively stable, ongoing control over our actions*. Authority will dominate us, legitimately. Our key analytic terms, the three siblings, are not as separate as we sometimes think.

These ambiguities are nowhere more apparent than in the influential writings of the historical sociologist Max Weber (1864–1920). Consider his attempt to define 'power' and 'domination' as he uses them:

A. 'Power' (*Macht*) is the probability that one actor within a social relationship will be in a position to carry out his own will despite resistance, regardless of the basis on which this probability rests.

B. 'Domination' (*Herrschaft*) is the probability that a command with a given specific content will be obeyed by a given group of persons. 'Discipline' is the probability that by virtue of habituation a command will receive prompt and automatic obedience in stereotyped forms, on the part of a given group of persons.

1. The concept of power is sociologically amorphous. All conceivable qualities of a person and all conceivable combinations of circumstances may put him in a position to impose his will in a given situation. The sociological concept of domination must hence be more precise and can only mean the probability that a *command* will be obeyed.

2. The concept of discipline includes the habituation characteristic of uncritical and unresisting mass obedience (1978: 53).

Given the preceding discussion, this is a remarkable set of assertions. First, although many have tried to use Weber's definition of power as an initial point of theoretical departure, he himself suggests that the term is too encompassing to be very useful. Instead he makes *Herrschaft*, translated here by Roth and Wittich as 'domination', the key analytic term in his lexicon. *Herrschaft* has manifold connotations (domination, dominion, reign, rule, authority, leadership, and all with an underlying implication of masculinity) that are not easily translated into a single English word. And scholars have disagreed about how best to translate it. Wrong, strongly influenced by Weber, and in contrast to Roth and Wittich (see also Bendix 1960) prefers 'authority', but as we have seen, his use of the term stretches into what many would call domination. There is textual justification for this in Weber however, when Weber says that *Herrschaft*

> may be based on the most diverse motives of compliance: all the way from simple habituation to the most purely rational calculation of advantage. Hence every genuine form of domination implies a minimum of voluntary compliance, that is, an interest (based on ulterior motives or genuine acceptance) in obedience (1978: 212).

So Weber's notion of *Herrschaft*, if we treat it as 'authority', is an authority that is not dependent on 'legitimacy'. If we treat it as 'domination', it is a form of domination defined by command–obedience relationships, which implies not cryptic control of behaviour but conscious compliance, however routine and habitual. The reciprocal element that secures *Herrschaft's* stability is not legitimacy in the first instance, but 'discipline', habituation among the obedient. The concept of legitimacy however, is an important element in Weber's theory of power (1978: 31–8; 212–16). Weber argued that specific systems of domination, or even more general patterns of social order, enjoy 'legitimacy' to the degree that these are supported by people's belief in the rightness and validity of commands and expectations imposed on them. He recognized that legitimacy in this sense is almost invariably intermixed with other motives, both instrumental and unconscious. And he argued that belief in the validity of commands and expectations tends to rest on one or a combination of these bases: (1) the sanctity of established tradition; (2) affective ties, especially to a charismatic individual (corresponding to Wrong's 'personal authority'); (3) ultimate, guiding moral or ethical values; and (4) rational and/or legal justification – in other words the commands are within the accepted rules of the game in question. Domination tends to seek out forms of legitimacy to enhance its stability, and Weber (following Roth and Wittich's translation of *Herrschaft*) spoke of characteristic types of 'legitimate domination', a phrase that might sound oxymoronic to an English speaker. But domination's stability, in Weber's view, is rarely entirely dependent on legitimacy, having other processes such as 'discipline' and self-interest also working in its favour.

To understand Weber's 'oxymoron' we have to appreciate his intent. Central to Weber's approach was his purpose, as much as possible, to separate normative evaluation from analytic description – to develop a social scientific language that was, in the first instance, as neutral as possible about the right and wrong of human affairs. It may sound strange to us to suggest that domination might be a normatively neutral concept, neither good nor bad. We tend to regard domination as implying harm and unjust treatment. But it can be argued that, to be useful for social analysis, a purely descriptive, normatively neutral concept is precisely what is needed. If relationships of domination are common features of our social landscape, then we need to be able to describe, analyze and comparatively study these, dispassionately, prior to any normative evaluation of the relationships in question. The key point is that, for Weber, the influence of a charismatic teacher on her pupils, conventions of deference between tenants and landlords in agrarian societies, the ability of an established democratic government to rule, the ability of monopoly businesses to set market prices, or the cultivation of widespread nationalist fervour by a dictator, are all equally instances of domination – phenomena of the same general form, regardless of how we might morally judge them. In keeping with this principle, Weber described most forms of domination as 'legitimate', meaning not that they should be approved of, but that those subject to domination frequently find their situation justifiable on some grounds, and that this is basic to the operation of domination. It is intrinsically difficult to translate Weber's value-neutral notion of *Herrschaft* when the English words at one's disposal, domination and authority, tend to be value laden, the former negatively, the latter positively.

## Recapitulation

The purpose of this review of divergent and conflicting uses of our key terms is not to suggest we should abandon them. Such terminological conflicts are in the nature of theoretical discourse. More crucially, 'domination', 'authority' and 'legitimacy' are part of our normal everyday language. If we want to develop more analytically effective ways of talking about power that matter for the real world, it makes sense to stick close to normal usage, while also seeking to both clarify and problematize that usage (cf. Morriss 2002: 8).

### Domination

Although this word tends to carry negative connotations, as when someone imposes their unwelcome will on others, we do use it sometimes in a neutral sense, for example when a team dominates the first half of the game, or when a cleverly designed product comes to dominate its market. Note, however, that in these neutral examples 'domination' arises out of a context of formalized competition in which it is 'legitimate' to attempt to dominate within the rules. Therefore, whether or not domination is acceptable depends on the conditions under which, and the context within which, it happens.

## Authority

When we talk of 'an authority', sometimes we simply refer to constituted bodies that have the capacity, like it or not, to issue binding orders, for instance a local government's ability to levy certain taxes, or a law enforcement agency's ability to issue tickets for traffic infringements. But this attenuated sense shades into other uses where principled acceptance of authority's power is more explicit: we believe our doctor knows her stuff, that our government office holders were elected 'fair and square.' There are 'thinner' and 'thicker' senses of authority.

## Command

Thanks to Weber, the notion of 'commands' or 'orders' is used to help clarify what we mean by both authority and domination. But what counts as a command? Paradigmatically, it would include a teacher's instructions to pupils or a general's order to soldiers. But there are 'chains of command' through which commands travel and get diffused and altered, and that sometimes originate in an ultimate locus of power in this world: the boss, the president, the legislature, and sometimes beyond, in a god or philosophical first principles. Moreover, there are quasi-commands, the origins of which are not so easily traceable. Economists often talk about fluctuating prices in markets as 'signals' that guide economic action. One can disobey such 'commands' at one's peril, but it can be difficult to identify an issuer of commands that can be challenged (cf. Weber 1978: 941–8).

## Legitimacy

As we saw above, notions of 'legitimacy' and 'legitimation' derive from the adjectival and transitive verb forms of 'legitimate'. This reflects our pragmatic relationship to the word because in the first instance what usually concerns us is whether a certain decision, act, status or object has been properly authorized. Legitimacy and legitimation tend to refer to how the power to authorize is constituted in the first place and how it is reproduced, respectively. There are two catches here. The first is that a narrower sense of legitimacy, as pertaining to recognized loci of authority, shades into a much broader sense of the acceptability of social ideas and arrangements in general. The second is that we tend to only notice problems of legitimacy and legitimation when the system manifestly isn't working, when the validity of authority is in question. Legitimacy fades into Weber's unthinking 'discipline' when things are running smoothly, disappearing from view.

*The tool kit*

The range of meanings that attach to each of these words invites some imprecision, but that very imprecision may also be a virtue, providing important
clues to how power actually works. For instance, authority does not need its
justifying principles on display all the time in order to operate, it needs them
just enough of the time and at crucial moments when it is called into question. In order to be useful, domination, authority and legitimacy don't have
to be utterly discrete and exhaustive of possibilities. Rather, through a kind
of triangulation, they help us get a handle on complex, real world situations,
which very frequently exhibit aspects of all three.

## Power, modernity and ambivalence

Running through the preceding, somewhat casual analysis of terms, is a theme
of distrust towards power. This is seen in the tendency for what I have called
cryptic domination to become a central, orienting conception of power, as
indicated in the influential work of Foucault, Bourdieu and Lukes. Barnes'
deeply ironic account of 'powerless' authority is another example, which ultimately points towards the hidden domination of genuine power. Correspondingly, notions of 'authority' and 'legitimacy' have a rather old-fashioned,
quaint ring about them – naive ideas from a more innocent age. This tendency
is particularly pronounced in fields such as general social theory, sociology
and anthropology, which lean toward universalizing, macro–micro linking assessments of human social relations. Tellingly, in fields such as politics and
international relations, with their steady focus on political institutions, concepts of authority and legitimacy have been more sustained, because of their
ongoing practical relevance for analysis regarding such things as the rise of
right wing parties, declining voter participation, 'failed' states, the European
Union, transnational civil society actors, international agreements and alliances, and so on. But if we think that there are some general principles of
power that can be articulated, and that these provide fundamentals of social
theory, then surely these should range across various distinct fields of substantive research.

So how can we account for this trend towards a deep distrust of power,
towards highlighting its occult and injurious side? Part of the answer involves
fairly recent history, and generational tensions and transitions within the academic field. Parsons, a major influence on social theory in the 1950s and
1960s, had no trouble assimilating power to legitimated authority, and making it a cornerstone of his conception of a healthy, well-functioning society,
particularly on the model of a capitalist liberal democracy. Lukes' alternative
conceptualization was one part of a generational challenge to an old guard
such as Parsons within the academy, inspired both by a revival of Marxist
ideas, and a general climate of social unrest and 'questioning of authority' in

the 1960s. Both Foucault and Bourdieu became influential in the Paris-centred French social sciences, amid the same general, transnational climate of student protest. In their cases they came up against a rather stifling communist–Marxist orthodoxy in the French academy, in which power was conceived largely in terms of relatively overt class struggles. Their strong turns toward the hidden processes of power reflected their frustration with the inadequacies of the reigning intellectual paradigm they encountered. These three figures, like all intellectuals, were creatures of their institutional and social environments, to which they responded, and in so doing set a new tone of thought for subsequent generations.

But my main contention is that this phase itself was a cyclical expression of deeper ideational tensions that are constitutive of the modern age, and that need to be introduced here, to take us to the heart of the matter and frame the rest of this book. In the next chapter we will begin with Machiavelli and Hobbes, as harbingers of a new, 'modern' view of power, and the natural starting point for an historical narrative of our own ideas. Here let me briefly suggest the triggers, cognitive and moral on the one hand, political and economic on the other, for that new, modern view.

In a typically bold fashion, Ernest Gellner characterized modernity as involving a fundamental transformation of human cognition (1991: 70–90). In pre-modern societies, referential knowledge about the natural world tended to be context bound and practice specific. Knowledge and skills around food production, tool making, protection from the elements, maintaining bodily health and so on were only loosely integrated. But cosmological beliefs, relating social order to world order through systems of symbols and values, were relatively more integrated. In short, the social group, for its practical survival, needed a shared moral view of social life and its internal relations more urgently than a unified understanding of the natural world.

In a first stage of transformation, agrarian state-societies of a much greater scale developed larger and more elaborate bureaucracies and political structures, and clerical/priestly classes to provide the theocratic ideologies to help legitimate these more complex systems. This process tended to develop much more elaborated and unified systems of thought that were designed to help explain the natural, social and moral order, but ones that were still only loosely, or sporadically, anchored in referential knowledge about the natural world. Thus, for instance, relatively accurate knowledge about the movement of the stars in the heavens provided both knowledge relevant to agricultural practices and symbolic support for religious beliefs about an afterlife, but not an element in an integrated system of physics and natural history as we would recognize them.

In the final, modern stage of transformation, there is a rupture. With the development of notions of empiricism, that all genuine knowledge is based on human experience, and the codification of scientific methods of inquiry, much greater development of an integrated, referential account of the natural world becomes possible. It also becomes a core social value. The tradition from the agrarian era of integrated cosmologies that aim to provide understanding of and moral orientation to the social world, whether through religion or secular philosophy, lives on. However, the relationship between systems of explanation of the natural and social–moral orders becomes permanently problematized. One of the first people to try to forcefully articulate this problematic rupture was the Scottish Enlightenment philosopher and historian David Hume (1711–1776). He argued that it is impossible to directly derive moral knowledge about what we 'ought' to do from referential knowledge about the state of the world (1978: 469–70). Instead we must content ourselves with our naturally occurring emotional responses and their moral implications, accepting these as the closest we will come to a foundation for our morality (see Mounce 1999: 84–90). About 150 years later, Max Weber would make a related argument, in the context of German debates about the proper role of academics and their relationship to politics. He maintained that while academic inquiry is normally motivated by social and political views, as a practice it must keep its distance, aiming to follow inquiry about the world as it is, wherever it will lead, without putting itself in the direct service of political or other interests (Gerth and Mills 1958: 32–74). In short, with Gellner's final phase of cognitive transformation, a permanent problem of moral relativism is established, in which the justification of moral and political order is constantly in question (see also Dupré 2004: Ch 5; Hall 1988: Ch 1).

The last stage of this cognitive transformation happens in tandem, in a complexly interdependent causal process, with transformations of political, economic and wider social structures. For our purposes this is stated most succinctly by Reinhard Bendix in *Kings or People: Power and the Mandate to Rule* (1978). Bendix recognizes the fundamental roles of the growth of commerce, trade, cities, and a more complex division of labour in reshaping medieval European society into its present day form. These processes by their very nature generated new interstitial classes with new competing and combining powers that forced the restructuring of society's basic rules and categories for managing power. Nonetheless, for him:

> It is easiest to define modernization as a breakdown of the ideal-typical social order: Authority loses its sanctity, monarchy declines, hierarchical social order is disrupted. Secular authority, rule in the name of the people, and an equalitarian ethos are typical attributes of modern society (1978: 10–11).

Of course this was not a single, smooth process. It played out differently in different places and at different times. The French executed a king and established a republic; the British killed their king, experimented with commonwealth and then reinstated monarchy, but in a reduced form that endures but dwindles to this day. Some parts of the globe brought 'the people' into the business of government through the gradual development of democratic institutions, others brought the people in a bit later, more suddenly and figuratively, as workers and peasants in whose name (but with limited voice) small cadres built and ran huge new bureaucratic states. But as regards basic patterns of domination, authority and legitimacy, Bendix rightly summarizes the underlying trend of human history.

This has several entwined implications. First, once again, this great transformation, far from being a story of processes of cryptic domination, is primarily one of agonized and highly explicit struggles over the nature of authority and legitimacy. I believe that this will also be true of any future 'great transformations'. Second, the rise of a world in which the people collectively have authority over themselves was at the same time the rise of a world in which individual liberty – personal authority over one's body, thoughts and possessions – became a core value. In this context, the very capacity of groups of notional equals to collectively govern themselves is also a capacity for the group, the wider society and its various institutions to dominate the individual. Our liberation has frustratingly delivered us into a world where domination continues, in elaborate forms, despite our elevated status. Third, there is a difficult relationship between the cognitive and moral rupture described above and this transformation of political structures. Together they have generated a world in which, simultaneously, we are forced to take on more responsibility for the relations of power we are involved in, because we have a greater hand in the collective making of those relations, but are chronically disabled in our capacity to formulate underlying or transcendent justifications for those power relations. It is less easy for many of us to palm this off on the will of a divine being or 'the logic of history'. Finally, this is a profoundly uncomfortable world, in which our desires to free ourselves and others leads only to the question, 'how shall we best dominate each other?' It is perhaps not surprising that in part, we deal with this question by disowning it, searching instead, almost habitually, for the hidden further sources of our domination, in the vain hope that an ultimate encounter with these will lead us either to absolute liberation, or at least an acceptable resignation to our condition. Our contemporary ways of thinking about power, explored in this book, arise out of traditions of grappling with these defining dilemmas of our modern situation.

# PART II

# Theorizing Power

The middle part of this book surveys various theorists and theories of power over a long stretch of time, running from Machiavelli five hundred years ago up to more recent figures such as Pierre Bourdieu and Michael Mann. I have aimed for a certain historical depth, and have had to be selective about whom to cover in each chapter. The narrative that emerges has some polemic intent. First, in Chapter 3, it seeks to flesh out some of the key progenitors of modern theories of power who are routinely referred to and invoked, but less often discussed in any detail. Part of my point here is that, for all the profound social transformations that have occurred since Machiavelli's day, we can see basic continuities between his concerns and ours. At the same time, we need to see each theorist as formulating ideas about power which are specific to their historical circumstances. What I have called the 'American debates' in Chapter 4 covers a series of discussions that emanated particularly from the US in the three decades after the Second World War, and have come to provide some of the core literature influencing contemporary theories of power. However I think that the original American historical, social and political context shaping those debates is often lost, so I have tried to recapture that, emphasizing how the question of the relevance of the concept of elites for the study of US society was central to those original debates. Chapters 3 and 4 provide, respectively, the historically deeper and more immediate discursive contexts for contemporary discussions and debates. But they also represent importantly distinct phases: the former helping us trace the development of power discourses through the formation of modernity, the latter exemplifying a fully modern, and academic, perspective on power.

The ordering of Chapters 5 and 6 may appear counter-intuitive. In Chapter 5, under the heading 'epistemological approaches' I examine a cluster of approaches, often (but not exclusively) emanating from the French academic context of roughly 1970 on, which have stressed the role of knowledge in the constitution of power. Some of these approaches have been conventionally labelled 'postmodern', a label not always welcomed by the theorists under consideration. Be that as it may, these theories have often been presented by their proponents as signifying serious ruptures with previous social theory, especially those of Marxist and positivist varieties. In contrast, the approaches surveyed in Chapter 6 under the heading 'evolutionary approaches', also dating from around 1970, are much more relaxed about carrying on in a tradition of social theorizing largely established by Marx and Weber (and, to a lesser degree, Durkheim), and developed by many that followed. Rather than rupture, theoretical advance is seen more 'as the strong and slow boring of hard boards' to quote Weber's description of the life of politics (1958: 128). I have deliberately put the chapters in this order to counter the tendency to assume that those that claim to represent rupture are necessarily intellectually subsequent to those that do not. In fact we are dealing with contemporary strains of theorizing that together evidence a strong bifurcation in theoretical tendencies, which is itself interesting. It is not my intention to pit these two tendencies against one another in a zero-sum contest, but neither can I honestly conceal my stronger sympathy for the approaches in Chapter 6. Just as I have tried to use the book's narrative to question the ultimacy of epistemological approaches, I invite the reader to question my own sympathies.

I provide Figure II.1 as a quick map of the historical and theoretical ground covered in Part II, highlighting the main theorists and some of their relationships. Before reading Chapters 3 to 6, Figure II.1 will necessarily be a bit cryptic and schematic. Hopefully, after reading them, it will provide a reminder of the main arc of Part II's argument and narrative.

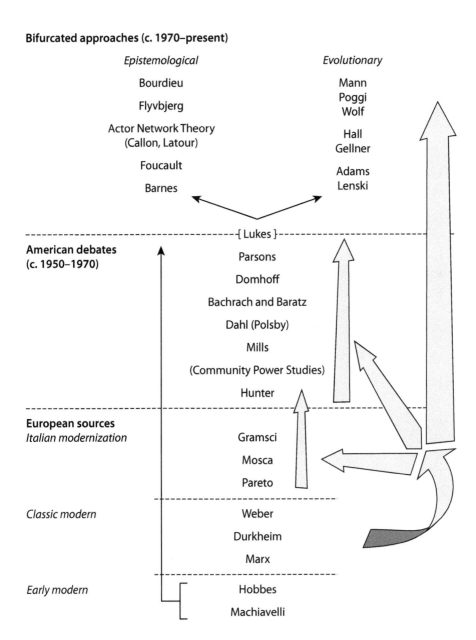

**Bifurcated approaches (c. 1970–present)**

*Epistemological*
Bourdieu
Flyvbjerg
Actor Network Theory
(Callon, Latour)
Foucault
Barnes

*Evolutionary*
Mann
Poggi
Wolf
Hall
Gellner
Adams
Lenski

{ Lukes }

**American debates**
**(c. 1950–1970)**
Parsons
Domhoff
Bachrach and Baratz
Dahl (Polsby)
Mills
(Community Power Studies)
Hunter

**European sources**
*Italian modernization*
Gramsci
Mosca
Pareto

*Classic modern*
Weber
Durkheim
Marx

*Early modern*
Hobbes
Machiavelli

**Figure II.1**   A genealogy of theories of power

# CHAPTER 3

# European Sources

## Introduction

This chapter begins with Machiavelli and ends with Gramsci's application of Machiavelli to twentieth century socialist politics. It provides a grounding in some of the classic figures in the European tradition of social theory that continue to provide key points of reference for contemporary discussions of power. It is 'Eurocentric', but with a purpose – to show how contemporary discourses about power have their origins in the upheavals of the European formation of modernity. A single chapter cannot provide comprehensive discussions of these thinkers. Instead I concentrate on how they conceptualized social power in ways that have had enduring influence. We will better understand current debates about power if we recognize their origins in this past.

The discussion is structured around three periods. First, we consider the early modern period (approximately 1500 to 1700), in which feudal and monarchical structures of power and authority were coming under strain and critical scrutiny, requiring new modes of legitimation. The focus is on Machiavelli's advocacy of city-state republicanism, informed by Renaissance humanism, and Hobbes' defence of royal absolutism amid the upheavals of the Reformation and the English Civil War. The second period is the heyday of nineteenth and early twentieth century modernization, in which the rapid growth of industrial capitalism and the expansion of the modern constitutional state posed an array of social problems and conflicts that stimulated the social analyses of Marx, Durkheim and Weber – studies which still serve as cornerstones of contemporary social theory. And finally, bringing us more fully into the twentieth century, we look at a line of Italian scholars who became particularly concerned with the concept of elites and the analysis of political leadership and following in mass society, in both conservative and revolutionary ways. Here the key figures are Pareto, Mosca and Gramsci who, each in his own way, moved from the more general concern with economic and social change to more purely political questions of how rulership is achieved.

# Early modern harbingers: Machiavelli and Hobbes

## *Niccolo Machiavelli*

The rise of modernity in Europe is often recounted as a macro-level shift from feudalism to capitalism, from monarchy to the constitutional state. It featured the great kingdoms of England, France and Spain, and the Holy Roman Empire which bound together a field of minor principalities in what would become Germany. But the Italian lands fit uneasily into this story. Geographical opportunity was afforded by a peninsula reaching into the Mediterranean Sea, advantageously linking access to trade with the Byzantine and Muslim worlds to trading networks in northern Europe. This helped sustain urban centres in northern Italy after the fall of the Roman Empire, cities which preserved aspects of Roman republicanism. Political struggles between an embattled papacy and claimants to feudal overlordship, often from beyond the Alps, created space for the economically powerful cities to negotiate and assert their relative independence. The resulting 'communes' – Florence, Venice, Genoa, Milan, among others – were quasi-republican city-states dominating their immediate regions. These centres of trade, banking and humanist scholarship were forerunners of modern commercial society.

Niccolo Machiavelli (1469–1527) was a native of Florence, born into a modest background, but well trained in the humanist scholarship of the day, which prepared him for a career as a 'civil servant'. In the centuries before Machiavelli was born, Florence's republican government, which contained elements of democracy, was in fact largely ruled by alliances among wealthy merchant families, each with its own patronage networks in the city and beyond. By 1434 Florence had come under the sway of the powerful Medici family (Hale 2001), first behind the scenes but then openly ruled by 'Lorenzo the Magnificent' (1469–1492), a great patron of the arts and master of statecraft. Lorenzo's son Piero II (1492–1494) was less competent, and was deposed by the city after a humiliating climb-down before a French army invading northern Italy. With this, republican rule was re-established between 1494 and 1512. It was in this context that Machiavelli advanced in a career as a diplomat for Florence, including a period of oversight for the Florentine militia. But these were geopolitically unstable times, and within the republican frame, the great families of Florence were becoming more of a mercantile aristocracy and more sympathetic to firmer rule from above. This prepared the ground for the return of Medici rule in 1512, only to be challenged again by republicanism from 1527 to 1530, just before Machiavelli's death. When the Medici returned to power Machiavelli, a staunch republican, fell out of favour and was briefly imprisoned and tortured, thereafter retiring to a life of independent scholarship, living on his small farm. Ever the political pragmatist, he immediately began seeking Medicean patronage, and was finally modestly successful when the Medici commissioned him to write a history of Florence in 1520. Machiavelli's main ideas were forged in this context of Florentine republicanism, which he held dear, compromised by Medicean wealth, reasserted but bungled, and then re-subordinated to the realities of Medici rule (Gilbert 1965).

Machiavelli is sometimes regarded as a founder of the modern science of politics, with his often cold, detached analysis of political affairs. But there is little in the way of scientific method in his writings. While they draw on his own experiences and observations of contemporary politics, and lessons drawn from classical sources such as Livy and Cicero, these are mobilized in an *ad hoc* manner, with no pretence of hypothesis testing or systematic comparison of cases. Machiavelli was a humanist scholar providing learned commentary on politics, both of his day, and in general (Coleman 1995; Plamenatz 1992: 36–45; Viroli 1998: 1–10). His ideas are striking precisely because of his liminality, drawing on ancient notions of republican patriotism, to comment on his contemporary world which seemed to be in a perpetual crisis of legitimacy, in ways that foreshadow the problems of government in modern, liberal, democratic nation-states. I focus on three themes: republican liberty, political leadership and morality, and fate and human agency.

According to Viroli, Machiavelli's overriding motive in all his work was patriotism: 'love of country' or city. He sought to live by this supreme value and inculcate it in his fellow citizens, despite any sufferings it brought him (1998: 148–74). The proper object of this love was the republic that achieves greatness and human flourishing by maximizing liberty. This was not the liberty of the individual's conscience or of minorities from majority oppression, as we might think of liberty today. It was the collective liberty of the citizenry, defined by their independence from foreign domination, from the internal domination of a tyrant, and more generally by a capacity for expansion and 'greatness'. He hyperbolically maintained that 'experience shows that no state ever extended its dominion or increased it revenues, any longer than it continued free' (quoted in Plamenatz 1992: 76). This requires high levels of public spiritedness and virtue, difficult to achieve given Machavelli's view that people are normally sectarian, self-interested and untrusting of others. But again, the virtue in question is not so much an individual as a collective quality. The political virtue of an individual leader might be consequential in shaping the wider public mores, and the greatest achievement of such a 'prince' is to lay down laws that will continue to cultivate public virtue in the citizenry after the prince is gone (Skinner 2000: 65–6). Thus, as we will see more closely in a moment, Machiavelli's love of republican liberty did not deny a role for strong leaders, even monarchs if need be, who might be crucial in fostering liberty. For him there were two great threats to the good state. The first was aristocracies and nobilities, whose self-interested factionalism tends to subvert the force of law and good social order (Machiavelli 1970: 118–24). And, drawing on his own experience in martial affairs, Machiavelli saw the second threat as mercenary armies, which had become a common means of city-state warfare in his day. Unlike citizen-militias motivated by civic purpose, mercenaries are 'disunited, ambitious, without discipline, unfaithful', in short, unreliable and in-it-for-themselves (Machiavelli 1985: 48–50). Nobilities and mercenaries are not oriented to the collective good of the city: this task falls to the dynamic between good leaders and virtuous citizens, which is our next topic.

Machiavelli's thoughts on republican liberty are most fully developed in his *Discourses* (1970), a series of commentaries on the first ten books of Livy's history of Rome, but he is best remembered for the much shorter and controversial text, *The Prince* (1985). This book followed an established medieval literary genre, further developed by humanist scholars, of offering 'advice to princes' by presenting an ideal model of the good king: possessing Christian virtues, placid and law abiding, and surrounded by wise counsellors (Gilbert 1939). But Machiavelli's 'prince' subverted the conventions of the genre, shocking both contemporaries and generations to come with its numerous assertions that effective princes must develop a more subtle and flexible understanding of 'goodness':

> And many have imagined republics and principalities that have never been seen or known to exist in truth; for it is so far from how one lives to how one should live that he who lets go of what is done for what should be done learns his ruin rather than his preservation. For a man who wants to make a profession of good in all regards must come to ruin among so many who are not good. Hence it is necessary to be a prince, if he wants to maintain himself, to learn to be able not to be good, and to use this and not use it according to necessity (Machiavelli 1985: 61).

This is sometimes interpreted as a counsel of sheer amoralism, the instrumental claim that any action that maintains power is warranted. But as we've seen, it is not that Machiavelli was without core, guiding values, but rather, there is a hierarchy of values. At the top is the maintenance of the (ideally republican) liberty of the city-state. The prince is called to countenance doing evil in certain situations, in order to preserve this highest good. And indeed, power-holders of all sorts often confront this dilemma, of choosing between ideal norms of conduct, and practical achievement of the collective good. This is now known as 'the problem of dirty hands', that politicians simply must do unseemly things sometimes (Coady 1993). It was Machiavelli's signal contribution to force this dilemma more fully into the open, to make it a legitimate object in our contemplations of power. The other key point about *The Prince*, setting it apart from earlier advice to princes, is that it is not simply about the prince and his strategies and virtues, it is about his role as a leader and thus his relationships to others. This includes other sovereigns, secretaries and courtiers (especially books xxi–xxiii), but crucially also the citizens (especially books xv–xix). Machiavelli stresses the prince's need to attend to how he appears to the people, how he is regarded, what opinion they hold of him. While he must avoid becoming an object of hatred or contempt, leadership will involve cultivating in the citizens complex attitudes of admiration and gratitude, and also fear and respect. Machiavelli marks a significant shift

towards regarding the problems of power as problems of the relationship between leaders and followers, between politicians and citizens. It is no surprise
that this happened in the context of the Italian city-states, which prefigured
the politics of the modern, mass-based, nation-state.

Finally, Machiavelli's attitude to religion has often puzzled (see Colish
1999: 597–9; Najemy 1999; Nederman 1999: 617–18). Some of his utterances seem deeply irreligious, or at least callously instrumental towards matters of faith (1985: 68–71), while at other times he is conventionally pious. We
cannot read Machiavelli's mind, but it would be an anachronism to imagine
him as a modern atheist dissimulating his way through a Christian world. He
was a creature of an environment in which the existence of God was common
sense, and yet humanism was affecting how some thought about the authority
of church and scripture, and their relationship to God, laying groundwork for
the Reformation. It is clear, however, that he saw a positive role for religion
in fostering the well-ordered state. Colish (1999) has analyzed Machiavelli's
deep antipathy for the influence of the Dominican prior Savonarola over the
restored republic during its first four years (1494–1498). Colish argues that
Machiavelli saw Savanorola's severe sermonizing to the people of Florence to
reform their religious observance as an inversion of the proper relationship
between religion and politics. Religion should serve the political good of the
city, rather than politics being bent to religious purposes (1999: 614). Nederman (1999: 620) has scrutinized the widely noted tension in Machiavelli's
writings between the concepts of *fortuna*, a pagan goddess that represents the
uncontrollable nature of events, the unpredictable and unintended outcomes
of clashing human actions, and *virtù,* the talents, skills and other qualities
that enable persons to prevail over the challenges *fortuna* presents. Nederman argues that these terms were mediated in Machiavelli's mind by a third
– God's grace. Thus the constant struggle between the human will and ability
and 'outrageous fortune' is itself framed by a divine plan; the deck is ultimately stacked. Whatever this may tell us about Machiavelli's religious beliefs,
it again suggests his pivotal position between pre-modern and modern ideas
about power. In the dialectic of *fortuna* and *virtù* we can recognize the ancestry of current ideas of 'structure and agency'. But where a medieval writer
would have been more likely to call for concordance between the wills of God
and humans, Machiavelli's God, anticipating eighteenth century deism, has
receded backstage, leaving more earthly struggles in the foreground.

## Thomas Hobbes

Renaissance humanism helped prepare the way for the Reformation, which
was the key context for our second harbinger, Thomas Hobbes (1588–1679).
Where Machiavelli was a humanist commentator on Italian politics, Hobbes was a system-building philosopher, of politics but also natural science,
optics and mathematics. He was widely regarded as brilliant, and seems to
have regarded himself in the same manner. Born into modest circumstances he

excelled in school, graduating from Oxford University in 1608. Thereafter he spent most of his career in the service of the noble Cavendish family, as tutor to two generations of Earls, and sometimes secretary. Hobbes' political theory was a response to his troubled times, in which Catholic and Protestant forces vied for supremacy and influence over the British monarchy. He lived through: the Catholic 'Gunpowder Plot' to blow up King James I and his Parliament (1605); the Thirty Years War (1618–48), a brutal continental struggle between Protestant and Catholic forces which began in Bohemia, but spread throughout the Holy Roman Empire and beyond; Presbyterian rebellion in Scotland against the 'papist' tendencies of the King (1638) leading to the English Civil War (1642–46) between parliamentarian and royalist forces, and the execution of Charles I (1649); the Cromwellian commonwealth and interregnum (1651–59); and the restoration of Charles II to the throne in 1660. Hobbes relocated to France from 1640 to 1651 during the worst of the conflicts, where he wrote *Leviathan*, the most influential of his many works. Amid this welter of political and religious upheaval, Hobbes tried to formulate a rational argument for the absolute, undivided sovereignty of the monarch, and the obligation of subjects to obey the monarch, except when doing so directly threatened their own lives. He sought to delegitimate religiously based challenges to kingly authority (see Curley 1994; Tuck 1989).

Hobbes thought and wrote in the context of rapidly developing 'scientific' knowledge about the world that was being produced by Galileo, Bacon and Boyle (Shapin and Schaffer 1985). But his approach to the study of politics was not inductive, but deductive, modelled on geometry, which he saw as the most superior of the sciences because it drew conclusions from axiomatic definitions. Hobbes was a materialist – arguing that everything that exists has material substance – and a nominalist – maintaining that the names of things are simply conventional labels for objects in the material world that do not rely on any abstract essences for their meaning. For him, studying power was a matter of beginning with basic definitions of terms, and reasoning on the basis of these to logical conclusions, that would then be applicable to the real world. Today we tend to think of induction and deduction as fundamentally contrary methods of inquiry. But, in Hobbes' day, such things as the great successes of the application of geometry and astronomy to the practice of oceanic navigation seemed to promise a much happier unity between these approaches to knowing, at least for Hobbes.

Hobbes begins with the premise that people normally seek to increase their power whenever possible, not because of a desire to dominate others, but out of chronic insecurity – safety means maximizing one's power where possible (Hobbes 1994: 58). He also claims that:

> The greatest of human powers is that which is compounded of the powers of most men, united by consent in one person, natural or civil, that has the use of all their powers depending on his will, such as is the power of a commonwealth, or depending on the wills of each particular, such as

is the power of faction or of diverse factions leagued. Therefore to have servants is power; to have friends is power; for they are strengths united (1994: 50).

In other words, we have here a seminal formulation of the idea that 'power over' maximizes 'power to', albeit in two versions, one 'tight', where several ('servants') consent to be united in one person, and one 'loose' where several ('friends') join together around shared interests. These basic understandings of power provide the foundation for his notion of ideal human government as the *Leviathan*, that is, the 'tight' version.

Hobbes' argument is presented as a narrative of the path out of the 'state of nature' where there is a 'war of all against all' and chronic insecurity, into the state of 'civil [that is, governed] society' (Hobbes 1994: 74–118). Although Hobbes drew on contemporary reports of non-European, pre-state peoples to illustrate his idea of the state of nature, it is clear that this is ultimately a logical category: the contrary of stable, governed society and something that was a present threat to civilized life in Europe as Hobbes understood it (see Ashcraft 1971). Given this insecurity and the way it undermines human power, Hobbes argued that self-interest would lead people to form a 'social contract' with each other, agreeing to place ultimate overarching power in the hands of one sovereign, who in turn was obliged to protect and serve the well-being of all subjects, but was unconstrained in how she or he did this as long as life and limb were protected. If the sovereign failed in their basic duty, the contract would be void. Hobbes expected the hypothetical people in the state of nature to reason as he did, that any division of power at the centre would inevitably lead to factionalism and destabilize the whole system of government, thus the rational, contracting subjects would agree to concentrate great power in the sovereign. Again, this 'social contract' is not so much an actual historical event as a logical derivative of the primitive dynamics of human power and motivations for peace, order, safety and stability (Curley 1994: xxi–xxxvi). Oddly, Hobbes can be viewed as a progenitor of both liberal and authoritarian ideas. He begins with individuals choosing to league together, to form a social contract for their own good, but he maintains that, once formed, this arrangement should bestow in a single sovereign extensive command over the making of laws, the establishment of religion and the content of public discourse. Having said this, Hobbes' ideal sovereign is, above all, a peacekeeper, whose powers are meant to control those things that lead to violent factionalism.

The last two of *Leviathan's* four books, on matters of religion and ecclesiastical authority, are usually given much less attention than their predecessors. This is because political theorists today are more interested in secular arguments for the legitimacy of the modern state, and thus the arguments about religion appear to be irrelevant baggage. Moreover, because of his unconventional beliefs, Hobbes was often accused of atheism. Recent writers have sometimes suspected he was an atheist, and that these latter books were simply necessary engagements with theological arguments at the time, but are now irrelevant. However, it is important to remember that Hobbes was responding to contemporary upheavals that were fundamentally framed in terms of claims and counter-claims of access to divine sanction and authority. Catholics were claiming that secular states stood under the authority of the Pope as the earthly emissary of God, while Presbyterians and other Protestant sects were claiming that their churches enjoyed direct authorization from God. Hobbes saw this as a chaotic situation in which irresolvable claims to authority would proliferate, driving society back into a state of nature, a war of all against all. His theological intervention was to cast extreme doubt on the plausibility of all claims to privileged access to God's will. Instead he argued that, all things being equal, the wisest course was to regard flesh and blood sovereigns as 'God's lieutenants' on earth, with appropriate authority over matters of interpreting scripture (Curley 1994: xxxvi–xlvii; Springborg 1975). In a sense he was articulating the core principle of the Treaty of Westphalia (1648) that concluded the Thirty Years War: *cuius regio, eius religio (whose realm, his religion)*. Put another way, the *Leviathan* forcefully supports Jesus' call to 'Render unto Caesar the things which are Caesar's, and unto God the things that are God's' (Matthew 22: 21), with the proviso that Caesar always knows best what things are God's.

With both Machiavelli and Hobbes I have ended on questions of religion. This is not an accident. We tend to read them as searching for theories of power that anticipate our modern, more secular understanding of the problems of rule, weeding out extraneous historical debates about religion. But to understand them properly, we need to appreciate that their attempts to understand and justify worldly power were reactions to societies in which traditional claims to divine authority were at once both weakened, whether discredited by corruption or the sheer proliferation of contesting claims to divine access, and overstimulated by ideological controversy and the very struggles for legitimate power and authority among earthly princes. We do both them and ourselves a disservice if we forget that recourse to transcendent divine authority to justify worldly political projects is alive and well today around the globe.

## Theorists of modernity: Marx, Durkheim and Weber

Our next three thinkers wrote in the context of the rapid growth of industrial capitalism and the state, which were reconstituting the social nature of power. Driven forward by capitalist development in Britain, the whole of Europe was being transformed by population growth, urbanization, the centralization and intensification of industrial manufacture, growth in global trade, and peasants becoming proletarians. These economic changes led new bourgeoisies and older traditional ruling classes into political struggles and the mobilization of wider populations behind their claims to power. At the same time, the administrative powers of states grew, especially in the latter half of the nineteenth century. In Britain, this was driven by a need to manage the socially disruptive effects of the capitalist economy; in Prussia, it was more a matter of creating the conditions for deliberate capitalist development, from above. The state's role in both fostering and regulating competitive capitalism became entrenched (Pounds 1990: Part IV).

## Karl Marx

Karl Marx (1818–83) came from a middle class Prussian background, and studied law, philosophy, history and languages at the University of Berlin, doing a PhD on Greek philosophy at Jena (1841). He soon abandoned plans for a career in university teaching to become a journalist and freelance radical intellectual and activist. His ambitions were enabled by the support of his financial benefactor and intellectual interlocutor, Freidrich Engels (1820–95) (see Collins 1994: 56–81, on the importance of Engels' contribution). Inspired by debates that raged within the Hegelian philosophy that dominated Prussia in his youth and encounters with the British political economists' (Smith, Bentham, Ricardo, Mills) theories of capitalism and markets, Marx articulated a vision of human history as a material struggle for emancipation, centrally manifested in economic activity. It is often remarked that Marx never systematically defined the concept of 'class', despite its centrality for his work (Bottomore 1983: 75–7). Similarly, although he can be regarded as offering one of the most strenuous critiques of power relations in his day, he never systematically defines what he means by power. We have to extract this as best we can from various uses of the term in his work. I focus on four key ideas: social labour, the mode of production, class conflict and alienation.

At the heart of Marx's perspective is a particularly complex and encompassing concept of labour. For him, labour is much more than just paid work or some measure of energetic output. It is the very essence of human existence as part of nature. Simply 'being' means engaging physically and sensually with one's environment, seizing it and materially transforming it, according to one's needs. The very idea of labour is imbued with self-realization for Marx. Furthermore, labour is an inherently social process. We work as social beings, making our world in both its physical and mental aspects for ourselves and for each other at the same time. More than just an acknowledgment that no-one lives and works in isolation, this is an assertion that our most substantial achievements arise out of coordinated, collectively organized labour. The most basic notion of power for Marx was this social capacity to change the world, in a word: labour (Marx in Tucker 1978: 88–91, 154; Wolf 1982: 73–5). Thus when Marx saw incipient forms of social and political mobilization by groups identifying as workers with a particular interest in the labour process, he saw this defining aspect of humanity emerging into active public consciousness, for him a matter of great historical consequence.

Marx placed this notion of social labour power at the centre of his analyses of capitalism and (a rather Eurocentric) human history leading up to capitalism. History became an evolving sequence of typically dominant ways of organizing social labour throughout a given society, what he called 'modes of production'. There are constant tendencies to both harness labour power and increase our productive capacity. This yields relatively stable systems of social relations oriented to the organization of social labour to core productive economic activities: growing food, making goods and commodities, deploying violence, generating and disseminating ideas. These social relations are at the same time regulated and stabilized by systems of beliefs about proper social and political order, right and wrong, natural or divinely sanctioned hierarchies of social power and so on. But in certain periods, transformations in economic productivity outstrip the belief systems that house them, leading to profound restructuring of the political, ideological, legal and cultural 'superstucture' that had previously helped hold the systems together (Marx in Tucker 1978: 4–5; Wolf 1982: 75–100). Thus Marx analyzed at length and in detail, often with great perceptiveness, the ways that the 'feudal' mode of production, based on a productive surplus generated by peasants working lands owned and controlled by a hierarchy of nobles, gave way to the capitalist mode of production in which surplus wealth was generated through commodity production and trade, with large numbers of poorly paid workers delivering their labour power to the owners of the means of production. Whereas the feudal mode was held together by notions such as human stations in life being part of a divinely ordained plan and the basic heritability of commoner and noble status, the capitalist mode relied on notions such as the rights of the individual, the naturalness of markets and the sanctity of private property. Thus the concept of the mode of production tracks major transformations in the overall increase of the productive power of social labour and in the fabric of ideas and beliefs about social order that serve to justify the ways in which the fruits of human labour power are allocated.

The concept of class operates within the concept of the mode of production. Marx shifted between socioeconomic analyses on the grand scale, in which only major classes mattered, such as peasants, wage labourers, great land owners and capitalists, and more historically and nationally specific analyses in which finer gradations of class interests, for instance state functionaries, small business owners, marginalized aristocracies and so on needed to be identified (Marx in Tucker 1978: 441–2, 608). The important idea for the present discussion is that classes are the key carriers of power within the mode of production, and thus transformations in the mode of production are driven forward by increasingly confrontational conflicts between the major classes in society. As medieval urban-based manufacturers and traders gradually increased the scale of their operations, accumulating wealth and becoming involved in the formation of modern banking, they increasingly displaced older landowning nobilities as key holders of the power and resources on which monarchs and their states depended. Thus over centuries, this 'bourgeoisie' created capitalist society in its own image. Similarly, Marx and Engels anticipated that industrial wage labourers, once sufficiently organized and strategically conscious of their position within the larger system, would hold the greater power when uncontrolled competition between capitalists sufficiently destabilized the capitalist system. This would allow class energies, focused in revolutionary political parties, to win control of the state and use it to build communist societies out of the wreckage of capitalism. Human productive power, having reached its full development, would finally be able to serve the needs of all equally, with no reason for class division and conflict.

This leads to our last concept, alienation, and in a sense back to the idea of social labour. This Hegelian concept is much more explicitly used in Marx's early work, particularly the *Economic and Philosophic Manuscripts of 1844*. However it informs Marx's mature discussions of capitalism and the way it disempowers and mystifies those subject to it (Marx in Tucker 1978: 292–3, 319–29). Marx's concept of alienation combines connotations of legal separation with existential self-estrangement. Ollman's detailed study identifies four dimensions of alienation for workers in capitalist society (1976: 131–52). First, workers lose control of their own labour power, forced to sell it as a commodity for employment. Second, they lose control of what they produce, the material commodity that is owned by the capitalist. Third, workers become alienated from their fellow human beings, in particular the capitalist class that dominates them through the control of their labour. Finally, they are alienated from their essential nature as human beings because, for Marx, what defines us as a species is precisely our power to transform nature through social labour, and that power appears to us under capitalism as an independent power controlling us, rather than as the direct, free expression of our natures. It is important to know that Marx drew this concept of alienation from contemporary analyses of religion, in particular Ludwig Feuerbach's argument that ideas of God and spirituality were alienated expressions of organic human consciousness. Our mental powers to know, imagine and explain the world give rise to notions of an omnipotent creator and law-giver, that in turn has power over us – but this is only our own mental powers estranged and turned against us (Aron 1968: 186–7; Marx in Tucker 1978: 107–8, 144, 169–72). This idea of the alienation of, and oppression by, our own natural, social powers is foundational for Marx's analysis of capitalism and his prediction of its demise. It implies the possibility of a world free of alienation, in which we can have as much 'power to' as we want without any problems of 'power over', of delivering our powers into the hands of others. Many doubt whether such a world is plausible, and in practice, a century of real-world experiments with communism has more often resulted in the alienation of social powers into the service of Leviathan-like states. Marx's acute diagnosis of the workings of capitalism has an Achilles heel in its emancipatory ambitions.

## Emile Durkheim

Emile Durkheim (1858–1917) was born 40 years after Marx, coming of age intellectually in a world where capitalism and the modern state were more firmly established. No freelance radical, he was a university professor (Bordeaux and then Paris), and founder of the first course in sociology in France. Much of his energy went into defining the field of sociology as one distinct from history, economics and especially psychology, with its own focus of study: the patterns of belief and behaviour that are emergent properties of society itself. Durkheim subscribed to a kind of progressive French republicanism, and a form of socialism that aimed not at overcoming capitalism but at counterbalancing its disordering effects on society and morality. Unlike Marx, Durkheim was relatively uninterested in social conflict as a causal process. He saw it more as a symptom of societal dysfunction. But just as Marx's fundamental conception of power was projected onto the general human capacity for transformative social labour, Durkheim's basic notion of power, and more particularly authority, was projected onto society as a whole, as a systemic property. He was particularly concerned with how moral order and authority could be regrounded in highly secular, individualist, competitive modern societies.

'Society' is the central idea in Durkheim's work, and yet, like Marx's 'class', it is not one he ever carefully defines (Poggi 2000: 84). Nonetheless, it is apparent that he conceives of society in a particular way. While Durkheim drew on biological analogies to discuss the forms and evolution of societies, in contrast to material bodies developing in space and time, he thinks of society as an inherently mental or ideational phenomenon (Giddens 1971: 66–7). It is the 'body' of ideas and sentiments that regulate and guide social behaviour, imbuing social relations with certain consistent patterns. Because these patterns are observable, despite being grounded in collective mentalities, he called them 'social facts'. They are facts also because they are 'caused': just as, in a game of pool, the cue ball transfers physical force to the eight ball, sending it veering toward the corner pocket, social rules and moral norms steer human behaviour in particular directions. Each individual mind maps its reality through various mental 'representations' of that reality, mapping both its natural and social 'laws'. Taken together, the aggregate of every individual's set of 'representations' forms something Durkheim called 'collective consciousness', which is not some kind of mysterious group mind, but rather the *de facto* coordination of individuals' representations into the larger patterns that define a society. But it must be added that for Durkheim the important part of this was not so much the coordination of beliefs about the natural and material world, but rather the social laws, the norms about how people ought to behave, and what should happen to them if they don't behave within accepted social rules. Society itself must supply the authority that binds its members together into a coherent whole (Poggi 2000: 90–3).

Durkheim saw a central trajectory in social evolution, which further unpacks this conception of society. His first book based on his doctoral dissertation, *The Division of Labor in Society* (1964 [1892]), picked up this term from political economy, but gave it an expanded meaning. Where 'the division of labour' had meant the separation of tasks in the production process, so that each worker can specialize on one part in coordination with others to achieve greater productivity overall, Durkheim used this idea to describe the historical transformation of society as a whole, in the process of modernization. It is not just that production processes in the modern factory become sub-divided and reorganized, but the various functions of government (executive, legislature, judiciary, military), of the economy (food production, commodities, trade, services, credit), and social needs and their provision more generally (education, healthcare, recreation) all become more sharply differentiated and elaborated. This process is summed up as a shift between two abstracted forms of society. In 'traditional' society, the social roles available to individuals were limited, and social segments (lineages, villages) were largely similar and self-contained in their structures and functions. Thus what bound larger populations together was precisely their 'collective conscience', their body of shared belief about the natural and social worlds. But in 'modern' society, with its extensive and intensive division of labour, society is made up of many different parts with highly different functions, which are also highly dependent upon one another to sustain society overall. Thus it is functional interdependence, rather than collective consciousness, that binds society together. A fundamental effect of this shift in Durkheim's view is that persons themselves become more differentiated, highly individualized, cultivated as unique, autonomous, private beings – in some sense more constitutionally cut off from their fellows. This, combined with the weakening of collective consciousness, creates a susceptibility to 'anomie', a sense of isolation and aimlessness that arises in the absence of clear, strong, binding social norms.

Durkheim was alert to how the complex division of labour greatly increased the powers of modern society, but simultaneously threatened to disempower individuals, enhancing their autonomy while also dwarfing them, setting them morally adrift. His prescriptions for how to address the dislocations of modern, individualized, industrial society arose out of his sociology (Aron 1970: 81–94; Poggi 2000: 121–40). Marx had predicted and prescribed the collapse of the capitalist system, the gradual disappearance of the state as its domination became superfluous, and the reconciliation of humanity with its estranged labour power. Durkheim, by contrast, sought the reform of modern industrial society, viewing the democratic state, somewhat naively, as a relatively impartial mechanism for coordinating diverse social interests. But for him the key problem was the weakness of moral authority, and here he prescribed neither the state nor the family as the prime source for re-moralization, but rather what he called 'occupational groups', a broad category which covered everything from professions to skilled labour. In his view corporate entities based on occupational groups (a cross between guilds, unions and professional associations) were best situated to articulate effective and meaningful group ethics, relating these to a wider civic morality, coordinated through a system of representative government (Durkheim 1964, 1992: 1–31). For Durkheim politics was a matter of reinvigorating moral authority, social codes of right and wrong, in a way that would map onto the complex division of labour, and be suffused throughout the social system.

Durkheim's last book, *The Elementary Forms of Religious Life* (1965[1912]), summed up his central concerns through a universal theory of religion. Its central ideas were that: (1) active participation in rituals and symbols that express emphatic social norms tend to make those very norms more compelling for the participants; (2) all religions are based on dividing the world into 'sacred' things, that are set apart and forbidden, and 'profane' things, that are worldly and accessible; (3) ritual/symbolic participation helps constitute and reinforce the sacred/profane divide; (4) societies create ultimate objects of sacredness, for example totems and gods; and, *crucially* (5) such objects are transfigured representations of society itself – in worshipping gods and acknowledging their moral authority, the members of society are in fact submitting themselves to society and its moral authority. Where Marx, following Feurerbach, saw in religion a form of alienation to be overcome, Durkheim saw evidence of the necessity of society's moral authority over its members, and some promise that this could be reconstituted in secular, individualized, modern society. His sociology sought to figure out how to do this. Durkheim is remembered for his criticism of those who, like Hobbes, try to derive all social and moral obligation from the primal practice of contracting between free agents, because, he argued, the initial willingness to enter into a contract implies some prior basis of social trust which is itself the actual foundation of obligation (Poggi 2000: 117). His arguments about the society hiding behind the god, and the trust hiding behind the act of contract, parallel each other in their search for sound moral groundings.

## Max Weber

Our third key theorist of modernity, Max Weber (1864–1920), was born into an upper middle class German family of textile manufacturers and linen merchants. His irascible and outgoing father was a jurist and municipal councillor on the political right, his more serious mother was liberal, cultured, socially conscious and of a deep Protestant faith. It is frequently suggested that the tensions between his parents' personalities deeply shaped his own, and played a role in his 'nervous breakdown' in 1897, from which he only partially recovered, returning to academic life in a limited capacity in 1902, until an inheritance allowed him to retire in 1907 and devote himself entirely to his studies. Weber seems to have been torn between a life of active political engagement and more detached sociological study, but his personality pulled him toward the latter, teaching at Berlin (from 1891) and Heidelberg (from 1896), both universities in which he had conducted his degree studies of law, history, economics, philosophy and theology. A liberal and nationalist, he became a very influential figure in German intellectual circles, as well as a behind-the-scenes adviser to politicians (Aron 1970: 303–6; Bendix 1960: 25–34; Gerth and Mills 1958: 3–31).

We have already encountered Weber in Chapter 2. This is because, unlike Marx and Durkheim, he did very specifically try to conceptualize and define power, thereby directly affecting subsequent theorizing. To recap the discussion from Chapter 2, Weber suggests that the term 'power' (*Macht*) is simply too broad to be of much analytic use. He therefore centres his analysis on *Herrschaft*, 'the probability that a command with a given specific content will be obeyed by a given group of persons' (Weber 1978: 53), which is variously translated as 'authority' and/or 'domination'. On balance I prefer domination, if we understand it as the broadest concept identifying contexts where social action is regularly and fairly stably controlled by some source of commands, also broadly defined. 'Authority' for Weber is a major component in social patterns of domination – it is part of how they work, in no way logically opposed to domination. But there are other principles besides authority that also bolster domination, including habituation and self-interest. Authority implies 'legitimacy', and Weber offered a basic typology here: (1) charismatic authority/legitimacy based on the personal devotion to and belief in the person of the leader by followers; (2) traditional authority/legitimacy based on time-honoured established practices as embedded in institutions, offices, routines and so on; and (3) rational or legal authority/legitimacy based on coherent and consistent reasoning from fundamental principles that have been accepted in the first place. These types are not axiomatic principles as with Hobbes, but are abstracted from Weber's vast historical knowledge to impose order on, and facilitate comparisons within, that body of knowledge. The other thing to remember about Weber's most basic definitions of these sociological terms – domination, authority, legitimacy – is that they are framed within a general discussion at the beginning of is magnum opus *Economy and Society* (1978: Chapter I) which emphasizes that social action should be situated within organizational contexts. For Weber these concepts are necessary for any fundamental understanding of how social action is organized, and how organization becomes formalized and routinized. Power for Weber is a matter of organization.

Weber put particular emphasis on three modes of organizing power (Weber 1978: 926–40; cf. Poggi 2001: 16–21). Firstly 'classes', or 'class situations', are possible bases for social action based on economic relations, that is, a group's shared position in the market by virtue of some particular resource: land, capital, specialized labour skills and so on. Whether the market position of a class bestows on it a strategic advantage in advancing its collective interests and, if so, whether the class becomes, on balance, collectively aware of this fact are open questions, not predetermined by economic logic. The second mode, 'status groups' (*Stände*), by contrast, are groups defined by a consciousness of their own collective identity and interests, particularly in terms of the honour or prestige its members enjoy within the wider society in which they are situated. Rigid social hierarchies in which racial, ethnic or caste groups are obliged to show deference or superiority according to their station are the sharpest examples. But more loosely defined status groups develop within more fluid systems of stratification, and of course, status and class situations are often closely aligned. Thirdly, Weber uses the term 'parties' broadly to mean not just modern political parties, but any organized faction within a wider field of political competition, which explicitly sees its purpose as the pursuit of power. And of course again, these may align themselves with classes or status groups. These three modes of power organization suggest points along a continuum, from the relatively *de facto* distribution of power opportunities by economic relations, to the conscious if often customary articulation of power as social standing by various status groups in regard to each other, to much more narrowly strategic alliances around political goals (Hearn 2002: 23–6).

Underlying much of Weber's work was a basic tension between 'charismatic authority' 'resting on devotion to the exceptional sanctity, heroism or exemplary character of an individual person, and of the normative patterns or order revealed or ordained by him' (1978: 215) and 'bureaucracy', formalized administrative domination through a system of depersonalized rules, offices, procedures and senses of duty, justified on rational and legalistic grounds. Although he never advances it as a simple hypothesis, there is a very strong sense across Weber's work of a long-term historical trajectory from small scale societies in which religiously based charisma (embodied by 'the prophet') was the main wellspring of ordering social norms, to modern states and economies in which bureaucracy inevitably becomes the dominant form, displacing charisma. Along the way, charisma can become routinized and generalized, associated with offices and institutions, for example the Pope and the Church, rather than individuals, contributing to patterns of traditionalized authority and legitimacy. At the same time, there is a sense of desperate hope in Weber that, within the modern context, capitalist economic structures will allow space for entrepreneurial innovation, and democratic plebiscitary structures will foster political leaders who can promote the innovation in social values that is needed. Thus bureaucracy, particularly in its most developed, rationalistic modern forms, is presented by Weber as the ultimate means of organizing power, and one with many virtues. But, it also threatens to submerge all original motivating purposes, mechanically reproducing itself through sheer efficiency (cf. Gerth and Mills 1958: 51–5).

Weber famously described himself as 'religiously unmusical', melancholically suggesting his own powers of reason undermined any nascent talent he might have for spirituality. This reverberates with his agonizing over the decline of charisma and the 'disenchantment' of an ever rationalizing world, and brings us back once again to the question of the grounding of 'ought' in a secular and scientific world. A basic starting point for Weber's mature sociology was a distinction between two types of rational action: one oriented toward the rational calculation of the best means to achieve a given end (*Zweckrational*), the other oriented toward the choice of ultimate ends and values (*Wertrational*) (1978: 24–6). Correspondingly, in a famous speech given to young, would-be politicians at Munich University in 1918, in the wake of the First World War, he argued that 'all ethically oriented conduct may be guided by one of two fundamentally differing and irreconcilably opposed maxims:

conduct can be oriented to an "ethic of ultimate ends" or to an "ethic of responsibility"' (Weber 1958: 120). In other words, he saw a tension between the principled pursuit of ultimate values, regardless of the costs to oneself and others, and conscientious regard for how one's decisions and actions may affect the well-being of others, even though this regard may compromise one's ultimate ends. He saw virtue in both ways of being, advising only that the life of politics would always compel hard, existential choices between the two (Aron 1970: 256–65).

Marx, Durkheim and Weber thought and wrote in a time when the rapid growth of the systemic powers of modern capitalist society and the state, and the society-wide conflicts this generated, were overwhelmingly apparent. Their main ideas of power were generally couched as system properties, rather than qualities of individuals and their relations. Marx located power in humanity's (alienated) capacity for social *labour*, which became historically focused and effective in particular modes of production and leading classes. Durkheim located power, and more specifically binding moral authority, in *society* itself, understood as a relatively integrated universe of value creation. Weber located power in social *organization*, which took myriad forms in human history, but became ever more concentrated in the bureaucracies of state and economy in the modern era, wistfully seeking some residual space for the ethical force of the individual person.

## Return to Italy: classical elitism and Gramsci

If northern Italy was in the vanguard of European developments in Machiavelli's day, leading in commerce, urban government and arts and letters, by the late nineteenth century it had fallen behind. The lead in commercial and industrial developments had passed to the Netherlands and then Britain. The country came under foreign Habsburg domination (1559–1796) and then became a client state of the French Republic during the Napoleonic era (1796–1814). In the middle years of the nineteenth century the older patchwork of cities and principalities were unified (the '*Risorgimento*') as a nation-state. In the end there was a compromise between progressive republican and conservative monarchical nationalisms, resulting in a monarchical constitution based on the Savoy dynasty of Piedmont. After unification (c.1861) Italian politics was characterized by radical socialist movements, with governments generally trying to appease and moderate these forces. Popular politics was shaped by tensions between the development of a more modern working class in the industrialized north, and the increasing impoverishment of a southern peasantry involved in underdeveloped agriculture, and often driven to emigration. Ideas of democracy based on an extensive franchise were slowly gaining ground. At the same time in intellectual circles there were many committed to a more classical notion of liberalism, in which freedom of thought and the 'freedoms' created by free market competition were more highly valued than those of democracy *per se*. This context of social change and political contestation stimulated a revival of interest in Machiavellian problems of political leadership, and new ideas about the nature and role of elites (Bottomore 1966; Kolegar 1967; Meisle 1965a; Olsen 1970: 106–79).

## Vilfredo Pareto

Vilfredo Pareto (1848–1923) exemplified the intellectual commitment to classical liberalism. Born in France to minor nobility, Pareto's father had fled Italy when his republican activism led to trouble, abandoning his fortune and marrying a French Calvinist, Pareto's mother. The family had all returned to Turin by 1859, where Pareto trained and worked as a civil engineer, like his father. In his twenties, Pareto moved to Florence where he became ensconced in intellectual circles, and an ardent advocate of *laissez-faire* economic policies. He provided journalistic commentary on the political issues of the day, and ran unsuccessfully for parliament. By the turn of the century he had established himself as a leading economist – his name today is most frequently associated with various rules of thumb he formulated for interpreting statistical data (for example, Pareto curves, Pareto optimality). But by the time he was fifty he had turned his attention to questions of political sociology, believing that, beneath the rational principles that seemed to account for economic behaviour, were more fundamental and 'irrational' forces that needed to be studied with the same scientific detachment. Like Hobbes before him, he saw himself as bringing science to bear on human irrationality. Like an engineer, he viewed societies as systems governed by law-like constants, expressed in equilibrating cyclical patterns (Powers 1987: 13–20).

In sociology and politics Pareto is best known for arguing that all societies of any scale and complexity are divided into those who rule, 'elites', and those who are ruled, and that it was useless to think it could be otherwise. He developed a ponderous and confusing terminology, particularly as put forward in his magnum opus *Treatise on General Sociology* (1963[1916]). I will avoid this and simply try to convey the main contours of his mature theory of elitism (see the two shorter and simpler works, *The Rise and Fall of the Elites* (1968[1901]) and *The Transformation of Democracy* (1984[1920]). Pareto believed that history was shaped by ebbs and flows in popular sentiments and mass psychology, but that because these are unobservable, we must estimate them through observations of major patterns in (1) social behaviour, and (2) discourses of all kinds – ideological, religious, political, philosophical – that provide justifications for the powers that be. He detected a macro-historical pattern to social change, great cyclical undulations between periods in which people seek innovation, adventure, change, and the opposite tendency, toward conservatism and preservation of tradition. Neither inclination is ever universal within a society, but in a given phase, one tendency or the other will have the upper hand. This ultimately expresses itself as alternating phases. In 'Phase A', economic growth and political decentralization are accompanied by sentiments, values and beliefs supporting consumption, gratification, liberality and decadence. In 'Phase B', economic contraction and political centralization are accompanied by frugality, conservatism, moral prescriptivism, and so on. As each phase reaches its limit of possibility, the other begins to come back in, as a response (Powers 1984, 1987).

Pareto's (1968[1901]) theory of 'the circulation of elites' needs to be understood against this backdrop. He believed that for any valued social practice, there will be those who excel, and these constitute the elite of that practice. He recognized that what skills and abilities are valued is culturally and historically relative, although he tended to blur normative and descriptive notions of 'the best'. Be that as it may, he distinguished between the sum total of elites leading their respective practices, and the 'governing elite' whose specialty is politics in particular. History for Pareto was a vast graveyard of such elites, which had acquired power, become decadent, complacent and over-extended, only to be displaced by a newer elite, which was more fit for the times. The criteria for excelling at political leadership tend to correspond to this grand cycle of phases. Phase A tends to cultivate political elites made up of 'foxes', i.e. those good at scheming, coopting, misleading, but generally 'on the make' and prepared to take chances. Phase B tends to encourage 'lions', i.e. those good at providing a stern moral vision, and prepared to use force where necessary. Foxes tend to give way to lions, because they become decadent and effete, and unwilling to use force. In their turn, lions lose out to foxes when the strong arm of rule becomes oppressive and resented, and people seek emancipation. As this suggests, Pareto's notion of a governing elite was not one of a permanently self-reproducing stratum, always in power and born to rule. Rather, while there must always be some elite 'at the helm', the terms of effective political leadership change. It is possible to have elites that combine the strategies of lions and foxes (although there is a tendency for one style to dominate), and new counter-elites are always forming, by appealing to and mobilizing the masses (Scott 1996: 139–46). Pareto's concept of elites, in its most mature version, was more a structural necessity than an accomplishment of politically gifted groups (Powers 1987: 133–4). He was a 'disaffected liberal' (Powers 1984: 22), fascinated and estranged by politics, but with a mission to disabuse people of their dreams of egalitarian transformation, whether based on democracy, socialism or both. He took Marx's idea of a ruling class, but turned it into a permanent fixture of history, which cannot be transcended, no matter how much the personnel may change. Mussolini saw his writings as justification for fascism, and made him a senator near the end of his life, but he had largely withdrawn from public life by this time, and whether he had any sympathy for fascism is highly debated (see Meisle 1965b: 34–6).

## Gaetano Mosca

Ten years younger than Pareto, Gaetano Mosca (1857–1941) was born to a middle class family in Palermo, Sicily. He studied law, and like Pareto, consciously saw himself as working in the fearless critical and realist tradition of

Machiavelli. But unlike Pareto, his political science was rooted more in comparative history and law rather than analogies to physical science, and he expressed his ideas with a more moderate tone. Although Mosca had advanced a theory of 'ruling classes' in the 1880s, Pareto's later theory of 'elites' was more widely recognized, causing an acrimonious dispute between them. Nonetheless, from the mid-1880s Mosca developed a prominent career in Italy as a scholar, university teacher, journalist and politician. Always a strident critic of parliamentary democracy and its corruptibility, he nonetheless became its cautious defender under the fascist regime (Albertoni 1987; Hughes 1965).

The root of Mosca's theory was the observation that 'the dominion of an organized minority, obeying a single impulse, over the unorganized majority is inevitable' (1939: 53). The fundamental dynamics of social organization generate ruling groups in all societies. Mosca preferred the terms 'ruling class' or 'political class' to 'elite', but this is problematic in that his 'organized minority' was not a group defined by a shared economic situation, but rather precisely by its hold on state power. Like Pareto, but without his cyclical vision of history, Mosca saw that political leadership requires skills and attributes, that the abilities needed change with the political and economic context, and that elites must maintain a degree of openness in order to rejuvenate themselves. He recognized different patterns of recruitment to the ruling class, particularly between aristocratic systems, in which heritability creates social closure, and democratic systems that recruit more openly and widely. He also appreciated that elites must make wider alliances through mobilizing 'social forces', by which he meant sub-elites in other institutional hierarchies (e.g. military, religious, economic, academic). These need to be enlisted, and provide both sources for recruitment and bases for the formation of counter-elites (Scott 1996: 131–6).

Mosca is also remembered for the idea of the 'political formula', a set of beliefs that legitimate political authority by grounding it in abstract principles. This was not a thin concept of ideology as deception of the masses, but rather linked to culturally embedded values. He began with a distinction between 'supernatural' formulas that grounded aristocratic rule in divine will, and 'rational' formulas that grounded democratic rule in the 'will of the people'. In his mature work this was elaborated by a distinction between 'autocratic' and 'liberal' formulas, the former seeing authority as radiating down from above, the latter as radiating up from below (Albertoni 1987: 23–5, 56–7; Scott 1996: 136–8).

Mosca is connected to Weber by their mutual friend Robert Michels (1876–1936), a gifted student of Weber's who left Germany to take up a post in Turin in 1907. Michels (1968 [1911]) developed Mosca's idea of the 'organized minority' in his extensive study of the bureaucratization of the Social Democratic Party of Germany. He formulated what he called the 'iron law of oligarchy', the premise that any organization, no matter how democratic its principles, will tend to generate a core leading group that monopolizes power within the organization and institutionalizes that monopoly. Again, as with Pareto and Mosca, there was a strong element of disenchantment in

Michels' work. His original socialist hopes and political activism were frustrated, leading him eventually to join the Italian Fascist Party in the vain hope that Mussolini's charismatic leadership might bring about proletarian politics uncompromised by bureaucracy.

It is important to grasp that these three theorists of elitism were not blind defenders of traditional or established elites, nor were they trying to invent fascism. They were ultimately driven by a profound scepticism about the aspirations of marxian socialism, fearing that utopianism unqualified by realism would lead to disaster, which in many communist countries it did. They sought to offer a hard look at the world as it 'is', countering those swept up in visions of how it 'ought' to be.

## Antonio Gramsci

The ideas of the Italian Marxist Antonio Gramsci (1891–1937) saw a remarkable revival and spread on the left and among academics in the UK and later the US, beginning in the late 1950s and reaching a peak in the 1970s and 1980s (Forgacs 1989). Gramsci provides an interesting counterpoint to the 'classical elitists', on the one hand highly critical of their aloof, conservative liberalism, but on the other sharing their Machiavellian inspiration, and a deep concern with political leadership. His father was a small town government functionary in Sardinia, whose five-year imprisonment for corruption pushed the family into relative poverty. Gramsci won a scholarship at the University of Turin in 1911, becoming active in the Italian Socialist Party and the socialist press by 1913. He eventually abandoned his studies, dedicating himself entirely to political and cultural journalism and party politics, helping to form the Communist Party of Italy in 1921 and becoming its leader in 1924. In 1926 he and other communist deputies were arrested by the fascist government, which sentenced him to 20 years in prison in 1928. He was freed in 1937 because of international pressure but, in poor health throughout his life, died of a brain haemorrhage within days of his release.

Gramsci argued from the perspective of revolutionary politics that Italy was in a particular historical situation, neither as backward as Russia nor as advanced as northern European societies. He believed a successful movement in these circumstances had to be built by harnessing grassroots industrial organizations to the leadership of a revolutionary political party, which could organically develop and promote new, or 'capture' existing, social organizations (unions, schools, clubs and associations and so on) throughout civil society. This infrastructure would provide the basis for a society-wide project of cultural education, instilling the moral values and aspirations of the communist project. He saw this as the necessary route to overcoming the deep divisions – between north and south, peasant and proletarian, intellectuals and the people – that characterized his country. I emphasize two central and related ideas. In communist circles *hegemony* was conventionally used to indicate the political leadership of the proletariat over other classes and groups, such as peasants and intellectuals, in the process of revolutionary mobilization. By Gramsci, it was defined as

> intellectual and moral leadership (*direzione*) whose principal constituting elements are consent and persuasion. A social group or class can be said to assume a hegemonic role to the extent that it articulates and proliferates throughout society cultural and ideological belief systems whose teachings are accepted as universally valid by the general population (Fontana 1993: 140; cf. Gramsci 1971: 12–13).

Hegemony is generally cultivated by groups within civil society, while direct domination, backed up by force, is the province of the state. Thus hegemony was central to Gramsci's idea of building a movement outside the state which would eventually have the means and momentum to 'conquer' the state, capturing the major means of domination as well.

This leads to the second idea. Evident in this concept of leadership is a broader programme of *intellectual and moral reform*. Arguments between Gramsci and the liberal Italian philosopher and historian Benedetto Croce are revealing here. Croce had argued that Machiavelli, in grasping that politics was about the leadership of the masses, had simultaneously discovered a radical rupture between a high culture of philosophy, ethics and reflective thought on one side, and a low culture of ideology, politics and instrumental action on the other. A liberal elitist, Croce believed that intellectuals and philosophers who were dedicated to truth must stand aloof from politics, which is about the necessary instrumental manipulation of the masses by political leaders. For Gramsci on the contrary, Machiavelli represented the politically engaged intellectual, who saw that politics must be about how 'the prince' achieves leadership through the moral elevation of the people, by educating them. Thus Croce contrasted the Renaissance, which advanced high culture precisely because it was a project of narrow aristocratic and courtly circles, with the Reformation, which became stunted as a philosophical movement precisely because it became immersed in mass politics. Gramsci's valuation is the opposite – the Renaissance was a narrow and incomplete intellectual movement, which left Italy weak and susceptible to foreign take-over, whereas the Reformation (associated with northern Europe's more advanced development) was a model of what genuine political mobilization is all about, a transformation of values leading to frontal assaults on the state (Fontana 1993: 1–51). It was in this light that he reworked Machiavelli's idea of the 'prince', making the revolutionary party the ultimate measure of value:

> The modern Prince [that is, the revolutionary party], as it develops, revolutionizes the whole system of intellectual and moral relations, in that its development means precisely that any given act is seen as useful or harmful, as virtuous or wicked, only in so far as it has as its point of reference the modern Prince itself, and helps to strengthen or oppose it. In men's

consciences, the Prince takes the place of the divinity or the categorical imperative, and becomes the basis for a modern laicism and for a complete laicization of all aspects of life and of all customary relationships (Gramsci 1971: 133).

Gramsci's influence on the left in recent decades is complicated by two factors. First, his most mature and well read work comes from the series of notebooks he wrote while in prison (1926–37), written in difficult circumstances and under the scrutiny of censors (Gramsci 1971). Thus he sometimes used obscure terminology, and addressed contemporary issues indirectly through historical analogies. His less read journalism and letters from before his imprisonment help give a more rounded view and sense of the evolution of his thought (Gramsci 1994). It is also the case that his more theoretical ideas developed in the specific context of trying to advance socialist and then communist projects in an Italy with a well established elite intellectual culture and constitutional integration, but socially fragmented and economically unevenly developed, indeed underdeveloped in some areas. Italy was in an unstable and revolutionary situation, but one that led to fascism rather than communism. Gramsci's rediscovery, particularly in the Anglophone academy from the 1970s, often transplanted his ideas rather awkwardly into the arena of left-wing politics in relatively stable capitalist liberal democracies, where they were used to soften the rigid economism of orthodox Marxism and advocate the need for a broadly left counter-culture, but found little strategic political application (Bellamy 1994).

In different ways, in turbulent times, Pareto, Mosca, Michels and Gramsci wrestled with the formation of modern mass politics, and conflicting relationships between political, intellectual and moral leadership. Each in his own way was somewhat ambivalent about democracy, at least in its liberal form. Thus it is somewhat surprising that, while they have been demonized in some quarters, their ideas have been to various degrees incorporated into more recent theories of liberal democracy, such as those seeking to understand American democracy, as we will see in the next chapter. It turns out it is not easy to entirely expunge the idea of elites, or do without hegemony.

## Conclusion

This historical sketch has had to be highly selective. Noticeably absent is greater attention to the eighteenth century and the Enlightenment, figures such as Montesquieu and Rousseau, the debates about federalism in the early US, and Tocqueville's acute observations on the American and French republics in the early nineteenth century. But limits of space, and the fact that these thinkers have had more influence on theories of government than power in general, are reasons for leaving them aside on this occasion.

I make two general points about this overview. First, these figures are like focused points describing a long historical arc, summed up in Bendix's (1978) phrase: 'from kings to people'. Machiavelli and Hobbes articulate their concerns about power in terms of princes' relations to citizens or subjects. Their problems are shaped by the particular paradigm of what it means to rule. With the great social theorists of modernity, Marx, Durkheim and Weber, the problems of power have become much more systemic – grounded in the very natures of labour, society and organization. There are roles for social agents that lead, such as ruling and revolutionary classes (Marx), and charismatic figures (Weber), but these are subsumed within larger theories of the workings of power. With the Italian elite theorists and Gramsci referring back to Machiavelli, the question of leadership returns to the foreground. But these are not individuals, but organized groups, elites at the helm of government bureaucracies or revolutionary parties mobilizing a movement against the state. By this final stage, the problem of power has been reconstituted as one of leaders and followers, now with the institutions of constitutional and democratic politics more fully formed. Thus the three periods move from the destabilization of the medieval–feudal monarchical paradigm, to the vast expansion of systemic social power by capitalism and modern nation-building in the nineteenth century, to the unsteady consolidation of the capitalist, liberal democratic regime under more formalized systems of competition for state power among elites, factions, movements and parties by the beginning of the twentieth century.

The second point is less of a development and more of a constant. All the thinkers considered above grapple with a world in which 'is' and 'ought' have been rent asunder. Some attempt to reunite them, while others are more resigned to the rupture. Machiavelli argues that the effective prince must distinguish between them carefully. Hobbes argues that whoever is king should be granted the power to determine 'ought', especially in matters of religion. Marx believes that in overcoming capitalism's alienation of labour, the distinction itself would become meaningless. Durkheim is very concerned that society should be able to generate a binding sense of 'ought', though not terribly concerned with contending conceptions of right and wrong. Weber faces the problem with resolve and resignation, arguing like Machiavelli that we must make a clear distinction, and take personal responsibility for the 'ought' we choose. Pareto and Mosca seem to almost revel in the rupture, taking an aloof pride in their own liberal values, and in their recognition of the distance between these and the realities of elites vying for power. Gramsci, like Marx, looks forward to a day when the rupture might be overcome, but until then seeks to make the revolutionary party the ultimate arbiter of ought, somewhat like Hobbes' 'king', and Durkheim's 'society'. The 'solutions' vary, but the problem is constant.

This historical sketch has dealt with intellectuals, scholars and revolutionaries, and only toward the end do they begin to appear as 'academics' in the sense we conventionally recognize today. The debates about power explored in the next three chapters all take place largely within the modern academy, among scholars working within modern universities that protect academic freedom, while delivering mass higher education. From here on in, the debates become in some sense domesticated and routinized within the educational regimes of the modern nation-state, now fully emerged and established, conducted mostly at greater remove from the actual dynamics of power in society. This has both advantages and disadvantages.

CHAPTER 4

# American Debates

## Introduction

Recent texts on the nature of power frequently begin with, or at least feature, part of the debates that are the subject of this chapter (e.g. Clegg 1989; Haugaard 1997; Hindness 1996; Scott 2001). These took place in a specifically American academic milieu, from the 1950s to the 1970s, and bear the impress of that social, political and historical context. While often presented as debates about the general nature of power, they were in fact debates about power in the United States, although with wider implications. This very conflation is telling. I begin with a bit of historical scene-setting, before launching into the debates themselves.

The Second World War transformed the United States, both consolidating internal political and economic processes that had been developing for decades, and fundamentally altering its geopolitical position in the world. The US had seen growth in manufacturing, industry and finance since the Civil War (1861–65), with the expansion of major business empires in various industries – oil, steel, railroads, banking – during what became known as 'the Gilded Age' (1865–1900). Agriculture and subsidiary small town industries also grew during this period and after, benefiting from the damage done by the First World War to agriculture in Europe and Russia. Growth is rarely smooth however, and there were serious economic depressions in the mid-1870s and mid-1880s, and finally, and most seriously, in the 1930s, triggered by the Wall Street Crash of 1929. Both the concentration of economic wealth and power and depression stimulated governmental action and change. The widespread Progressive Movement (c.1890–1918) responded to poor urban and industrial conditions amid prosperity, calling for industrial regulation, anti-trust laws, and a federal income tax. Franklin D. Roosevelt's presidency (1933–45) during the Great Depression established the 'New Deal', a raft of federal legislation aimed at regulating industries and banking, stimulating the economy through federally funded projects, and providing welfare and economic relief to citizens. These measures began the recovery, but it is widely recognized that the United States' involvement in the Second World War completed it. The incredible stimulus to industry and employment required by the war effort rebooted the economy, at the same time giving a powerful push to scientific and technological research, and to the coordinating powers of the federal government. By the end of the war the US had a revivified industrial economy, a homeland infrastructure undamaged by warfare, and a leading international role to play in the economic reconstruction of Europe and new transnational bodies such as the United Nations. This was also a kind of 'moral victory' for the US, which could claim to have made sacrifices to save Europe from the demon of fascism it had unleashed, and to be the main defender of capitalism, liberalism and democracy (and Christianity), as the Soviet Union regrouped its power and the long Cold War set in.

Outgoing President Dwight D. Eisenhower's famous farewell *Address to the Nation*, delivered on 17 January 1961, remains one of the most trenchant comments on post-war developments in the US, so I cap off this scene-setting with an extended quote:

Now this conjunction of an immense military establishment and a large arms industry is new in the American experience. The total influence – economic, political, even spiritual – is felt in every city, every statehouse, every office of the federal government. We recognize the imperative need for this development. Yet we must not fail to comprehend its grave implications. Our toil, resources and livelihood are all involved; so is the very structure of our society.

In the councils of government, we must guard against the acquisition of unwarranted influence, whether sought or unsought, by the military–industrial complex. The potential for the disastrous rise of misplaced power exists and will persist. We must never let the weight of this combination endanger our liberties or democratic processes. We should take nothing for granted. Only an alert and knowledgeable citizenry can compel the proper meshing of the huge industrial and military machinery of defense with our peaceful methods and goals, so that security and liberty may prosper together. Akin to, and largely responsible for the sweeping changes in our industrial–military posture, has been the technological revolution during recent decades. In this revolution, research has become central; it also becomes more formalized, complex, and costly. A steadily increasing share is conducted for, by, or at the direction of, the Federal government.

Today, the solitary inventor, tinkering in his shop, has been overshadowed by task forces of scientists in laboratories and testing fields. In the same fashion, the free university, historically the fountainhead of free ideas and scientific discovery, has experienced a revolution in the conduct of research. Partly because of the huge costs involved, a government contract becomes virtually a substitute for intellectual curiosity. For every old blackboard there are now hundreds of new electronic computers. The prospect of domination of the nation's scholars by Federal employment, project allocations, and the power of money is ever present – and is gravely to be regarded. Yet, in holding scientific research and discovery in respect, as we should, we must also be alert to the equal and opposite danger that public policy could itself become the captive of a scientific–technological elite (Eisenhower in Ledbetter 2011: 215–17).

Given this context of a massive expansion of national power, it is perhaps not surprising that the American social sciences and academic world, itself stimulated by post-war economic growth and the GI Bill, tended to be a bit insular and inward, and to view the US and its problems as representative of the world as a whole. The three main sections that follow examine: (1) a set of debates about whether the US is ruled by elites at the local and national levels; (2) an intervention by Talcott Parsons about the social nature of power; and (3) an intervention by Steven Lukes about how we can infer the presence of power, when it is often obscured.

## Power: community structures and national elites

Floyd Hunter's *Community Power Structure: A Study of Decision Makers* (1953) started a wave of similar studies in the 1950s and 1960s that aimed to grasp the nature of power and decision-making in (mostly) US cities of various sizes (see Aiken and Mott 1970; Hawley and Svara 1972; and various articles reprinted in Scott 1994). Hunter was unusual, having begun a doctorate in sociology at the age of 37, after a considerable career in social work administration in Indianapolis and Atlanta. 'Regional City' was the fictitious name he gave to Atlanta, the focus of his seminal study that grew out of years of practical experience in city politics in that setting. He argued that urban power was structured by small networks ('cliques' or 'crowds'), featuring people prominent in downtown land ownership, real estate development, public utility management, department stores and banking. New policy initiatives began as ideas among these groups, floated in discussion in private clubs, sounded out with actors in mid-level city organizations and government bureaucracies, and only then made into public governmental issues advanced by the Chamber of Commerce or other civic organizations. In this way a fairly small, affluent stratum of people, a network of smaller networks, took the lead in defining the city's business development and public service agendas. Hunter did not see these people as a tightly defined, self-conscious elite, but rather the occupants of advantageous structural positions in the local community, who shared a greater frequency and intimacy of social interaction. His aim was to give a realistic, unvarnished account of how power works at the local level, not to suggest dark conspiracies.

Not surprisingly, as community power studies proliferated, they revealed variation in their findings (for some good examples see: Pellegrin and Coates 1956; Miller 1958; Schulze 1958). Rossi (1960) detected an emergent pattern of three main types in these studies: (1) larger cities with major business interests and 'pyramidal' structures that focused decision-making in the hands of one or a few (as in 'Regional City'); (2) smaller towns and suburbs in which a 'caucus' cultivates consensus among a 'cozy few' of the community leaders; and (3) 'polylithic' structures, in which power hierarchies are more divided, with professional politicians and government agencies more separate from business and professional leaders influencing community organizations. This last type seemed to be associated with cities in which party politics articulated with local class structures in such a way that 'capturing' local government arises as an explicit strategic issue. In these studies there was often an implicit assumption that the city might provide a microcosm for understanding the national political order, with major business interests being deeply involved in local decision-making. But such major employers often turned out to be rather aloof from local politics. It gradually became clear through subsequent studies that, because major businesses were often based outside the city, they had limited interest in the nitty-gritty of local politics, and were more interested in general conditions amenable to their own business profitability. The leaders of city politics on the other hand are 'place entrepreneurs', part of a 'growth coalition' interested in attracting external investment (from businesses or government) to bring revenue into the city and, often crucially, to raise urban land values (rent) (Domhoff 2007; Molotch 1976).

Hunter, and many of those after him, based their research on what came to be known, rather pejoratively, as the 'reputational method'. This involved starting with a baseline list of plausible community leaders from the registers of key organizations (Chambers of Commerce, League of Women Voters, city newspapers and so on), presenting this list to identified local government insiders and asking them to select or rank from this list the most important people. Those most frequently identified became the target population for interviews about who holds power, who knows who, and how local policy issues get formulated. This was of course not the whole method, but rather a way of generating an appropriate sample of subjects with which to do elite interviews. The content of those interviews, along with relevant documents and other observations, made up the complex body of data for most community power studies (Domhoff 1983: 159–60).

In 1956, the radical sociologist C. Wright Mills published his controversial study of national power structures in the US, *The Power Elite* (1956; 1958 summarizes the argument). Based on a combination of original research and surveys of journalism and other public documents, Mills painted a portrait of American society in which three great interlocking bureaucratic hierarchies of corporate business, government and the military had come to dominate society. Through the cumulative effects of expanding turn-of-the-century business empires, the Great Depression and the New Deal, and finally mobilization for the Second World War, power, previously more widely dispersed, had become concentrated in, and more coordinated between, these three hierarchies. Alongside this process he also identified the rise of a nationwide system of celebrity that at once rubs shoulders with, and adds lustre to, 'real' power, while also providing an alternate arena of symbolic status competition, misdirecting public attention. By using the term 'elite' Mills signalled that he was defining a small stratum of society in which there was considerable similarity of social background and socialization, careers pursued through large scale organizations that often led individuals to move across the boundaries between the three hierarchies, and enough common interest and mutual benefit to motivate the coordination of action, at least some of the time. Mills saw this stratum as sitting atop a vast social pyramid, the middle layers of which, captured partly by the urban community power studies but also involving Congress, state governments and regional economic actors, operated as a contained arena of balanced power struggles between various organized interests. But beneath this he saw a much larger 'mass society' forming that was apathetic, politically disengaged, and distracted by the celebrity industry.

It is an image that is intuitively believable in its broad outlines, but also frustratingly underspecified. As Wrong (1957) noted shortly after the book was published, Mills infers a range of shared interests and policy initiatives from the convergence of institutional hierarchies and social networks, but never really demonstrates it. He highlights the tendency of the executive branch of government to take decisions about war and military related foreign policy without adequate Congressional scrutiny, but fails to illustrate instances of coordinated elite action within the national arena. G. William Domhoff, who has subsequently been a leader in the tradition of national power structure research that Mills could be said to have started, observes that it is not unreasonable to think, as Mills did, that 'the highly skewed distributions of wealth and income in the direction of the corporate rich, and their over-representation as appointees in the executive branch of the federal government, are indicators of their power' (2007: 6). Nonetheless he also dissents from some of Mills' arguments, suggesting that the military is not on an equal footing with the corporate and government power hierarchies, and that Mills overstates the cooptation of the party system and the labour unions by the 'power elite', the permanent de-politicization of the masses, and the capacity of the media to hoodwink and control a passive population (2006).

Mills read widely and was influenced by several theorists, including Mosca, but his perspective can be characterized as an odd mixture of Marx and Weber. With Marx he felt a kind of moral outrage at human alienation, and while eschewing what he called Marxism's 'labor metaphysic' (1962), he saw the processes of capitalism as central to the analysis of power. But his deepest antipathy was not toward class structure or markets *per se*, but rather toward bureaucracy in all its forms. Weber was very troubled by the effects of bureaucracy on the individual, but he nonetheless also saw positive aspects in its institutionalization of rationality. With Mills however, there is an overwhelming sense of the 'little guy', the individual of integrity, being dwarfed and muted by the expanding bureaucracies – corporate, military, governmental – that organize the modern nation-state. In a sense, while his aim was to disabuse the public of the idea that the United States actually operated according to the ideals of open and enlightened 'town hall' democracy, his own indignation seemed to be fuelled by a romantic yearning for precisely that lost past, whether real or imagined. Paradoxically, when we look around the US of 2012 for popular examples of his viewpoint, we find it resonates in certain respects with the discourse of the Tea Party, a grassroots right-wing movement hostile to interfering 'liberal elites' and 'big government'. Mills would have abhorred this comparison, perhaps preferring to cast his lot with the 'anti-capitalist' protesters and their critique of corporate power. But the point is that a common cultural paradigm of anti-elitism is available for use on both the left and the right in US politics. However, the right has frequently been much more effective at mobilizing this idea and associated sentiments, and deploying it through the democratic political process.

The most strident critics of Hunter, Mills and associated approaches have been the school of political scientists variously labelled 'pluralists', because they emphasize the idea that power is widely distributed among various groups in society, or 'behaviorists' because of their emphasis on research methods that provide observable measures of power. In an effort to provide an empirically based challenge to 'elite' theories, Robert A. Dahl led an in-depth study of New Haven between 1957 and 1959, which became a landmark of US political science (1961). During the research he published 'A Critique of the Ruling Elite Model' (1958), accusing Hunter and Mills of formulating a notion of elite rule that was impossible to disprove because it offered no clear diagnostic test of a ruling elite's power. He argued that:

> The hypothesis of the existence of a ruling elite can be strictly tested only if:
> 1. The hypothetical ruling elite is a well-defined group.
> 2. There is a fair sample of cases involving key political decisions in which the preferences of the hypothetical ruling elite run counter to those of any other likely group that might be suggested.
> 3. In such cases, the preferences of the elite regularly prevail (1958: 466).

Thus, for Dahl the proof of an elite's existence hinges on scrutinizing decision processes and their outcomes. He made several further stipulations. First, while the normal rules of representative democracy generate governing minorities, these in themselves do not constitute self-reproducing elites. Second, although some groups, such as city based business communities, have a 'high potential for control' because of the resources they command, 'political effectiveness' requires unity of purpose as well, and this is by no means guaranteed. Third, different groups have different interests and 'scopes' of influence. In a true elite these scopes of influence would be aligned in one group, but this rarely happens in a democracy. Fourth, it is in the nature of human organization that some will be in a position to have greater influence over decisions than others, but this in itself does not make them an elite. And finally, if a group manages to achieve its political preferences, not in the face of opposed preferences from other groups but because of widespread indifference of the masses, this cannot be taken as evidence of their dominance. An elite must be able to override resistance on key political issues. The upshot of Dahl's argument was that Hunter and Mills had only succeeded in showing a degree of correspondence between the possession of wealth and high status, and the occupancy of positions of organizational leadership, indirectly inferring that this constituted an ability to realize preferences and accrue benefits, and defined a social group that was able to coordinate its interests. Dahl was unconvinced.

Dahl's student and researcher on the New Haven study, Nelson Polsby, elaborated some of these arguments in a book-length critique of those he called 'stratification theorists' (Hunter, Mills and others). This work promoted the 'pluralist' approach, and helped to set the dominant tone in the social sciences from the mid-1960s on (1963, see Polsby 1960 for a précis of the argument). He argued that the 'stratificationists' attempted to illegitimately deduce elite rule from a set of quasi-ideological assumptions that:

> (1) the community is divided horizontally, into ranked layers, with a single layer on top; (2) power is a collective attribute of classes indexed by the per capita economic and status value positions of class members; (3) classes are oriented to the goal of maximizing their long-run share of values; (4) the total supply of values in the community is smaller than the demands of the various classes (1963: 111).

The fact that Polsby's re-analysis of eight key examples of stratificationist studies seems to undermine this set of assumptions might be taken to indicate that he had rather crudely aggregated and stereotyped the studies in question. Be that as it may, he uses this as a basis to advance the pluralist approach, the essence of which is that for purposes of research one should presume at the outset that:

(a) power is not monopolized by any group but rather dispersed, situational, and issue-specific; and
(b) only higher frequencies of prevailing in a direct conflict over decision outcomes, and not merely higher levels of participation in or gain from, decision-making processes, is reliable evidence of power.

But the depth and subtlety of Dahl's work is best conveyed by the study of New Haven itself, *Who Governs: Democracy and Power in an American City* (1961). Dahl and his colleagues found that over the preceding two centuries New Haven had evolved from a system of rule by a patrician oligarchy (a true elite) that monopolized multiple values – wealth, prestige, education, organizational leadership – to one characterized by 'dispersed inequalities' in which different groups tended to control different resources. The 'patricians' had been displaced, first by a small class of business entrepreneurs, then by the growth of several ethnically and religiously defined working class communities whose votes were courted by 'new men', a more professionalized class of politicians oriented toward these various voting blocs. To cap off the argument Dahl showed that there was relatively little overlap between the 'social notables' of contemporary New Haven, those descended from the patrician class and associated with local high society, and the 'economic notables', i.e. the leaders of the contemporary business community. Examining three 'key issues' at the time of the study – political nominations, urban redevelopment, and public education – he found that different constituencies took particular interest in different issues, and that the economic notables, far from dominating through their wealth, were relatively disengaged from local politics. In short, he found a shifting plurality of political interests and mobilizations, and no local elite.

More broadly the study served to support a series of observations about pluralist democracy in the US. First, politics involves a small 'political stratum' that is much more involved in the ideas and ways of politics than the majority of the population. While almost all subscribe to a general cultural creed of democracy, the political stratum is much more deeply versed in, and committed to that creed (1961: 90–4). Second, there is an interplay between the direct influence of a small minority of leaders on decision-making and the indirect influence on those decisions by the bulk of citizens who are variously disengaged, or episodically enlisted as constituents, according to issues and the political climate (*Ibid.*: 163–5). Third, this process is heavily mediated by 'subleaders', who act as brokers between leaders and constituencies, and must be rewarded for their services (*Ibid.*: 95–7). And fourth, not all those with strategic resources use those resources for political ends, and when they do, the values they aim to maximize are multiple and diverse (*Ibid.*: 271–5). Thus Dahl's overall account emphasizes that direct decision-making is concentrated in the hands of the few, a professionalized political stratum, but that this stratum is relatively open to new recruitment, and that the larger mass is relatively apolitical most of the time. This is seen as a virtue of representative democracy:political leadership has to be responsive to the mass of the citizenry to a degree, but also in turn moderates mass politics and creates a healthy space for relatively apolitical daily life (*Ibid.*: 311–25).

These arguments are underpinned by a particular conception of power. Dahl generally prefers the term 'influence' to that of 'power' (1963: 50), although he also treats them interchangeably. He rather influentially defined power thus: '*A* has power over *B* to the extent he can get *B* to do something that *B* would not otherwise do' (1957: 202–3, see also Dahl 1968), and this conception informs his writings on the subject. Thus power abides in the relationship, in the event of one actor altering the behaviour of another. This definition almost prescribes that to study power one must look for events (decisions) in which wills are opposed and only one can win. This is a very different conception from the one we saw in Chapter 1, put forward by Peter Morriss (2002: 14–19) and which I endorse. It perceives power as a 'dispositional concept', one that identifies a general propensity of an object (person, group, organization) to have certain effects, to be able to make a difference in the world, leaving the specifics of power relationships an open question. I would simply point out that Dahl's conceptual decision here appears to take a defining problematic of democracy – the resolution of disagreement between actors – as a starting point for the definition of the more general concept of power, and this appears to be the wrong way round. Democracy is a way of managing power, not its origin.

Of course, the pluralist position itself came under scrutiny almost immediately. Bachrach and Baratz (1962; 1963) heartily endorsed the pluralist critique of elite theories, in particular the assumptions that all communities contain a 'power structure', that these tend to be stable over time, and that a reputation for power is a reliable indicator of power (1962: 947–8). But they also highlighted two defects in the pluralist position:

> One is that the model takes no account of the fact that power may be, and often is, exercised by confining the scope of decision-making to relatively 'safe' issues. The other is that the model provides no *objective* criteria for distinguishing between 'important' and 'unimportant' issues arising in the political arena (Bachrach and Baratz 1962: 948, emphasis in original).

They argued that power is not just about winning a decision, but about preventing decisions from being made, by shaping the public agenda (cf. Scoble 1964: 315). In other words, pluralist democratic politics doesn't just respond to diverse, conflicting interests, it mobilizes and directs those interests as well (see Schattschneider 1960, a key inspiration for Bachrach and Baratz's argument).

Dennis Wrong pays particular attention to the problem of 'anticipatory influence', namely, that actors may adjust their actions in advance in the face of power, thereby avoiding confrontation and obscuring the operation of power. He takes Polsby to task for refusing to recognize that economic resources and advantage may elicit submission before matters can come to a head in a moment of 'decision'. Dahl on the other hand recognizes the role of anticipatory influence, but primarily in the sense of political leaders anticipating how constituencies will stand on an issue and acting accordingly, in ways that concord with the democratic process. The possibility of powerful minorities inhibiting opposition is underplayed (2002: 127–30).

The most direct challenge to the pluralist position, and sustained defence of the basic intuitions of the elite model, has been presented by G. William Domhoff (1967). His study of New Haven, completed in 1978, using some of Dahl's original data as well as new data, found, *contra* Dahl, that: the social and economic elites of New Haven were significantly interconnected; business leaders had reasons for being relatively uninterested in political nominations and public education, but were very interested in, and influenced, urban renewal; Yale University, as a major landowner, also had deep interest in urban renewal, was interconnected with the business community, and instrumental in attracting government funding. Dahl had suggested that Yale was a marginal player in city politics. Methodologically, Domhoff concluded that Dahl's original strategy of examining decision processes through interviews with those involved at the time severely underestimated their capacity to misrepresent what was going on. Domhoff claimed the advantage of hindsight through the public and archival documents that he had used to reconstruct the wider power processes from some temporal distance (Domhoff 1978; 1983: 184–96; 2005a).

This brings us back to basic and conflicting conceptions of power, and how to study it. Domhoff maintains that 'power can be thought of as an underlying trait or property of a collectivity. As with any social trait, it is measured by a series of indicators, or signs, that bear a probabilistic relationship to it' (1983: 10). In other words, power is a dispositional concept, not a phenomenon that can be directly observed. Therefore researching power involves defining indicators that can be taken as evidence of the trait. He suggests that the main ones are: 'who benefits', i.e. the powerful are more likely than most to obtain what is normally valued in a given society; 'who governs' i.e. the powerful are more likely to occupy institutional positions with direct control over decisions affecting society; 'who wins' i.e. in direct conflicts over issues, the powerful will tend to get their way; and 'who stands out', i.e. the disposition of power in society is something important and therefore known to many, and it is possible to draw on the knowledge of well-informed observers. In other words, there are reasons to have some confidence in the 'reputational method'. Domhoff is quite clear that these indicators, like most in the social sciences, are imperfect. For instance, the powerful may let the weak win some battles for strategic reasons, or an ineffectual fool may inherit a windfall or win the lottery. Nonetheless, if several indicators are used, and show probabilistic correlations with certain social groups, then he believes we are warranted in using this as a way of defining elites that monopolize social power (1983: 7–13; 2005b). The key point here is that Dahl and Domhoff begin from fundamentally different conceptual and methodological starting points, and this strongly affects their collection and interpretation of data.

I conclude this section on a paradoxical note, which complicates the elitist–pluralist debates. Jack L. Walker's 'critique of the elitist theory of democracy' (1966) accused Dahl of being representative of a scholarly trend that endorsed elitism as a necessary component of modern representative democracy. How could this be, given Dahl's attack on the 'ruling elite model' (1958)? Walker argued that there had been a shift in recent decades from a 'classical' theory of democracy that emphasized widespread, well-informed public debate guiding public officials and their decisions, to a 'revisionist' theory. This approach, which he associates with figures such as Joseph Schumpeter (1976 [1943]: 269–302), Seymour Martin Lipset (1968) and Dahl (1961), that belied a distrust of an often naive and volatile popular will, instead emphasizing the management of democratic plurality by institutionalized procedures and a professionalized cadre of political leaders. The new perspective was perhaps epitomized by Schumpeter, who frankly described representative democracy as based not on 'rule by the people', but on competition between leading groups (elites) for the people's votes, in a sense rephrasing Pareto's idea of a 'circulation of elites' (see Chapter 3; cf. Bottomore 1966: 48–68, 112–28). For

Walker this was a revision both of descriptive accounts of how democracy really works (especially in the US), and of normative aspirations for what a democratic society should aim to achieve. He finds the shift troubling, worried that it serves to legitimate passivity and apoliticism among the citizenry, approves a form of elite rule, and that it was causing researchers to neglect important contemporary aspects of US politics, such as the black civil rights movement. Dahl (1966), unsurprisingly, was indignant, countering that no such 'revisionist school' existed, and that his own concern was with a realistic account of the institutional conditions for good leadership in pluralist democracies, and hardly 'elitist'. It is the very possibility of the disagreement and the ambiguities it implies, rather than its resolution, that is interesting. To invoke the Tea Party once more, just as Mills' radical analysis of US power structures seems to ironically resonate with their grievances, Dahl's more conservative endorsement of US democratic institutions is designed to show how that system can moderate and diffuse this kind of ideologically charged popular insurgency. In this instance, Mills and Dahl appear to switch positions across a left–right spectrum.

## The power of positive function

Meanwhile, the leading American sociologist Talcott Parsons had levelled a trenchant critique of Mills' *The Power Elite* from a more theoretical angle (1994 [1957]). Parson's theoretical writings are notoriously abstract, but this piece is one of his most accessible, and revealing of his fundamental perspective. As we saw in Chapter 2, Parsons ties the idea of power to legitimate authority. For him, power does not 'lie behind' the surface of authority, as force, but rather is generated by the social agreement to constitute institutionalized authority. His critique of Mills' notion of a coherent national power elite begins with several substantive disagreements about ongoing historical processes. Broadly, he sees the growth in economic, governmental and military bureaucracies, not as a burgeoning Leviathan, but as necessary functional adaptations to the growth in scale and complexity of the US economy, and the country's altered position on the world stage. Like the pluralists, he also thinks Mills exaggerates the cohesiveness of the upper classes, failing to appreciate, for instance, the significance of the separation of ownership from professionalized management for the constitution of power in the modern corporation. But the heart of his argument challenges how Mills conceives of power. He claims that Mills subscribes to a 'zero-sum' concept, in other words, as in a game where there can be only one winner, power is always a matter of one gaining at the expense of another. (Note that Mills has this in common with Dahl.) But power for Parsons is not just about the 'distribution' of limited goods, but also the 'collective' capacity to achieve ends. Mills sees only 'power over', whereas Parsons wants to add, and heavily emphasize, 'power to'. He suggests that behind Mills' analysis is a 'utopian conception of an ideal society in which power does not play a part at all' (1994: 266). He is worth quoting at length here:

> This is a philosophical and ethical background which is common both to utopian liberalism and socialism in our society and to a good deal of 'capitalist' ideology. They have in common an underlying 'individualism' of a certain type. This is not primarily individualism in the sense that the welfare and rights of the individual constitute fundamental moral values, but rather that *both* individual and collective rights are alleged to be promoted only by *minimizing* the positive organization of social groups. Social organization as such is presumptively bad because, on a limited, short-run basis, it always and necessarily limits the freedom of the individual to do exactly what he may happen to want. The question of the deeper and longer-run dependence of the goals and capacities of individuals themselves on social organizations is simply shoved into the background. From this point of view, both power in the individual enterprise and power in the larger society are presumptively evil in themselves, because they represent the primary visible focus of the capacity of somebody to see to it that somebody else acts or does not act in certain ways, whether at the moment he wants to or not (1994: 266, emphasis in original).

Thus Parsons detects in Mills' radical attack on elitism and yearning for a 'Jeffersonian' past, not simply a socialist critique of the power of big business over the state, but a thoroughly American individualism that cannot articulate a positive conception of collective 'power over'. Parsons' elaborate structural functional theories, on the other hand, were designed precisely to highlight the systemic functionality of major social institutions for individuals. His intellectual programme was to explain how diverse individual social action becomes integrated into a larger social order, placing considerable emphasis on the role of shared values in generally orienting social behaviour toward common, or at least coordinated, ends. While the image of the 'social system' that dominated his work suggests a very static, self-equilibrating conception of society that is often criticized, it should be recognized that this was also a device for understanding long-term historical change – how societies succeed or fail to adapt in the process of social evolution, a point that became clearer toward the end of his career (Parsons 1977; Holton 2003). In terms of the classical theories of modernity examined in Chapter 3, Parsons took from Weber a concern with the orientation of social action to values, especially economic action to non-economic social values, and perhaps Weber's matter-of-fact, 'value neutral' conception of *Herrschaft*, which Parsons preferred to translate as 'authority' or 'imperative control' rather than 'domination'. From Durkheim he took a concern with the cohesion of society through shared values and the primacy of 'society' as a unit of analysis. From both he took the increasing complexity of society, the division of labour and bureaucracy as posing core problems of adaptive social order.

But it has been argued that Parsons' conception of power errs in the opposite direction to Mills'. Parsons placed great emphasis on the virtues of social order, value consensus and trust between members of society, which indeed are necessary to some degree for a society to persist. But this tends to marginalize the role of social conflict and power struggles in generating social change, and the additional roles of coercion, deception and ideology (or 'shared values' with a bias towards the interests of certain groups) in maintaining social order. As Giddens remarked:

> By treating power as necessarily (by definition) legitimate, and thus starting from the assumption of consensus of some kind between power-holders and those subordinate to them, Parsons virtually ignores, quite consciously and deliberately, the necessarily hierarchical character of power, and the divisions of interest that are frequently consequent upon it. However much it is true that power can rest on 'agreement' to cede authority which can be used for collective aims, it is also true that interests of power-holders and those subject to that power often clash (Giddens 1994[1968]: 79)

While I think it is truer to say that Parsons was just not bothered by the 'hierarchical character of power', Giddens' objections have force.


## Power hides its face

It took a Briton to bring these American debates to a head. Steven Lukes' highly influential essay *Power: A Radical View* (1974) both summed up and, in a sense, redirected the debates we have been discussing. The original essay was republished in 2005 with two new chapters that restate, develop and qualify the original argument, and I cite from the new edition. But, because the essence of the argument remains the same and because I am interested in this chapter in reviewing the original trajectory of debates, I focus mainly on the original argument (2005: 14–59).

Lukes constructs a logical narrative that leads from the 'liberal' or 'one-dimensional view of power' of Dahl and Polsby, through the 'reformist' or 'two-dimensional view of power' of Bachrach and Baratz, to his own 'radical' or 'three-dimensional view'. In short, as we have seen, the 'one-dimensional view' focuses on overt, observable conflicts in the decision of key issues of public politics and policy. The 'two-dimensional view' focuses on both decision-making and the marginalization of decisions in the agenda-setting process, allowing that some issues may remain 'potential', and some conflicts of interest submerged or diverted. Luke's 'three-dimensional view', on the other hand, critiques both of the other views, suggesting not just that overt political agenda-setting gets manipulated, but that social conflicts can be 'latent' and not apparent to anyone, and that one must articulate counterfactual hypotheses about people's 'real interests', which they may not be aware of themselves, in order to fully analyze power relations (2005: 29). To make this argument he reformulates Dahl's definition of power:

> I have defined the concept of power by saying that *A* exercises power over *B* when *A* affects *B* in a manner contrary to *B*'s interests. Now the notion of 'interests' is an irreducibly evaluative notion: ...if I say that something is in your interests, I imply that you have a prima facie claim to it, and if I say that 'policy x is in *A*'s interest' this constitutes a prima facie justification for that policy. In general, talk of interests provides a license for the making of normative judgments of a moral and political character. So it is not surprising that different conceptions of what interests *are* are associated with different moral and political positions. Extremely crudely, one might say that the liberal takes people as they are and applies want-regarding principles to them, relating their interests to what they actually want or prefer, to their policy preferences as manifested by their political participation. The reformist, seeing and deploring that not everyone's wants are given equal weight by the political system, also relates their interests to what they want or prefer, but allows that this may be revealed in more indirect and sub-political ways – in the forms of deflected, submerged or concealed wants and preferences. The radical, however, maintains that people's wants may themselves be a product of a system which works against their interests, and, in such cases, relates the latter to what they would want and prefer, were they able to make the choice. Each of these three picks out a certain range of the entire class of actual and potential wants as the relevant object of moral appraisal (2005: 37–8).

This quote presents several themes that are worth further comment. First, by starting from Dahl's formulation, Lukes commits himself to a concept of power as domination, as 'power over'. I have already suggested some of the problems with this approach. In the first edition, Lukes argued that '[c]onsensual authority, with no conflict of interests, is not, therefore, a form of power' (2005: 35), which put him squarely at odds with Parsons' more anodyne conception of power. In the second edition, Lukes acknowledges that his original focus had actually been domination, and that he had reduced power in general to this aspect, although this does not stimulate him to reconsider Parsons' position (2005: 85–6, 109–10). More generally, this move locks Lukes into an argument about decisions and debates that never happened, and why they didn't. This generates much ambiguity about the relationship between structure and agency. According to the 'radical view' the exercise of power may involve 'inaction', be exercised by a 'collectivity', and be 'unconscious' (2005: 52). Now, 'conscious inaction' is not too problematic, and lands a serious blow on the pluralist strictures. If, for instance, a regulatory body is aware of serious risks to the public, but chooses quietly to take no action when it could have, this neglect to use power is itself a manifestation of power. The term 'collectivity' has ponderous breadth – it is much easier to imagine a committee

exercising power than a whole social class. Without making an absolute dichotomy, the former is more of an agent, the latter more of a structure (see
Chapter 1). But the real difficulties arise with the matter of consciousness. For
Lukes, power, as distinguished from the sheer operations of social structures,
consists in agents, knowingly or unknowingly, affecting the interests of others,
when they could in theory have acted otherwise (2005: 57, 68). This is a very
broad conception not just of power, but of agency, which is stretched to cover
all possible actions, not just those deliberately done or left undone. Combined
with an expansive notion of agents that includes classes and institutions, it is
an idea of power that shades into the very idea of social order itself (Hearn
2008; Layder 1985; Wrong 2002: 184–9).

A crucial effect of Lukes' approach is to turn the problem of power into a
problem of knowing. It is noteworthy that he labels Dahl and Polsby primarily as 'behaviorists' rather than 'pluralists', thus emphasizing the problem of
what evidence counts in the study of power, rather than a thesis about how
power is distributed in society. He examines Crenson's (1971) study of how
the company US Steel impeded the development of clean air legislation in
Gary, Indiana, by refusing to actively engage with local protests around the
issue, and by playing on reasonable anticipatory fear that the company would
economically harm the city if it relocated in the face of restrictive legislation.
Lukes compellingly argues through this case that 'evidence' of power must
include broad descriptive accounts of issues which, in light of comparison
with similar cases and guiding assumptions about normal human interests,
can be construed as cases of interests in conflict, no matter how muted and
submerged that conflict (2005: 44–8). His emphasis on identifying 'real interests', however unarticulated, has brought him in for accusations of wielding
a patronizing, quasi-Marxian concept of 'false consciousness' (Benton 1981;
Hay 1997) that seems to privilege the perspective of the 'objective' researcher
over the subjective understandings of those enmeshed in the power relations
in question. Lukes counters, effectively I think, that we cannot do without
the ideas of deceiving and misleading as mechanisms that serve the interests
of the powerful. To deny their role is as much an error as reducing power to
them (2005: 144–51). But the 'problem of knowing' is most fundamentally
evident in Lukes' insistence that power is 'an essentially contested concept'
(2005: 14, 61–5, 110–11; after Gallie 1955–56). By this he means, as suggested in the long quote above, that the very definition of power has implications
for power, and thus can never stand outside the contest among interests that
may want to define power quite differently from one another. Morriss (2002:
202–4) has objected that this kind of invocation of 'essential contestability'
confuses disagreements over the meaning and use of words with the nature
of concepts. 'Radicals' and 'conservatives' may use the word 'power' to label
quite different concepts, as we have seen, but the contest here is between political positions and sets of interests, not a property of the concept itself. As a
philosopher, Morriss worries that this way of posing the matter will condemn
us to an instrumental rather than a principled use of language. Once again, it

seems that among those who define power as a relationship *between* agents, rather than as a dispositional property *of* agents, endless contestation about that definition is much more likely.

These are all important theoretical issues. However, it is slightly odd that for many students of power today, Lukes' essay has become the primary summation of the American power debates of the 1950s–1970s, because much of what those debates were about recedes into the background in his argument. The question of whether liberal democracies have genuine elites, or are governed by a more widely distributed plurality of interests, gets lost. The debate itself may be tendentious on both sides, but at the same time it has been productive, driving a lot of empirical research. The whole idea of community power structures focused attention on the complex relationships between power, wealth, organizational position, social prestige and so on. Lukes' turn to the third dimension tends to focus questions of power on the roles of belief, ideology and hegemony, and how we take account of them in research. These are very important questions, but can also divert attention from less ideational and less obscure structures of power that may be just as important for explanation. Whatever its limits as a summation of previous debates, the original 1974 essay anticipated one of the major trends in subsequent research which we explore in the next chapter, which is to ground the study of power in questions of epistemology. Thus it is not surprising that Lukes selects two of the major figures in this trend, Michel Foucault and Pierre Bourdieu, as primary interlocutors for the new chapters in the 2005 edition of *Power: A Radical View*.

## Conclusion

I have emphasized the national, social and historical context of these debates from the 1950s to 1970s, and some of the substantive issues at stake are now a bit dated. Intervening decades of neoliberal policies and further globalization have reconfigured many aspects of power, between cities and states, between economic, governmental and civil society organizations, between corporations, shareholders, trade unions, and so on. But many of the underlying theoretical disputes that drove these debates remain fundamental and relevant, and much can be gained from further empirical attention to these same research contexts of local, urban and national power structures, and especially how the tensions between economic and political organizations of power play out.

The whole set of debates explored in this chapter points us back to basic conceptual issues raised in Chapter 1. First, whether or not one finds 'elites' depends partly on how we define them along a continuum from 'agency' to 'structure'. The more we think of elites as highly cohesive groups with a unified will that they collectively seek to realize, the less likely we are to identify something that fits the bill. But the more we think of elites as an artifact of social structure, as a necessary aspect of leadership in complex bureaucratic organization, the more likely we are to find them (Burton and Higley 1987). Second, those who perceive elitism and are critical of it are more likely to think of power as 'power over', as one group dominating others. Those who instead perceive good, necessary, institutionally bounded political leadership are more likely to think of power as 'power to', as a general social capacity to get things done. Our argument that power normally involves both 'over' and 'to' aspects, suggests that the real issue here is not 'whether' some have 'power over', because this is unavoidable, but how openly they get it, how disinterestedly they use it, on what grounds their power is justified (cf. Domhoff 1983: 209–10). This leads us to more nuanced questions about patterns of asymmetry and balance in actual distributions of power: how these operate, how stable they are, and whether or not their effects are desirable. Third, Lukes' engagement with the behaviourism of the 'one-dimensional' approach has a complicated relationship to the question of whether power should be conceived of as a potential of certain entities, or as only existing in its actual manifestation. In essence, Lukes argues that many manifestations of power may not be recognized as such because the ideological processes that bring them about obscure the workings of power. But to the degree that Lukes commits himself to Dahl's relational definition of power as such, the question of power *in potentia* does not arise. Thinking of power as a potential is logically linked to defining it as a disposition of an object.

Finally, despite the labels of 'radicals', 'conservatives', 'liberals' and 'reformists' that have populated this chapter, it is important to grasp that, in many ways, these are debates among liberals of various stripes. All the disputants would contend that they are arguing for how best to realize human freedom, for groups and individuals. On the 'conservative' side, Dahl and Parsons are defending the capacity of the institutional forms of US democracy to realize these goals, while on the 'radical' side Mills and Lukes are concerned with the concentration of power undermining the autonomy and self-realization of the individual. Indeed, Lukes had strong interests in Durkheim (1973a) and the problem of individualism (1973b) that preceded his work on power, and become more apparent in the revised edition of the 'radical view'. The debates explored here, however generalizable, arose out of specifically American aspirations and anxieties about the fate of individual and collective freedoms in a burgeoning superpower with increasing institutional concentrations of power. They are as much about whether the US was succeeding in its historical mission to advance liberty and democracy, and how best to pursue these goals, as they are about power in general. They should be read in this light.

CHAPTER 5

# Epistemological Approaches

## Introduction

Consider two quotes about the relationship between knowledge and power from Francis Bacon (1561–1626), early modern proponent of scientific methods, and Michel Foucault (1926–84), critical philosopher of the modern human sciences:

> Human knowledge and human power come to the same thing, because ignorance of cause frustrates effect. For Nature is conquered only by obedience; and that which in thought is a cause, is like a rule in practice (Bacon 2000: 33).

> The important thing here, I believe, is that truth isn't outside power, or lacking in power: contrary to a myth whose history and functions would repay further study, truth isn't the reward of free spirits, the child of protracted solitude, nor the privilege of those who have succeeded in liberating themselves. Truth is a thing of this world: it is produced only by virtue of multiple forms of constraint. And it induces regular effects of power (Foucault 1980: 131).

At first glance these might appear to be saying similar things. Both assert the unity of knowledge, or truth, and power. But Bacon's legacy is the conviction that by better knowing the natural world, we will be able to control it to our benefit, while Foucault sought to expose the way claims to knowledge invariably endorse particular regimes of power. A crucial difference between them is that Bacon was mostly concerned with knowledge about the non-human, natural world, whereas Foucault was primarily concerned with knowledge about human beings as such. Although developments in genetic science tend to blur the boundary, the distinction remains important. Knowledge claims about human nature have implications for the social ordering of power and inter-human morality. However there is also an affective shift between these positions, to which Foucault himself alludes, from a confidence and faith in knowledge ('knowledge will set you free'), to an attitude of distrust and suspicion, or at least extreme relativism about truth. For the moment I simply want to suggest that this is more than just a difference between Bacon and Foucault, that it is diagnostic of the whole career of human knowledge over the last four hundred years from Bacon's time to ours.

This chapter examines approaches to the study of power that emphasize the role of knowledge in the constitution of power. Chronologically, it picks up roughly where the last chapter left off. However, it presents one of two broadly contemporaneous tendencies in the theorization of power, what I call 'epistemological approaches' as opposed to the 'evolutionary approaches' discussed in the next chapter. These labels are meant to highlight basic themes, differences of approach and, to a degree, patterns of intellectual influence among theorists. But of course I am imposing these categories on a messy reality that could be organized differently. I am trying to explore a general style of thought, and for this reason will examine several theorists and theories in a discursive rather than simply chronological order, and in ways that are not necessarily proportionate to their wider influence. In particular, I address aspects of how Foucault and Pierre Bourdieu have conceptualized power, with the aim of placing them in the general context of my argument. But those wanting a more comprehensive view of their highly influential works will need to turn to the large literature on them, as well as their original writings. (As starting points, on Foucault see: Foucault 2000, Gutting 2003, McNay 1994, Rabinow 1984; on Bourdieu see: Bourdieu 1990, 1991, Jenkins 2002, Shusterman 1999a.)

The shift in the terms of theorization between the 'American debates' of the last chapter and this one is striking. There the language was one of organizations, bureaucracies, classes, elites and power structures, all generally brought to bear on the relationship between society and fairly conventional notions of public politics. Here, the key terms are such things as *epistemes*, discourses, fields, networks, habitus, subjectivity – generally concepts with a more abstract (which is not to say illegitimate) relationship to the human reality they aim to analyze, and with formal politics being less central, but not absent, as the object of study. There continue to be concerns about the problem of the method of studying power but, in keeping with the general trend I am identifying, these are often pitched at the rarefied level of how it is possible to have sociological knowledge in the first place, rather than simply how we define and measure power.

Attention to the interconnections between power, knowledge and ideas has been a theme in much of what we have already covered, often articulated through concepts of 'ideology' (Eagleton 1991: 1–31; Plamenatz 1970). Some examples we have seen are Marx's argument that modes of production include corresponding sets of legitimating beliefs, Mosca's idea of the 'political formula' underpinning systems of political authority, Gramsci's concern with intellectual and moral leadership leading to hegemony, and Mills' critique of the role of the celebrity industry in distracting the public from the dynamics of social power. However, in all these perspectives ideology takes the role of something that supplements, augments and steers power relations, and, to varying degrees, is subject to falsification. With the theorists considered in this chapter there is a distinct shift in conceptualization, from knowledge as something that bolsters power to knowledge as something that constitutes power in the first instance. This is not an absolute dichotomy, but a clear trend in emphasis.

Two figures are particularly important in laying some of the groundwork for these approaches. Karl Mannheim (1893–1947) was an important influence on C. Wright Mills. In *Ideology and Utopia* (1936) he sought to transform the concept of ideology from one that specified the mystifying ideas underpinning the power of a dominant class to a more general property of social structure in all times and places. He was interested in how the structural positions of all social classes and groups, particularly intellectuals, conditioned their characteristic ideas and worldviews, so he promoted a more complex and pluralistic approach to the study of ideologies. He also made a distinction between 'ideologies' – sets of ideas representing partial perspectives, sometimes cloaking political interests, but with a tendency to misrepresent and thereby conserve, or at least not disrupt, a given social order – and 'utopias' – idea complexes that, in the course of history, have revealed themselves to have radical transformative effects on society. He came to present his approach to ideology as a 'sociology of knowledge', and sought to overcome its implicit relativism by arguing that, while all perspectives on reality are interested and partial, some are nonetheless broader and more comprehensive, and thus better able to inform critical judgments about more embedded ideologies and their relationships to one another. Thus there was a distinct and, to a degree, transcendent role for intellectuals in the study of ideology (Freeden 2003: 12–19; McLellan 1995: 35–43).

Louis Althusser (1918–90), a leading French Marxist philosopher in the 1960s and 1970s, also helped to broaden the concept of ideology. Like Mannheim, he sought a firm foundation for the objective study of ideology, but rather than privileging one social perspective among others, he made a sharp distinction between 'ideology' and 'science'. Althusser thought of science as, by definition, independent of historical and social context, and considered Marxism to be the science of society. His conception of ideology stressed the practical role of ideology as not simply an image of reality, but a guide to action in that reality. Thus, however objectively false, capitalist ideology will embody certain pragmatic truths about how to get by in that kind of society. In contrast to the traditional Marxian opposition of the ideal to the material, he emphasized the way ideas become materially embodied. Human thoughts and actions are material events taking place within material social settings (buildings, rituals, games, for example) that encode and induce ideologies. Finally, he also stressed the way that ideology constitutes individuals as subjects, playing on the double meaning of 'subject' as autonomous person and as one subordinated to another (Althusser 2000). To be realized and effective, ideology must take the form of self-understanding, of a sense of who we are. One implication of all this is that the entire emancipatory project of revolutionary Marxism, with its raising of class consciousness, is itself something of an illusion. If such transformation came about, it would be because the scientific laws of history prescribed that subjects acquired the appropriate revolutionary ideology, in keeping with the contradictions of capitalism. Human will and agency are rendered an irrelevance, or at best a by-product – a difficult idea to deploy in mobilizing people politically (Freeden 2003: 25–30; McLellan 1995: 28–30). Although Althusser has fallen out of fashion, aspects of his way of thinking about ideology and subjectivity carry on in the works of those we examine next.

## Barnes: self-fulfilling prophecies

I begin with the theory of Barry Barnes (1988) because he provides a particularly stark example. Barnes was instrumental in developing the 'sociology of science' (1977), a perspective which explains his interest in the role of knowledge, and which we will return to in the section on Actor-Network Theory. He starts from the insights of Talcott Parsons that we have already encountered, that power is a collective capacity, not just 'power over', and that it is a system property, basic to the creation and maintenance of social order. But he departs from Parsons' assumption that rational, calculative action is individualistic and self-interested, leading to social strife, and needs to be counterbalanced by the *morally* integrating effects of shared values and norms. On the contrary, Barnes sees rational action within a shared *cognitive* framework, a universe of knowledge, as the best explanation of social integration (Barnes 1993: 209–10). He asserts that the 'social power of a collective is a function of the *distribution of knowledge* over the collective' (1993: 211, emphasis in original). Barnes distinguishes knowledge, as socially accepted or acceptable belief, from belief itself, which can be highly individual and quixotic (1988: 181). In short, power is constituted by what people know, and knowledge is not a private mental state, but rather a collective phenomenon. Thus the 'power to' of any organization, for instance an army, is constituted through an ensemble of technical know-how and abilities – operating weapons, military intelligence, logistics and so on. But so too is its 'power over', its organizational hierarchy and chain of command. For an officer to give effective orders to a soldier entails that both know their respective roles within the organization, and the behaviours appropriate to those roles. Without this shared knowledge, the power over would dissolve. Although the roles and associated duties are different, they correlate, they are different sides of the same coin of knowledge. Barnes makes much of the fact that knowledge about socially defined objects is 'self-referring' and 'self-validating'. That the earth has a natural satellite in the moon, or that whales are the largest mammals, can be confirmed by observation and clarification of terms. Knowing that someone is 'a leader', or that a particular currency has a particular value in relation to other currencies at a given point in time, is different, because it is the collective knowing that makes it so. In calling someone 'the leader' we refer not to some objective property, but rather to the conventional understanding that they are the leader, and in accepting this knowledge, the very leadership is constituted (1988: 47–9). Barnes likes pondering examples of autocratic leaders such as Stalin and the Shah of Iran, arguing that when they were in power the 'overall system of domination and obedience had the character of a vast monumental self-fulfilling prophecy' (1993: 215). When they lose power, as the Shah did in 1979, it is because the context of constituting knowledge crumbles and the prophecy fails.

One objection to Barnes' account is that it is too cognitivist, placing too much emphasis on reason and intention and neglecting the roles of affect and ultimate values (Haugaard 1997: 39). I would add that he rather overplays the distribution of knowledge. It is not just that the various roles within a system of knowledge are differentiated and positional, but that some of the people only know their own part, what they need to know, and are ignorant of the much larger interlocking complex of knowledges, while others do have a grander view, often to their advantage. Power is also constituted by the *distribution of ignorance*. Barnes also makes too much of the difference between 'natural' and 'social' objects of knowledge. He offers, as a quintessential example of knowledge about society, the fact that a red traffic light 'means' stop (1993: 214). But this is understood as an arbitrary convention. Knowing that Stalin is the leader, and must be obeyed, is likely to rest on practical knowledge about the objective suffering experienced by those who have disobeyed. Such knowledge, even though it is about human, social affairs, is rather more like our knowledge about the brute facts of nature, that fire burns, than it is like knowing and thereby confirming the rules of chess, or other social conventions. The social world exists for us also as a natural object.

## Foucault: power/knowledge

Michel Foucault is probably the most widely influential of the theorists considered here. A philosopher and historian, his work has influenced several disciplines, challenging more conventional notions of history and social theory, and was itself formed in resistance to the Marxian orthodoxy of the French intelligentsia, represented by figures such as Althusser. His writings are often viewed as falling into three main periods (Haugaard 1997: 41–2; McNay 1994: 2–8), and his thoughts on power develop in ways that correspond to those periods. At first the concept of power is fairly implicit in his writings on the formation of the medical (1965, 1973) and human sciences (1970, cf. 1980: 115), then it is explicitly critiqued in the middle period that sought to explore the historical formation of modern subjectivity through institutions of incarceration (1979), and sexuality (1990). In the last period his attention increasingly turned to the nature of liberal forms of government (2008) and the ethics of self-making (1988), continuing to contemplate power, in terms of both institutions and subjectivities. These three periods roughly correspond to the 1960s, the 1970s, and the late 1970s up to Foucault's death in 1984, although much of his early work was not published in English until the early 1970s, minimizing his impact on Anglophone scholarship before then. Let's look at this phased development of his ideas more closely.

Two interdependent ideas were central in Foucault's early work. The first is that, to achieve a clearer understanding of human history, we must reject forms of subjectivism (humanism, existentialism, phenomenology) that place human consciousness at the centre of the production of meaning, resulting in a reified and romanticized notion of the individual agent's role in shaping social life. Instead we should attend to the historically formed discourses (the parameters of perception, thought and utterance possible within a given field of knowledge) and practices (the realization of discourses through social action), as we reconstruct these through the archival record. Second, this emphasis implies that people are subject to the discursive practices that make up their social worlds, and that these entail, and make actual, relations of power. The power to do certain things and the power of some over others are constituted through discourse (Layder 2006: 116–20). Moreover, discourses (about health and illness, botany, politics, the supernatural and so on) are ultimately bound together in larger epochal forms that Foucault called '*epistemes*', systems of implicit rules of discourse setting the very limits of claims to scientific knowledge in that epoch (Canguilhem 2003; Flynn 2003: 30–4). Thus Foucault (1970) identified three distinctive *epistemes* in European history. In the Renaissance (c.1450–1650), inquiry into the natural world was driven by principles of resemblance, and language itself was regarded as one more object in the God-given world. In the 'classical period' (c.1650–1800), the division between language and what it represents became explicit, generating multiple and competing systems of logical classification of natural objects. In the modern period (c.1800–present), a reflexive awareness develops that language and mind do not just 'read off' order from the natural world, but impose order on the world. Moreover, humankind itself, formerly outside the systems of classification, becomes an object of inquiry, thus opening the possibility of new ways of dominating people through scientific knowledge (Gutting 2003: 16–18; Haugaard 1997: 60–5).

In the 1970s Foucault began to grapple with the idea of power much more directly (see Foucault 2000). Two key assertions defined his work in this period. First, power is 'productive' or 'positive' (in the non-normative sense of asserting something), not inherently 'repressive' or 'forbidding'. He believed the study of power had been misled by a dominant model of juridical sovereignty: 'we must eschew the model of Leviathan in the study of power' (1980: 102). By thinking of power as that which negates freedom, we miss a much more fundamental truth, that power works by enabling, by cultivating and channelling abilities; and it does this especially through forms of knowledge. The second assertion is that power creates subjectivity, moulding identities and modes of self-awareness in ways that, again, are productive and not necessarily repressive. Thus, while his earlier work had tended to suggest the human subject, as a category of knowledge, was a contingent historical creation, this

period posed the subject, in the sense of individual subjectivity, as more substantial, but at the same time malleable. Foucault asserted in a late interview
that his primary concern was always with the formation of subjects, the concern with power arising out of that as a secondary problematic. He described
his work overall as 'a history of the different modes by which, in our culture,
human beings are made subjects' (2000: 326). In addition to these two key
themes of productivity and subjectification, Foucault argued that we should
take as 'the object of analysis *power relations* and not power itself' (2000:
339, emphasis in original), and tended to offer methodological prescriptions
for the analysis of power: (1) it should be viewed as dispersed, decentred, and
always circulating through the 'capillaries' of the social body, not as emanating from particular centres of 'sovereignty'; (2) one should begin by looking for its mechanisms and manifestations from 'below' in a 'microphysics of
power' tracing matters upwards; and (3) intentionality should figure not as
an explanation (in keeping with his earlier rejection of subjectivism), but only
as that which gives rise to patterns of 'relations of force', of 'strategies' and
'tactics' in 'games' of power, which is the most appropriate paradigm for conceptualizing power processes (see Foucault 1980: 92–108; 1990: 81–102).

In this period Foucault emphasized the mutuality of power and knowledge
to the point of fusing them in the term 'power/knowledge' (Foucault 1980;
Rouse 2003), a conception that informed two of his most influential studies,
both originally published in the mid-1970s. In *Discipline and Punish* (1979)
Foucault reconstructed the formation of modern penal systems that concentrate on incarceration and reform rather than bodily punishments. He saw
this trend as a fusion of law and human sciences that helped to create criminal
and deviant subjectivities through techniques of surveillance and study, which
could then become the objects of treatment, or 'discipline'. He situated this
institutional development within a larger social complex of surveillance and
subjectifying institutions (factories, schools, militaries, hospitals and so on)
that disciplined people in myriad ways. He shifts the emphasis of meaning in
'discipline' from 'stricture' and 'imposed order' to 'mental self-control' and
'bodies of knowledge'. In *The History of Sexuality, Vol. I* (1990) Foucault
counterposed the conventional late-twentieth century idea that Victorian attitudes toward sexuality sought to repress more or less natural urges, which
had since become liberated, with the idea that new sciences of sexuality, and a
proliferation of discourses about sexuality and its control, were in fact bringing sexuality as we understand it today into being. On the one hand, this was
part of the wider modern *episteme* in which human bodies, both as individual
people and populations, became objects of study, and understood as sources
of 'bio-power' (especially as labour). On the other hand, it was yet another
episode in the cultivation of subjectivities, susceptible to regulation from both
within and without, through the power of knowing.

During the last seven or so years of his life, Foucault's work on discursive practices and subjectivities took a new turn. He began to analyze what
he called 'governmentality' and 'governmental rationalities' (Foucault 2000:

201–22, 2008; Gordon 2000: xxiii–xxix; Hindness 1996), by which he meant the business of states taken not as the policies and actions of a single sovereign power, but as a bundle of discursive practices concerned with the 'art of government'. He saw a distinct shift, around the eighteenth century, from discourses addressing the problems of how a sovereign can control territories and populations (as in Machiavelli's *The Prince* and subsequent critiques of it), to a more complex set of practical knowledges about the care and management of populations and 'things' (Foucault 2000: 208). On the one hand this continues the theme of bio-power, with populations viewed as resources to be cultivated through attention to such things as demographics, public health, labour fitness and policing; on the other, it laid the basis for the development of 'political economy' as the theory of the administration of national resources. This led Foucault to reflections on the nature of liberalism, as the fullest expression of governmentality:

> It is here that the question of liberalism comes up. It seems to me that at that very moment it became apparent that if one governed too much, one did not govern at all – that one provoked results contrary to those one desired. What was discovered at that time – and this was one of the great discoveries of political thought at the end of the eighteenth century – was the idea of *society*. That is to say, that government not only has to deal with a territory, with a domain, and with its subjects, but that it also has to deal with a complex and independent reality that has its own laws and mechanisms of reaction, its regulations as well as possibilities of disturbance. This new reality is society. From the moment that one is to manipulate a society, one cannot consider it completely penetrable by police. One must take into account what it is. It becomes necessary to reflect upon it, upon its specific characteristics, its constants and its variables (Foucault 2000: 352, emphasis in original).

It is in this context that one of Foucault's last formulations of power should be understood: power as 'action upon action' (2000: 340), that is, not as the negation of agency, which it requires, but rather the shaping and direction of agency. He grasped that liberalism quintessentially orders society by bestowing controlled freedom on its members. Correspondingly, in his final work on philosophical reflections on sexual mores in ancient Greece and Rome, his interest in subjectivity began to explore this sphere of individual autonomy in terms of an 'ethics of the self' (1988: 39–68; Davidson 2003). Foucault thought of ethics as the self's relationship to itself, the way it judges, orients and transforms its own conduct. Thus the process of 'action upon action' becomes internalized, and a sphere of power/knowledge 'over' oneself, albeit one that aimed at constant self-transformation, seemed to provide Foucault with a sense of power that was positive in the normative sense.

Foucault's bold historical interpretations and enigmatic critical stance have elicited many criticisms. Some have worried that his close identification of truth and power entails a relativism that undermines any kind of critical or normative standpoint (Kelly 1994; Taylor 1986; cf. Rouse 2003). More specifically, some have argued that this, combined with a general disregard for the problem of women as subjects of power, makes his approach debilitating for any kind of emancipatory feminist project (Fraser 1985; Hartsock 1990; cf. Sawicki 2003). Steven Lukes has accused Foucault of appearing to adopt an 'ultra-radical' stance which calls all power and knowledge into question, but ultimately boils down to sociological commonplaces: individuals are socialized, internalizing cultural norms and practices that they experience as freely chosen (2005: 97; cf. Wrong 1996: 871). Along these lines, in the context of this book, I would note that Foucault developed his ideas through idiosyncratic and selective engagements with other scholars and historical materials, in ways that tended to obscure the similarities of his ideas on power with those of others. As we have seen, the idea that power is 'positive' and 'productive' was central to Parsons' concept. Foucault's insistence that power exists only in relations, in its actual exercise, is clearly reminiscent of arguments made by Dahl. John O'Neill (1987) has argued for the complementarity of Foucault's notion of disciplinary society and Weber's analysis of the power of bureaucracy. Given Foucault's final arrival at an ethic of the solitary, self-creating intellectual project within the context of liberalism, it would seem that there are further parallels with Weber to be explored. This is not to deny Foucault's distinctive and original contribution, but to question a certain air of exoticism that surrounds his work and to suggest that more engagement with similar ideas put forward by others might have enriched his work.

Because it bears on discussions in the next chapter, I would question one aspect of Foucault's approach to doing history. He placed great emphasis on 'singularity' and 'discontinuity' in history, for instance on the uniqueness of *epistemes* as systems of thought delimited by their own rules. He was especially concerned to reconstruct these thought worlds, in all their strangeness. In trying to understand modern penal systems and sexualities, he tried to identify the various epistemic conditions that had to be in place for these to operate as discursive practices, but eschewed clear arguments about causation. This commits him to one version of 'historicism', which approaches historical periods and settings the way an anthropologist approaches an unfamiliar culture, seeking to discover its uniqueness and difference from the known, its internal coherence. It also separates him from the other sense of 'historicism', the search for underlying causes and overarching patterns in the long sweep of history (Foucault 1980: 70). The problem is that, if *epistemes* and discourses are so bounded by their own logics, it becomes difficult to understand why they change – why history happens at all (Burke 2005: 157). If power is conceived as so ubiquitous, it becomes simply a constant accompaniment to social life, but of little utility in understanding why things happen the way they do.

My final point is that the language Foucault uses to characterize and talk about power, despite his opposition to treating it as a 'substance' located in 'centres' of sovereignty, nonetheless frequently treats it as a kind of ethereal, omnipresent being that 'does' things as though it had a will of its own. Thus we get phrases such as: '[t]his form of power that applies itself to immediate everyday life' (2000: 331), and 'power establishes a network through which it freely circulates' (1980: 99). The king lives on in supernatural form. Moreover, Foucault's account of power as decentred, endlessly circulating, not the product of intention but realized through myriad local negotiations and struggles, is in fact a fairly well accepted characterization of how language and knowledge develop and operate, into which he has placed the concept of power. I would argue that Foucault's 'insights' about power are more an effect (perhaps an illusion) of this cognitive positioning than of a systematic search for utility in the concept.

## Actor-networks, '*realrationalität*' and the ghost of Machiavelli

Next I consider some approaches, heavily influenced by Foucault's ideas, which became prominent from the 1980s on. Foremost is a cluster of researchers (Callon 1986, 1991; Latour 1987; Law 1992) working under the mantle of 'actor-network theory' (or ANT, also called the 'sociology of translation' or 'enrolment', see Callon 1986). This perspective developed within the fields of the sociology of science, and 'science and technology studies' (STS), out of attempts to solve what were seen as basic problems in established approaches to the sociology of science. Theorists had rejected the view that science is characterized by universal principles of objectivity and rationality, arguing instead that science is largely socially determined by interests, situational perspectives, conflict dynamics and so on (Barnes 1977; Bloor 1976). In effect ANT argued that this simply reversed the bias, from the view that true explanation lies in nature, objectivity and the material to locating it in an appreciation of the social, subjectivity and ideas. What was needed was an approach that rejected and transcended these dichotomies: natural/social, objective/subjective, material/ideal (see especially Latour 1993, 2000). This is what ANT was designed to do. It has generated a number of idiosyncratic methodological terms, and I will not try to do justice to them all here (see Crawford 2004). Instead, I aim only to outline the main thrust of the ANT approach, and then what it has to say about power.

The ANT approach focuses on 'networks', sometimes described as sociotechnical, sometimes as heterogeneous (Law 1992). This means a cluster of relatively stable (though always potentially volatile) relations between humans, human made artifacts (tools, machines, formulas, architecture), the animal world (scallops, fruit flies, chimpanzees, viruses) and the inanimate world (water, coal, climate). This conception of a network manifests typical STS research concerns with scientific research settings, such as labs and field sites, but the argument is that this irreducible combination of animate and inanimate, human and non-human elements, is actually the stuff of all social research. When we privilege the human and the social, we skew our understanding of the processes under observation. This conception of networks is very different from the more standard and restricted idea of 'social networks', webs of interpersonal relationships, in the social sciences. Thus in ANT, for methodological reasons, one speaks of 'actants' in general, and attributes agency to any element in a network – an insect, a computer, a table, not just humans. Some object that this fails to appreciate that human intentionality is definitional of agency (and I would agree), but it is something of a 'red herring', in that the core of the approach is to treat the network as a whole as a causal process that defines its elements, not as by-product of the agencies of various actants. Alive to problems in specifying networks for examination, ANT also argues that the things to which we normally attribute agency – persons, organizations, social movements, for example – can always be disaggregated into heterogeneous networks. Conversely, networks typically coalesce into unified agents (such as when a 'research laboratory' achieves an advance in the understanding of cancer). This principle of commutation between networks and agents is called 'punctualization', and again underscores the point that, in ANT, agency is more significant as an aspect of networks than of actants *per se*. Ultimately ANT calls on researchers to observe a strict and extensive impartiality, applying the same ontological assumptions and methodological approaches to everything in a network, refusing to make distinctions between the natural and the social into a basis of analysis (Callon 1986: 198–201).

Callon's (1986) study of the domestication of scallops and the fishermen of St Brieuc Bay in France is widely seen as the paradigmatic example of the ANT approach. The study focuses on the efforts of a group of three researchers to address the problem of declining scallop populations due to predators, climate changes and over-fishing. Working from a Japanese example, they postulate that scallops anchor themselves on sub-aquatic surfaces in the larval stage, and that intervening in this process to protect and cultivate the scallop larvae will address the problem of declining scallop stocks. Callon presents this problem – do St Brieuc scallops anchor like the Japanese ones, and if so, how? – as the thing that brings the temporary network that is the object of his study into being. The researchers, the local species of scallop, the fishermen and outside scientific experts are all brought into a relationship around this problem. The question itself is labelled an 'obligatory passage point' because each set of actants is oriented to an outcome that hinges on it: researchers solve the assigned problem, scallops get to reproduce, fishermen secure long-term profitability and the wider scientific community advances its knowledge about the scallop species. Callon takes a particular interest in how the three researchers define the problem and mobilize the interest and cooperation of the other actants involved, including the scallops. In the end the project fails:

initial evidence that the St Brieuc scallops do anchor and can therefore be cultivated turns out to be equivocal, and the few successful experimental beds are raided by impatient fishermen, thus undermining the project. The network falls apart.

What does all this have to do with power? In one sense it is an account of how the three researchers make a failed bid for the power that would come with enhanced reputations if they had succeeded in solving this complex problem, and their success would have in some sense empowered the other actants. And we can easily analogize our way to other examples in which the issue of power seems more obvious: a large corporation trying to mobilize various other actants (suppliers, governments, coastal communities, workers, endangered species, crude oil, ocean floors) around a project of deep sea oil-drilling to grow profits, or a government mobilizing popular support for a high-tech war that relies for its legitimacy on the 'cooperation' of various violence-delivering technologies. However, we have to recognize that the ANT approach is more concerned with the general efficacy of heterogeneous networks, with the circumstances that bring them into being and their capacities to stabilize and create 'order', than with attributing power to actants, human or otherwise. It is the network itself that makes things happen, and thus networks are the loci of power (see Law 1991). On the other hand, Latour has suggested that power is an 'empty' concept, best done away with (1986: 278). He understands power as a property or resource of the powerful, emanating from them, and guiding the actions of others (as we saw in Chapter 1). In short, Latour argues that 'power' and even 'society' are not 'causes' that explain events and bind people together, but rather 'effects' of the ongoing performance of associations between elements of a heterogeneous social-material network. As he puts it:

> Social scientists have mistaken the effect for the cause, the passive for the active, what is glued for the glue. Appealing to a reserve of energy, be it 'capital' or 'power', to explain the obedient behaviour of the multitudes, is thus meaningless. This reservoir is full only as long as you do not need it, that is only as long as others dutifully fill it. It is empty when you need it, that is when the others are no longer filling it (1986: 276).

This argument strongly resembles Barnes' self-fulfilling prophecy, in which power exists only to the extent that people believe it does, but with the added dimension that such beliefs are also bolstered and induced by the myriad material elements of the macro-networks we call societies. Ultimately, instead of assimilating power to knowledge, in the way Foucault often does, ANT disregards and dissolves power as an inter-human issue, dispersing it into heterogeneous networks.

ANT presents various conceptual problems. There is a tension between the call to make no methodological distinction between the material and the ideal, the human and the non-human, and the manifest focus on human behaviour.

This would seem to imply that there is something specific about humans that interests us, and if so, why not have methods and perspectives specific to studying them? Physical and natural sciences normally define their respective subject matters – astronomy, geology, zoology, entomology – as having properties and dynamics specific to them, why not the social sciences? It is true, as Marx stressed long ago, that humans uniquely engage, transform and embed themselves in the natural/physical world, and this is fundamental to how they generate and distribute power. But can we both preserve this insight and obliterate the natural/social distinction? Moreover, although ANT prescribes methodological 'symmetry', the actants in question are generally neatly divided into human, animal and technological categories, which implicitly preserves the very distinctions one is supposed to be overcoming. Another claim in the ANT approach is that we need to get beyond positing hidden 'structures' and 'dynamics' that explain social process. Instead, in a more phenomenological fashion, we should 'stay on the surface', with what's really there. But the ultimate difference between a set of hypotheses about 'underlying structures' and a set of methodological prescriptions about how to analyze social behaviour is difficult to parse. Both ask us to begin with certain assumptions about how the world works, that direct our attention in particular ways. Certainly notions of social structure often suffer from reification, but strict methodological prescription may have much the same effect. Finally, as with Foucault, there is a resistance to the idea of causation, and a puzzling tendency to talk about power as an 'effect', while neglecting the fact that effects are normally understood to have causes, and in turn are themselves causes of further events (Latour 1986; Law 1992). We have no access to 'first causes' or 'final effects'. This predilection seems to be related to the resistance to underlying structures, but causation as it is prosaically understood is routinely implied in ANT analyses with their generous attributions of agency, so it is not clear at what point the idea of causation becomes suspect for ANT theorists.

Working in a similar though less methodologically prescriptive vein to the actor-network theorists is Bent Flyvbjerg, who specializes in the study of urban planning and 'megaprojects' (Flyvbjerg1998a; Flyvbjerg *et al.* 2003). He has been particularly concerned with the ways in which supposedly objective democratic rationality, that is presumed to guide such large projects, is in fact undermined and distorted by the multiple positional and strategic rationalities through which various actors pursue their conflicting goals. In *Rationality and Power: Democracy in Practice* (1998a) he offers a detailed case study of how an award-winning urban planning project in the Danish town of Aalborg, which sought to redevelop the city centre and relieve traffic congestion, went awry over a decade and a half, as various special interests redirected the process. It is worth noting the similarity to ANT studies, which typically focus in detail on projects which are driven by bodies of specialist knowledge, although Flyvbjerg does not share their close concerns with science *per se* and overcoming natural/social dichotomies. Nonetheless, one of his key (though not very elaborated) analytic concepts is what he calls '*realrationalität*'

(1998a: 6), by which he means rationality as it actually happens in real life, always wedded to power processes. He adapts this term from the idea of *realpolitik*, used in the tradition of international relations to designate a pragmatic approach to foreign relations that refuses to be bound by fundamental normative principles (cf. Carr 1939). He argues that social science has often been led astray by unsafe assumptions about universal reason guiding human behaviour. Thus he counterposes the approaches of Jürgen Habermas, who has sought to ground ethics in universal principles of human communication, to that of Foucault, which he prefers because of its rejection of universalizing ethics and recognition of the power-laden nature of knowledge and reason (1998b). I would argue that it doesn't make much sense to contrast explicitly normative (Habermas), with manifestly descriptive (Foucault) projects in this way. Be that as it may, Flyvbjerg wants to disabuse us of any innocent invocations of rationality in the study of social life as it actually happens.

Following on from his work in Aalborg, Flyvbjerg, as part of a research team, has studied the phenomenon of cost overruns in large public work projects ('megaprojects') more widely, arguing that there is a convergence of incentives among those commissioning and those delivering such projects, such that unrealistic proposals are likely to win approval. He poses the question:

> Which projects get built? We found it isn't necessarily the best ones, but those projects for which proponents best succeed in conjuring a fantasy world of underestimated costs, overestimated revenues, undervalued environmental impacts and overvalued regional development effects. Our survey, the first and largest of its kind, looked at several hundred projects in more than 20 countries.
>
> Machiavelli seems to have been Chief Adviser on these projects with his observation that 'princes who have achieved great things have been those ... who have known how to trick men with their cunning, and who, in the end, have overcome those abiding by honest principles' (Flyvbjerg 2005: 18).

This invocation of Machiavelli is part of a wider pattern. In his later work, Foucault sometimes invoked Machiavelli as playing a seminal role in the idea of the art of government (2000: 202–12). The Florentine has become a touchstone for the approaches considered in this section. He is presented as a champion of quasi-ethnography doing participant observation in close proximity to power, as prepared to detach himself from normative perspectives, and as advocating a non-essentializing attention to the strategies and tactics of power, unconcerned with sources of power (e.g. Callon 1986; Clegg 1989: 21–38; Flyvbjerg 1998a: 5, 37). My brief account of Machiavelli in Chapter 3 suggests that this is a fairly superficial invocation of Machiavelli as a legitimating figurehead for current theoretical positions. Machiavelli's writings were in fact spurred by the tension between the normative and the practical, his commitments to republicanism and the search for effective leadership.

Nonetheless, he now gets mobilized as a proto-Foucauldian because of his suspicion towards notions of disinterested power.

## Bourdieu: the practice of power

The nature of domination was a central concern running throughout Pierre Bourdieu's (1930–2002) work, from the beginning to the end of his career (Bourdieu 1979, 1984, 1990, 1996; Bourdieu *et al.* 1999). Trained as a philosopher and self-taught as an anthropologist, like Foucault, he was a creature of the French academic milieu, an environment in which he excelled, while also being deeply ambivalent about its claims to status and authority. He also resisted the Marxian orthodoxy that was dominant in his early career, but, unlike Foucault, was more inclined to take core Marxist categories of analysis, such as 'capital' and 'class', and radically rework them rather than marginalize them. Curiously, Bourdieu and Foucault rarely engaged each other's work.

Theoretically and methodologically, Bourdieu's work was defined by an effort to resolve, or at least negotiate, the tension between objectivism and subjectivism in the social sciences (1989). That is, between a positivist scientism that naively assumes it can construct an objective account of reality and its causes, and a perspectivism that reduces all knowledge to incommensurable personal understandings. Throughout his career he called for reflexivity in social scientific practice, arguing that we must both discover the ways in which subjective perspectives inform supposedly objective representations, and find ways to objectify our own subjective experience (see Dreyfus and Rabinow 1999; Jenkins 2002: 45–65; Pinto 1999; Shusterman 1999b). For the present argument the important point is that this leads Bourdieu to make the mediating concept of 'practice' absolutely central to his work. Drawing on the analytic-linguistic philosophers J.L. Austin and Ludwig Wittgenstein, he argued that all social behaviour, including social scientific research, is structured not so much by the internalization of strict social rules, whether consciously or unconsciously, as by the acquisition of more flexible and situational strategies of interaction that allow for some play and manoeuvre, while nonetheless enabling the adjustment of behaviour to the given social context. Life is more like jazz musicians improvising on a song form than an orchestra being conducted according to a score. How to behave is learned more through the practical 'doing' than through systematically assimilating knowledge. This conception of practice bears directly on Bourdieu's understandings of power and domination. Whatever hope for self-determination that this notion of practice might seem to suggest, Bourdieu tended to emphasize the way it renders most aspects of social structure common-sensical and difficult to question for social actors, at the same time making them unconsciously complicit in the reproduction of those same structures. It was the structuring of power relations through practice that most captured Bourdieu's attention.

To further elaborate, let us consider two key concepts in Bourdieu's work: 'habitus' and 'symbolic violence'. Taking habitus first:

> The conditionings associated with a particular class of conditions of existence produce *habitus*, systems of durable, transposable dispositions, structured structures predisposed to function as structuring structures, that is, as principles which generate and organize practices and representations that can be objectively adapted to their outcomes without presupposing a conscious aiming at ends or an express mastery of the operations necessary in order to attain them (Bourdieu 1990: 53).

The density of the prose is not untypical of Bourdieu (cf. Jenkins 2002: 162–4), and this is about as straightforward a definition as he offers of this key concept. As the name sounds, habitus involves patterns of habituation oriented to particular aspects of social life that map the common sense possibilities in familiar situations, and enable the possessor to act in those situations spontaneously, but within appropriate limits, in ways that are not rigidly prescribed. There is a strong accent on how habitus becomes encoded in the body, as engrained habits of posture, comportment and so on, such as lowering one's gaze in the presence of authority, that correspond to social roles and relations (the special term for this aspect is hexis). In principle there are multiple habitus oriented to all kinds of social interaction, but Bourdieu overwhelmingly focuses on those that are involved in the maintenance of class and other forms of domination. It provides a fundamental explanation for the durability and toleration of systematically unequal power relations, because these are experienced not as unnatural imposition or challengeable doctrine, but rather as deeply familiar and constitutive of the self and its relationship to the world.

Bourdieu also often spoke of 'symbolic power' and 'symbolic violence' (1989, 1990: 122–34), by which he meant 'the imposition of systems of symbolism and meaning (i.e. culture) upon groups or classes in such a way that they are experienced as legitimate' (Jenkins 2002: 104). This 'misrecognition' of power relations is brought about through various forms of learning, from informal socialization to formalized education. Although, compared to habitus, the emphasis here is on the acquisition of more explicit bodies of knowledge, nonetheless these have a way of bedding down into habitus. Thus, as specific examples, Bourdieu offers the way speakers learn to privilege and devalue certain dialects and pronunciations (normally class marked) within a common language, or the way those inculcating dominant values will shift to the inclusive indexical 'we' ('believe in value $x$, $y$ or $z$...') rather than 'I', as a way of falsely drafting the listener into shared beliefs (1991: 51–2, 209–14). In these examples relations of domination become embedded in habitual speech, leaving its marks on patterns of expression and meaning, almost like scars on the body, subtly contorting the subordinate's symbolic universe to the needs of domination.

Analytically, habitus and symbolic violence operate in conjunction with Bourdieu's multiplex concepts of capital and social fields. Expanding on Marx, he posited four primary forms of capital:

1. *economic*, in the usual sense of material resources and wealth;
2. *social*, that is, networks and other useful social relations;
3. *cultural*, recognized forms of valued knowledge and expertise; and
4. *symbolic*, markers of honour and prestige.

Thus, in a manner reminiscent of Weber's distinction between class, status group and party, he sought to show that key goods and resources, over which people compete to accrue power, take multiple forms that cannot be directly reduced to the economic, although it is possible to parlay some forms of capital into others, as when a successful business person is able to buy an elite education for their children (which actually involves all the other three forms of capital). People and institutions enter into various arenas of competition with one another over these various capitals, or combinations of them. Bourdieu calls these arenas 'fields' (*champs*), and the connotations of spaces in which people meet to play a sport or engage in battle are apt. Essentially, whenever people or institutions are oriented towards each other in competition over the same limited goods/capitals, a field exists. Although Bourdieu insisted that fields have a concrete, objective existence, he was rather vague about how differentiated and bounded they can be. Nonetheless, the idea usefully directs analytic attention to diverse forms of social interaction and struggle over power, or the resources that Bourdieu treats as underpinning power. Fields cultivate habitus appropriate to them – imagine the different styles of interaction among stock market traders on the floor versus academics in a seminar debate – but, as Jenkins notes,

> [i]n places he writes as if each field generates its own specific habitus. Elsewhere it seems to be the case that actors bring to whichever field they are a part of their own preexisting and historically constituted habituses (2002: 90).

The way these concepts bear upon concrete empirical study is perhaps best exemplified in Bourdieu's celebrated study of the contemporary French class system, *Distinction* (1984). Beginning with a statistically informed analysis of French class structure into bourgeois, petit bourgeois (middle), and working classes, further divided into class fractions centred on economic sectors, professions and so on, Bourdieu investigates the myriad ways people use taste, the ability to make aesthetic judgments and refined distinctions, in regard to art, food, knowledge and all kinds of consumption, to build class-appropriate symbolic capital, either bolstering or attempting to reposition their own class-based status. As Bourdieu nicely puts it elsewhere: 'nothing classifies somebody more than the way he or she classifies' (1989: 19). In other words, the way we classify objects in our world reflects our class location, expresses claims to symbolic capital, bears the impress of symbolic violence, and becomes manifest through class habitus. So again, power as domination for Bourdieu is particularly a matter of how we come to know the world, and how that knowledge becomes implicit and habitual. This perspective leads Bourdieu to differentiate the three major classes in terms of their respective capacities to 'capitalize' on symbolic capital. The bourgeoisie enjoys the leisure time and historical reservoir of resources and opportunities to cultivate refined taste in its members from infancy. The working classes, circumscribed by necessity, have very limited scope to express aesthetic judgment through consumption, and therefore channel symbolic claims to status into more bodily forms, such as the machismo of sports. The middle classes are caught in between, desperate to distinguish themselves from those below, usually unable to 'pass' as bourgeois, and perennially inclined toward crass displays of taste that fail to emulate the refined tastes of those above (Jenkins 2002: 136–47). This is only the briefest summary of a vast study (one of many by Bourdieu). Although he may underestimate how specific to France his findings are, many of his core observations are wickedly recognizable.

I have already raised one reservation about Bourdieu's approach in Chapter 2, under the heading of 'cryptic domination'. Through concepts such as habitus and symbolic violence, Bourdieu's entire understanding of power is heavily skewed toward embedded and tacit forms of knowledge that are highly intractable and tend to conserve the *status quo*. He is clearly on to an important aspect of how power relations are reproduced, but he gives minimal attention to, and leaves limited analytic space for, equally important public and explicit forms of power struggles. Thus concepts such as 'authority' and 'legitimacy' tend to be invoked ironically, implying mystification by power, rather than as actual aspects of some forms of power. Although his emphasis on practice and habitus is meant to recover human agency from overly structuralist accounts, other social phenomena that mediate agency, such as self-identifying social groups, organizations and institutions, are relatively under-theorized (Jenkins 2002: 92). Finally, Bourdieu's driving interest in why class domination succeeds (and generally it does) leads him to an account of social order and its stable reproduction, with minimal consideration of why things change, of why power sometimes fails and falls apart (Bohman 1999; Butler 1999; Connell 1983: 155). The result, like that of his compatriot Durkheim before him, is a fairly static model of society that misses the process of human history.

## On language and culture

I began by observing certain continuities between the study of ideology and the epistemological approaches to power that are the focus of this chapter. Before concluding I want to also address the affinities between these approaches and some others that treat language and culture as crucial mediums through which power is constituted (see Connolly 1993; Shapiro 1984). Discourse is a key, mediating concept here. On the one hand, the term 'discourse', particularly under the influence of Foucault, has taken on a rather generalized sense as 'large, historical meaning-structures that shape and "govern" human interaction' (Farfán and Holzscheiter 2011: 139). Thus it covers not just language in the usual sense, but other meaning-laden human creations such as architecture, landscapes, visual arts, etiquette, sports and so on *ad infinitum*. However the term has its roots in the study of language as spoken and written utterances, and a considerable amount of work in the broad field of sociolinguistics has focused on the relationship between language and power, on 'discourse' in this more specific sense (e.g. Chimombo and Roseberry 1998; Fairclough 2001). Sociolinguists have long been concerned with aspects of power such as how dialect variations within a language mark class boundaries, and how rules of politeness encoded in speech – as in who gives and receives the formal and informal variants of the pronoun for 'you' (e.g. *tu* and *vous* in French) – reinforce hierarchical social roles (see Wodak *et al.* 2011). Two approaches to the study of language and power that have been prominent in recent years are 'critical discourse analysis' (CDA) (Toolan 2002) and the theory of 'conceptual metaphor' (Kövecses 2002; Lakoff and Johnson 1980).

CDA has developed in various national and institutional strains, particularly British, Dutch, German and Viennese (Wodak *et al.* 1999: 7). But the common defining elements are: (1) a focus on real everyday discourse found in talk and various communicative media; (2) a concern for how the relatively close analysis of samples of such discourse provide insights into the constitution of social power relations; (3) a locating of such discourse in wider social and institutional contexts; and (4) an underlying emancipatory motivation, to use these methods to reveal, and make subject to critique, power relations. Thus CDA studies address the use of language in regard to such things as nationalism and national identity (Wodak *et al.* 1999), racism (van Dijk 1993; Wodak and Matouschek 1993), the spread of marketizing language into academic contexts (Fairclough 1993), and doctor–patient relations (Wodak 1997). More generally, certain kinds of institutionalized practices – for instance education, medicine, law, policing, news media and literature – lend themselves to CDA research, because they generate characteristic texts (court transcripts, articles, textbooks) and institutionally and ritually framed verbal interactions (interviews, diagnoses, speeches) that are serviceable for close analysis. This is not an unreasonable way to proceed with empirical research, but does tend to steer it in certain directions. Nonetheless, CDA generally exemplifies attempts to get at discourse and its significance in an empirically grounded way, informed by sociolinguistic theory.

The theory of 'conceptual metaphor' is more rooted in a combination of linguistics and philosophy, and perhaps not as widely practised as CDA. Its most basic premise is that much of what we know, think and say about the world around us is governed by the fact that we tend to 'experience one kind of thing in terms of another' (Lakoff and Johnson 1980: 5). We talk about emotional 'highs' and 'lows' as if they were spatial phenomena. We talk about time as if it were a precious substance ('time is money'). We describe arguments as if they were a form of warfare ('she attacked my position'). A basic contention here is that abstract and intangible things – feelings, time, arguments – are made sense of by relating them to more tangible domains of experience, with such things as the human body, space and physical forces being fundamental. It is pretty easy to see that, while this may just be a general condition of how we experience and talk about the world, language is never entirely neutral, and the choice of metaphors may have consequences for power relations, how they are understood and engaged.

One of the first and main proponents of this approach, George Lakoff, has applied these ideas to the realm of politics, particularly in the US (1995, 2002). He argues that underlying liberal (Democratic Party) and conservative (Republican Party) political discourses are core, governing metaphors that encode notions of moral order, and succeed or fail according to their intuitive appeals to voters. Conservatives mobilize what he calls the 'strict father' model, while liberals deploy the 'nurturant parent' model. This corresponds to conservative defences of the 'traditional family' and liberal openness to variation in family forms and gender roles. But more deeply he suggests that the 'strict father' model may, on balance, serve more effectively in bids for political leadership, resonating with people's more concrete experiences of morality and authority as constituted in familial relations. This is an analysis that places great emphasis on the power of metaphorical rhetoric in shaping politics, leaving aside many other factors, such as material and sectional interests. Lakoff writes not just as an analyst, but as a liberal trying to contribute strategically to the formulation of liberal political rhetoric, convinced that US conservatives have tended to 'have an edge' on this front. Whatever the limitations and biases of the analysis, it is provocative and suggestive about the role of language in politics.

Alongside these language-based approaches lies the development of what has come to be known as 'cultural studies' (Dirks *et al.* 1994; During 1999; Hall 1980), in which the key term or focus is culture. Here, 'culture' is understood in a way that resonates with the idea of discourse, and has been strongly influenced by Foucault, Bourdieu and, earlier on, by the Marxian analysis of literature and culture developed by Raymond Williams (1958, 1977). Too sprawling and shifting to cover here, I would simply point out that again there has been a central concern with the critical analysis of power (Gibson 2007), often approached through the analysis of aesthetic forms in high and popular culture (museums, literature, musical subcultures, children's games, the popular press, pop idols, soap operas and so on). In my view the concept of culture one often finds in this field is too compressed into the realm of representations and discourses. It is treated as something that by definition lends itself to critical interpretive readings, and this treatment loses touch with an older, more holistic and anthropological conception of culture as the general, rough congruence of symbolic systems, modes of social organization and material conditions of livelihood. Be that as it may, the main point of this section is that several fields of social research that have marched under more specific banners of linguistic and cultural study have strong affiliations with at least some of the epistemological approaches to power that we have been exploring in this chapter.

## Conclusion

As I indicated at the outset, I cannot offer comprehensive treatments of these thinkers in the narrow scope of one chapter. Instead, my aim has been to bring out a common theme: a preoccupation with defining power in terms of knowledge. This epistemological focus is twofold. On the one hand, it is about how human knowledge in general creates power, whether it is Barnes' shared cognitive worlds, Foucault's discourses, epistemes and subjectivities, the knowledge-making that tends to be the focus of ANT's sociotechnical networks, Flyvbjerg's rationalities or Bourdieu's symbols and habitus. On the other hand, running through most of these is also a strong reflexive concern with social scientific knowledge itself, and the basis for its claims to authority. In particular there is a strong preoccupation with the dichotomization of subjective and objective approaches to sociological knowledge, and a belief that, because both perspectives present limitations and distortions, they must somehow be abandoned, or synthesized at a higher level (cf. Giddens 1984; Haugaard 1997: 98–115; Layder 2006: 155–88). Whereas Foucault generally tries to by-pass the problem, flattening everything into discourse for purposes of study, ANT attempts to remove the problem through methodological strictures, and Bourdieu searches for magical mediating terms – practice, habitus. But it may be that we are simply stuck with these imperfections, and the best we can do is to play objectivity and subjectivity off of one another in our research, each supplying some degree of corrective to the other (see Smart 1982). Regarding the concept of power, removing clear distinctions between subjects and objects, and agencies and structures, ultimately prescribes that it must become a highly elusive phenomenon, permeating relations in general, but rarely clearly located. (Bourdieu's notions of 'capitals' and 'fields' counteract this somewhat.) Moreover, as I have already suggested, it is difficult not to see in this notion of power a certain projection of the social scientist's, or perhaps more generally the intellectual's, ambivalence about the basis of their own claims to authority, and thus a kind of power. With Foucault in particular, one senses that his strong identification of knowledge with power means that he also unavoidably identifies any strong claims to explanation, especially in causal terms, with domination, which he sought to evade. The epistemological problems and assumptions driving these approaches are very different from those that tend to inform the 'evolutionary approaches' addressed in the next chapter.

Once again, we should consider the historical context. These perspectives have arisen and become influential since about 1970, in a period that has seen massive growth in information, communication, cognitive, linguistic and computing sciences. Related technologies have transformed economies and many aspects of daily social interaction. Political leaders and economists in the advanced nation-states strive for post-industrial knowledge-based economies. At the same time there is a diffuse climate of anxiety about the capacity of science, technology and out-of-control knowledge to dominate our lives, posing new social and political problems (identity theft, rapid financial meltdowns, Wikileaks and so on). So there is a general fit between economic and material trends in recent decades and the notions of power we have been exploring here. The question is, are these epistemological approaches to power 'keeping up with reality' or simply 'mirroring' the dominant discourse? It is also worth considering the more specific institutional contexts within which these ideas are being generated. The period since 1970 has seen the massification and domestication of academia. There has been a general shift in the role of scholarship from a relatively 'pure' intellectual pursuit – justified in terms of its inherent good on the one hand and as a pragmatic adjunct to the needs of power and government on the other – carried on by a relatively small cadre of intellectuals, to a much larger profession charged with provisioning society in general through higher education with the various kinds of knowledge it requires, but in ways that are often only loosely connected to the demands of actual centres of power, especially for the 'softer' social sciences and humanities. There is a sense in which, as institutionalized knowledge-mongers, we may have a tendency to model the rest of the social world in our own image, as a vast welter of knowledge-mongering. In a fascinating and pertinent essay, Mary Douglas (1986) argues that when intellectuals and spiritual leaders find themselves institutionally marginalized from real power and authority, they are more inclined to develop epistemologies that are deeply sceptical about reality and our ability to know it. When they have greater access to power, they become more pragmatic and realist in their worldview.

Finally, picking up again on the arguments of Chapter 2, power in these approaches is presented primarily in the form of domination, with concepts of authority and legitimacy relatively marginalized. Bourdieu explicitly connects habitus and symbolic violence to class and other forms of domination. Foucault seems to suggest that knowledge itself dominates us, or creates relations of domination in the first instance. The actor-network theorists simply see heterogeneous networks as the foci of action, with little use for a concept of domination that would privilege human-to-human relations in a causal nexus. Authority and legitimacy on the other hand, taken not as normative but as descriptive concepts for analyzing how people regard the power relationships they find themselves in, have little role to play. But this is not surprising given that the attention is so predominantly on modes of knowing that people cannot possibly, or just barely, think (let alone feel) beyond. Authority and legitimacy can only arise in regard to power relations that are explicitly posed as such. Moreover, their indispensable analytic utility comes in precisely because authority does come into question, and legitimacy does weaken and fail. This is a crucial part of both major and minor processes of social change, from reformations and revolutions to political realignments and the destabilization of traditional hierarchies, and to routine organizational dysfunction. But the approaches we have considered here (less so ANT because of a relative disinterest in the specifically human) are so preoccupied with how social order is imposed and maintained through ubiquitous knowledge deeply embedded in practice and subjectivity that contrary, but equally important, questions about how social order changes become marginalized. We should recognize the role of knowledge in enabling power and stabilizing power relations, but we should not confuse them. Foucault makes this point himself (2000: 337–8), but I would argue that his approach overall tends to confound power and knowledge. Knowledge is a fundamental means of coordinating human experience and behaviour. Power concerns the capacity of agents to realize their wills, a capacity that is often unevenly distributed, and realized by some imposing their wills on others or simply enjoying structural advantages over them. Whether, how and to what degree this occurs via knowledge should be open questions, and not prejudged by collapsing the idea of power into that of knowledge, which in fact makes it impossible to pose these questions effectively.

# CHAPTER 6

# Evolutionary Approaches

## Introduction

Pondering whether to call the approaches in this chapter 'historical' or 'evolutionary', I chose the latter for more than just the alliteration of 'epistemological' in the previous chapter. 'History' indicates a concern with the past, either in part or as a whole, but usually with a light touch in regard to the search for underlying 'principles' and 'factors'. 'Evolution', on the other hand, implies a concern with underlying patterns and what mechanisms account for them. As my concern in this chapter is with approaches that examine the unfolding of human history as a means to better understanding the nature and dynamics of power, I've decided that 'evolution' is the more appropriate label. However, the theorists I discuss vary in whether they invoke rubrics of history or evolution. Sensitive to these labelling problems, Ernest Gellner prefers the middle-ground term 'philosophic history' (discussed further below (pp. 114–20)), which he justifies thus:

> [H]uman ideas and social forms are neither static nor given. In our age, this has become very obvious to most of us; and it has been obvious for quite some time. But any attempt at understanding of our collective or individual predicaments must needs be spelt out against the backcloth of a vision of human history. If our choices are neither self-evident nor for keeps, we need to know the range of alternatives from which they are drawn, the choices that others have made or which were imposed on them. We need to know the principles or factors which generate that range of options. The identification of those principles or factors is not beyond our capacities, even if specific prediction continues to elude us (1991: 11).

To reiterate, the theorists discussed here represent a contemporaneous stream to that covered in the last chapter. But whereas 'epistemological approaches' often couch their arguments as radical theoretical and methodological breaks with earlier approaches, 'evolutionary approaches' tend to work within a more established tradition, one in which figures such as Marx and Weber are more prominent as interlocutors and progenitors. Although new things are being said, and previously regnant ideas rejected, arguments generally develop within this tradition. This might suggest that the evolutionary approaches are just 'more of the same', while epistemological approaches

represent a 'new turn', and should be viewed as somehow intellectually subsequent to the former. But this would be a mistake. Again, the theorists in
question are largely contemporaries, none are trapped in a time warp. From
a future vantage point, what appears *avante-garde* at present might be seen
more as an intellectual *cul-de-sac*, and what appears ploddingly conventional
may nonetheless turn out to yield enduring insights. I am more sympathetic
to the approaches discussed in this chapter, but I also think that it is useful to
consider both approaches in parallel, comparatively and respectfully. The very
divergence of approaches itself is an intriguing issue in the historical sociology
of intellectuals (though one we cannot pursue very far here).

Once again there is a shift in terminology, to historical periods and societal types, production and class, energy capture and technologies. Notions
of organization and ideology stage a return. Unlike the epistemological approaches, human prehistory enters the frame, as necessary for understanding
the long-term trajectories of social power, while concerns about integrating
objective and subjective perspectives are relatively absent. I begin with approaches that are explicitly framed in terms of evolution (Lenski, Adams),
then contrast the 'philosophic histories' of Ernest Gellner and John A. Hall,
and lastly I compare the different analytic concepts used by Eric Wolf, Gianfranco Poggi and Michael Mann to track the dynamics of power.

## Energy, technology and evolution

I begin with some clarifying remarks, first on the relationship between biological evolution and human social evolution, and then on the generalizibility
of evolutionary theory beyond the biological. The association of the concept
of evolution with the biological sciences can lead to confusion. Our concern
here is with power and changing patterns of social relations and organization,
not with human biological evolution. The latter, while providing preconditions for social evolution, pre-eminently the capacity for language and symbol
use, appears to have largely stabilized in the last 35,000 years or so, and need
not concern us. However, it is worth noting the features that set our species
apart from the rest, especially our fellow primates. Michael Tomasello (1999)
and colleagues have argued that the unique human capacity for cumulative
cultural evolution over time has its roots in a genetic/cognitive shift in how we
learn. While many of our closest primate relatives display rudimentary forms
of culture, that is, sets of adaptive, learned behaviours that are imitated and
passed on within the social group, this capacity appears to stay within narrow
limits. A crucial difference is that other primates appear to learn merely by
copying processes they observe in their environment, including the actions of
their fellows, while humans, from about one year on, also attribute *intention*
to the fellow humans they are learning from. This adds a distinctive capacity
to direct and focus joint attention as others become sources of knowledge
and will, not just objects of emulation. This also appears to greatly enhance

our capacity to acquire and use linguistic symbols in a social context. It is not just that we can traffic in abstract representations, but that these achieve significance in an intersubjective world of intentional beings. It appears that something genetic, in terms of brain structures, accounts for this basic species difference, but it opens the door to the possibility of the highly complex, cumulative and non-biological social evolution that we have inherited. It is striking that the perception of intentionality, a contentious issue in regard to the definition of social power, is also basic to what defines us as a species.

If that's how we got this way, how do we conceptualize and model processes of social evolution? Our sharpest and most developed ideas about evolution come out of the Darwinian tradition of theorizing about genetic evolution. In outline, Darwin's idea of 'descent with modification' implies a set of elements and mechanisms: (1) a unit of analysis, be it a gene, an organism or a population (there are arguments about which makes the best unit of analysis), (2) a process of reproduction, sexual or otherwise, (3) a degree of variation in the units, for instance through genetic mutation, (4) the 'natural' selection of some variants over others because of adaptive advantages specific to environments, and (5) the inheritance of selected characteristics in the next generation. Many have attempted to transpose the Darwinian model to sociocultural evolution through strong analogies (Dawkins 1989; Hodgson 2005; Hodgson and Knudsen 2006). Building on well developed conceptual foundations is sensible, but there are fundamental difficulties with this approach. Most basically, with societal evolution it is even less clear what the core unit(s) of analysis should be – what is it exactly that evolves? Is it societies, organizations, institutions, social groups, bodies of knowledge and belief? These are so complexly interrelated it is very difficult to analytically disarticulate them. Moreover, they do not 'reproduce' in the same punctuated manner that biological organisms reproduce, and processes of 'selection' are severely complicated by human foresight and intention. Nonetheless, more loosely, it is difficult to dispense with the general idea that human sociocultural forms are subject to processes of competition, adaptation and elimination. Whether examining scientific theories, languages, economic firms, political parties or countless other 'fields' of competition (to invoke Bourdieu's term), we can usefully imagine these as 'complex adaptive systems' (Lansing 2003), in which cognitive and organizational forms and strategies are advanced, modified, synthesized and eliminated, in ways that at least echo the struggles for survival found in the natural world. In short, a general, transposable ecological paradigm, in which entities are seen as adapting to environments in ways that help to account for longer-term directional change, is often useful for getting some analytic purchase on social processes.

Two interrelated factors – energy and technology – loom especially large in the approaches of Lenski and Adams, discussed below, returning us to the fundamental relationship between physical and social power broached in Chapter 1. Theorizing connections between harnessing energy and societal forms goes back at least to Herbert Spencer (1880[1862]), and was perhaps most vividly summarized in Leslie White's assertion that *'culture evolves as the amount of energy harnessed per capita per year is increased, or as the efficiency of the instrumental means of putting the energy to work is increased'* (1949: 368–9, emphasis in original). Broad-brushed as it is, the general assertion holds for the overall trajectory of human history, from small foraging bands in relative ecological balance with their environments, through ever larger and more complex forms of society based on agriculture, with industrial forms of production becoming predominant in the modern era. Along the way human labour power fuelled by food calories is progressively augmented, by energy derived from fire, water, wind and draft animals (which also require food calories), on up to fossil fuels and nuclear energy (Rosa *et al.* 1988). This brings us back to the dialectic between 'power to' and 'power over'. If this were simply a matter of ever greater amounts of energy at human disposal, with corresponding alterations of society, so much the better. But sources of energy are often finite, leading to conflicts over the control of those sources and the technologies for harnessing them, and increases in 'power to' (raw energy capture) tend to correspond to increases in social complexity, organization and hierarchy, that is, 'power over'. Moreover, the equation works both ways – not only does pursuit of energy lead to conflict, but the prosecution of conflict through evolving armed forces provides another stimulus to the capture and technological delivery of energy, in the form of lethal violence (McNeill 1982; Rosinski 1965).

Gerhard Lenski's (b. 1924) evolutionary view of human society grew out of an initial involvement in debates about the nature of twentieth-century stratification in the US (1952, 1954), which led him to deeper questions about the origins of social stratification and the distribution of power (1966). He begins in Hobbesian fashion by postulating certain human constants: that people are inherently self-interested, particularly in their own self-preservation, and that they pursue valued goods, both material and symbolic, under conditions of chronic scarcity. He recognizes our inherently social nature (including possibilities for altruism), but thinks that individual egoism and instrumentalism also need to be recognized as fundamental. Like Pareto and Mosca, he assumes the existence of elites in large, complex societies. In such societies, 'controlled by a dominant class which has the power to determine the direction of the coordinated efforts of the society, *the goals of the society are the goals of this class*' (1966: 41), *'societies, like individuals, are basically self-seeking units'* (*Ibid.*: 42, emphasis in original). Moreover, such societies are oriented toward two primary goals: (1) maximizing production and the capture of resources, and (2) minimizing internal political disruption. Thus societies for Lenski become rather like self-seeking individuals writ large.

Fundamentally, Lenski argues that it is not the distribution of wealth that determines the distribution of power, but *vice versa* (Collins 2004). The ultimate guarantee of power is force, especially the ability to take a life (1966: 50), which Lenski treats as a kind of power. However, by 'power' he usually means institutionalized power, which has become 'socially acceptable' and 'impersonal' (1966: 56–7). In other words it involves forms of authority, legitimacy and bureaucratization. Although power is often initially seized by 'might', there is always a need to reground it and reduce the costs of maintaining it by associating it with 'right', by justifying and institutionalizing it. Thus power for Lenski is primarily the occupancy of a strategically advantageous position. Another of his key starting points is the observation that the distribution of wealth over the long arc of human history describes a lopsided curve, beginning with the minimal forms of wealth found very evenly distributed in small foraging bands, with increasing inequality in larger horticultural societies (horticulture = smaller scale, village-based agriculture without the plough), on up to maximum inequality in the large, ancient agrarian states. These unequal distributions reduce, but do not disappear, in later industrial societies. Lenski seeks to account for this historical pattern in terms of the constitution of power. In summary, he argues that the most fundamental factor is *technology*, first as applied to food production, because this is conditioned by other environmental and demographic factors, and later in the arts of war and the production of commodities for markets. New technologies that increase production (such as irrigation and the plough) bring the possibility of a society creating a *surplus*, that is, more than is needed for the basic subsistence of society. This generation of a surplus, which may arise for quite contingent historical and environmental reasons, can lead to population increase, but if it is sustained, also leads to problems in the control, *administration* and application of the surplus. What activities does it support? – elite leisure, temple building, standing armies and so on. In general Lenski's answer is that it tends to go to activities that enable the elite to preserve their power and control over the surplus.

The appearance of a substantial and sustained surplus creates the conditions for institutionalized power, reaching its most exaggerated forms in the ancient agrarian states. Eventually, as new technological inputs bring forth more modern forms of commercial and industrial society, a more complex division of labour and a larger surplus of wealth develops. This creates the basis for agitation from those lower down in society, pressuring elites to distribute wealth and power more widely, through institutions such as democracy and constitutionalism:

> Periodic concessions to the lower and middle classes could help elites preserve much of their power and privilege. By giving ground in relative terms (i.e., by conceding a larger share of total income to nonelites), they could even improve their economic position in absolute terms (i.e., their total income and wealth actually increased). This was possible because technological advances had transformed the old zero-sum game that prevailed in most preindustrial societies into a positive-sum game. Elites apparently concluded that it was better to settle for a smaller share of a much larger pie than to fight to preserve their historic share and, in the process, risk an end to economic growth and the loss of all the benefits it afforded (Nolan and Lenski 2006: 270).

Lenski tries to explain our present situation in terms of basic mechanisms of social change that also describe previous and quite different forms of society. He tends to rely on a paradigm of elites as very coherent groups pursuing their own interests. This helps make the theory work, but elitism is a much messier process than his language often suggests. And in modelling the concept of societies on individuals (with elites as the linchpin), he rather sidesteps one of the conceptual problems of social evolutionary theory mentioned above – societies are rendered as clear units of analysis, the ultimate things that are evolving in competition with each other, in ways that make the process seem much cleaner than it actually is (see Nolan and Lenski 2006: 54–5).

In anthropology and archaeology there are many variants on the kind of argument Lenski offers, taking the evolutionary trajectory of major societal forms as the main frame of analysis (Fried 1967; Wenke and Olszewski 2007). Unlike Lenski, many of these have drawn on Karl Polanyi's (1971: 148–58) distinction between three modes of economic distribution – reciprocity, redistribution, and market exchange – which provide conceptual links between changing forms of economic organization and institutionalized power. Briefly, *reciprocity* indicates the generalized exchange of goods and services, on assumptions that 'one good turn deserves another', and 'it will all even out in the end'. It is typical of interactions among family, friends and colleagues. *Redistribution* involves the centralization of valued resources in some person or organization, and their reallocation, usually among the population from which they were originally drawn. It implies some sort of agency with the authority and administrative capacity to do this. When we pay our taxes and receive government services, we participate in redistribution. With *market exchange*, goods and services (commodities and labour) are exchanged more directly between those who want or need to sell or buy, through mechanisms of money and pricing. This is the basis of the capitalist economy within which most of us pursue our livelihoods. Compared to redistribution it is decentralized, although market exchange relies on the central power of states to create and sustain credit and money, and police practice, in order to develop beyond a certain rudimentary level.

All these processes go on at once in modern societies, interacting and compensating for each other, and this was part of Polanyi's point. However, they have proven to be highly relevant for understanding the general evolution of societies. In small-scale, relatively egalitarian societies, reciprocity is the dominant principle of distribution. As societies grow larger, from horticultural tribes to agricultural states, various institutions of redistribution develop (from ritual communal feasting to tithing, taxation and drafted labour), often with forms of market exchange developing at the margins. Finally, as commerce and production for the market take off, societies take on a recognizably modern form dominated by market exchange. This pattern generally fits with Lenski's paradigm, but places it in a somewhat different light, suggesting less the machinations of elites and more the *ad hoc* institutional development of distributive systems, which then present new opportunities for elite formation and control. It also places more of an accent on the role of commerce and trade, as social institutions involved in the final transformation, and less on technology *per se*, as implied by the characterization 'industrial society'. Nonetheless the core of the 'story of the surplus' remains the same: with the formation of centralized institutions that accumulate and redistribute resources over and above the needs of subsistence, we have the conditions for serious social stratification and institutionalized power in the form of the state, and with the development of industrial production and wider fields of market exchange, the redistributive power of states becomes both augmented and countered by organizational bases of power rooted in the market economy itself.

For Richard Newbold Adams (1975, 1988), it is the concept of energy, rather than technology, that plays the central role in his theory. Whereas Lenski's main emphasis is on the capacity of technologies to expand production and wealth (including capturing sources of energy), Adams is more specifically concerned with the 'flow' of energy through sociocultural systems. Working in the tradition of Leslie White, Adams is theoretically eccentric in his determination to construct a theory of power and society out of the building blocks of theories about material energy, that is, to make his theory of social evolution congruent with the theories of physics. I present his ideas not because I think they are entirely successful, but because they force us to contemplate the deeper relationships between physical energy and the organization of social power. As with Lenski, the domestication of plants and animals is seen as a pivotal juncture in societal development, providing a surplus that can be commandeered by a subset of the population involved (Adams 1988: 111–13). This and other developments (e.g. industrialization, colonial expansion) that bring more energy (food calories, slave labour, fossil fuels) into the system will tend to promote the development of what Adams calls 'operating units' (1975: 52–67). The most basic of these are aggregations of individuals pursuing common ends. These can become more complex through a series of steps: first defining themselves as having a common identity, then pooling and coordinating their individual powers, then centralizing power and decision-making in a leadership, which becomes progressively independent of the group and able to delegate powers on its own behalf. (There are echoes of Michels' 'iron law of oligarchy' here.) Adams sees this general ramping up, from the coordination of separate powers to the institutionalized centralization of power, repeating itself at different levels of units. In the small village-based community it is individuals that aggregate; on larger scales, kin groups, oligopolistic firms, nation-states (in the European Union for example) can and will form more complex operating units if this yields competitive advantages in the quest for energy. Of course specific operating units, including whole societies, expand, achieve relative stability, contract and fragment according to specific historical conditions of ecology and competition with other units. But the overall effect is a 'ratchet' that steadily raises the stakes of energy capture, and the scale of operating units.

Underpinning this is a commitment to the relevance of the Second Law of thermodynamics:

> The First Law [of thermodynamics] states that energy can neither be created nor destroyed, but that it can change its form [through conversions of matter into energy and *vice versa*]. The Second Law ... essentially holds that in making its changes in form, energy is necessarily reduced from a higher organization ... to a lower organization (1975: 109).

This decrease in organization, or entropy, is the one-way tendency of energy in a closed system to degrade to a maximally dispersed and chaotic state. Adams acknowledges debates about whether the universe or parts of it can constitute closed systems, but argues that for heuristic purposes we should consider the Sun, the Earth and life on it as a closed system. He observes that many have claimed that life in general, and human society, appear to contradict, or stand outside, the Second Law, transforming the organic parts of the world into higher levels of organization (biotic or social) rather than lower ones. But this is an illusion. The order we perceive in complex human society (arts, sciences, cities, markets, governments and so on) is in fact part of a 'dissipative system' that appears orderly to us according to our cultural systems of meaning, but ultimately involves the steady transformation of material energy into more exhausted and less usable forms, and material energy ultimately sets the limits of what is culturally possible (1975: 122–5). Ultimately human civilization becomes simply a highly ornate process of dissipation of the sun's energy. Added to this is Lotka's Principle which 'states that, in evolution, natural selection favors those populations that convert the greater amount of energy, that is, that bring the greater amount of energy form and process under their control' (Adams 1975: 126). For Adams, social evolution is an extension of biological evolution, and follows the same general rules. Human history, at its core, is a process of competitive energy capture and deployment that favours those operating units that are most successful in doing this over the long term, weeding out those that are less successful.

This perspective yields a rather bleak view of humanity's future, fated by our evolutionary natures to constantly compete to escalate our energy consumption, although Adams also suggests that the natural limits of non-renewable energy resources may force us to devise something more like a society based on 'steady state' energy depletion, with corresponding implications for the dynamics of social power (1975: 301–4; 1988: 242). Many aspects of Adams' theory are contentious, and too involved to go into here. But even if one rejects the agenda of deriving social theory from natural science, it helps to focus our attention on the undoubtedly important relationship between the harnessing of material energy and organizational development of social power, which becomes very apparent when we take the long view of human history, and when we consider impending global struggles around energy resources as fossil fuels are depleted. The integral relationship between power to, here in the form of physical energy, and power over, in the guise of centralized institutions of power, is again underscored.

## Two philosophic histories

In the early 1980s Ernest Gellner, John A. Hall and Michael Mann jointly ran a seminar at the London School of Economics on historical sociology, called 'Patterns of History', that significantly influenced the texts considered in this chapter (Gellner and Hall in this section, Mann in the next). Both Gellner and Hall describe their approaches as 'philosophic history', making power a central analytic concept. We saw Gellner's justification for this approach at the outset of this chapter. Similarly, Hall professes a concern 'with distinguishing different types of society and explaining the transitions from one type to another in order thereby to reflect systematically on the nature of power and human life chances' (1986: 3). Both theorists tend to invoke history rather than evolutionism, but the more open sense of evolution suggested above, of looking for patterns in the competing adaptations of societies and institutions, is in evidence throughout their work.

### Ernest Gellner

Gellner's *Plough, Sword and Book: The Structure of Human History* (1991) is designed around a basic matrix of the three major forms of human society: hunting and gathering (or foraging), 'Agraria' (pre-modern agriculture-based states) and 'Industria' (modern industry-based states); and the three analytic themes of production (plough), coercion (sword) and cognition (book). In broad outline, his take on hunting and gathering societies and Agraria, including the significance of the emergence and control of the surplus, resembles those of Lenski and Adams. I focus on what he says about the transition from Agraria to Industria, including the possible causes of the transition and associated changes in the natures of coercion and cognition. Gellner uses the word 'power' primarily to mean coercion, which can take two forms: the threat of physical harm or the 'bending of the wills' of those coerced through socially imposed rules and norms. He focuses on 'power over', taking 'power to' largely for granted under the headings of production and cognition (1991: 146–9).

Gellner offers a good short survey of major theses that have been advanced to try to explain the emergence of modern industrial forms of society out of agrarian societies, and why it developed first in Europe, more specifically northwestern Europe, and even more specifically England (1991: 158–70). As he puts it:

> Our problem is to understand how, on one occasion at any rate, the entire structure can be modified, as opposed to a mere change of personnel within it. How can it happen not merely that the weak, the swordless, overcome the swordsmen, but that the whole organization and ethos of society changes, that Production replaces Predation as the central theme and value of life? (1991: 158)

He suggests that the explanation probably lies in some unique historical conjuncture of propitious conditions. Some of these involve ideological changes, such as increased openness to technological and scientific discovery, the possible role of religious orders in cultivating a spirit of individualism by offering an opt-out from the close ties of kin-based communal life, and the well known idea associated with Max Weber of the Protestant Ethic thesis – that the Reformation reoriented religious and social values in a way that encouraged industriousness and reinvestment, stimulating capitalist development. But below I concentrate on those explanations, often overlapping, that more directly involve the disposition and dynamics of social power.

- The feudalisms of western Europe, though not driven by commerce, nonetheless were 'contractual' in their nature, allowing and even affirming 'a curious free-market in loyalty' (1991: 158) among monarchs, vassals and relatively independent urban communities of burghers. Unlike the agrarian empires to the east, this system included greater flux in the patterns of allegiances.
- Western Europe was unusual in its 'church/state dualism', with the centralized religious bureaucracy of the medieval Catholic Church involved in spiritual matters and the legitimation of worldly powers, ranging over a fragmented system of political units. This may have set limits on the centralization, and 'rapaciousness' of the secular state (*Ibid.*: 159).
- It seems that the aristocracies in this part of the world, particularly England, were more open to new blood than more closed, caste-like stratification systems elsewhere (*Ibid.*: 160).
- At the other end of the social scale, it has been argued that peasants in northwestern Europe were, atypically, more independent both from strongly constituted kin-groups and despotic landlord power, and thus a population predisposed to transform toward a more dynamic and mobile society and economy (*Ibid.*: 162–3).
- The 'plural state system' of Europe alluded to above was one in which these states competed with each other for supremacy, but were also constrained by a relative balance of power, thus stimulating interdependent economic, technological and military changes. This situation also provided escape routes between polities for persecuted minorities (such as Jews and Huguenots) to find niches for entrepreneurial activity (*Ibid.*: 168–9).
- Within states, internal balances of power among social forces (institutions, ideologies, interest groups) may have been eventually conducive toward ideologies of pluralism and toleration, which in turn supported the dynamism of society (*Ibid.*: 169).
- Finally, the emergence of the nation-state was a key part of this process: 'An island society, served by the sea in the office of a moat, and enjoying civic liberties granted not to individual towns but to a national parliament – a country with a national rather than merely civic bourgeoisie – was perhaps uniquely fitted to constitute the launching pad for the new order. Holland, an association of urban republics, also played a great part; but it may be significant that the central locus of the transformation was England' (*Ibid.*: 170).

As ever with historical explanation, each of these theses tends to suggest preconditions rather than exact mechanisms of transformation, preconditions that in turn need to be accounted for. Nonetheless, the perspective Gellner outlines, taken as a whole, provides an argument about what was different in the heartland of industrial capitalist development, which must be a part of any explanation. The main motif here is that, while there are various centres of power for a series of historically specific reasons, social power was more distributed and balanced, albeit with tension and conflict, and less concentrated in one great centre than had been the main tendency of agrarian civilizations for millennia. This fundamental disposition of power matters for social change.

Gellner also tries to characterize the nature, problems and possible developments of 'coercion' in the industrial societies we now live in. There is a basic difference between people fighting over shares of a huge and expanding pie and people struggling simply to maintain their share, or to get any share at all. He ponders what happens to power when generalized affluence replaces chronic scarcity of material necessities, when power is no longer rooted in monopoly control of the surplus and its use. He is fully aware that poverty persists, both within and beyond the most 'advanced' nation-state economies. But within those societies, the poorest are generally minimally maintained through redistribution, they are not allowed to starve. Coercion, in its most brutal sense, becomes less of an issue. Gellner speculates that 'possessions' become significant, less as the basic means to survival and more as the means for symbolic competition for social position and status (1991: 224–32).

Be that as it may, he argues that the basic context for modern life is the industrial nation-state (see Gellner's major statement on this, 1983). Coercive power is primarily grounded in centralized state bureaucracies administering relatively homogenized populations through complex infrastructures, and with decisively superior means of physical coercion – weapons systems, prisons, standing militaries and police and so on – at their disposal. Because Gellner conceives of power as coercion, and physical threat as the nub of coercion, I think he tends to underplay the coercive potential of other, non-state bureaucracies in modern society, especially large economic organizations such as firms and banks. While they rarely deliberately advance their purposes through the threat of physical harm, nonetheless they can manipulate and induce decisions and behaviour through their control of wealth, patterns of investment and other resources. At any rate, Gellner's argument is also that the harder forms of coercion are generally unnecessary in order to maintain social order. First, as Durkheim argued, the complex division of labour and interdependence of society's parts regulate behaviour, inhibiting regional or sectorial rebellion. Second, modern citizens are highly habituated to being administered by impersonal bureaucracies. Finally, the middle class has been largely 'tamed', achieving enviable livelihoods, and aware of its dependence on the given regime for the goods it values most – educational opportunity, decent employment and so on. Thus the stratum that is often best equipped to effectively mobilize against a regime is disinclined to do so (1991: 232–8).

Running parallel to these transformations of coercion have been deep changes in social cognition. I touched on this aspect of Gellner's argument at the end of Chapter 2. To recap, Gellner sees modernity as involving a 'dethronement of the concept' (1991: 122–8), by which he means a shift from a world in which the entire system of ideas and concepts through which a society operates is oriented toward 'implementing' social order, presenting an integrated view of the human and natural universe sanctified by ritual and doctrine, to a world in which concepts become 'instrumental' tools for grasping and manipulating the natural world. Humans are regarded as part of the natural world, but understandings about the natural and social orders are only weakly bound to one another. In Agraria, big concepts (a monotheistic god is perhaps the biggest) reign supreme, providing a gravitational force that binds society together, and to its relationship with its environment. In Industria, concepts multiply and are levelled, and must prove their value through utility, without recourse to metaphysical justification. And as we noted before, this levelling and instrumentalizing of thought tends to disable the concept as a means of legitimating power and constituting authority. For instance, we can evaluate a given state of affairs in relation to an ideal notion of democracy, but what ultimately legitimates democracy remains an open question. Gellner advances this argument largely through discussions of major figures in the 'western' philosophical tradition (Plato, Descartes, Hume, Kant), but he treats their ideas not as socially detached takes on reality, but as symptomatic of the contexts of production/coercion/cognition that shape them (1991: 113–44). Although there is an underlying materialism to Gellner's perspective, privileging changes in production in the explanation of social change overall, there is no simple, unidirectional priority in the causal relationships between production, coercion and cognition in his argument. It is more a matter of maintaining that any society will contain all three dimensions, and there must be a degree of correspondence among them such that changes in one will induce changes in the others. The argument tends to follow these macro-level changes, observing parallels and speculating about their interactions without trying to treat them as 'levels' that can be logically reduced one to another.

In his conclusion Gellner asserts: 'The truth of agro-literate society is essentially different from the truth of scientific-industrial society' (1991: 276). This invites comparison with the ideas of Foucault we encountered in the previous chapter. Foucault also presents history as a succession of regimes of truth, in which knowledge is inseparable from power. But Foucault's '*epistemes*' and 'discourses' are understood mostly in terms of their own internal logics, the set of ideas and knowledges that must be genealogically in place in order for them to take shape. While Gellner intends to suggest that cognition matters and is not just epiphenomenal, by the same token he makes sense of changing ways of knowing, of transformations of truth, precisely by seeking correspondences with the relatively autonomous dimensions of production and coercion. Gellner and Foucault have fundamentally different explanatory strategies. Moreover, for Foucault, truth, or knowledge, constitutes power in different ways at different times, but for Gellner it is not just that there is a difference, there is a single critical rupture. We move from a world in which the tendency is for centralized authority to justify knowledge to one in which the tendency is for democratized knowledge to corrode authority, and this irrevocably alters the nature of human power relations. (For commentary on Gellner's work see: Hall 2010, Malesevic and Haugaard 2007.)

## John A. Hall

In *Powers and Liberties: The Causes and Consequences of the Rise of the West* (1986) John A. Hall explicitly makes power central in accounting for the growth of capitalism and European domination in the modern period. He distinguishes between *enabling power* 'as a capacity created by social agreement' (1986: 22), a sense very close to what we have meant by 'power to', and situations of *blocking power* 'in which a power stand-off ... prevents the release of social energy' (1986: 23). Blocking power suggests not so much 'power over' as situations in which contending claims to such power tend to cancel each other out. In general his aim, *contra* Marxian economic determinism, is to formulate a social evolutionary account in which economic, political and ideological ways of organizing power are all given their due, describing his approach as a kind of 'organizational materialism' (1986: 21). Having said this, these different modes of organizing power come to the fore in different circumstances. One of Hall's main contentions is that ideological power, represented in the book primarily by the major world religions, has seen two great periods of productivity, which were associated with the upheavals of the two great socioeconomic transitions: first to agrarian and then to industrial forms of society (1986: 20). Thus Buddhism, Hinduism, Confucianism, Christianity and Islam are all bound up with the social tensions engendered by early state formation and imperialisms, and the modern ideologies of liberalism, conservatism, socialism, communism and fascism arise out of the conflicts and uncertainties engendered by industrial capitalism and the modern bureaucratic state. As Hall puts it: 'In conditions of crisis intellectuals can assume great power, less because of their ability to explain to fellow citizens some confusing situation than on account of their ability actually to *create a society in the first place*' (1986: 20–1, emphasis in original).

Hall summarizes his argument as an attempt to rethink the 'shape of history' by replacing the classic Marxist stage model of development through modes of production – primitive communism, ancient slavery-based society, feudal society based on serfdom, bourgeois society based on capitalism and wage labour, communism/socialism – with one that emphasizes the three great societal forms we have already encountered – pre-agrarian (i.e. hunting and gathering), agrarian and industrial – while also highlighting differences between the major world religions/civilizations, and the bifurcation between capitalism and state socialism in the twentieth century (see Figure 6.1).

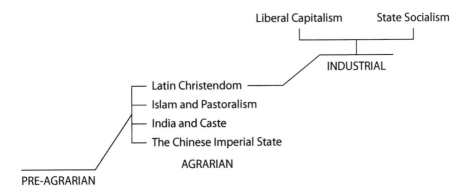

**Figure 6.1** Hall's model of history
*Source*: Hall (1986): 18.

Thus he picks up on Weber's (1964) attention to the role of religion in shaping societies and their trajectories, while suggesting that Weber placed too much emphasis on the ideological content of religious beliefs, and not enough on the mutually shaping effects of religious, political and economic institutions. Again, the key historical question becomes, why did industrial capitalism emerge out of the European branch of Latin Christendom? Hall's argument is neither that Christianity alone made the difference, nor Protestantism in particular, as in Weber's famous thesis. Rather it is that the organization and institutionalization of Christianity, polity and economy in Europe interacted in ways that became uniquely conducive to the transformation, in contrast with other civilizational patterns that tended to obstruct such change. Boiling chapters down to sentences:

1    The succession of Chinese empires were characterized by what Hall calls a 'capstone state' (1986: 51–3). A bureaucracy run by an imperial mandarinate, professionally trained and bound together by Confucianism, sat atop a fragmented field of fairly insular agrarian communities, jealously guarding against the formation of secondary bases of strong social organization within society.

2    Hall describes the classical pattern of Hindu India as having a 'free-floating custodial state' (1986: 71–8), in which daily local communal life, structured through a shifting complex of castes and cults, was very much regulated by an integrated Brahman caste, which, though providing legitimation, stood at some distance from the overarching, sometimes imperial, states that came and went. The key effect was to maintain local traditional hierarchy, and stunt economic change.

3    Islam is presented as being integrated by an *ulama* elite, sitting atop a series of syncretic folk variants of the religion, and ranging across several cultures and polities. Here the pattern of rising and falling state formation was 'cyclical', and had much to do with the fact that claimants to secular

rule emerged out of communities of tribal pastoralists, traditionally on a kind of permanent war footing and distrustful of sedentary and urban life (1986: 91–8). This sociological background also made the *ulama* itself habitually distrustful of political power, and aloof from it, thereby preventing coordination of religious and political leadership in the development of society.

4    Finally we come to Europe and Christianity, where things went differently. Hall echoes many of the factors featuring in Gellner's account of the European transformation. For him the crucial structural difference is that the collapse of the Roman Empire left Latin Christendom as a 'transnational' bureaucracy and social ethos with relatively deep social penetration, across a wide range and variety of polities. Underneath this carapace of ideological integration, a patchwork of political and economic powers was constituted through a web of relatively autonomous market-based towns, run by burghers, and feudal lords controlling manors and peasants. The result is what Hall calls 'the organic state' in which a balance of forces and interests, instead of resulting in a 'power-stand-off', leads to fuller integration of state and society. From about 1300 on, this begins to coalesce into a system of nation-states in chronic political and economic competition with one another, driving forward, indeed enabling productivity, and eventually capitalism (1986: 133–44).

Summing up, Hall sees the 'rise of the west' as attributable to a unique conjuncture of circumstances which promoted the overall development of concentrated and systemic powers (economic, political, ideological) within western European societies, in patterns which have since radiated out to shape power formation throughout the globe. In contrast, in the other civilizational matrices considered, the over-concentration (China) or under-integration (Hindu India, Islam) of political and ideological powers and institutions tended to yield states and elites that were mainly predatory and extractive in regard to economic powers, rather than cultivating and enhancing them. (For alternative explanations of the 'rise of the west' and the overtaking of Asia, see Goldstone 2002, Goody 2004, Hobson 2004 and Pomeranz 2000.) Both of the books by Gellner and Hall that we have considered were published in the mid-1980s, and include reflections on the fate of the Soviet Union and its relationship to 'the West', capitalism, liberalism and democracy that are now a bit dated. Concluding reflections in the early twenty-first century might focus on the evolving relationship of tension and interdependence between China and the US. But the deeper historical hypotheses are unaffected by subsequent events, and the basic analytic ideas, remain relevant. Both Gellner (1996) and Hall (1988, 1995) are also champions of liberalism and civil society, and need to be understood as not just describing the rise of liberal society, but also advocating and defending it. This normative position itself rests on particular analyses of social power and the causes of its maximization, various modes of distribution and potentials for conflict.

# Modes, forms and sources of power

*Eric R. Wolf*

Our last three figures provide further contrasting strategies for the macro-analysis of power and its historical manifestations. Eric R. Wolf (1923–1999) was one of a cohort of anthropologists who were influenced by the revival of evolutionary theory in anthropology after the Second World War. (On Wolf's work in general, see Schneider and Rapp 1995.) The ideas of Marx were a key point of departure for him, although as an intellectual eclectic he was more 'Marxian' than 'Marxist' in his thinking. While he can be counted among those anthropologists preferring a more 'materialist' approach to the study of humankind, he was also keenly interested in the 'idealist' aspects of social life, in how power-laden symbols and rituals serve to constitute, support and challenge social orders (2001a). The problem of adequately dealing with both the material and ideological dimensions of power found in the anthropological and historical record became a central concern in his later career.

Wolf was a strong critic of how anthropology had come to deal with questions of power, arguing that the method of treating sociocultural groups as analytic isolates, detached from world history and its power dynamics, made anthropologists complicit in obscuring power relations (2001b). As a general analytic starting point, he suggested that power should be regarded as operating in four interacting 'modes': (1) as a personal attribute of potency or capability; (2) as the ability of one to impose its will on others in social interaction (a sense very akin to Dahl's definition); (3) as that which 'controls the settings in which people may exhibit their potentialities and interact with others', a conception he attributes to Adams' idea of 'operating units' discussed above; and most crucially (4) 'structural power' which in turn shapes social settings, and fundamentally concerns 'the power to deploy and allocate social labor'. Here Wolf's debt to Marx becomes clear, although he also saw this fourth mode as resonating with what Foucault meant by 'governance', the power to cultivate and guide the actions of others (2001b: 384–5). This paradigm echoes Steven Lukes' three dimensions of power, but without the same methodological preoccupations. I would take issue with how Wolf seems to locate 'power to' strictly at the personal level, tending to treat more complex levels of power relations as only a matter of 'power over'. This is probably the imprint of a critical Marxian disposition that normally regards power negatively. Nonetheless it is a useful initial guide for any concrete analysis of power relations.

His last two books elaborate on his approach to the study of power. *Europe and the People Without History* (1982) sought to expand on a 'world systems' approach to history (Braudel 1973; Frank 1978; Wallerstein 1974). It paid particular attention to the myriad, 'non-western' cultural groups that have been the traditional focus of anthropological research, locating them as active, if often disadvantaged, agents in the world historical process. In case after case, Wolf shows how contact and interaction with the expanding forces of capitalism, first mercantile and later industrial, had transformed 'traditional societies', thus questioning the very idea of 'societies' and 'cultures' as adequate units of analysis in and of themselves. Without erasing the analytic distinction between a Europe with a distinctive historical trajectory and 'the rest of the world', he argues for a globally integrated perspective on major social processes. The key analytic device for Wolf is a reworking of Marx's concept of the mode of production (discussed in Chapter 3). For Wolf it is 'a specific, historically occurring set of social relations through which labor is deployed to wrest energy from nature by means of tools, skills, organization and knowledge' (1982: 75). This phrasing is meant to capture at once the material, social organizational and ideational aspects of the concept. Marx's various writings formulated up to five main modes of production, noted above in regard to Hall. Wolf reduces modes of production to three major types that roughly correspond to the foraging, agrarian and industrial models we have seen above (1982: 75–100; 2001c).

In Wolf's 'kin-ordered mode' kinship is

> understood as a way of committing social labor to the transformation of nature through appeals to filiation and marriage, and to consanguinity and affinity. Put simply, through kinship social labor is 'locked up,' or 'embedded,' in particular relations between people. This labor can only be mobilized through access to people, such access being defined symbolically (1982: 91).

Of course dominant kinship principles featuring descent exist in tension with principles of spatial propinquity based on co-residence, but there are strong tendencies to fictively liken co-residents to kin-like roles. Wolf observes that the kin-ordered mode spans a range of societal forms, from highly egalitarian foraging bands where kinship calculations are usually loose and not historically deep, to incipiently stratified lineage systems where one chiefly lineage has become permanently elevated in status and authority above the other lineages. This mode is not intrinsically egalitarian. The point is that symbolized kinship constitutes the socially recognized and sanctioned language for allocating social roles and labour. The forms of kinship we experience in modern society have become highly attenuated, and while there are echoes of this capacity to organize labour and mobilize resources, kinship ceases to be a dominant principle of power organization.

The 'tributary mode' encompasses classical European feudalism, systems based on slavery and other forms of agrarian-based states and empires. Here social labour is mobilized primarily through political structures by which a ruling class has detached itself from the wider kin-networks, and exercises control over the productive process through command of key resources, such as irrigation systems, armies and access to rituals perceived as necessary to social reproduction. The ruling class extracts labour power and/or its products through various forms of coercion. Kinship may persist as an organizing principle within the elite class and localized communities, but these are disarticulated as a system, embedded within the larger structure of political authority and economic extraction. Such systems can be highly centralized and expansive, as in China's 'capstone' empire, or much more fissiparous and unstable, as in European feudalism, where monarchs were often less able to control, and more reliant upon, their vassals. As already suggested, such systems will contain forms of commerce and trade with the potential to generate alternate bases of power but, for precisely this reason, these tend to be tightly controlled from above.

The 'capitalist mode of production'

> shows three intertwined characteristics. First, capitalists detain control of the means of production. Second, laborers are denied independent access to means of production and must sell their labor power to the capitalists. Third, the maximization of surplus produced by the laborers with the means of production owned by the capitalists entails 'ceaseless accumulation accompanied by changes in methods of production' (1982: 78).

This lines up with Marx's formulation, although Wolf eschews the further Marxist hypothesis that this system must necessarily drive itself to its own destruction through the unbridled competition of capitalists. He recognizes the capacity to institute countervailing measures to sustain the system and rescue it from crisis tendencies. But Wolf is also adamant that capitalism in the proper sense is not merely the accumulation of wealth, as happens when a merchant 'buys cheap and sells dear', but must involve the reordering of production, such that labour power itself becomes primarily a commodity for sale on the market. Wolf of course recognizes that his three modes are in a sense 'ideal types', that on the ground there would be intermediate forms, periods of transition between them, and complex contemporaneous interactions between actual historical manifestations of different modes. Indeed, the transformative impact of the capitalist mode on the other modes it encountered (and *vice versa*) as it expanded out of Europe, was his core concern. But he also believed that the wide view of human societies over time suggested gravitation toward one of these three broad ways of organizing and deploying labour power.

If *Europe* was magnificent in its global historical sweep, Wolf's last book *Envisioning Power: Ideologies of Dominance and Crisis* (1999) was meticulous in its attention to the specific ethnographic and ethnohistorical detail. It revolves around three cases, each corresponding to one of Wolf's three modes of production, and chosen for the way they offer 'extreme expressions' of culture (1999: 16–17). In each case, complexes of symbols and rituals, and the cosmological visions of a unified natural, social and supernatural order in which they were embedded (1999: 280-5), were elaborated in response to various pressures – ecological, economic, political – that came to bear on those systems, and the groups that monopolized power within them. Wolf considers the Kwakiutl chiefdoms of Vancouver Island in British Columbia. Here the 'potlatch', a traditional system of ritual redistribution of goods that

played a role in the reproduction of tribal lineage hierarchies, became de-
ranged and subject to massive deflation of values as European trade goods
flooded the system, and external trade relations created alternate bases for
power. The case of the Aztecs of fifteenth and sixteenth century Central Mexico, just before the arrival of the Spanish Conquistadors, reveals 'numerous
material sources and causes of crisis, ranging from the ecological instability
in the Valley of Mexico to the organizational stresses brought about by rapid
urban and imperial expansion' (1999: 194). Here chronic social anxiety was
induced by a combination of material circumstances, a cosmology that called
for endless ritual propitiation in the face of uncertainty and struggles by a
new cadre of rulers to legitimize their expanding authority. The effect was to
ratchet up the demands for ritual human sacrifice, dramatically escalating a
long-standing cultural practice in Mesoamerica. His final case is provided by
the Third Reich of Germany (1933–45), an example of crisis and extremity
within the modern industrialized nation-state. The crisis was conditioned by
longstanding political fragmentation and localized codes of honour and status
in the German lands that tended to inhibit or grind against the levelling effects
of industrial modernization. These factors combined with the rise of romantic notions of the German *Volk* in the nineteenth century and the country's
humiliating defeat in the First World War. Wolf likens the Nazi project to a
'revitalization movement' that sought to

> restore a world 'turned upside down' to health and vitality ... This view
> was grounded in a cosmology that saw the world as a scenario of strife in
> which the strong were rewarded and the weak destroyed. Germany had
> lost the last war because it had grown weak; to rebuild its strength it was
> first necessary to make war on weakness (1999: 270).

As we know, that war was waged on both internal (Jews, Gypsies, socialists,
communists) and external fronts, becoming an all-consuming endeavour from
which Hitler and his followers could not draw back.

Throughout the analysis of the three cases, Wolf is at pains to show that,
while material factors such as labour power and valued and strategic resources are being harnessed in the interest of dominant groups, the harnessing – the
organizing of social action – relies on, and must operate within, the parameters of culturally available repertoires of ideas. He sought to examine how
crises of power for leading groups in these societies lead to the ideological
elaboration of cultural assumptions and ideas in efforts to shore up or reclaim
power. For anyone interested in how ideology works substantively, in practice,
it is a book that will repay close reading.

## Gianfranco Poggi

We can contrast Wolf's Marxian approach with Gianfranco Poggi's (b. 1934)
Weberian one. A social and political theorist, Poggi addresses much of his work
to the historical development of the modern state (1978, 1990). In *Forms of
Power* (2001) he begins by arguing that there is good reason to characterize

our species as '*homo potens*' because we are 'uniquely enabled, or condemned, to self-*determination*' (2001: 3, emphasis in original), with exceptional control over our environments and fate. However the question of 'social power' for Poggi more specifically concerns 'power over', institutionalized asymmetries of power between individuals and collectivities (2001: 8–14). As I did in Chapter 2, Poggi observes that the key concept for Weber is *Herrschaft* (a notion of domination which includes authority) rather than power (*Macht*). He draws on Weber's distinction between three primary resource bases for organizing power relations – classes, status groups, parties – elaborating these into three corresponding 'forms' of power: economic, ideological/normative, and political. For him the analysis of power implies different kinds of social groups, to some degree elites, ensconced in major social institutions (states, businesses, churches, media), from which they control key resources. For each form there is a corresponding principle for how goods are allocated: by the market, by customs associated with statuses and by command. Thus, where Wolf approaches the subject through complex historical packages of all three of these forms bundled into the notion of modes of production, Poggi's approach is to disarticulate them analytically, looking for basic principles of 'confrontation and accommodation between the holders of various forms of social power' (2001: 28).

Poggi concentrates mainly on modern, 'western' society. He focuses on the interdependencies between these three main groups/institutions, and what they need from each other that locks them into certain patterns of interaction. States need revenue to operate, and unless they attempt to formally incorporate all economic activity, as in the failed Soviet model, they find themselves dependent on their economies, and particularly powerful organizations within their economies, for support. Political power is also in chronic need of moral legitimation from some higher, less earthly authority. Although basic success in rulership can win some pragmatic legitimacy for power, there is always a deficit of moral authority which needs to be imported. For its part, economic power based on wealth, property and control of the flow of investment needs the auspices of the state to create stable conditions to conduct its business. At times this will include the ultimate resource at the effective state's disposal, the monopoly, and state-of-the-art delivery, of violence, when sheer coercion becomes necessary to prosecute interests. Finally, those who specialize in the creation of ideological visions of moral order, be they the leaders of formal religious institutions or more secularized and footloose 'creative intellectuals' (2001: 100–2) as Poggi calls them (for example ideologues, philosophers, social critics/commentators, some academics and artists), need patronage to practise, whether it is the Medici funding public arts or a modern state's system of mass higher education. In return, in addition to the explicit ideological legitimation of regimes, creative intellectuals can 'give splendour to the realm', help 'construct political community', and 'divert the citizenry' from more critical attention to the regime it lives under (2001: 103–9).

Poggi leans towards two main interpretations of current tendencies. First, with secularization, the producers of normative and ideological power are increasingly in the weaker, more dependent position in regard to the state, for various reasons (2001: 119–22). Increasingly the state gains its legitimacy directly from its husbanding of the economy, its role in 'delivering the goods'. Moreover, modern, liberal creative intellectuals, unlike their forerunners operating out of integrated churches, are a diverse and fragmented lot, with no 'party line' to give them collective clout, and increasingly they speak a rarefied language with limited purchase on the popular imagination. And the media through which ideas are communicated have themselves become forms of big business, dominated by purposes of entertainment ('diverting the citizenry'), and in which the sheer technique of the media tends to overwhelm the messages. Secondly, and perhaps more simply, economic globalization, the transnational mobility of investment capital and business operations, has weakened the state's claim on economic powers which have more latitude to escape those claims. It's not that corporations have no national ties or priorities, but rather that they have increasing freedom to loosen those constraints when it is advantageous to do so, thus enhancing the overall bargaining power of major corporate interests (2001: 177–9). Poggi concludes with a note of trepidation at the possibility of any one form of power decisively trumping the other two (2001: 204).

## Michael Mann

Perhaps the most monumental and influential attempt to formulate a macro-historical analysis of power has been Michael Mann's (b. 1942). The first two volumes of his *Sources of Social Power* (1986, 1993) survey human history 'from the beginning to A.D. 1760' and 1760–1914, respectively. The third and final volume (forthcoming at the time of writing) brings the story up to the present, with intervening books on the nature and development of fascism (2004) and the relationship between the emergence of democracy and ethnic cleansing (2005) arising out of groundwork for that volume. Mann lays out basic principles and a model for his approach at the outset (1986: 1–33), to which he has remained remarkably faithful, most later qualifications of his argument concerning the interpretation of historical particulars to which the model is applied (see Mann 2006). Broadly speaking, he resists approaches that reduce power to economic processes, operate with a strong distinction and preference between 'materialism' and 'idealism' as forces in history, and neglect the importance of war and violence for sociological analysis (see Mann 1988). Altogether this tends to make him a Weberian, with undertones of Marx and social theorists of war (for example Andreski 1971).

Mann's guiding premises include:

- Causality in human affairs is highly complex, and not likely to reduce to any single 'primary' underlying causal process apart from the very general human need for power, 'the ability to pursue and attain goals through mastery of one's environment' (1986: 6).

**Table 6.1** Continua of organizational reach

|  | Authoritative | Diffused |
|---|---|---|
| **Intensive** | Army command structure | A general strike |
| **Extensive** | Militaristic empire | Market exchange |

Source: M. Mann (1986) *The Sources of Social Power, Volume I: A History of Power from the Beginning to A.D. 1760*, p. 9. Reproduced with the permission of Cambridge University Press.

- Power is a matter of social organization, involving both 'collective' and 'distributive' aspects, that is, both the aggregated 'power to' of the social group and the hierarchical 'power over' that comes with social complexity. He tellingly acknowledges Mosca's principle that the organized few will tend to dominate the disorganized many (1986: 7).
- 'Human beings are social, not societal' (1986: 14), that is, they require social relationships but not neatly bounded community. With this assertion Mann distances himself from overly integral conceptions of society as a systemic whole. When he uses 'society' it is as shorthand for a particular density and interdependence of a variety of social networks, which are not strictly separate from other 'societies'.
- It is frequently useful to distinguish between forms of organizational reach highlighting two continua: (1) from 'intensive' (smaller bands of the highly committed) to 'extensive' (populations more geographically dispersed and less tightly controlled); and (2) from 'authoritative' (involving clear command–obedience relations) to 'diffused' (in which behaviour is coordinated spontaneously and unconsciously, often through shared beliefs) (cf. de Jouvenel in Wrong 2002: 14). Mann illustrates with a matrix (see Table 6.1).
- Shifts in power frequently exhibit a process of 'outflanking' in which small innovations, for instance in technology or social organization, substantially alter the previous balance of power between groups. These outflankings often originate 'interstitially', that is among groups and their ways of life that hitherto had been more marginal to the main axes of social power in their environment.

These principles are put in service of a fourfold paradigm of 'sources' of social power. Mann seems to prefer the term 'sources' because it emphasizes that powerful groups get their powers in different ways (metaphorically, from different points of origin). Known as the 'IEMP model', he treats power as originating in four kinds of institutionalized social networks of actors: Ideological, Economic, Military and Political. He emphasizes that wide investigation of history suggests these as analytically useful ideal-types, but also that they are 'functionally promiscuous', meaning that, in practice, social organizations will sometimes combine these sources. For example, the medieval religious brotherhood of the Knights Templar was also a major regional economic force and a military unit. To elaborate:

- *Ideological power* is the capacity to construct and organize meanings, social norms and aesthetic and ritual practices. It makes sense of the natural, social and moral orders, in ways that cannot be reduced to questions of truth and falsity. It comes in two main types: (1) 'sociospatially transcendent', that is, as a system of ideas and practices that can spread and range across a variety of social networks and settings; and (2) as 'immanent morale', 'intensifying the cohesion, the confidence, and, therefore, the power of an already established social group' (1986: 24).
- *Economic power* rests on the human capacity to seize and transform nature to meet subsistence and other needs. It involves organized circuits of production, distribution, exchange and consumption, binding manifold forms of labour power to multiple, extensive and ramifying markets. Economic power organizes people into classes (a strictly economic concept for Mann) with differential powers in the overall economic process.
- *Military power* is 'the social organization of concentrated lethal violence' (2006: 351, slightly refined from his original definition). As suggested in Table 6.1, it can have a core of intensive command and control radiating out into a more extensive, if sometimes sporadic, sphere of efficacy. For Mann, the technologies, arts and skills of lethal violence are sufficiently distinctive to require specialized social networks and institutions, and thus warrant being defined as a distinctive source of power.
- *Political power* 'derives from the usefulness of centralized, institutionalized, territorialized regulation of many aspects of social relations' (1986: 26), the paradigm being the state. Like military power, it also is 'sociospatially dual' (p. 27), but divides more sharply into internal/domestic and external/international spheres of action. While societies are ultimately unbounded networks, states are by their nature more bounded (thus we often confuse 'society' with 'the citizens of a state').

Mann uses these principles and his IEMP model to provide narrative order and comparative structure to his vast survey of social evolution, the main thread of which runs from the ancient civilizations and empires of Mesopotamia and the eastern Mediterranean up to the rise of capitalism, modernity and European domination of the globe. Contra Wolf's ironic title, Mann's work is mostly about Europe and the people *with* history. It attempts to build up an account of the emergence of our contemporary world, organized by nation-states, classes and ethnic groups, capitalism and major economic actors, and modern political and religious ideologies.

Poggi (2001: 180; 2006) objects to Mann's separation of military from political power, preferring his three 'forms' to Mann's four 'sources'. Essentially Poggi follows very closely Weber's definition of the state as that institution which monopolizes the use of force; for him the bottom line of the state's power is over life and death. The tendency of militaries to become institutionally differentiated from the rest of the modern constitutional state is a specific historical development that belies an underlying unity. Mann counters that the state's administrative powers have a unique basis in the social order and net power capacity they can bring to social relations which is separate from the ultimate threat of force. Moreover, the distinctiveness of military power is attested to by the relatively autonomous actions of military coups, mercenaries, terrorist organizations and the private security industry abroad (Mann 2006: 351–8).

Some suggest that, despite claiming a balanced view of the four sources, Mann in fact privileges the state/political power (Hobson 2006; Weiss 2006), downplays the role of ideology (Bryant 2006; Gorski 2006), and is ultimately a kind of materialist (Reus-Smit 2002) or political 'realist', insensitive to the social construction of reality (Hobson 2006). In regard to the European transformation in particular, he indeed tends to emphasize the growth of the modern nation-state and interstate fiscal and military competition, suggesting that religions and ideology more generally have weakened in this period (1993: 35). Mann generally pays more attention to how ideas are concretized and put into action towards ends than to reconstructing the universes of meaning that shape understanding in the first place. In response, Mann acknowledges that sometimes his language has misled, and that he had underestimated the continuing force of religion and ideology in the world. However he reasserts his resistance to a strong division between the material and the ideal, arguing that his underlying emphasis on the simultaneous organization of both dimensions is often misinterpreted as instrumental and materialist (2006: 344–50). Regarding Europe's rise to power, many argue that Europe pulls ahead of Asia quite late, in the nineteenth century, because of, for instance, the acquisition of New World resources via colonialism, easier access to coal to fuel industrialization and the impact of scientific thought on technological practice (Goldstone 2002; Pomeranz 2000). Against this, Mann defends his emphasis on a deeper history of structural differences accounting for European advance (1993: 373–517), arguing for a more gradual transformation of ways of organizing the four sources which led to capitalism (economic), an interstate system with multiple, rival, but roughly balanced, centres of power (political), dynamic growth in the means of controlled lethal violence (military), and a Christian ecumene issuing forth a more secular system of interstate norms and diplomacy (ideology) (2006: 365–84) .

Finally, given the sheer mass of historical detail Mann mobilizes in his arguments, some, perhaps especially sociologists, will wonder if he hasn't become essentially a historian, the theory-building aims of sociology dwarfed by particularistic arguments regarding specific historical processes. On one hand, we might counter that that is precisely what good theory should do – explain a lot with very little, provide a parsimonious set of postulates that can help assimilate and make sense of diverse data. On the other hand, we might also note that, with his four sources of power and rejection of the primacy of any one source (such as 'capitalism'), Mann provides himself with a conceptual tool kit that can easily be adapted or rebalanced when new historical facts or arguments come to light. Some will see this as improving its explanatory reach and flexibility, others as diffusing its explanatory power.

I have presented Wolf, Poggi and Mann as contrasting examples of how very large, encompassing concepts of power organization can be brought to bear on historical and cultural analysis. Poggi's forms and Mann's sources bear obvious resemblances, despite the difference in number. Both owe a considerable debt to Weber, although Poggi's historical scope is narrower, and betrays a very particular interest in the nature of power in the modern, liberal, constitutional and capitalist state, whereas Mann seeks to explain all possible concatenations of power from the year nought. Wolf, by contrast, rather than devising intertwining threads (forms, sources) that can be traced through various social formations, conceives complex, historically particular 'packages' of power, although nonetheless organized into three overarching types (modes). Despite his wariness of the ahistoricism of some ethnography and his scrupulous attention to historical context, this approach exhibits that classic anthropological concern for 'descriptive integration' (Wolf 1999: 18) in regard to particular cases, as a way of capturing the combined material and ideological circumstances in which people make sense of and act upon their worlds.

## Conclusion

The macro-perspectives considered here have the virtue of addressing the widest possible body of evidence available to us. Strikingly, they tend to converge on the division of human history and social forms into three great periods and types. Correspondingly, some of the profoundest questions about social power concern the transitions between these periods/types, what leads us into a world of stratified classes in agrarian states, and later into one of competitive and escalating patterns of production and consumption, housed increasingly in a network of constitutional states internally stratified by markets. And, as Fried (1967: 227–42) pointed out, the first entrants into these new conditions do so for different and more contingent reasons than those who follow after, responding to pressures created by those who went first. While these approaches may seem too macroscopic and remote to afford any purchase on the more localized questions of power relations that concern some researchers, I would argue that such encompassing frames are necessary for contextualizing more focused analyses of power.

Let me complete this conclusion by making some comparative observations in regard to the previous chapter. First I note an absence. Anthony Giddens, who we have touched on in previous chapters, places power among the primary concepts of social science, and in the context of questions about social evolution and change (1984: 227–80, 283). He emphasizes the differences between 'allocative' (economic) and 'authoritative' (political) forms of power, and the variable effects of different 'power containers', that is, major forms of social organization, especially cities and nation-states (1981; 1987: 7–17). But he also explicitly distances himself from the idea of evolution, assimilating this idea with Marx's historical materialism and dubious ideas of a universal, progressive human history, emphasizing instead the discontinuities between modern and premodern eras (1987: 31–4). Thus he takes little interest in power as central to the causal dynamics of social change. Giddens fits awkwardly into the present chapter because his work, while empirically informed and concerned with the formation of industrial and capitalist society, is primarily about theorizing societies as systems, with limited engagement with the complexities of human history. Ultimately power becomes an embedded issue in his larger project of reconstituting social theory in a way that synthesizes micro, agency-oriented theories that emphasize the creation of meaning, with macro, structure-revealing theories that objectify sociological data. In many ways, his project is closer to Bourdieu's, considered in the last chapter, with a similar preoccupation with the tension between subjectivity and objectivity, and with overcoming the analytic distinction between structure and agency (see Layder 2006: 155–88; Mouzelis 2008: 115–21). It is notable that our evolutionary approaches routinely invoke, implicitly and explicitly, distinctions between structures and agents (often as elites) operating through those structures. They appear to find no utility in challenging a clear distinction here.

Another contrast is the greater presence here of concepts of domination, authority, and legitimacy compared to Chapter 5 in which they tended to dissolve into problematics of knowledge. This is partly due to the strong influence of Weber, for whom these concepts are central. But it also reflects a more naturalistic perspective on social life, in which command–obedience relations are regarded as ubiquitous, normal, and analyzable as objective, institutionalized patterns of behaviour, not in need of any deeper explanation. Again, in Chapter 1 I argued that ideas of concentrated centres and patterns of symmetry and asymmetry between various loci of power are indispensable for the analysis of power, and this assertion fits very well with the approaches explored in this chapter. (For instance, Mann's sources are ultimately various institutionalized centres for the production of power.) But it is clearly at odds with Foucault's injunction to treat power as de-centred, constantly trafficking through the capillaries of society but never settling anywhere. Bourdieu's social fields through which people compete over economic, social, cultural and symbolic 'capitals' clearly suggest a kind of centre. But these are convergence points for social action defined by the pursuit of certain 'goods', whereas in the work considered in this chapter it is more often organizations and institutions that provide the centres of power. Both ideas – social fields and organizations – have analytic utility, but they invoke the centring of power in very different ways. Finally, as suggested above in comparing Gellner and Foucault, it is not that those considered here are uninterested in matters of knowledge (cognition, ideology and so on), but rather that knowledge to be such needs to be understood as being 'about' something that is not itself knowledge. Problems of power include, but do not reduce to, problems of knowing; and the fact that any claim to knowledge implies some sort of bid for power, is regarded as commonplace, and not necessarily problematic.

# PART III

# Investigating Power

The last part of this book offers a more thematic approach, moving on to consider some of the areas of life in which we might want to investigate the specific nature and dynamics of power. What has gone before has been a critical survey of key ideas and theories, but I have not attempted to generate a tightly formulated 'theory of power'. Nonetheless I have indicated preferences for some ideas and approaches along the way, and these will broadly inform what follows.

Given my opening contention that power is ultimately the central concern of social science, it follows that any topic or field of study provides an opportunity for developing the analysis of power, and that one cannot offer a comprehensive account of possible applications. So, in Part III, I have chosen four broad topics that together represent some of the issues that have been central in debates about power, but are sufficiently different from one another to suggest the broad range of social phenomena for which the study of power is relevant. Moreover, at points they will also afford us opportunities to move between macro and micro levels of analysis, and to suggest connections between them.

Chapter 7 explores the complexities of domination, authority and legitimacy in modern liberal societies. Particular attention is paid to the evolving relationship between state, economy and civil society, and how notions of a public/private divide and competition help to organize and legitimate power relations. Chapter 8 looks at the role of power in religion, its definition, institutions, ideologies and movements. It concludes by considering the implications of power for moral argumentation more generally. Chapter 9 turns to the question of gender and power, because gender differences provide a unique opportunity to examine questions of power cross-culturally. Particular emphasis is given to the ideas of patriarchy and, again, public/private dichotomies. Finally, Chapter 10 explores aspects of identity and personhood, arguing that power is fundamental to how these take shape, interact, change and acquire significance for their bearers. Each chapter is in the form of an essay that seeks to provide a general take on the topic, and raise some key questions. Because the topics are very broad, I have not attempted an exhaustive review of the relevant literature. Instead, my aim is provoke interest and ideas, and to offer a good starting point for further reading and inquiry.

# CHAPTER 7

# Domination, Authority and Legitimacy in Liberal Society

## Introduction

This chapter examines processes of domination, authority and legitimacy in the specific context of liberal society. By 'liberal society' I mean the variety of societies, housed in nation-states, in which power relations are primarily organized by a combination of capitalist economic structures, democratic political institutions and liberal cultural norms. I choose this focus for two reasons. First, the liberal nation-state is in the ascendancy for the time being – it is a dominant form, spreading, however haltingly, across the globe (cf. Dahl 2000; Dunn 2006). For this reason it warrants special attention. Second, the variable interactions of capitalism, liberalism and democracy in these societies give them patterns of power relations that are particularly complex. Scrutinizing these kinds of societies in particular will help reveal some of the subtleties of modern power relations. Crucially, liberal society is characterized by a deep and dynamic tension between the high valuation of individual freedom and autonomy, that is, personalized power, and the generation of highly concentrated yet flexible forms of organized and institutionalized power.

I view the subject from four converging perspectives. First, I discuss the peculiar interdependencies of state and economy in the liberal system and their conjoined historical emergence. This provides, in a sense, the largest frame for the discussion. I then use three other diagnostic features of liberal society – civil society, the public/private dichotomy and ritualized competition – as alternate routes into the same terrain, as complementary ways of getting analytic purchase on the subject. Each of these provides certain insights into how power relations in liberal societies, both implicit and explicit, are created, reproduced and legitimated. My aim is to build up a composite picture of liberal society and its power processes.

## State, economy and the 'memorable alliance'

While politics and government have been defined as objects of comparative study since the fourth century BC at least (Aristotle 1988), it is worth reminding ourselves that the idea of the economy emerged more slowly. It appeared first as an aspect of households, then cities, and only much later in the modern era, as a system of markets governing national and even global relations (Polanyi 1957). Rather than treat politics and economics as highly distinct, relatively autonomous fields of inquiry, I will be emphasizing their interdependence. I do this because most of the readers of this book are likely to live in some form of liberal society, and I think doing this is essential to having an accurate 'map' of where we live, and some assessment of its characteristic problems. Put bluntly, I am opposing a common sense image we tend to carry around in our minds: of modern liberal society being made up of a body of citizens with a special relationship to their own government, that manages and mediates power relations among citizens, amid an encompassing quasi-natural environment called 'the economy', to which it is also supposed to manage society's relationship, while simultaneously not despoiling the economy by interfering too much in its natural workings. The contrary image I will be advancing comprises two symbiotic and interpenetrating organizational complexes with features of bureaucracy and hierarchy, those of state and economy respectively (see Figure 7.1). In complementary but also conflicting ways, these serve the needs of a citizenry, which is actually very 'lumpy', sometimes acting as individuals, but much of the time clumping together around common interests, ideologies and identities, and opposing and competing with each other on these bases as well (cf. Beetham 1991; Bowles and Gintis 1987; Crouch 2004, 2011; Reich 2008; Scott 1997).

In short, we should not privilege the relationship between state and citizens when considering patterns of domination, authority and legitimacy, because

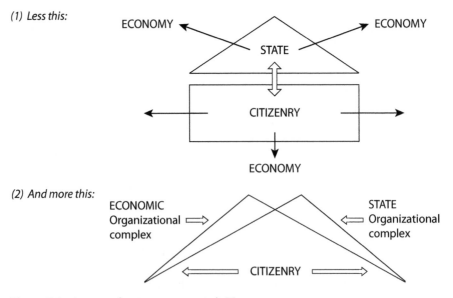

**Figure 7.1**  Images of state, economy and citizenry

these terms apply equally well to the citizenry's relationship to the economic organizational complex. Having said this, how the two hierarchies function together is shaped by the fact that they and their relationship are normally perceived in terms of the first, rather than the second, model above. Thus, while I argue that there is a basic underlying pattern of 'triangularity' between state, economy and citizenry, in which both state and economic organizations dominate citizens, construct authority over them and seek legitimacy from them, this triangularity is asymmetrical. Economic organizations occupy a quasi-naturalized space in the social imagination, obscuring their artificial, human-made natures, and their position in the overall production of social power. We know from our own histories that we have had some hand in making the states that rule over us, and that we have some means to recall unsatisfactory governments. But the economy and its centres of organized power appear to have 'just grown there', to be less obviously our own creations.

Weber argued that modern rational capitalism was the unintended outcome of the 'memorable alliance' of early modern mercantile bourgeoisies creating money through lending to monarchical European states locked in mercantile and military competition (Ingham 2008: 32–3, 126–7, passim; cf. Arrighi 1994: 85–158; Weber 1927: 337).

> Weber believed that capitalism would flourish as a global economic system in which neither the state nor capital subordinates the other. Capitalism would not collapse under the weight of its economic contradictions, as Marx predicted. Rather, it involves a perpetual political conflict between states and an increasingly cosmopolitan bourgeoisie in which the balance of power swings from one to the other. The subordination of capitalists to the interests of the state would destroy the dynamism of the system; but the converse subordination of the state to the interests of the capitalists would lead to excessive, debilitating exploitation and turmoil (Ingham 2008: 33).

This schematic image of a balance of power between capitalists and the state perhaps misses out the degree to which key personnel move back and forth between the institutional hierarchies and the role of key intermediate institutions such as central banks, but the basic model is illuminating.

Modern banks and corporations have their origins in this process. Machiavelli's nemesis, the Medici family (see Chapter 3), established one of the first banking networks through the city-states of Italy and key trading cities of Europe in the fourteenth and fifteenth centuries. Another early banking family, the Fuggers, were major bankrollers of the Spanish state and its imperial wars in the fifteenth and sixteenth centuries, and were bankrupted by the Spanish state defaulting on its loans. Soon after, the governments of trade-oriented states began establishing their own banks, such as the Bank of Amsterdam (1609) and the Bank of England (1694). By the 1700s multiple private banking houses, or 'merchant banks', began to appear under such family names as Rothschild, Morgan and Baring, contributing to a more complex system of state and private banking operations (Allen 2001: 155–72). These banks took in deposits from the wealthy and, as time went on, from further down the social scale. They invested in monarchical states, particularly bankrolling the costs of international wars in Europe, and advanced money for trading ventures, first centred on the Mediterranean Sea, and later on transatlantic and far eastern trade. In regard to the latter, by developing 'bills of exchange' and 'credits of account', the forerunners of our paper money and bank accounts, they enabled merchants to reduce the need to exchange precious metal coinage in payment, thus greatly lubricating the wheels of commerce and the means to generate and accumulate economic power. Modern money, as a system of debts underwritten by the state, has its origins in this process (Ingham 2004).

At the same time as these banks were evolving, so were antecedents of the modern business firm. In England joint-stock companies, in which various parties pooled their money to invest in trading ventures, proliferated from the late sixteenth century. Some of these had royal or government charters, such as the English East India Company (1600) or the Dutch East Indies Company (1602), involving particularly close relations between the state, offering naval protection, and the investing merchants. But other companies involved more private arrangements between groups of merchants and 'adventurers'. These trading ventures laid some of the technical and legal groundwork for the development of modern commercial and manufacturing enterprises, such as accounting by double entry bookkeeping and notions of the limited liability of investors for losses. In Britain the large family-owned enterprise became an important part of the burgeoning industrial economy in the nineteenth century. Meanwhile the US liberalized laws for the establishment of private companies in the early nineteenth century, and eventually pioneered the large modern corporation, based on public investment in stocks, vertical integration of different stages of production in a single organization, and trans- or multinational operations (Allen 2001: 15–39; Ingham 2008: 126–33). This has become a dominant model throughout capitalism, although of course, under pressures of capitalist competition, it has seen adaptations, such as periods of 'outsourcing' and 'flattening' of management structures. And these big players sit amid a complex economic ecology that includes many smaller and diverse kinds of firms and enterprises. So we now find ourselves in a world composed of two interpenetrating hierarchies; on the one hand private banks and financial investment companies, major corporations, medium, small and family businesses, and on the other, states, composed of executives, legislatures and legal systems, with multiple government agencies assisted in their work by various para-governmental bodies. Central banks occupy a kind of intermediate position between the two hierarchies. And of course various activities and forms of employment, such as in the voluntary sector, education, healthcare and the arms industry, are also complexly intermediate between these two hierarchies in terms of their structural position and orientation.

The fundamental point I want to make here is that both these hierarchies, and the specific organizations within them in which people are ensconced as employees or on which they are otherwise reliant, exert power over people's lives. They both dominate us. And they are, as Weber suggested, highly inter-dependent. The power and authority of the state relies on the productivity and robustness of the economy, and capacity for wealth creation by economic ac-tors is underwritten by the state's administration and protection, and in some cases, purchasing power. And yet our public vocabulary for talking about power, authority and legitimacy is skewed towards the state. Because states lay down the laws and their personnel are routinely appointed, scrutinized and replaced through electoral processes, we naturally recognize them as sources of authority and objects of legitimacy, respectively. While the power of the economic sector, especially as concentrated and manifested in major actors such as banks and multinational corporations, is obvious, the mechanisms for scrutiny, for assessing the competency of their rule, are much less developed. Because they do not so much issue commands and make laws and policies as inculcate and channel activity, the question of the authority through which they shape social life is less subject to question. Only in rather special circum-stances, such as the role of bankers in precipitating the post-2007 economic downturn and credit shortage, does the legitimacy of their power and author-ity in regard to the economy become a more focused, if rather inarticulate, public question.

Somewhat provocatively, I would suggest a curious structural echo here of those antecedent western European polities, in which legitimation revolved around a dualistic reciprocal dynamic between the secular and sacred powers of the state and church (see Poggi 2001: 74–96). Popes provided kings with divine sanction for their rule, and kings provided popes with military protec-tion and support. With secularization and the growth of the modern economy, increasingly it is the economy and its mediators, rather than the divine and its priests, which claim the closest proximity to ultimate power, the holy grails of 'productivity', 'competitiveness' and 'wealth creation'. It is the corporate leaders and star economists that claim the capacity to mediate between the ultimate powers of the economy and the worldly civil powers of the state. In both cases, then and now, power and its legitimation is represented as dual and differentiated, with the state/secular powers ultimately accountable for worldly politics, societal administration and so on, while economic/religious powers are less explicitly accountable to those they govern, instead interced-ing between transcendent sources and earthly, civic institutions of power.

## Civil society

A moment ago I described the citizenry as 'lumpy', and this is the nub of the idea of 'civil society', which came back into the social scientific and public political lexicons in the 1980s (see Bobbio 1989: 22–43; Gellner 1996; Hall and Trentmann 2005; Seligman 1992). This term identifies the capacity of individuals to freely associate, organize and form groups around common values, interests and goals. Some uses treat it as a structural concept that demarcates a certain social 'space', a portion of society as a whole. All definitions treat civil society as separate from, and a counterpoint to, the state, with its inherent power to compel. Some distinguish it from the economy and social action oriented to markets, because these are again seen as conditions of compulsion, while others view civil society as interpenetrating, even deeply dependent upon, markets, understood as enablers of free association and the pursuit of goals. This points up different perceptions of the market economy, as a process of domination versus as a realm of independent action, both of which contain truth. Most also separate civil society from ties of kinship and the family. Here the pressures of affect and obligation that come with these kinds of bonds are seen as incompatible with the civil society's characteristic freedom of association. So, structurally, we get a kind of 'layer-cake' image, with the state on the top, kinship and family on the bottom, and civil society in the middle. And this middle layer, precisely because it is a zone where people are supposedly less constrained, is highly dynamic, an area where people and groups align and realign, conflict and cooperate, defend status quos and mobilize for reforms. So the idea of civil society aims partly to direct our attention to where power struggles take shape in society.

The idea of civil society is also used prescriptively, carrying a normative load. It is almost universally regarded as a good thing, but there are differences of opinion over what's good about it. From the perspective of classical liberalism, the emphasis is on 'negative liberty' (Berlin 1969: 122–31), that is, freedom from constraint, to act and associate as an autonomous individual, as one chooses. In short, this is freedom from others having too much 'power over' us. Here civil society is identified with market society, as a bulwark against the unwanted intrusions of the state. From the perspective of a more progressive liberalism, or communitarianism, the emphasis is more on civil society as supporting a capacity to coordinate social action, as a basis for the formation of social solidarity; in short, on the collective 'power to' achieve things. On this side civil society is identified with efforts to oppose or transform the state and its policies. Thus, for some its 'goodness' has to do with its separateness and distance from the state, and for others it has to do with its orientation to and effects on the state.

In the eighteenth century and earlier, in writings such as Adam Ferguson's *Essay on The History of Civil Society* (1966 [1767]), the term referred to a general form of society, including the state, in which commerce and the rule of law were highly developed, and effectively regulating social relations. But in the intervening period, under the influence especially of Hegel and later Gramsci, the term shifted towards its present dominant meaning, as a middle layer of society defined by commerce, capitalism and markets, and opposed to the state. Accepting that this is now the conventional way of understanding the concept, we can nonetheless observe ambiguities in this civil society/state dichotomy. By their nature, political parties are designed to move back and forth between state and civil society. When successful, they acquire the offices and powers of government, and when unsuccessful, they lose these and are thrown back down into civil society. Thus smaller, cause-oriented 'third' parties, such as the Green Party, manage to seem more 'of' civil society, precisely because of their limited access to state power. But the major parties, especially in two-party systems, oscillate between state and civil society, gaining authority and legitimacy when they are 'out of power' and 'closer to the people', and then in a sense slowly being drained of these the longer they are 'in government', and inevitably shown to be limited in their capacity to control events. Thus, in the liberal democratic system, they function like dredges, scooping up legitimacy in the realm of civil society, and delivering it to the state, which suffers from chronic depletion of legitimacy.

This sense of civil society as oriented to politics, as opposed to its other sense as a private realm of action shielded from politics, points us to its connections to the idea of 'publics'. Formulated decades apart, John Dewey's notion of 'publics' and Jürgen Habermas' idea of the 'public sphere' both attempted to articulate a positive conception of the role of the public in social life:

> Publics are spontaneous groups of citizens who share the indirect effects of a particular action. Anyone affected by the indirect consequences of a specific action will automatically share a common interest in controlling those consequences, i.e., solving a common problem (Dewey 1927: 126).

> By 'the public sphere' we mean first of all a realm of our social life in which something approaching public opinion can be formed. Access is guaranteed to all citizens. A portion of the public sphere comes into being in every conversation in which private individuals assemble to form a public body (Habermas 1974: 49).

In these definitions we can discern a tension between the idea of the public as the whole of the citizenry, or as a kind of common social and institutional space, versus the 'lumpiness' and fractiousness of civil society. These passages suggest multiple and shifting publics, with no guarantee that their interests and actions are compatible and won't come into conflict. In this sense, civil society becomes not simply a solution or counterweight to the powers of the state, but a terrain in which bids for power are constantly being made and unmade, often with an ultimate aim of affecting the state and its policies.

How people understand the relationship between civil society and the economy is even more mixed and ambiguous. The distinction I have been drawing between 'the economy', as a more abstract term for the entire web of market-based relationships we operate within, and an 'economic organizational complex', a dense network of organizations and institutions in which power is concentrated to varying degrees, can help us examine this ambiguity. On the one hand, the modern liberal economy provides many of the conditions that facilitate the freely associating actions supposedly characteristic of civil society. Whether it is simply privately buying and selling goods and services, or cooperating to form economic ventures or economic protections, such as those offered by trade unions, all these activities go on in civil society, broadly defined. But on the other hand, if we think not so much in terms of action within the 'neutral' space of the economy, but rather under the dominating influence of a hierarchy of powerful economic organizations, then it is not surprising if civil society comes to be seen as opposed to the economy, as well as to the state. Neither of these characterizations on its own is adequate for conceptualizing economic life. Minimally, we should be careful to distinguish between domination through the economy by powerful groups and organizations in the economy, and domination by the economy itself, as a set of market-based norms of interaction. The latter sense of domination is problematic, offering no clear conception of who is doing the dominating, and being poorly distinguished from more general processes of socialization and social convention.

We are better off not burdening the concept of civil society with a normative load, instead using it to direct our attention to the structures and dynamics through which domination, authority and legitimacy operate. On the one hand, it can support the consolidation of the power of major institutions of state and economy, providing the myriad forms of organization of daily public life that facilitate their operations. On the other, it can provide the means for the development of new organizational bases for power, for new social movements that potentially radiate out, influencing the wider society, economy and the state itself. Civil society can underpin fundamental challenges to the social order, especially where states attempt total control over society. But in the liberal societies that are our specific concern in this chapter, its very capacity as an alternate sphere for the generation of social powers, beyond the upper reaches of our two great hierarchies, ultimately has system-reinforcing effects, enhancing the aggregate mobilization of social energies and providing means for both defraying, and articulating and responding to, social discontent. Civil society 'cultivates' social power beyond the state, in the full sense of that word – increasing, developing and channelling that power.

## Public and private

The tensions between state and economic hierarchies are built into one of the most fundamental and problematic conceptual distinctions shaping liberal societies, that between 'public' and 'private' (Benn and Gaus1983; Bobbio 1989: 1–21; Weintraub and Kumar 1997). While the term 'civil society' is mainly used by those politically engaged and active, and less a part of ordinary speech for most people, the distinction between public and private is deeply rooted in common sense and everyday language. The distinction is part of the deep structure of the social organization of power in liberal societies. While some such distinction is quite widespread culturally and historically (Moore 1984), it becomes particularly pronounced in liberal society, in which power is managed and negotiated by: (a) defining the state as a public form of power in which the citizens have an interest and a say, and (b) defining zones of private power that are supposedly off limits to the intrusions of the state. In this way aggregate power is increased, and systemic legitimacy is enhanced through a 'double movement', in which private citizens are allowed influence on public power and yet spheres of limited private 'sovereignty' are allowed to multiply, within bounds. However, this same principle that facilitates legitimation of power, also defines the central axis of social conflict in liberal societies. Conflicts over freedom of speech, the rights of parents over their children, the influence of religion on public education, government regulation of business practices, to name just some prime examples, all hinge on disputed understandings of the proper boundaries between public and private.

The distinction we have inherited has its origins in Roman Law, as codified by the Emperor Justinian in the sixth century AD: 'Public law is that which regards the condition of the Roman commonwealth, private, that which pertains to the interests of single individuals' (quoted in Weintraub 1997: 12). This comes down to us as the distinction between 'public' or 'criminal' law concerning the interests of the state, and 'private' or 'civil' law concerning contracts and disputes between private citizens, which can include corporations as artificial legal persons (Weber 1978: 641–4). Our highly developed concept of private property (which implies corresponding notions of public property) arises out of this same legal nexus, spurred on by capitalist development (see Hann 1998; Reeve 1995). In the English language of the fourteenth to sixteenth centuries, the word 'private' indicated withdrawal from public life, as in the case of some religious orders, or the lack of public standing, in terms of office or position (Hirschman 2002: 121; Williams 1983: 242). But by the seventeenth to eighteenth centuries, the public/private distinction was being actively reworked by natural law and social contract theorists such as Pufendorf, Locke and Hutcheson, as part of a general attempt to rethink and reground power, authority and legitimacy in the evolving early modern state. Across this period there is a gradual shift between two models. In the first, the private is all that comes under the domain of a head of household (the *dominus*, normally male), both property and persons, and the public is the community of heads of households, with rights to participate equally in matters of collective concern. In the second, emerging model, private becomes associated with each individual's domain over their own person, body, thoughts and actions, and the public becomes the more general, unbounded sphere of human interactions (Gobetti 1997). However, many aspects of the earlier model persist, even while the second model has taken shape, a key issue for the feminist analysis of gender relations, as we will see in Chapter 9 (cf. Pateman 1989). In contemporary liberal society, privacy is associated with the domestic sphere, but it is individuals that carry the ultimate rights to privacy. Meanwhile 'public' tends to carry a range of connotations, more narrowly associated with the domain of the state, more widely with opinion formation among a citizenry, and more widely still, with that which takes place within the general view of humanity.

We often use spatial language to talk about the public/private distinction, treating these as separate 'spheres', 'realms', 'domains', or simply 'spaces' (Habermas 1974). I suggest that this is because of the close association with concepts of power. Just as power is normally conceived in terms of its extension and limits, its domain of sovereignty, so public and private are imagined as separate spaces. But of course, as suggested above, the boundaries are highly contested, and the private in fact blends into the public by degrees. For heuristic purposes, instead of two great 'spheres', it is more useful to think of four, entangled levels. First, the individual, with their own private domain of thought, belief, opinion, tastes and preferences. The contemporary scope for autonomy of belief was forged in the European wars of religion in the sixteenth and seventeenth centuries. In a sense, the agreement in the Treaty of Westphalia (1648) to allow each ruler to decide the sanctioned form of confession in their own lands devolves over the centuries into the present freedom to individually choose one's religion, or none at all, along with various other ideological convictions. We are individual in both mind and body. The growth of the notion of the personal sovereignty of the private self includes the body – how we use it (for instance sexually, reproductively), how we modify it and adorn it and so on. Greater latitude in these personal decisions is a key marker of liberal society, although sometimes a flashpoint of public/private conflict, as in rights to reproductive self-determination or to assisted suicide (cf. Okin 1991: 87–90). However, this should not blind us to the material elaboration of individual expression afforded by liberal society. The modern economy, especially in its most advanced forms, is calibrated to facilitate self-realization through the provision of consumer goods that appeal to both the body and the mind. Our experience of making free choices, of embodying our individuality, is embedded in consumer behaviour much of the time.

At the next level is the household. The proportion of single occupancy households has been increasing since the 1970s, in those cases making the domains of the individual and the household largely congruent. But in multiple occupancy households, often made up of families, broadly defined, one frequently has a sphere in which strategies for income and consumption are combined, under the leadership of a head or heads of household who exercise a certain authority over children or other dependents. Thus the household is quite literally a private space in which, with adequate resources, personal tastes and consumption preferences can be realized with minimal outside interference. However, in families and some other forms of multiple occupancy households, the question arises of the authority and domination of household heads over dependants. Here there is a tension between the private right of, say, parents to make independent decisions in the upbringing of their children and the private right of child (or other dependants), notionally protected by the state. Conflicts over the right of parents to prescribe religious or other beliefs, or impose marital choices, are classic examples. This axis of conflict is partly managed by having designated ages at which, by stages, minors achieve majority and legal autonomy from their parents or custodians. But of course, the control of heads of household, based on their control of key resources such as household income, means that they have considerable scope to coerce those within the household, whether or not they are children. This is a fundamental issue in the male domination of women and households, given the general advantages for men in the economy (see Chapter 9). The public appetite for the privatization of public housing in the UK in the 1980s and more recently the flawed attempt in the US to expand private home ownership through sub-prime mortgage lending are both evidence of the centrality of the idea of home and household as defining a sphere of private sovereignty.

Leaving the household we come back to civil society, the level of the public sphere, the economy, the marketplace. There are two main modes in which we occupy this space: leisure and work. On the one hand, to the degree that we are free from some of the micro-dominations of the household, we are able to realize our individuality, through consumption and association with others. As already indicated, this can run the gamut from apolitical recreation for personal enjoyment to politicized mobilization around public issues and disputes. On the other hand, most of us are obliged to find income, to work, and very often that involves us in another set of subordinations to the relatively private rule of the firms, institutions and bureaucracies we work under. It is not that notions of individual private interests are entirely absent from the realm of work. Ideas of craft, career and profession enable some of us to find degrees of self-realization in our work, and of course monetary income provides a primary means of action in the private sphere. But work is also a matter of compulsion, and normally entails subordination to an organizational hierarchy of some sort. A few of us will find our way to dominant, elite positions in the organizations where we work (which we perhaps even own), but most will not.

This is the level where the distinction between public and private is most fraught, where conduct is governed by public norms and laws which are also designed to protect the private autonomy of actors, particularly in the economy. It is the realm of both conflicting and coordinated interests, at once stimulated and regulated by law and economy, where power is episodically concentrated and mobilized. This generally involves the public assertion that certain issues are matters of public concern: the rights and political representation of women, working condition standards, basic public provisioning of needs for education, healthcare and employment, and movements around civil rights, anti-discrimination, rights to sexuality and environmental issues. In each case movement leaders have articulated public opinion and mobilized power through various tactics – votes, strikes, boycotts – to bring pressure to bear on states and other power actors. As we can see from these examples, contestation causes conventional understandings of the public/private boundary to shift over time. Interestingly, A.O. Hirschman (2002) has speculated that modern liberal societies characteristically oscillate through cycles of coordinated public action and withdrawal into the private sphere, suggesting that the experience of alternating disappointments with the satisfactions of public engagement and private consumption propel generations back and forth over decades between public and private domains. Given my argument that liberal society is defined by the twin powers of state and economy, it follows that class-based politics should be particularly central to the social dynamic. It has been very important at various stages of the evolution of state and economy, most centrally in the general promotion of labour rights and the welfare state (Pierson 1991). But we should be sceptical about reifying classes, especially the working class, as unified historical actors endowed with enduring powers. It is much more difficult for mass working classes, distributed across diverse economic sectors and regions, to act in a coordinated and sustained way than it is for much smaller strata occupying the upper reaches of institutional hierarchies. This was a key point for the elite theorists we encountered in Chapter 3. In practice working class power has been episodic, and largely a matter of influencing and mobilizing state power for the expansion of rights, not a stand-alone locus of persistent social power in the political economic system (see Mann 1988: 146–65; 1995: 16–22).

Finally, there is the ultimate 'public' level of the state, charged with protecting the autonomy of private domains, but also placing publicly agreed limits on what can go on in those domains, and where necessary being the champion of private individuals when they have come under the oppressive domination of another private agent (employer, household head and so on). In theory, the state monopolizes certain crucial powers – violence, coercion, incarceration, and execution – holding these in public trust for the collectivity of citizens. It also helps to supply key conditions for the operation of a productive economy, for example, the rule of law, enforcement of contracts and a stable currency. Failures to monopolize violence and facilitate a stable economy are the main diagnostic features of a weak state. Correspondingly, the state becomes corrupt precisely by becoming subject to the undue influence of private power. The state has an inner and an outer face (Hearn 2006: 118). In this chapter we are primarily concerned with its inner face, which it presents to its citizens as the steward and manager of the collective power they have notionally invested in it. But of course the state also faces outward into a geopolitical arena of states and other international actors, in which it must also negotiate and defend its powers. Just as the state shows signs of weakness if it cannot adequately control other centres of power within its own domain, it must also protect the whole against external incursions against its power which may come in the form of military threat, such as terrorism, or economic domination, such as by the IMF, or legal subordination, which is an ongoing issue between the European Union and its member states. The viable state must demonstrate adequate power in both the inner and outer domains.

As I have presented it here, the public/private distinction defines a series of trophic levels of power, of embedded domains of domination, authority and legitimacy. Part of the genius of liberal society as a form of state is that it allows the maximization of these embedded spheres of power and sovereignty, gaining some of its overarching authority and legitimacy precisely by farming out the same in smaller, more circumscribed packages. But of course, this builds in the constant threat that some of those packages will become powerful enough to coerce the state itself or declare autonomy from it. This brings us back to the state/economy relationship we began with. There is a convention, evident in much of the preceding, of notionally aligning the state with the idea of public power and the economy with that of private domain. This is reflected in the common distinction within the economy of public and private sectors, and notions that these are in a kind of zero-sum competition for resources. In neoclassical economic theory, the state, and the state-led employment sector, is seen as tending to be predatory and a drain on the private sector of the properly capitalist free market economy. But in light of all I've said so far, this is a dubious argument as a general principle. While there is no doubt that the state can become predatory on economic resources, it is clear that the entire evolution of the capitalist economy and liberal society has hinged on the symbiotic growth and strength of powers lodged in both political and economic institutions. While the capitalist market-based economy thrives partly because the state allows considerable scope and freedom for manoeuvre by private actors, nonetheless the entire economy is irreducibly a public concern and an object of macroeconomic management. Moreover, the capacity of economic organizations to dominate the lives of employees and public life more generally is something that can only be counterbalanced by the power of the state under the mobilized pressure of its citizenry. An exaggerated association of the economy with the private is misleading. We are better off recognizing that we live under twinned Leviathans that must be played off against each other in order to reduce either's capacity for domination.

## Competition as legitimation

I want to highlight one more aspect of the management of power in liberal societies. A key idea, or procedure, and I will go so far as to say 'ritual', for the legitimation of allocative outcomes in both the economic and state spheres is competition (cf. Helle 2008; Simmel 1964: 57–85). A standard online dictionary definition provides an initial view into the significance of the idea:

**Competition**
the activity or condition of striving to gain or win something by defeating or establishing superiority over others:
• *there is fierce competition between banks*
• *the competition for university places is greater than ever this year*
[*count noun*] an event or contest in which people take part in order to establish superiority or supremacy in a particular area:
• *a beauty competition*

[*in singular*] the person or people over whom one is attempting to establish one's supremacy or superiority; the opposition:

- *I walked round to check out the competition*

*Ecology* interaction between animal or plant species, or individual organisms, that are attempting to gain a share of a limited environmental resource.

**Origin:** early 17th century: from late Latin *competitio(n-)* 'rivalry', from *competere* 'strive for' (see compete) (*Oxford Dictionaries Online* 2011b, entry 'competition')

From this definition we can see the diverse range of applications of the term, from banking to education to beauty. A moment's reflection reveals the ubiquity of competition in modern society, particularly in its liberal variety. Missing or only suggested in the definition above is the absolute centrality of competition to the operations, authority and legitimacy of our two great institutions: state and economy. Both are validated by power being won through forms of competition that have been institutionally channelled and regulated. Intriguingly, 'ecology' is set off as a distinct sphere of application of the term, and yet we know that the boundary between ecological competition and, say, economic competition is constantly being blurred by metaphor and analogy.

The word 'competition' appears to enter the English language in the early seventeenth century. Of course this is not to say that competition is a modern invention. The previous chapter's focus on social evolutionary approaches to the study of power implies that competition in various forms has been present throughout human history as one of its driving forces (Hall 1986; Mann 1988; Tilly 1975). But it does suggest that our ways of thinking about competition may have undergone a transformation around the beginning of the seventeenth century. We variously attribute the formation of European modernity to the rise of industrialization, capitalism, individualism, mass politics, science and so on. I am cautiously suggesting that overarching these processes was another: the emergence of a much more reflexive conception of competition in which it became not just a fact of life, for example that monarchs wage war on each other, but an aspect of reality to be captured and harnessed. Our complex package of inherited ideas about markets, democracy, science, biology, and even art, have been defined by, and institutionally developed through, competition, as both practice and governing metaphor.

For the present argument I would emphasize the link between the 'memorable alliance' and competition. The rise of the liberal system has hinged on the translation of *de facto* competition within economic and political spheres into a legitimating creed of competition. Capitalism and democracy are unimaginable without it. Competition is highly imperfect, with various kinds of monopolies constantly threatening to undermine market competition (Fligstein 1996), and democracy perhaps more a competition between elites to rule than the direct articulation of popular wills (Dahl 1971; Schumpeter 1976). Nonetheless we turn to competition to ensure the best and fairest outcomes, and the failure of fair competition in either sphere threatens to invalidate outcomes and elicit calls for reform. If politics and economy provide the twin pillars supporting and sanctioning a culture of competition, as a social form competition permeates society. There is a huge variety and dispersion of forms of competition throughout the system, from the macro to the micro, naturalizing socially constructed forms of competition through sheer pervasiveness. Access to opportunities, support and prestige in education, the arts and sciences, the voluntary sector are all routinely regulated by competitions. Popular culture, from sports to television reality shows ('The X Factor', 'Big Brother' and so on), celebrates competition as entertainment. Here we move beyond competition as a mechanism for determining outcomes and allocating rewards, and into the realm of cultural representations. Competition can reach almost parodic levels in which society represents itself to itself, 'worshipping' its own form.

I would argue that competition frequently takes the form of ritual, in the sense of 'a symbolic-expressive aspect of behavior that communicates something about social relations, often in a relatively dramatic or formal manner' (Wuthnow 1987: 109). However I would also argue that rituals very often are not just about 'social relations', but also more specifically about the social organization of power, providing means to both validate and challenge power relations (Gluckman 1954). 'Ritual' is used in a range of senses, from solemn, often religious, ceremonies to mundane routines, and I apply it here in a way that covers this range. Some rituals of competition are elaborate public displays, such as major sporting events and election night results, and others more routine, such as applying for grant funding or bidding on a house. But all are rituals in the sense of formalized procedures, charged with some drama, whether highly public or personal, that by their very operation legitimate their outcomes. In common with performative rituals that effect a change in social statuses, such as weddings and initiations, competition rituals don't just dramatize power relations, but help to create them, yielding results in terms of winners and losers. And whatever the attempts to soften the blow of losing by framing it in terms of the value of participating in competition regardless of the outcome, winners generally gain, in prestige, material rewards, new opportunities and so on. In short, ritualized competition allocates power, legitimating that allocation in the process.

There are other aspects to how ritualized competition achieves legitimating effects. One is simply by the multiplicity of forms. We can posit three 'ideal types' (Swedberg 2005: 119–21), competition rituals decided by: (1) experts or panels of experts who make a judgment (such as arts prizes), (2) votes from a concerned constituency (such as elections), or (3) by the very outcome of the contest (such as a football match). Of course there are many hybrid forms between these types, but all involve notionally fair, rule-governed selection between contenders. But this very spread of procedures within the ritual form tends to fuse by degrees one mode of legitimation, the socially constructed right of experts to make authoritative judgments, with another, the sheer

ability of contenders, by their own might and natures, to achieve supremacy
in a given contest. The ritualization of competition helps elide the tensions
between 'right' and 'might', 'artifice' and 'nature', as bases of power. And finally, all these various constructed, ritualized forms of competition bleed into
a more general, encompassing environment of competition in social life that
in some sense is more naturally occurring and beyond the bounds of ritual.
In this way, reinforced by the identification of competition with the supra-
human order of biology, ecology and evolution, a key aspect of the social
order appears to emerge inevitably from the natural order.

## Conclusion

I have tried to convey a general take on power within liberal systems via a set
of admittedly schematic images. The first describes the two great overarching
hierarchies of political and economic institutions. The second shows the 'layer
cake' of civil society, sandwiched between state and kinship, and the third,
overlaying and reprising the second, the image of society as a private/public
continuum, defined by heuristic levels ranging from the individual to household to civil society/public life to the state. Finally and rather differently, there
is the image of competition as a ritual practice that recurs in myriad forms
throughout the social body, replicating and diffusing throughout the system.
My purpose in this chapter has been to sketch a structural, systemic account
of liberal society, to abstract basic features of the type, through a focus on selected themes. If my aim had been an empirical, historical, comparative study,
I would need to mobilize other concepts that map more closely onto social action, such as social movements, classes and class fractions, elites, institutional
logics and so on. More empirical analysis of specific cases requires a somewhat different conceptual tool kit. Nonetheless, I offer a general perspective
which can be scrutinized through more particularistic research.

Let me conclude with some brief comparisons between the account above,
and the approaches of theorists explored in the last two chapters. In Chapter 6, Gellner (1991), Hall (1986), Poggi (2001) and Mann (1986) all place
strong emphasis on conceptualizing economy and politics as distinctive major
modes of power, as I have done here with my heavy emphasis on the 'memorable alliance' of economy and state. However, each of these adds a third
'form' or 'source': ideology (or 'cognition' in Gellner's formulation), although
ideology is often regarded as a somewhat weaker or episodic form of power.
My account has not had much to say about ideology *per se* and the various
institutional forms that sustain it. I agree that there is an essential place for
ideology in any analysis of power, but I see its institutional embedding as
rather different from what happens in the cases of economics and politics.
My treatments of the public/private dichotomy and competition as ritual are
meant to capture the way these social institutions encode ideological premises,
fundamental understandings about the social order, fusing ideas with social

organization and routine practice. But I have left aside ideology in the more conventional sense of the claims that are made about the nature of reality and moral order, those of opinion-formers ensconced in political, religious, educational, media or other institutions, or aligned with social movements. Finally, Mann, in contrast to the other three, distinguishes a fourth source of power, the military, but this tends to fall outside the present discussion simply because my focus has been inward, on the internal working of the liberal nation-state, rather than outward toward its geopolitical horizons.

Clearly my account, with its emphasis on the historical emergence of new forms of political, economic and social organization, owes more to the 'evolutionary' approaches in Chapter 6 than the 'epistemological' ones in Chapter 5. However, there is a degree of resonance with Foucault's idea of 'governmentality' which, as we saw, is concerned particularly with the formation of liberal society, in which governance is achieved precisely by devolving substantial degrees of autonomy of action. In Foucault's double-edged phrase, this involves 'action upon action' (2000: 340), both allowing and directing 'free' activity. But I have been trying to anchor my account of liberal power in institutional concepts that more specifically shape the dispersion of governance: the economy, civil society, the public–private continuum and competition as ritual. Whatever the similarities with Foucault's notion of governmentality, I am offering an account that is more structural and functional, and less purely ideational. At base, my approach has perhaps been more like that of Eric Wolf (see Chapter 6), in trying to characterize a complex social whole and the institutional embedding of cosmologies of power, rather than proceeding by breaking power down into analytically discrete forms: ideological, economic, military and political. Again, this has partly, but not entirely, to do with the purpose of schematizing a type of society, rather than tracing very long-term historical developments across societies. In the end, regardless of these differences of approach, I would underscore the relationship of this chapter to one of the basic themes of the book: 'power over' versus 'power to'. The argument here has been that liberal society has prevailed so far through its ability to generate a greater aggregate of 'power to' by loosening the hold of 'power over', that is, the suppression of alternate bases of power from the political centre. But this ultimately increases 'power over' as well, albeit in the uneasily bifurcated form of the symbiosis of political and economic institutional hierarchies. The liberal strategy is to both split power and distribute it more widely in ways that return power to these two great hierarchies.

# CHAPTER 8

# Religion and Morality

## Introduction

Religion provides a fruitful field for exploring multiple dimensions of power. There have been numerous and divergent attempts to define religion theoretically (see Evans-Pritchard 1965; Guthrie 1993: 8, 205 fn1; Morris 1987). As a working definition for present purposes, I suggest that religion is a pattern of beliefs, ideas, institutions and practices oriented to ultimate sources of power, usually conceived as supernatural, in the forms of a god, a pantheon of deities, spirits or other impersonal supernatural forces, sometimes combining several of these. Although this is not unlike many definitions of religion, I admit that by including 'power' in the definition I have loaded the dice in my favour. This is because the definition is in fact a hypothesis that I will be trying to support in what follows; put neatly, that religion is about power (Poggi 2001: 63). The chapter begins with religion and works toward considerations of the implications of power for morality. Making this connection is not to say that religion is ultimately about morality, or that morality requires religion, but to acknowledge that they are complexly entwined and mutually implicated.

The thesis once prevalent in social science, that with modernization religion would decline and eventually be eliminated by a process of secularization and increasing rationality, is not tenable. Religions variously persist, grow and undergo revival around the globe. A more sustainable conception of secularization is that of religion becoming more private, pluralist and optional, particularly in the context of liberal societies (Bruce 2002). But even here there are questions. Formal religious participation, as measured by such things as church membership and attendance, appears to be in long-term decline in Europe, especially Britain, but remains very high in the US. Moreover, it is unclear whether receding formal religious participation leaves in its wake a set of looser but nonetheless supernatural beliefs (Davie 1990; Heelas and Woodhead 2004), or whether these are in retreat as well (De Graaf and Te Grotenhuis 2008; Glendinning 2006; Glendinning and Bruce 2006). How one approaches these questions will of course depend on how one defines and accounts for religion in the first place. Although a non-believer, my position is that religion is pervasive and persistent because it is grounded in human nature, at a level that runs deeper than ideology and explicit beliefs. Thus I reject

152

at the outset arguments that treat religion simply as an instrumental device, an ideological trick played on the masses by elites. While it can certainly serve and bolster given power structures, which I will address, I don't think this adequately explains its deepest origins in our basic experiences of power.

The next section discusses various theoretical explanations of the origins of religion that emphasize how it arises as a response to the limits of human powers. I then examine the idea that religions tend to symbolically reflect and validate the power relations found in a given society. Then I look at religious institutions and movements as mediums through which power struggles are enacted, both ideologically and materially. The next section starts to shift toward questions of morality and power. It argues that there has been a shift in Christian theology, away from a focus on power *per se*, and toward a focus on problems of meaning, reflecting the general impact of modernity and science on the constitution of knowledge and social authority. This shift has corollaries in social science thinking about religion, which has tended to submerge concerns with power under problems of meaning. In the last section I turn more generally to the relationship between power and morality, and the necessary conditions of any critique of power.

## Human limits and explanations of religion

In his book *Faces in the Clouds* (1993) Stewart Guthrie provides an excellent overview of the main tendencies in attempts to explain the existence of religion in secular terms (*Ibid.*: 8–38). First there are what he calls 'wish-fulfilment' approaches that place a strong emphasis on the emotional dimension. These view religion as serving to allay fundamental fears and anxieties arising from risk and uncontrollability in our environment, and more existentially, the imponderability and socially disruptive effects of death. One of the classic advocates of this perspective was the anthropologist Bronislaw Malinowski, whose ethnographic study of the Trobriand Islanders included the observation that they did not engage in magic to ensure relatively safe lagoon fishing, but did use magic when preparing for the much riskier activity of deep sea fishing. However, it was death and the rituals surrounding it that Malinowski saw as the very core of religious experience (1979). This basic reading of religion as responding to primal fears and helplessness also appears in treatments by David Hume, Karl Marx and Sigmund Freud. Freud sees religion as a kind of mass delusion that seeks to supplant reality and its suffering with something better. In Guthrie's first tendency of wish fulfilment there is a kind of psychological functionalism that sees religion as helping people to cope mentally and emotionally with life's strains.

The second tendency Guthrie calls 'social functionalism', in which religion is seen as serving the more general needs of society itself, and is less anchored in personal psychological needs. The premier figure in this approach is Emile Durkheim, who argued that all religion rests on a categorical opposition between the *sacred*, something 'set apart and forbidden' (1965[1912]: 62), and the *profane* world of everyday life (*Ibid.*: 52–7). Crucially, the sacred gets symbolized by clan totems, gods or other supernatural entities, which Durkheim believes are ultimately representations of society itself. Through ritualized sanctification and worship of these sacred objects, which are also seen as the source of ultimate and binding moral injunctions, society constitutes its own moral authority over its members, creating social solidarity to counter the fractious tendencies of human individualism. For Durkheim, as we saw in Chapter 3, the problem of explaining religion was bound up with the problem of maintaining social integration and cohesion in modern industrial society – how to find a way to do what religion does, in a secular world.

Guthrie's own theory of religion arises out of the third, 'intellectualist' or 'cognitive', strain of explanations. 'These theorists emphasize the task of interpretation faced by humans (as by other animals) in perceiving and acting in the world. They see the world of experience as inchoate and our first necessity as making sense of it' (Guthrie 1993: 21). The early anthropologist, E.B. Tylor (1832–1917) was a leading figure in this approach, explaining beliefs in spirits and supernatural forces as attempts to rationally explain what is happening when we dream, or when animation leaves the body at death. In this rationalist tradition, religion shares the same explanatory impulses as science, drawing on analogies and making causal inferences, but without the more rigorous empirical methods of modern science. It tends to suggest that science should replace religion, at least in the realm of naturalistic explanation. Developing Robin Horton's (1967) thesis that both religion and science aim to explain diverse and complex reality by reducing phenomena to a more limited set of theoretical entities (gods or gravity, for instance), Guthrie argues, unlike Horton, that religion is simply anthropomorphism. He reasons that evolution has given us deep, innate predispositions to perceive and interpret the world as fundamentally humanlike, because other human intelligences are among the most important aspects of our environment for our survival. By orienting ourselves to the ordering effects of the human mind, and over-generalizing it to the natural world through various kinds of anthropomorphism (mischievous spirits, God's will and so on), we maximize our ability to discern pattern and order in the universe. The benefits of maximizing our recognition of other minds, both real and imagined, outweigh the harm of misrecognizing mind, will, intelligence, intention and so on where they don't exist (1993: 39–40, *passim*). This concords nicely with the findings of Tomasello (1999), discussed at the start of Chapter 6, that, as humans, we are set apart from our closest primate relatives because in social learning we assume the presence of will and intent in our fellows, directing our attention accordingly.

Guthrie presents the influential formulation of Clifford Geertz (1973: 87–125) as a synthesis of these approaches, with a strong element of functionalism. I think Geertz has much in common with Durkheim's quest for social solidarity. However, I would also view him as exemplifying a somewhat different fourth strain that emphasizes moral order and to a degree theodicy, that is, the problem of reconciling the existence of evil and human suffering with a world supposedly made by a benevolent god. Geertz defined religion as:

> (1) a system of symbols which acts to (2) establish powerful, pervasive, and long-lasting moods and motivations in men by (3) formulating conceptions of a general order of existence and (4) clothing these conceptions with such an aura of factuality that (5) the moods and motivations seem uniquely realistic (1973: 90).

In other words, religion is a complex of symbols that bridges the gap between the world as we know it is, and as our beliefs, morals and ethos tell us it ought to be, and how we ought to act in it. It creates and anchors meaning in a world that constantly threatens to become meaningless. The themes of emotional reassurance, consolidation of social ties and making cognitive sense of reality are all present in Geertz's elaborations of this definition, but pride of place is given to how religion addresses the problem of making moral sense of an amoral world (1973: 105–8, 123–4). Religion, as he puts it, is a frame of interpretation that provides the believer with both a 'model of' how reality works, and a 'model for' appropriate action within that reality (1973: 93–4). It helps us to confront our cognitive, emotional and, particularly, moral limitations all at once (cf. Parsons 1979: 65–6).

Guthrie notes various trenchant criticisms of these approaches, among them:

- some religious ideas are as terrifying as the fears they are supposed to allay;
- not all religions make clear distinctions between the sacred and the profane (for example Shinto);
- religion is not always closely linked to moral prescription (consider the capricious gods of ancient Greece);
- religion persists, despite the rise of supposedly rationally superior science; and
- the creation and maintenance of meaning and moral orientation pervades many aspects of culture – science, arts, ethics, common sense – and is not a unique feature of religion.

In short, these criticisms all seem to capture some widespread aspects of religion, while over-generalizing their theses. What I want to suggest here at the outset is that underlying all these explanations is a concern with power, although it has been variously transmuted into the power to face suffering and fear, the power of society to hold itself together, the power to make sense of causal processes, and the power to find meaning or goodness in a meaningless or evil world. Whatever its variable social and psychological functions, I am inclined to view religion as a complex of both meditations on the nature of power, and searches to harness or align oneself or one's social group with power. Again and again when we observe religious behaviour, we see people appealing to 'higher powers', however these are imagined, in search of capacities to heal the sick, ensure essential crops, endure catastrophe, throw off oppressors, prevail in war, ground one's morals and so on. The point is often made that belief, even in the imaginary, can have real effects. As Malinowksi argued, confidence in supernatural protection may actually enhance real-world powers. And compelling claims to privileged access to supernatural power can enhance the capacity for some to dominate others in the real world. But matters are not always this directly instrumental. Sometimes religious thoughts, teachings, ceremonies and rituals seek to harness spiritual power to human needs, and sometimes these seek to reconcile us to our weakness and helplessness. But, either way, religion is *about* power, and reflects on its nature. Indeed, it is the limits of human powers that lead us to seek the greater power. In a sense, and possibly because they have been developed mostly by academic intellectuals, our accounts of religion perhaps lay too much stress on the need for explanation, whether cognitive, emotional or moral, and not enough on the need for power.

## Religion as reflecting the social constitution of power relations

If religion addresses fundamental human needs in regard to power, it also provides a legitimating account of power. Basic to Durkheim's view is the idea that religious symbolism somehow reflects patterns of social organization, as well as reinforcing social cohesion. There are indeed fascinating correspondences between how supernatural or divine power is imagined and how actual social power is organized. In a classic cross-cultural study Guy Swanson (1960) sought to demonstrate some of these correspondences. Using a sample of fifty pre-industrial societies, from foragers on up to early agrarian states, Swanson begins from the premise that supernatural beliefs tend to fall into two main types: (1) belief in 'mana', 'a substance or essence which gives one the ability to perform tasks or achieve ends otherwise impossible' (p. 6), often accessed through magical practices, and (2) belief in 'spirits', personified supernatural beings with 'purposes and intentions of their own as well as the power to achieve their objectives' (p. 7). He also maintains that social life is regulated by two kinds of structures: (1) 'primordial', the affective ties and implicit norms that guide relatively close, small scale relationships, and (2) 'constitutional', the explicit organization of society and its relations into groupings with recognized powers and spheres of competence (pp. 22–31). Swanson argues that beliefs in mana tend to correlate with primordial structures, and beliefs in spirits tend to correspond to constitutional structures. In other words, as social structures become more complex, and powers more formally distributed and concentrated, supernatural beliefs shift from a focus on capturing diffuse substances or forces to the idea of relating to supernatural beings who are agents in their own right.

Through statistical comparison, Swanson identifies three broad correlations. The first, not surprisingly, is that societies structured by strong corporate kin groups (lineages, clans) above the nuclear family are likely to practise ancestor worship, treating ancestral spirits as active in human affairs. Thus the spirits that need to be placated correspond to the key social units governing the distribution of resources and power (pp. 97–108). Secondly, polytheism, belief in a pantheon of 'superior gods' that are more abstract than the spirits associated with particular places or people, tends to correspond to societies in which there is a more complex division of labour and specialization in terms of economic activities and public/ceremonial offices. Thus the group of gods with their individual skills and provinces seems to reflect the similar division of society into key groups and leading members (pp. 82–96). And thirdly, monotheism, belief in a single 'high god', is associated with societies that have a hierarchy of three or more levels of 'sovereign groups', that is, groups with their own sphere of legitimate authority and control. Out of a sub-sample of 39 cases, Swanson found that societies that had several embedded levels of sovereign groups, such as families, lineages, villages, districts, provinces and central levels of authority and administration – those that have a certain degree of political hierarchy and social stratification – are more likely to have high gods (pp. 55–81) (see Table 8.1).

Swanson also asked what factors might account for spirits being understood as regulating moral behaviour through supernatural rewards and punishments. He found that 'supernatural sanctions for interpersonal relations are more likely to appear in societies in which there are interpersonal differences according to wealth' (p. 174). Particularly significant positive correlations were found with the presence of 'considerable debt relations', stratification into distinct social classes, personal property and primogeniture, which presumably concentrates power and resources in the hands of first-born inheritors (pp. 166–8). There is also a suggestion that such sanctions are more elaborated in societies that maintain fairly rigid separation from neighbouring societies. Thus spirits seem more likely to intervene in moral life when there are sharp power differences within relatively closed societies.

Swanson's findings are obviously partly a matter of how he coded his ethnographic data, raised questions about the definition of discrete cases (societies),

**Table 8.1** Number of sovereign groups and presence of high god

| Presence of a high god | Number of sovereign groups | | |
| --- | --- | --- | --- |
| | 1 or 2 | 3 | 4 or more |
| Present | 2 | 7 | 10 |
| Absent | 17 | 2 | 1 |
| Total | 19 | 9 | 11 |
| Percentage present (%) | 11 | 78 | 91 |

*Source*: Swanson 1960: 65. Reprinted with kind permission of University of Michigan Press.

and privileged structural over more particularistic and historical notions of causation. Nonetheless they abstract well-recognized patterns in the vast field of historical and ethnographic data, and are highly suggestive about the relationships between the social distributions of power and supernatural beliefs. Moreover, his interpretations are strengthened by being based on comparisons of globally and historically dispersed cases. A later attempt to analyze why the Reformation took hold in some European countries rather than others, by reference to political and social structures (Swanson 1967), has been considered less convincing by many (Wuthnow 1987: 299–330). Part of the problem is that the sheer social complexity and interdigitation of theoretically separate societies and polities on the European peninsula make it very difficult to assess causality in terms of discrete cases. The wider point is that, as societies increase in scale and complexity, they are less likely to have 'a religion' or set of supernatural beliefs, but rather will exhibit religious pluralism. Correspondingly, difficult questions arise about whether large modern polities, nation-states, are better understood as containing one or many societies, based on class, ethnicity, religion and so on. But this doesn't prevent us from considering relationships between social organization and religious beliefs in these more complex settings, it simply requires that we take account of that complexity.

An interesting question has been posed here in regard to religion in the US in the late twentieth and early twenty-first centuries. People are often struck by the apparent contradiction of a society with a constitutional separation of church and state having such high levels of religiosity. In a major survey in 2007 by the Pew Forum on Religion and Public Life, 92 per cent of respondents indicated that they believed in 'God or a universal spirit', about 82 per cent of adults indicated a religious affiliation, and a further 5.8 per cent described themselves as religious but unaffiliated (Pew Forum 2008). One explanation is the idea of a religious 'economy' or 'marketplace', in which inter-religious and inter-denominational competition is seen as stimulating religiosity and religious involvement (Finke and Stark 1992). The argument is that 'to the degree that religious economies are unregulated and competitive, overall levels of religious commitment will be higher' (Finke and Stark 1998: 762). This is seen as being especially true of the US, when compared with more secular Europe, but also applicable to Latin America in the context of growing evangelical Protestantism in recent decades (Burdick 1993; Selka 2010; Trejo 2009). The Pew Forum survey tends to support this thesis in the case of the US, finding that 'constant movement characterizes the American religious marketplace, as every major religious group is simultaneously gaining and losing adherents' (2008: 7), albeit at different rates. While the domination of traditional mainstream Protestant churches in the US has been in decline for several decades, leading to greater religious pluralism, especially if we distinguish Christian denominations, being religious in some sense remains normative. (Only 3 per cent identify themselves as atheist or agnostic, although another 6.3 per cent describe themselves as 'secular unaffiliated'.) People appear to 'shop around' for their faith, but religiosity overall appears to be holding up in the US.

There is dissent from this thesis (Bruce 1993; Hill and Olson 2009; Olson 2002). But whether or not it provides an adequate causal explanation of varying levels of religiosity, it fits with Swanson's broad Durkheimian thesis that religious beliefs reflect social organization, as well as the general analysis of liberal society I was developing in the previous chapter. In a form of society premised on the maximization of private choice, an active civil society and the legitimating effects of competition, religion accommodates itself, forming a complex and fluid landscape of religious options of varying intensity. But much like Henry Ford's famous quip that the customer can have 'any color of Model T they like, as long as it's black', Americans can have any religious beliefs they like, as long as their beliefs include religion (with a few exceptions). Access to supernatural power is not controlled by the state, but thrown on to the market, which stimulates the production of religious institutions and ideologies, binding diverse believers together in an *agora* of faith.

## Religion as a medium of power struggles

So far we have been looking at religion primarily as something that mirrors or bolsters power structures in society. But we must also take account of its more dynamic role in challenging power relations. Indeed, in the history of religions it is particularly apparent that established religious institutions usually have origins in movements of dissent, reform and resistance in the past (Wallace 1956; Weber 1964: 46–59, *passim*). As in other walks of life, bureaucratic organizations crystallize out of more fluid social movements and alliances between groups, and in due course tend to find themselves challenged again, either from within or without. I want to suggest that this is not just a matter of periodic spiritual renewal, but of an interaction between earthly power struggles and human attempts to draft the powers of gods and the supernatural into those struggles. Conflicts can develop within a common arena of established religious institutions, or be articulated in supernatural terms, between culturally and religiously distinct groups. After prefatory remarks, I illustrate these points with three cases.

In *Forms of Power* (2001) Poggi argues in a Durkheimian vein that religion is intimately connected to power because of the way it articulates a general view of reality and normative order, supporting these with ultimate supernatural authority. But he goes on to pay particular attention to the relationship between religion, as embodied in churches, and the state, a 'variable but always significant relationship' (2001: 74). Churches can 'consecrate', 'hallow' and legitimize the given social and political order, and in exchange, through policy and law, the state can support a church's rights, privileges, and to a degree moral prescriptions, in an ongoing dance of shifting, negotiated claims from both sides (2001: 63–86). In contrast to this specific image of church and state as uneasy bedfellows, in a programmatic statement Mart Bax (1987) calls for a more general integration of research into politics and religion, advocating a concept of 'religious regimes' to parallel that of political regimes (see also E.R. Wolf 1991). The point is to direct attention to a complex of power dynamics: between religious institutions and the state (as with Poggi); between different religions competing for state patronage; and between organizational segments within religious institutions. Bax also argues that religions and their sustaining organizations will compete for adherents and to monopolize resources, both material, such as tax-free lands, and spiritual, such as the claim to offer salvation. Unlike Swanson's interest in the fit between religious ideas and social structure, Bax is more concerned with putting religious and political institutions on the same analytic footing, to make their mutual concerns with worldly power more apparent.

In June 1981 six children playing on a hillside outside the town of Medjugorje in Bosnia-Hercegovina saw a vision of the Virgin Mary. She was still appearing to the visionaries in 2012, making the place a major site of religious pilgrimage. Bax (1991) explores the institutional tensions that helped to foster this development. It is important to know that the Catholic Church contains a major division between diocesan priests, who work under the direct authority of a bishop and are primarily responsible for administering parishes and spiritual care, and the religious orders, governed by a Father Superior in their provincial order, who are more autonomous and concerned with maintaining support institutions such as schools and hospitals. In the spread of Catholic Christianity, religious orders (most famously the Jesuits) often play an advance-guard, missionary role, with diocesan hierarchy moving in once presence is established. In the diocese of Mostar, where Medjugorje is located, the order of Franciscan Fathers had been particularly strong since the middle ages, partly due to alliances with local political leaders and partly due to protection under Ottoman rule, which tolerated their presence but opposed further encroachments from Rome, inhibiting the development of diocesan structures. After the Second World War the new communist government of Yugoslavia weakened the Franciscan 'regime', taking property and control of many schools and healthcare organizations. In the mid-1960s, a cautious rapprochement between Rome and the Yugoslav government paved the way for development of the diocesan regime under the Bishop of Mostar. However, the Franciscan Fathers resisted this new encroaching religious authority. Moreover, they were more aligned with, and representative of, the Croatian peasants of the region, whereas the new wave of diocesan priests were seen as aligned with an urban petty bourgeoisie, as well as the Yugoslav state itself. In this embattled context the Franciscan leadership began to cultivate more charismatic and visionary strains in the religious tradition, creating conditions conducive to the six children's vision of the Virgin, whose core message was for 'peace and forbearance among God's people' (Bax 1991: 36). The apparitions served to consolidate the authority of, and popular support for, the Franciscan Fathers in the region, effectively blocking the combined efforts of state and diocese. (On the role of the Franciscan orders in subsequent Croatian nationalism around the Bosnian war, see: Aleksov 2004; Bax 2000.)

In the post-Yugoslavia state of Bosnia-Hercegovina, the economic importance of the religious pilgrimage to the region appears to be a factor sustaining the apparitions.

At base in Bax's account is a network of religious and political organizations in conflicts and alliances. On one side were the Franciscan Fathers, aligned with village-based agrarian life, and with an uneasy relation to Rome, which suspected the organization's autonomy, but also didn't want to lose a strong Catholic foothold in the region. Additionally, the Fathers had an international Franciscan network that they were able to draw on in spreading knowledge of the apparitions and stimulating the pilgrimage process. On the other side, Rome had an interest in strengthening its better-controlled diocesan structures in the region, but this involved uneasy alignments with a communist state, and played into rural/urban political tensions, which also had an ethnic dimension. Bax is less interested in the visions of the Virgin as a direct symbol of power relations themselves, and more as an instrument for manoeuvre in power struggles within and beyond the Church.

In 'Spirits and the Spirit of Capitalism' (1991) Jane Schneider has argued for a shift in focus in the study of the Protestant Reformation in Europe, viewing it not just as a struggle around religious authority within the Church and between church and state, but more broadly as a confrontation between a more urban 'salvationist' Christian ideology and more rural 'animistic', syncretic folk beliefs. The crux of Schneider's argument is that livelihoods which depend on very direct human–nature interactions, on practical engagement with a local ecology, tend to induce animistic beliefs, that is, belief in a multitude of supernatural beings and forces closely associated with the natural environment. Emphasizing the continuities between historical European peasantries, whose Christian beliefs were often fused with earlier supernatural ideas, and our wider ethnographic knowledge of religious ideas in foraging, horticultural and agrarian societies, she argues that where people must perforce live in balance with a local ecology, this tends to induce beliefs in a parallel moral ecology with the supernatural, based on principles of equity and reciprocity both within the peasant community and with supernatural beings. She describes how inequities in local communities are liable to give rise to regulating beliefs such as fears of the 'evil eye' or accusations of malign magic and witchcraft. At the same time, interactions with the natural environment, especially innovations such as opening up new lands to cultivation, frequently involve various placating rituals and offerings for spirits associated with places or dead ancestors. Local Christian saints were often transmuted in the popular imagination into something more like traditional supernatural beings inhabiting places and relics. In general the peasant ethos is one of maintaining a power balance between community members, and between them and myriad supernatural beings that represent relations with the natural world.

Schneider contrasts this agrarian folk cosmology with more orthodox Christian salvationism, always central to the religion, but reinvigorated in the Reformation. Salvation religions (for example Judaism, Christianity, Islam) have roots in rapidly expanding urbanization around the eastern Mediterranean in the first millennium BC. They characteristically stress the moral relationship between the individual and God, and the search for personal redemption, usually in an after-life. Rather than constant negotiated exchanges with multiple supernatural beings, they emphasize a generalized ethos of abstract love and self-sacrifice, concentrating the variable populations of spirits into basic principles of good and evil (God and the devil) and a problematic of sin and divine forgiveness. Of course everywhere, just as with medieval European Christendom, these more philosophical 'high' traditions of religious belief have merged with pre-existing supernatural beliefs. The key point for Schneider is that the Protestant Reformation represents a new wave of urban growth and power, opposed to the rural folk traditions. A revivified salvationist ideology sought to demonize folk beliefs, particularly through redefining traditional folk beliefs as 'witchcraft' and then persecuting it. More generally, this worldview was more conducive to the growth of agrarian capitalism and proto-industrialization which, because of their more dynamic and distant relationships to the places and resources being exploited to meet market demands, could not afford to be tied down by embedded local notions of reciprocity and equity with nature. Unlike Weber's classic thesis that Protestant, and particularly Calvinist beliefs, helped orient believers to an ethic of work, productivity and saving that was conducive to capitalism, Schneider focuses on an incompatibility and conflict between views of the natural world and its exploitation, with the Reformation preparing the ground for subsequent capitalist growth (cf. White 1967).

Religious innovation often arises out social conflict and stress. The religious practice of the 'Ghost Dance' (or Spirit Dance), a reformulation of other dancing ceremonies, arose among the Northern Paiute Indians of Nevada in 1889, and spread among other Plains Indian tribes, in varying forms. It was a response to the undermining of the means of subsistence and ways of life among native groups being forced out of traditional lands by the encroaching Euro-American farming settlers, backed by the US Army. It began with a vision by the Paiute prophet Jack Wilson (a.k.a. Wovoka) in which God appeared, giving him the new dance to take to his people, and showing him a vision of life in which land was restored and plentiful, ancestors returned from the past, and there was no sickness and old age. The prophet's message called on followers to perform the dance, and practise peace and love, weaving together traditional Paiute and Christian themes. The dance and its message spread and differentiated among various Plains Indian groups. When the US government broke its treaty with them, the Lakota Sioux of South Dakota, facing severe loss of reservation lands and livelihoods, forced acculturation and famine, took up the Ghost Dance in a particularly millenarian form, which envisioned the magical removal of the whites, and attracted large gatherings of followers in 1890. The ensuing tensions led to the massacre of 153 Sioux men, women and children at Wounded Knee Creek in a botched attempt by the army to confiscate Indian weapons. In subsequent armed conflict between some of the

Lakota and the US Army, some Lakota warriors donned 'ghost shirts' which were believed to protect the wearer from bullets. Eventually the rebellion was broken, and public outcry in the east contributed to the reinstatement of the broken treaty (Kehoe 2006; Neihardt 1979: 230–70).

These events conform to a well-known pattern called 'revitalization movements' by Anthony Wallace (1956), in which communities under extreme stress, making traditional ways of life untenable, will often turn to supernatural guidance for a way forward. As in the differences between the Paiute and Lakota contexts and forms of the Ghost Dance, this process may lead to a fairly pacific re-ordering of communal values and synthesis of new and old customs, or it can take more desperate and militant forms, seeking profound supernatural transformation of the troubled situation. For the present discussion what matters is the way the severe loss of communal power triggers a collective search for, and receptivity to, messages of new or renewed power from the spirit world to address social crisis.

## Meaning eclipses power

Before moving on to questions of power and morality *per se*, I will make some observations about these themes in regard to our social scientific understandings of religion. Talal Asad has made a probing and sustained critique of Geertz's definition of religion presented above, and of anthropological approaches to the study of religion more generally, including a failure to interrogate secularism (1983, 1993, 2003). Asad (1983) argues that Geertz treats religion as a *sui generis* system of symbols that address human problems of meaning, order and morality without adequate attention to how those religious symbols are formed in the first place. Geertz is concerned with the needs that religion meets, to the neglect of the forces that induce religion; he elevates meaning, and forgets about power. Asad's rejoinder is that we should 'begin by asking what are the historical conditions (movements, classes, institutions, ideologies) necessary for the existence of particular religious practices and discourses. In other words, let us ask: how does power create religion?' (1983: 252). Owing much to Foucault (see Chapter 5), Asad's conception of power is largely one of domination through the power of religious institutions to inculcate disciplines, knowledges and senses of self. He chides Geertz for following in an anthropological tradition that treats religion as a matter of expressive, as opposed to instrumental or technical, social action (p. 251). For Asad, this cleaves off the instrumentalities and techniques that create religious knowledge in the first place, and which also need attention. Beyond his immediate critique of Geertz's concept, Asad argues that anthropological and social scientific theories of religion illegitimately generalize from the perspective of Christianity in the secularized 'West'. The problem is twofold. First, modern western Christianity is constituted through its relationship to secularism, with which it forms a particular understanding and regime of religion and power, exemplified by such things as a notion of the appropriate separation of church and state. And second, modern Christianity, with its characteristic concern with existential meaning and morality (matters that secular practices such as science tend to remain silent about), becomes the implicit but misleading model for understanding religion in general. This leads Asad to deep scepticism about the possibility of a general definition of religion, fearing an essentialized conception based on recent western history, and advocating instead particularistic investigations of cases (cf. Weber 1964: 1). It has also led him to call for the systematic study of secularism, as not simply the absence or privatization of religion, but as part of a social configuration of power itself (1993).

I don't share Asad's doubts about the possibility and utility of a general concept of religion. His call for particularistic studies implies at least a working definition of religion to guide investigations. I also think his Foucauldian notion of institutionalized disciplinary power, while a good corrective to Geertz, misses underlying continuities in religious behaviour – a general human impulse to try to comprehend and grapple with power. Religion happens from the 'top down' and the 'bottom up' at the same time. I argue that humans face a permanent problematic of power, and that religions, or more loosely supernatural beliefs, both confront and address that problematic, and become instrumental in the social constitution of power and its institutionalization, that is, caught up in modes of domination.

However, I think Asad's observations about the combined impress of secularism and modern western Christianity on social scientific theories of religion are acute. On the one hand, religious belief has been rejected from a secular perspective as the position from which to understand and analyze religion and social life more generally, and on the other, mainstream Christian authorities themselves have abdicated to the sciences, social and otherwise, claims to provide a superior account of causation. In this context, religious discourse becomes more narrowly focused on problems of meaning, moral orientation and spiritual solace, and less concerned with providing access to (now suspect) supernatural power itself. The confluence of philosophy, Christian theology and developing social science in the west since the nineteenth century helps us to understand how this situation came about. By the early 1800s Hegel (1770–1831) had proffered an optimistic philosophy in which human reason could be understood as a path to grasping the ultimate reason of God or 'world spirit' (Hegel 1977[1807]). But by the later nineteenth century and early twentieth century, in terms of influence on Christian theology, such optimism was being displaced by the more agonized philosophy of existentialism, as exemplified by Kierkegaard (1813–55) and Heidegger (1889–1976). Existentialism offered not a happy congruence of faith and social life, but a chronic condition of severe uncertainty and a call to decide and act despite the lack of evidence or sure knowledge. It was in part a response to the hemming in of religious explanation by advancing science. Thus reasons for faith were given a different basis, in primary spiritual or psychic needs, separate from other kinds of more 'objective' knowledge and belief oriented toward the natural world. This problematizing of belief greatly influenced many of the key Christian theologians of the twentieth century, such as Karl Barth, Reinhold Niebuhr, Rudolf Bultmann, and Paul Tillich (Allen and Springsted 2007: 187–207, cf. Percy 1954).

Meanwhile, theories of hermeneutics – how to interpret texts and other cultural materials to achieve understanding – had also been developing. With origins in the study of biblical exegesis and its problems, hermeneutics was applied to more general problems in the study of language and history (Mueller-Vollmer 1988; Palmer 1969: 33–45), and to understandings of social science practice (Rabinow and Sullivan 1979). Here the key idea is that the 'hard' sciences concerned with the non-human natural world could aim to explain objective processes, but when studying other people, especially from other times and cultures, one is obliged to take into account their worlds of meaning, and somehow translate these into one's own. Indeed, likening the problems of anthropological research to those of hermeneutics, as ultimately more a matter of interpreting other cultures than explaining them, was central to Geertz theoretical project (1973).

I am suggesting that the social science we have inherited, and its attitudes toward religion and power, has evolved in a kind of conceptual ecology with these philosophical and theological trends. This general sense of a deficit of meaning and stable moral grounding haunts both modern Christianity and social science. There is a strange parallel between two divisions of labour in making sense of the world: between 'spiritual' religion and 'secular' science, and within the latter, between the 'hard' natural sciences and the 'soft' social sciences. Somehow the problems of modern religion and social science, particularly in its more humanist guises, gravitate towards one another, revolving around problems of meaning in an uncertain world. We can see this in previous chapters, in Durkheim's preoccupation with the source of modern moral order and authority that so shaped his theory of religion, and in Weber's concern with the waning of meaning-generating charisma in the face of expanding bureaucratic routine. Oriented to these same themes in Durkheim and Weber, Talcott Parsons, and his student Robert Bellah, who specialized in the study of religion (1964, 1979), were both deeply concerned with the need for shared orienting values to make society work. Geertz's ideas arise out of this same current of thought, and he explicitly grounds his own approach in his reading of Weber as particularly concerned with problems of meaning and interpretation (1973). I am not trying to reduce social science to this particular nexus of intellectual influences, but it is a central one, indicative of a core trend in social theory. That trend sees religion and social science as both involved, however differently, in the search for meaning and values to underpin social order and give individuals a sense of purpose. But in doing so it tends to forget about the centrality of power for human problems, both social and personal. It remembers God's omniscience, but forgets God's omnipotence.

Having said this, even within the supposedly secularized West, this is a rather esoteric view of the matter, as though highly educated Protestant theologians and professors of anthropology were typical of religious belief and practice in 'the West'. In fact, actual religious practices and supernatural beliefs are highly diverse and robustly oriented to the pragmatics of power, as any survey of contemporary Christian evangelism, Pentecostalism and various animistic 'new age' beliefs will quickly attest. While a congregation of comfortable, liberal Episcopalians may roughly correspond to the perspective outlined above, for many others, their religious or spiritual beliefs and practices will be oriented to searches for healing, support, protection, guidance, good fortune and empowering infusions of the Holy Spirit. They will be invoking a god or other supernatural forces that do act and have effects in the real world. The stoical intellect that faces a cold disenchanted reality, seeking only the most theoretical comfort in religious ideas, is not all that common. Most people are less consistent and more pluralist in their beliefs, and often prepared to entertain the possibility of powers beyond those that science will admit, especially when the need for those powers is great.

## Power and morality

In a Machiavellian vein, the American Protestant theologian Rienhold Niebuhr once asserted that 'Goodness, armed with power, is corrupted; and pure love without power is destroyed' (Niebuhr 1938: 185). Having proposed this connection, let me set religion to one side and consider more specifically the implications of power for morality. As we have seen, there is a central problem that 'the good', however we might understand it, needs power to be made a reality, and that power cannot cleave too closely to moral principles if it is to survive. One response to this dilemma is to try to clean up matters by acts of definition. This is what the philosopher Hannah Arendt does when she distinguishes between 'power' and 'violence' in an attempt to counter the view that violence is the ultimate ground of power. Influenced particularly by the rise and impact of Nazism and Stalinism in her lifetime, Arendt sought to make the case for a positive form of public spirited politics against tendencies to become cynical and turn inward, faced by such horrific political developments. For Arendt, politics is not just an instrumental means to ends, but an end in itself, inherently good, leading to the fuller realization of human dialogue and potential. She rejected the ideas that politics is a matter of harnessing natural laws of society and history, as in Marxism, or that it is primarily a matter of safeguarding space for private activities, as in liberalism. She saw politics as a matter of human self-creation and virtuous public engagement. Her work emerges out of the same sense of a fundamental existential need to create meaning in the potentially meaningless world that we have just been discussing (Haugaard 2002: 132–7).

Making this argument in *On Violence* (1969) Arendt offers these definitions:

> *Power* corresponds to the human ability not just to act, but to act in concert. Power is never the property of an individual; it belongs to a group and remains in existence only so long as the group keeps together...

> *Strength* unequivocally designates something in the singular, an individual entity; it is the property inherent in an object or person and belongs to its character, which may prove itself in relation to other things or persons, but is essentially independent of them...

> *Force,* which we often use in daily speech as a synonym for violence, especially if violence serves as a means of coercion, should be reserved, in terminological language, for the 'forces of nature' or the 'force of circumstances' ... that is, to indicate the energy released by physical or social movements...

> *Authority*, relating to the most elusive of these phenomena and therefore, as a term, most frequently abused, can be vested in persons – there is such a thing as personal authority, as, for instance, in the relations between parent and child ... or in offices ... Its hallmark is unquestioning recognition by those who are asked to obey; neither coercion nor persuasion is needed...

> *Violence* ... is distinguished by its instrumental character. Phenomenologically, it is close to strength, since the implements of violence, like all other tools, are designed and used for the purpose of multiplying natural strength until, in the last stage of their development, they can substitute for it (Arendt 2002: 137–8).

Thus Arendt disarticulates more complex and conventional notions of power. At one end we have 'power' associated with our essential sociality and the formation of collective purposes, and at the other end 'violence', not simply as a kind of harmful action, but as the distillation of instrumentality in the pursuit of strength, logically contrary to power. In between are the mediating concepts of 'strength' as sheer capacity, 'force' as that capacity in action, and 'authority' as the routinization of power, which she recognized as necessary, but also as dangerous if not susceptible to questioning and challenge.

Arendt makes a strong case for not reducing power to violence, but by her own admission, in reality these are chronically bound up with one another, with power rarely appearing in its pure form as she defines it. Although she wants to take full account of the real world, her definitions are ultimately governed by the demands of her normative theory, in which power and violence are opposing points on a moral compass. Although not exactly assimilated with 'good' and 'evil', they appear as proxies for these concepts – power is to be preferred, and violence abjured. Whatever moral guidance this might provide, it renders these concepts awkward for more descriptive and analytic purposes. But even within a normative frame, one wonders if a notion of power purified of its instrumental dimension is wise. Power simply as 'the human ability to act in concert' seems a bit thin and general, putting the purposive and intentional aspects we usually associate with power and action out of focus. Correspondingly, intentionality unsupported by some instrumentality is difficult to imagine. The normative theorist faces a decision about whether it is better to turn power into a purified ideal that we aim for or to leave it tarnished and dangerous, something that must always be handled with care, with its own kind of 'original sin'. I argue throughout this book that there is a dialectic of 'power to' and 'power over', that increasing our capacity to achieve collective ends brings with it degrees of hierarchy and subordination. Arendt's conceptual disaggregation obscures this problem.

Even if power and violence are separable, power and responsibility are not. If we regard power as something like the capacity to produce intended effects, then the incorporation of intention into our definition implies responsibility for the outcomes of actions. One of the great paradoxes of political discourse, particularly in complex liberal democracies, is that when we assign blame and responsibility for negative events to those other than ourselves, we implicitly assert our own powerlessness. The post-2007 banking and economic crisis and its aftermath in the US and the UK can reasonably be viewed as stemming partly from the abuse and mismanagement of power by key agents (banks, individuals) in the financial sector. But it also stems from the failures of government to sufficiently regulate banking practices, and the willingness of citizens to accumulate unwise levels of consumer debt. To confront the issue it is not sufficient simply to 'blame the bankers'. Societies such as those found in the US and the UK do distribute power more widely, which is not to say evenly, and with that comes a wider distribution of responsibility for events (Hearn 2011b). At the same time, the link between power and responsibility depends on a conception of power as a dispositional property of agents, individual or collective, which can be held accountable for their actions. The more we conceive of power as a diffuse system property, not anchored in any agents, the less we can link it to responsibility (Hay 1997). The 'problem of dirty hands' (Coady 1993), that is, that even powers aligned with what we regard as 'the good' will sometimes need to compromise morally in order to preserve their power and continue to serve the good, implies the link between power and responsibility. Although we cannot logically derive statements about how the world 'ought' to be from those about how it 'is' in reality, moral statements that assign responsibility only make sense given certain actual distributions of power. When we assign moral responsibility, we are also, by implication, saying something about how the world 'is', asserting that those 'responsible' had the power to do otherwise. Conversely, to define ourselves as 'innocent' is also to define ourselves as 'helpless'. It may be that a tendency towards moral compromise is a price we have to pay if power is to be, at least in principle, both accessible and accountable.

Peter Morriss (2002: 36–46) argues that discussions of power and morality tend to get confused because they fail to distinguish between three distinct contexts in which power matters in different ways: the practical, the moral and the evaluative. In a practical context we need to know the extent and limits of people's capabilities, both our own and those of others. We need to be able to judge, or reasonably estimate, for instance, whether we can accomplish a task before us, or whether an opponent can carry out a threat made against us. In this context, right and wrong are not the issue, but rather what, in causal terms, is likely. In a moral context we are interested in 'blaming, excusing and allocating responsibility' (2002: 38) to agents, and thus the central question becomes whether agents could have done otherwise, or acted where they failed to act. If so they are held responsible; if not, they are off the hook. Interestingly, as in Morriss' examples we think first here of responsibility for acts we disapprove of, but of course when bestowing praise we are often also making moral statements, which depend on the power of the agent to have done otherwise. Finally, there is the evaluative context. Here judgments are made not of individual agents, but entire social systems, or conceivably complex parts of them, such as large bureaucratic organizations. Thus we may judge societies and political systems according to how effectively they empower their citizens, or how they limit their potential, without reducing these to moral judgments of agents. We judge them in terms of how conducive they are to desired ends, not in terms allocating responsibility, although a thoroughgoing normative assessment of a particular case might invoke both moral and evaluative contexts. Morriss accuses Steven Lukes (1974) and William Connolly (1983), both radicals critical of the systemic domination that occurs in capitalist society, of neglecting the practical and confusing the moral and evaluative contexts.

> Lukes and Connolly, as radicals, want to emphasize the plight of the powerless and thus to persuade people of the evils of contemporary capitalism. But they fail to achieve their aim, because they mistake their target. They think that what is wrong if you are powerless is that you are thereby in someone else's power, and that someone else must be responsible for your powerlessness if you are to have a valid complaint. Both of these assumptions are wrong, as I have argued. What is wrong with being powerless is that you *are* powerless – that is, lacking in power. And if people are powerless because they live in a certain sort of society – that is, they would have more power if the social arrangements were changed – then that, itself, is a condemnation of that society. A radical critique of a society requires us to evaluate *that society*, not distribute praise or blame to *people*. The two are very different procedures, and must be sharply distinguished (2002: 41–2).

Lukes addresses this criticism in the second edition of *Power* (2005: 64–9), but ultimately rejects Morriss' distinction between moral and evaluative contexts, reading it as an assertion of tidy divisions in the real world rather than as a distinction between purposes of inquiry, which I think was Morriss' intention. As I have already suggested, it would be perfectly possible to pass properly grounded moral and evaluative judgments in regard to different aspects of the same socially complex whole. But what Morriss is objecting to is the failure to distinguish between them, to talk as though showing that a particular form of social organization has reprehensible effects on its members suffices to assign responsibility and moral blame.

I finish with two points. First, our discussion in Chapter 2 of the relationships between concepts of domination, authority and legitimacy is highly germane to the present discussion. Theories of power that are anchored in socially diffuse notions of domination are not very serviceable for either: (1) making moral judgments, as Morriss argues, because they under-specify competent agents who can be held responsible; or (2) descriptive analyses of the interactions between power and moral systems, because they privilege modes of domination that are, by definition, beyond conscious moral scrutiny. Theories that allow more space for concepts of authority and legitimacy as descriptive features of the social landscape, by virtue of that fact, will direct more attention to conscious, public conflict and confrontation over power arrangements when these are challenged, and thereby perhaps teach us more about the relationship between power and morality. Second, criticism, whether aesthetic or moral, is always a matter of making judgments according to criteria applied within some domain, but not to the domain itself. A jazz critic may argue for particular reasons that one musician is superior to another. Someone who deplores all jazz cannot be a critic of jazz, they are just someone who objects to it. Likewise, a critic of power must make distinctions between good and bad forms of power, power relations that are acceptable and those that are unacceptable, and give their reasons, a common set of criteria for making these varying judgments. People who offer blanket condemnations of power, or hope that it can be replaced by something altogether different, are not critics of power, just unhappy.

## Conclusion

I began by defining religion somewhat loosely as a pattern of beliefs, ideas, institutions and practices oriented to ultimate sources of power, usually conceived as supernatural, in the forms of a god, a pantheon of deities, spirits or other impersonal supernatural forces, sometimes combining several of these. This primarily suggests the idea of religion as both a system of meditations on power and as an ideological mirror of power. But of course, as shown, these meditations and ideologies can become dynamic elements in social conflict and change, within, between and beyond religious institutions. Toward the end I have moved toward the issue raised at the end of Chapter 2, the modern rupture of the supernatural and mundane worlds, and problematic re-grounding of authority in chronically contested secular institutions of science and politics. Here I have tried to address the fact that that re-grounding is only partial, that religion lives on in an awkward division of labour with those new secular institutions. At a more rarefied philosophical level, particularly in the Christian tradition, claims have become attenuated, restricted to existential moral guidance, leaving the business of power to the secular field. But more generally in social life, the need for supernatural power is unquenchable, and religious modes of appealing to such power are alive and well. I have also tried to suggest that we are uneasy with power, and one of the things religion does is to imaginatively locate power ultimately in a separate realm, at a safer distance, out of our hands. And similarly, even when we grapple with power in secular terms, we are often inclined to conceptualize it as diffuse domination 'out there', rather than as part of who and what we are. The very idea of secular, and especially democratic, authority forces us to contemplate our own hand in wielding power over ourselves and others, and this can be deeply uncomfortable.

Many of the framing concepts broached in the first chapter have arisen in this context, and I conclude by noting some connections. First, we noted the dangers of conceptualizing social power on the model of physical power, and the puzzles of conceptualizing power as existing in both actual and potential forms. These theoretical problems are prefigured and anticipated in the idea of supernatural power, which conceives of power as something that lies beyond the natural, actual world, but nonetheless enters into it. We also argued that, however much power relations may become embedded in social structures, nonetheless the idea of agency and intention is inherent to our understanding of power. The tendency to conceptualize power as embodied in spirits, supernatural agents, especially so as social structures become more complex, suggests a general human intuition of this point, shaping religious ideas. Meanwhile, the struggle outlined in Schneider's article, between peasant animism and reformed salvationist beliefs, suggests that differences between relatively balanced and relatively asymmetrical power structures in society will be echoed in religious ideologies. Finally, I have emphasized the uncomfortable trade-off that lies at the heart of our relationship with power. Paradoxically, we maximize our 'power to' achieve things, by allowing the collectivities we are a part of to increase their 'power over' us, thus enhancing overall power while diminishing our individual part in it. A moment's reflection shows that this is also a central religious motif, particularly heightened in the great salvation religions, in which the believer is called to achieve the greatest power, of life over death, precisely by subordinating themselves entirely to their god.

CHAPTER 9

# Gender, Power and Patriarchy

## Introduction

The reason for addressing gender in a book about power is not simply to acknowledge an important field of research. The dimension of gender provides an unparalleled opportunity for making broad comparative observations about social power. Sex differences and their cultural encoding in terms of genders are human universals. Male domination, patriarchy, is and has been extremely widespread, but not universal, and highly variable in the forms it takes. This invites us to consider what it is about distinctions between genders that so frequently get caught up in hierarchies of power, and what might explain variations in when and how that happens (cf. Connell 1987; Davis *et al.* 1991; Flammang 1983; Halford and Leonard 2001).

The chapter comprises three main sections. First, I take a broad historical and comparative perspective, looking at what we know about the variability of gender and power, and some of the main attempts to explain it. Here I draw especially on the anthropological literature. Then I focus on the idea of the public/private dichotomy as an explanatory framework for understanding diverse forms of patriarchy, past and present. This also extends the discussion of the public/private dichotomy in Chapter 7. Finally, I look at feminism, as a political and social movement and as an approach to social theory shaped by that movement. My aim here is not a comprehensive discussion of feminist theory, but rather an examination of the interaction between theory and practice in concrete contestation over power relations. Across these sections the chapter moves from a more historical to a more contemporary perspective.

Before proceeding I should offer some clarification of terms. I use the fairly conventional distinction between 'sex' as biological difference and 'gender' as sets of ideas about proper social roles that are attached to the sexes, but are in fact culturally and historically variable and evolving. Although there are some individuals who are ambiguously sexed, by and large human bodies fall into recognizably female and male forms. But not only are the gender roles culturally assigned to female and male highly variable, but some societies allow for more than two genders, such as the 'two-spirit people' found among some Native American groups. These individuals were usually morphologically male, but engaged in forms of dress, work and religious activity associated either with women or the distinctive 'two-spirit' gender role (Wiesner-Hanks

2011: 204–6). This underscores the socially constructed nature of gender. It is also important not to confuse the study of gender with the study of women – there are minimally two genders, and our interest is in their relationships. In recent years greater attention has been paid to 'masculinity' as a phenomenon in need of explanation, and not just the unmarked standard against which 'femininity' is understood (see Connell 2005; Gardiner 2002; MacInnes 1998). Having said this, the pervasiveness of male domination has meant that the critical study of gender has understandably been driven from the female point of view, centred on questions of 'women's status' (Mukhopadhyay and Higgins 1988; Quinn 1977). Finally, I will use the term 'patriarchy' as shorthand for male domination, to identify social contexts where men as a social group have ongoing power advantages over women as a social group. Patriarchy, as we will see, can also be highly variable, in some contexts with elaborate ideological justification, and in others more of a *de facto* structural condition, with weaker ideological legitimation.

## Comparative perspectives

The long development of gender roles and male domination maps onto the 'great arc' of human history defined by Lenski (1966) and others, and its three main phases, which Gellner (1991) called 'foraging, Agraria, and Industria' (see Chapter 5). The historical shift is from: (1) quite diverse gender relations, but often with a relative balance of power between men and women, though with incipient formation of patriarchy in some cases, to (2) the extreme expansion of patriarchy with the arrival of plough agriculture and larger, more urbanized and stratified political systems, to (3) variable effects of the modern era – colonialism, capitalism, industrialization, more extensive/intensive states and legal systems – which have variously introduced, intensified, reconfigured and amelioratated patriarchy according to specific social and historical conditions, without fully abolishing it anywhere. There is no good evidence of there ever having been any matriarchal societies. Nor does the evidence suggest any single, initial key cause of gender inequality. What it does suggest is that as stratification begins to happen gender is one of the first things to be affected and incorporated into structures of stratification, in various ways. I will elaborate this broad outline, bearing in mind that our knowledge about foraging, horticultural and pastoral ways of life rely heavily on archaeological, historical and ethnographic records of cases from the last 200 years, but many of those societies, especially foragers and horticulturalists, have been radically transformed over the last century by the encroachments of the modern state and economy (in general, see Klein 2004; Sanday 1981; Wiesner-Hanks 2011).

In foraging societies it is often the case that men and women have relatively undifferentiated roles and equal access to power and group influence. Prime examples include the Mbuti pygmies of the Ituri rainforest in Zaire, the Semang inhabiting the tropical forest of the Malay peninsula and the !Kung San of the Kalihari. However, this seems particularly the case when subsistence depends more on gathered foodstuffs. When hunting large game is crucial, as among the Inuit of the Arctic, gender roles are more sharply differentiated, and men gain in power within the group. In horticultural and pastoral societies, in which conventions of group leadership are more developed but stable political structures are absent or limited, the picture is mixed. One more often finds pronounced differentiation of gender roles, with men tending to have a greater role in hunting, working with hard and heavy materials (mining, felling trees and so on), trade and inter-societal exchanges, and women more closely linked to 'domestic' tasks such as childrearing, weaving and ceramics. In some cases this promotes systems of gender parallelism in political and religious roles. The five Iroquois Nations of the Great Lakes region were composed of matrilineal clans, with an economy in which women ran sedentary farming villages and men lived highly nomadic lives involved in hunting, trapping and intertribal warfare. The political role of inter-clan and inter-nation representatives (called *sachems*) was a male prerogative, but the 'electors' of the *sachems* were clan matrons, with powers to recall them. Thus men and women had rather different provinces of power, but also mechanisms of checks and balances between them. In other cases there are clearer patriarchal tendencies, with men monopolizing political and religious power, as among the Yanamamo of the Brazilian Amazon, whom Chagnon called 'the fierce people' (1968) because of the way they prize male hunting and intergroup feuding. In horticultural societies one sometimes finds that women are regarded as having gender-specific supernatural powers associated with fertility and menstruation, which can both indicate a kind of social value and power, and also mark them as 'dangerous' in the view of men, for example among the Papagoes of southwest North America.

Pastoral societies again take variable forms, and usually exist in a complex symbiosis with other sedentary agricultural societies with which they make exchanges. Among the matrilineal Navajo, sheep pastoralism introduced in the 1600s involves considerable overlap in both genders' contribution to herding, and relative gender egalitarianism. However in many of the nomadic, patrilineal herding societies in and around the Arabian Peninsula dating from the first millennium BC, pastoralism seems to be associated with a sharp decline in women's status because herded animals, the key source of wealth, became male property. The patrilineal Tswana of East Africa provide a recent example in which women tend crops and men control herds and the wealth and prestige they bring. Women are largely excluded from public political life.

With the formation of ancient agrarian states, the power of women generally seems to decline. It must be borne in mind that such states were stratified into heritable class statuses (nobles and commoners), and thus gender hierarchies were crosscut by class hierarchies. Such societies are associated with plough agriculture, an activity normally controlled by men, and the elaboration and promotion of other activities associated with the state and usually

restricted to men: military service, long distance trade, and literacy and clerical activities. Moreover it appears that by this stage religious specialization
and authority is largely monopolized by men, although complex systems may
allow a role for subordinate female cults. Correspondingly, it appears that
state formation brings with it the masculinization of deities worshipped or
the superordination of masculine over female deities, overturning earlier gender parity or even female-centricity in religious symbolism (Wiesner-Hanks
2011: 113). There are interesting exceptions to the pattern however, such as
the Greek city-state of Sparta (c.650–146 BC), in which the highly militarized
and segregated role of men combined with a remarkably independent role for
women, who were able to own property, run households, divorce and remar-
ry, were not restricted in their movements, and were expected to be physically
fit and outspoken (*Ibid.*: 31).

Many anthropologists and archaeologists believe that 'chiefdoms' may
have been the antecedents of the first archaic states. In chiefdoms a series of
tribally connected lineages living in multiple communities involved in horticulture and regional trade have undergone an initial process of structural stratification, such that the members of certain lineages are permanently
ranked higher than those of lesser lineages, and the top ranking lineage and
its members monopolize access to supreme political authority. Chiefs tend to
be titular landholders in such systems, and while high-ranking women can be
quite powerful, chiefdoms overall tend to promote male power (Klein 2004).
However, such chiefdoms appear to be highly variable in their actual abilities
to materially concentrate effective power, and sometimes appear to develop in
response to contact with more organized state/imperial systems, rather than
through endogenous processes of power accumulation (Earle 1987; Wolf
1982: 96–9).

One thing to note before proceeding is that in the long path from foraging
communities to archaic dynastic states, it is kinship and descent relationships
that provide the key symbolic infrastructure for representing social and political organization. Whatever its various causes, patriarchy up until the modern
period was put in practice through the malleable idiom of kinship, by men
monopolizing the symbolisms of hierarchy and descent that kinship affords.
This sketch of the 'pre-modern' development of gender stratification provides
a basis for considering some efforts to explain its causes next. The following
sections will pick up questions about patriarchy in the modern era.

Various explanations for the differences in female and male power have
been put forward. Physiologically, men on average have greater strength than
women, and this seems to play a role in some gendered divisions of work
tasks, with men predominating cross-culturally in pre-industrial societies in
large game hunting and heavy manual work such as wood cutting. But the
differences here are not universal – for instance among the Mbuti and Agta
(Luzon, Philippines) women participate in hunting. Moreover, technology can
often minimize the importance of strength differences, and it is not obvious
why a division of labour based on this factor would necessarily translate into

a pattern of patriarchy. And indeed it doesn't with any regularity in foraging and horticultural societies. Men also have a greater biologically based propensity towards aggression. This may make men more suited to organized violence and warfare. And male violence against women, especially husbands against wives in domestic contexts, is culturally widespread, but again far from universal. Physiological aggression is subject to complex cultural mediation. It can be channelled, sublimated, regulated and forbidden. Moreover, one of the hallmarks of domination is that it does not rely solely on direct coercion for its social reproduction. While physical differences between the sexes of strength and aggressiveness may provide some of the raw material out of which patriarchy is built, these are insufficient on their own to provide explanations of the diverse cultural patterns of belief and behaviour that constitute male domination (Quinn 1977: 186–90; Mukhopadhyay and Higgins 1988: 469–75).

Biological and social reproduction have also been focuses of attention. Regarding the connections between maleness, aggression, warfare and large game hunting, it has often been noted that, for the viable biological reproduction of the group's population, males are more expendable – the group can afford more easily to risk male lives in dangerous activities (Friedl 1975). But more often attention is paid to women's role in childbearing and childrearing, and how these may constrain the mobility and task-repertoire of women, leading them to become more tied to a 'domestic sphere'. Women may take on such activities as food processing and tending domestic animals because these are more compatible with looking after young children (Rosaldo 1974). Two counterpoints are often made. First, while pregnancy, childbirth and nursing do put some real constraints on activities, these are not constant, and such things as slings for carrying children can facilitate the combination of food gathering and childcare. And second, social reproduction, childrearing, is a separate matter from childbearing. Men can and often do participate in childcare, particularly in small foraging bands with mixed plant and animal subsistence. Although there is a general pattern of association of women with activities closer to the domestic base and of men with activities that take them further afield, within this pattern there is great cultural variability, which suggests that more specific matters of environment, ecology and subsistence are ultimately more determining of gender roles.

Lineality, how societies tend to trace ancestry and reckon the intergenerational transfer of possessions, rights and duties, is a matter of cultural models and rules rather than simple biological facts. Matrilineality, tracing group inheritance through mothers and daughters, is associated with more equal power between men and women, as are patterns of matrilocality, where couples move to live among the wife's kin upon marriage. Patriliny and patrilocality, on the other hand, are associated with patriarchy and lower status for women. Thus the consequences of lineality are not symmetrical. Ways of tracing lineage, which become more elaborated with sedentarism and plant and animal domestication, are themselves outcomes of environmental, including political and economic, adaptations. They tend to encode balances of power between men and women, as much as cause them (Martin and Voorhies 1975; Schlegel 1972).

Many have sought explanations for gender inequality in economic factors, such as contributions to subsistence and the control of strategic resources. Clearly contributions of labour to production do not translate directly into higher status, or else slaves would dominate slave-holding societies. The control of strategically important resources, including labour power, appears to be the more crucial issue (Sanday 1973). Thus, if food such as meat is more highly prized, is more instrumental in forging relations of dependence, and this is more controlled by men, then it will enhance male status, even if women's labour contributes more to subsistence (Quinn 1977: 202). Similarly, control of trade goods is important, and it has been noted that men with their greater mobility tend to dominate trade connections. Correspondingly, in societies where women play a strong role in market activities, as in several West African cases such as the Yoruba of Nigeria (Barnes 1990), they tend to hold an improved power position.

As already suggested above, intensive agriculture and the archaic state appear to be the clearest determinants of lower status for women (Ember 1983; White 1978). Typically, in horticultural societies in which root crops grown and harvested year-round provide a food staple, men tend to hunt, fish and trade, while women stay close to the domestic settlement tending the gardens and looking after children. With the shift to the plough agriculture of cereals, which must be planted and harvested with intensive labour at certain points in the year, men tend to supply the agricultural labour, while women become more closely tied to the household and tasks such as food processing, tending animals, pottery and weaving. The increased scale of agricultural production and the larger population it supports intensifies the demand for these other productive activities in which women come to specialize. The distinction between female/domestic and male/public activities sharpens, to the detriment of women's power and status. At the same time intensive cereal agriculture is associated with the rise of early states, such as those in Mesopotamia, Egypt, the Indus Valley, the Valley of Mexico, which put further gendered demands on labour power. Such things as draft labour for monumental building projects, military service, long-distance trade, as well as clerical and religious roles in the state bureaucracy, all tend to be male-dominated activities. With this historical shift to greater scale and complexity, the variable and incipient gender differentiation of smaller and simpler societies seems to crystallize into a much clearer gender hierarchy embedded within the stratified agrarian state (Reiter 1975; Sacks 1975).

There have also been attempts to explain gendered power differences in terms of essential cognitive patterns, most controversially Ortner's (1974) claim that women are universally associated with the forces of nature because of their manifest role in childbearing, while men are associated, in contrast, with culture, understood as human opposition to and mastery over nature.

Thus male domination becomes a manifestation of mental structures lodged deep in the human mind. The argument has been extensively critiqued, with detractors noting that in some cases the gender association of nature and culture is reversed, for example women as bearers of culture and civilizing influences that domesticate 'natural' male aggression, and that not all societies make clear distinctions between concepts of 'nature' and 'culture', which tends to be a 'western' paradigm (MacCormack and Strathern 1980). A more intriguing, though speculative, theory, that synthesizes many of the above themes, arises out of Peggy Reeves Sanday's (1981) cross-cultural survey of pre-industrial societies in search of underlying patterns of association with gender inequalities. She argues that gender ideologies in pre-industrial societies tend to fall into three broad types shaped by ecological circumstances:

1   Societies that are primarily oriented to the gathering or cultivation of plants, in which fathers tend to be more closely involved in childrearing, and group creation myth symbolism treats women as the generative source of the group.
2   Societies that are more oriented to hunting large animals, in which fathers tend to be more distant from children, and creation myth symbolism treats men as the generative source of the group.
3   'Dual orientation' societies in which both food sources are important and creation myths feature a generative male/female couple.

However, Sanday argues that societies ultimately gravitate towards one of two models: one with an 'inner orientation' to sources of power associated with femaleness, fertility and plant life, and one with an 'outer orientation' to power associated with maleness and hunting animals (1981: 67–8). She suggests that conditions of stress and resource competition will tend to amplify the androcentric 'outer orientation' as men are by nature more prepared to respond to stress with aggression and life-risking behaviour, while women are more inclined seek survival through conciliation, acquiescing to male domination (1981: 89–90, 210–11). Sanday's sample of 156 pre-industrial societies may not sufficiently distinguish between pre-agrarian and agrarian societies, and may downplay the significance of the historical shift between them. Nonetheless, in a bold interpretation she finds many correlations between biological differences, ideological patterns and environmental conditions that are thought-provoking, if not conclusive.

## Public, private and patriarchy

Running through the previous section is a recurring distinction between a 'domestic' or 'private' sphere more associated with women, and a 'public' sphere associated with men, echoed to a degree in Sanday's distinction between 'inner' and 'outer' orientations. Some have seen this as a near universal principle of gender relations, possibly rooted in the requirements of childbearing and rearing (Rosaldo 1974, 1980). But the distinction is difficult to apply to small scale foraging societies, although it becomes more pronounced as we move up the scale in size and organizational complexity toward stratified states. I doubt that the public/private dichotomy provides an adequate explanation for *why* patriarchy develops in the first place, but it seems to be deeply implicated in *how* it develops across human history, and therefore deserves closer attention.

A *prima facie* reason for looking more closely at the public/private divide is that it, and the complex interaction between the public and the private, is implicated in most of the standard indicators we use to assess women's position in society in comparison to men. Data compiled in the *The World's Women 2010: Trends and Statistics* (United Nations 2010) help to frame the issue, bearing in mind that global statistics can mask considerable regional and national variations. In terms of occupying positions of power, leadership and decision-making, despite slow and steady progress since the 1960s, women hold only 17 per cent of the parliamentary seats in lower or single chambers (29 per cent for western Europe, with the highest representation in several Nordic countries). In 2009 only 7 of the 150 elected Heads of State in the world were women. Women's representation is similarly low in local government, and judiciaries. In the 'private sector', women are around 12–16 per cent of the directors on boards of large companies in Europe and the US, and 'only 13 of the 500 largest corporations in the world had a female CEO in 2009' (United Nations 2010: 124). In terms of work, in Europe women tend to earn 15–25 per cent less than men for comparable work, and this is related to informal segregation into lower-paying service sector jobs. Worldwide, women are found in vulnerable forms of employment in the informal sector, family businesses and as own-account workers more frequently than men. In the household, 'women spend at least twice as much time as men on domestic work, and when all work – paid and unpaid – is considered, women work longer hours than men do' (*Ibid.*: 75). Education has been one of the main areas of recent improvement in women's status, with the global gender gaps in primary enrolment and literacy closing among the young. In tertiary (higher) education women now outnumber men, although they are underrepresented in the fields of science and engineering, remaining predominant in education, health and social welfare, social sciences, humanities and the arts. Steady growth in the service sector and women's employment in it appears to be a factor in this difference. Poverty is normally assessed at the level of the household, and gender correlates with poverty. Single-parent households with young children are more likely to be poor when the parent is a mother (the vast majority) than a father, and women are more likely than men to be poor when living in one-person households. In less developed regions, statutory and customary laws often limit women's access to land and other property (especially in Africa and Asia), and women tend to have less access to cash income. When married, they tend to have less control over the cash they do earn and household spending decisions. Finally, statistics on violence against women can be very difficult to collect. However, across a range of countries the number of women reporting experiences of physical violence in their lifetimes runs from about 11 per cent (China, Hong Kong SAR) to 59 per cent (Zambia), with no strong correlation to the level of economic development (Australia just under 50 per cent). Moreover, overall rates of women experiencing sexual violence are only slightly lower, and intimate partners are often the perpetrators of violence, both physical and sexual. Surveys have also found ideological acceptance of these conditions among some women, reporting that in 33 less developed countries, on average 'around 29 per cent of women agreed that being hit or beaten for arguing with the husband was justifiable, 25 per cent for refusing to have sex with the husband, and 21 per cent for burning the food' (*Ibid.*: 137). Taken together, such statistics indicate complex patterns of male domination running from the public to the private domain.

Before going further, let me make some conceptual points. The public/ private distinction is not simply about the division of genders into separate social spheres with associated activities. Despite the characteristic language, it is not strictly a spatial concept, but concerns also scopes of command and sovereignty. An Ottoman ruler could live entirely within his own palace compound, bringing the outside world to him as needed, through agents, and commanding a complex household as well as the wider society (Wiesner-Hanks 2011: 99). Here sequestration in the 'household' is a demonstration of power, because it is the ruler's choice, a ruler with instrumental reach into the 'outer' realm through his subordinates. Wherever he stays, his command ranges over the public domain and into the private. As I argued in Chapter 7, the public/ private distinction is about the overall constitution and distribution of power, and involves hierarchical notions of embedded levels of domain and control. Moreover, it is associated especially with the form of the state, and there is always an uneasy balance in the public/private relationship. Ultimately, public power can extend its reach into the private, overriding private rights in some instances, but if private power extends too far into the public (as with the influence of private money on electoral politics), the very nature of public power is undermined. Also, liminal, gatekeeper positions are intrinsic to embedded levels of public/private structures. Just as the head of state, and the state as such, faces inward to the citizenry and outward into the international arena, heads of households face both inward toward the 'private' domain in the household and outward toward participation in public life.

We need to understand public/private divisions as something socially variable and historically evolving (see Benn and Gaus 1983; Landes 1998). As I have argued, in some form they reach back at least to the early formation of stratified states, but our general model of the distinction, outlined in Chapter 7, is heavily shaped by western political and economic thought that has developed since the seventeenth century, in conjunction with ideas about private property and political representation. Earlier versions operated in quite different ideological settings, although generally supporting patriarchal orders. A crucial difference here is the conception of the 'public' as the manifestation of the will and domain of the collectivity, or 'demos' in modern constitutional states, versus the traditional authority of a ruler as the ritual embodiment and personification of the group. For various reasons, political cephalization characteristically involves the formation of a hierarchic network of men (although women can be inserted or there may be parallel women's structures) monopolizing 'public' rights and obligations, with embedded household/domestic spheres of command over women. As for the future, I do not take the view that public/private distinctions intrinsically require gender hierarchy, only that they have historically been strongly allied with such, and that their disentanglement is a very difficult thing. But it is perhaps even more difficult, and frightening, to imagine a form of extensive and complex society that does not manage power by drawing and protecting boundaries between the massive, socially aggregated powers of the state, and the more circumscribed, distributed and counterbalancing power of its various parts and members (cf. Okin 1991).

To explore this idea further we need to consider concrete examples. We can start with Irene Silverblatt's (1980, 1987) study of gender and power among the Inca, before and after the Spanish conquest. She traces the historical development of patriarchal structures in two stages, first with the growth and expansion across the Andes of the Inca Empire (c.1450–1532) centred in Cuzco, and then with the imposition of Spanish imperial colonialism (1532–1826). Although sources are fragmentary, there is evidence that prior to the spread of the Inca Empire, women often enjoyed higher status in various Andean communities. At the time of Inca conquest the predominant pattern of Andean social organization involved a kind of gender parallelism. Women traced their descent through mothers, and men through fathers. Through their mothers women enjoyed rights of access to community land, water, herds and so on. Marriage was seen as the formation of a new household in which the partners had a mutual interest, although their labour contributions were gender-defined. Some evidence suggests that local elite women served as community leaders, either in parallel with, or at least in the absence of, men fulfilling these roles. Similarly, Andean cosmology featured reciprocal male and female deities: Illpa, god of thunder, lightning and rain (and associated with conquest), and Pachamama, goddess of the earth and its generative forces. Accounts indicate that religious cults and ritual forms tended to further reinforce this gender parallelism (Silverblatt 1987: 3–39).

As they conquered outlying groups, the Inca reoriented gender roles, and grafted their own version of Andean gender cosmology onto pre-existing ones in ways that increased men's power over women. The idea of complementarity of women's and men's contributions to households was preserved, the household being the minimal unit subject to imperial tribute. However, in censuses designed to assess capacities for imperial tribute and service, it was a married adult man's capacity to bear arms and serve as a soldier that was crucial, and the expanding imperial administration selected local elite men as the public figures to hold authority. According to Silverblatt:

Men and not women represented the household to the imperial administration. And the men who now became public figures for state purposes
were characterized as arms bearers with wives. In building their empire,
the Incas froze certain aspects of gender – attributes that had been part of
the construction of maleness and femaleness – to facilitate imperial governance ... As the Incas tightened their grip over others, the imperial ideal
of Andean malehood increasingly became the norm (1987: 15).

Meanwhile, Inca imperial cosmology featured two deities, the male sun
and female moon, issuing from the supreme androgynous divinity Viracocha.
The male hierarchy of rule, from Inca noblemen down to subjugated village
headmen, was symbolically likened to the line of the masculine sun god and
his descendents, while women were likened to the line descending from the
moon, linking Inca noblewomen to peasant women. Pachamama, the guard-
ian of local powers of fertility, was also incorporated into the Inca cosmology,
but 'no longer a local sponsor, Pachamama had become the benefactress of
the empire through her bond with the lords of Cuzco' (1987: 49). Thus the
Inca transmuted Andean gender ideologies and symbols, from separate but
relatively equal to separate and unequal.

With the Spanish Conquest women's position in the social hierarchy wors-
ened further. The Inca had built up a trans-communal network of male power
and authority, politically binding its provinces together, but had left households as units that acknowledged the combined values of male and female
labour inputs to production, largely intact. The Spanish brought with them
Iberian gender norms and conceptions of property rights. Quickly abolishing
the Inca state cults of the Sun and the Moon to be replaced by Christianity, they also reconfigured property relations, treating Inca nobility as feudal
owners of all the land, rather than as tribute-takers from relatively autonomous communities. Some noblewomen were able to parlay this into positions
of power in the new empire, especially through intermarriage with the new
Spanish ruling class. However, for the average Andean peasant women the
imposition of Spanish law meant that married women were reclassified as
legal minors, with property and resources traditionally controlled by women
transferred to their husbands by law. There was resistance to this, including legal contestation from elite women, and more traditional notions of
women's rights to property within marriage have persisted among the Andean
peasantry. Regardless of this, the sheer pressures of colonial taxation and labour extraction meant that women's labour became much more dedicated
to production for markets (agriculture and textiles) and domestic service to
the new Spanish elite, further undermining male/female complementarity in
household-based production. Peasant women's resistance to the new order,
expressed partly through the preservation of indigenous religious practices,
was compared to European notions of witchcraft, idolatry and devil-worship,
and prosecuted by the conquerors (Silverblatt 1980). We know from various accounts of the effects of European colonialism that women's power and

status often declined as European patterns of patriarchy and property rights were imposed on indigenous populations (see Etienne and Leacock 1980). Although not as well understood, it seems likely that state formation in various premodern contexts, like the rise of the Inca that Silverblatt describes, often involved an earlier wave of patriarchal power consolidation. One of the basic processes of state formation is that the state and its elites have to gain control over communal resources normally regulated through local norms of kinship. For various reasons we have seen above, men may be the most susceptible point for attaching and subordinating kin groups to state hierarchies of power and resource extraction (see Reiter 1975: 275–82).

Let us turn now to a more contemporary view. Examining the cases of Britain, Australia and the US, the political theorist Carol Pateman (1998) has argued that the modern welfare state institutionalizes a form of patriarchy through the public/private divide. These systems have legally defined the roles of household 'breadwinner' and 'worker' as male. They have developed two-tier systems of benefits: one directed at 'public persons', those included in participation in labour markets, normally 'male breadwinners'; and one directed at 'private persons' dependent on breadwinners for support, usually women and children. Thus benefit entitlements were conceived in terms of 'living' or 'family' wages aimed at male breadwinners, whether or not they had families, tending to lock women into their dependent status (1998: 250–3). As Pateman puts it:

> The widely held belief that the basic structure of our society rests on the separation of the private, familial sphere from the public world of the state and its policies is both true and false. It is true that the private sphere has been seen as women's proper place. Women have never in reality been completely excluded from the public world, but the policies of the welfare state have helped insure that women's day-to-day experience confirms the separation of private and public existence. The belief is false in that, since the early twentieth century, welfare policies have reached across from public to private and helped uphold the patriarchal structure of familial life. Moreover, the two spheres are linked because men have always had a legitimate place in both. Men have been seen both as heads of families – and as husbands and fathers they have had socially and legally sanctioned power over their wives and children – and as participants in public life. Indeed, the 'natural' masculine capacities that enable them, but not their wives, to be heads of families are the same capacities that enable them, but not their wives, to take their place in civil life (1998: 246).

Although the number of women in paid employment has grown in recent decades, welfare systems continue to shunt them into the role of dependants on the state, rather than of unemployed breadwinners, because they tend to be in lower paid and more precarious jobs, have poorer pensions and continue to bear the brunt of responsibility for children. Pateman notes the paradox

184 *Theorizing Power*

that women's preponderant role in unpaid work in the private sphere of the household involves a massive unrecognized contribution to social welfare, and yet they often find themselves with lesser entitlements to state welfare when in need (1998: 255).

In a similar but more elaborated argument, Sylvia Walby (1990) argues that the public/private distinction is crucial for understanding both the structures and development of patriarchy in advanced capitalist economies, focusing particularly on Britain in the nineteenth and twentieth centuries. While forms of patriarchy historically precede capitalism, once the latter arises, they evolve in interaction with one another. Walby looks at the way structures of patriarchy develop in regard to the structures and practices of households, waged employment, the state (laws and policies), sexuality, male violence against women and roles in cultural institutions (religion, education, media and so on). She traces a general shift in Britain from patriarchy grounded in the private/household sphere in the nineteenth century, to patriarchy grounded in the public/state sphere in the twentieth. From earlier patriarchal norms in which, despite male domination, men and women were more mutually involved in household production and public activities, she sees the rise in the nineteenth century of an intensified private patriarchy, especially as a middle class ideal, in which men gained in public roles through the expansion of the franchise, while women were increasingly sequestered into households to deliver unpaid labour there. Women's labour was characteristically expropriated by individual men as heads of households, and women were relatively excluded from public life and legally constituted as dependent upon men. In the twentieth century, through a combination of the changing labour demands of capitalism and the political pressures of 'first wave feminism' (see next section), 'private patriarchy' is relatively displaced by 'public patriarchy' in which, while still providing the bulk of household labour, women's labour is further expropriated by job markets and the state. Women become politically enfranchised and, again, particularly in the norm-setting middle classes, have greater participation in paid employment (poorer women had always had to work). But there is nonetheless a *de facto* segregation in public life, as indicated by the UN statistics outlined above, giving women less access to genuine power than men. Walby emphasizes that patriarchy is an historical process, and that 'private and public forms of patriarchy constitute a continuum rather than a rigid dichotomy' (1990: 180). Moreover, she sees feminist agitation as a significant factor in social change, and makes an analytic distinction between the 'degree' and the 'form' of patriarchy. As she puts it: 'British feminists have won significant reforms which ameliorate a number of the features of patriarchy, but some have eventually resulted in a different form of patriarchy' (1990: 174).

In a similar spirit, this section offers an outline of how patriarchy has formed and evolved into the present, not a static model. The possibility of greater gender equality is not logically excluded, and has been positively implied as an historical tendency by some developments in women's rights over the last century. This is consistent with the trajectory of Lenski's (1966) long historical arc from egalitarianism through stratification to 'stratified egalitarianism'. The point is that gender has been deeply bound up with stratification *per se*, and stratification itself, in whatever form it takes, appears to be linked to public/private distinctions.

## Feminism and power

So far I have been tracing a broad history of gender and power relations, with particular attention to the public/private dichotomy. I now want to turn to a history of feminist thought since the mid-nineteenth century, and some of the issues it raises in regard to our understanding of power. While not attempting a thorough engagement with feminist theory, which is very diverse, a brief examination of feminist thought provides an opportunity to consider some issues that arise when the theorization of power is entwined with the existential circumstances of those doing the theorizing. The major marxian theorists of working class oppression and liberation were not, for the most part, industrial workers. But the vast majority of those contributing to feminist thought have been women. Does this make a difference to how power is understood?

I use the fairly conventional periodization of feminism into three historical 'waves' of social movement, beginning in the nineteenth century, as a frame to raise key issues (Walters 2005). We should note first, however, that women have become conscious and mobilized as women at various times across history and cultures. Silverblatt's account of the Spanish conquest of the Inca clearly suggests that some Andean women formed distinctive oppositional identities in regard to the Spanish conquerors and their religion. First wave feminism (c. 1850–1920) arose, principally in the UK and the US, out of the manifest contradictions between expanding democratic rights for men and continuing legal and constitutional subordination of women. Although there were many issues at stake, including access to education, women's health and control over their own bodies and property rights, the central focus of the movement was women's suffrage. There is no doubt that women's political pressure was crucial to the staged expansion of this central democratic right for women. The claims made during the 'first wave' were in many ways prefigured in terms of eighteenth century discourses on rights, as articulated in such writings as Olympe de Gouges' *Declaration of the Rights of Women and Female Citizens* in Revolutionary France in 1791, and Mary Wollstonecraft's *A Vindication of the Rights of Woman* in 1792. Correspondingly, first wave feminism anticipated many aspects of the later civil rights movements, in terms of claims to rights made through a variety of political protest methods and directed both at the state and a wider public imagination.

What came to be known as the 'second wave' of feminism (1960s–1970s) developed in the milieu of the civil rights movements and student radicalism of that period. The second wave renewed the struggles of the earlier period, but the right to vote having been won in the US and the UK, focused more on the idea of equal rights, and the removal of *de jure* and *de facto* forms of discrimination against women in regard to such matters as education, employment, wages and access to positions of power. In the US the National Organization of Women (est. 1966) was instrumental in advancing these issues. The Equal Rights Amendment, which was passed by the Congress in 1972, was also a key focus of political energies. (It remains three states short of ratification and incorporation into the federal constitution, but has been incorporated, with some variations, into 21 state constitutions.) Influenced partly by the sexual politics of the 1960s, the second wave was also concerned with bodily self-determination. Key issues included reproductive rights to birth control and abortion, the power to refuse men sexual access and to identify rape as such, and control over the representation of women's bodies in regard to pornography and hegemonic notions of feminine beauty.

The second wave tended to develop on two distinct fronts, popular and academic. Several key and often polemical texts have had very wide audiences, among them Simone de Beauvoir's *The Second Sex* (1953), Betty Friedan's *The Feminine Mystique* (1965), Germaine Greer's *The Female Eunuch* (1971) and Naomi Wolf's *The Beauty Myth* (1991). In a more strictly academic context, feminist theory has developed mostly within the social sciences and humanities, in particular in fields such as history, anthropology, sociology, politics, philosophy, psychology, literature and law. The literature of this period was often concerned with positioning feminism with regard to other political and theoretical stances, such as radicalism, liberalism, socialism and Marxism (Jaggar 1983; Tong 1989). Radical feminism (Brownmiller 1976; Daly 1978; MacKinnon 1987) tended to place patriarchy centrally in the social organization of power, to argue that essential biological and psychological differences between men and women were at the root of conflicts between them, in some versions advocating women's separatism from male-dominated society. Liberal feminism (Cornell 1998; Nussbaum 1999) has worked within the liberal tradition, seeing feminism as a reformist project of the expansion of equal rights and the removal of discrimination, but not as a fundamental challenge to liberal society *per se*. Socialist/Marxian feminism (Delphy 1984; Leacock 1972) has tended to treat patriarchy as an effect of capitalism, with the exploitation of women's lower paid and unpaid labour as central to the wider capacity of capital to exploit labour power and achieve class domination. As with Walby discussed above, there are also 'dual-systems' theories (Hartmann 1979; McLaughlin 2003: 51; Young 1981) which recognize the relative independence of capitalism and patriarchy, but also acknowledge their complex and reinforcing interactions. The key point here is that second wave feminism in the academic context produced not so much a single field or body of theory as a set of concerns ranging across disciplines and articulating with various theoretical traditions. And this academic discourse shades into a wider popular discourse, much more so than many of the theoretical traditions of power research we have discussed in earlier chapters, precisely because women's status is an ongoing 'live' issue in modern liberal society, and feminism is, at base, a social movement.

I want to highlight two ideas emerging out of this period: 'the personal is political', and the view that theory can be justified by its relationship to the 'standpoint' of the theorist.

## The personal is political

This phrase is often traced back to the title of an essay by Carol Hanisch (Firestone and Koedt 1970), although it was probably already in currency within the women's movement (see Hanisch 2009). Hanisch argued that the consciousness-raising meetings and discussion groups that were characteristic of the movement at that time were not 'therapy', as sometimes dismissively described, or personal in the sense of apolitical. Her point was that power, in the fullest sense, was present in the most personal aspects of people's lives, especially in regard to women's disproportionate responsibility for households, childcare and 'emotional work' more generally (Komter 1991; Meyer 1991). Feminism has been particularly concerned with tracing power from the micro to the macro (Davis 1988), and from more 'internal' psychological (Chodorow 1978) to more 'external' sociological (Halford and Leonard 2001) processes. Hanisch's argument has much in common with C. Wright Mills' (1959) assertion that sociology needed to be concerned with the interface of personal problems and public issues, of biography and history.

Because of this orientation, feminism has fought on two distinct fronts that we have encountered in this book's discussion of theories of power. On the one hand, there has been great concern for making explicit the myriad, often micro-level, implicit supports of patriarchy, such as gendered language and control of conversation, aesthetics and norms of bodily beauty, and the work of caring, and thereby rendering it subject to criticism. In other words there are confrontations with what I have called 'cryptic domination', which I treated as symptomatic of more 'epistemological approaches'. But, as we've seen, much of feminist politics has also been concerned with questioning the legitimacy of various widely recognized patterns of power, authority and discrimination. It has been engaged with a full-on public confrontation with institutions, in the pursuit of social change. This aspect resonates more with what I have called 'evolutionary approaches'. Having made this distinction, it is important to grasp that, because of its politically engaged nature, feminism's approach to the implicit, habitual, subjectifying and cryptic aspects of power has not been simply to observe that this is how power works, but to bring these issues to conscious awareness. Thus there has been both an attraction to, and dissatisfaction with, the conceptions of power proffered by, for instance, Foucault (Hartsock 1990; McNay 1994) or Actor Network Theory (Faulkner 2001; Wajcman 2000).

## The feminist standpoint

Another theme has been to argue that theorizing emerges from the actual conditions of the theorist, and that women have a particular 'standpoint' that is the ground of feminist theorizing (Harding 1986; Hartsock 1998; Smith 1987). This position reworks the Marxist argument that worsening conditions for labour under capitalism would put the proletariat in a privileged position to understand the dysfunctions of capitalism, and articulate a revolutionary solution. It transposes this epistemological argument to women's situation in regard to patriarchy (Hartsock 1983). The essence of the argument is that those with less power, in the oppressed and subordinate position, are better situated to understand power than the powerful, who need to convince themselves of the justness and inevitability of their own position. It is not that the female perspective is essentially or naturally superior, but rather that conditions of patriarchy are conducive to feminist ethical and political insights into reality. Thus there is a tendency in standpoint theories to justify knowledge pragmatically, according to its usefulness, and to relativize notions of 'objectivity', rejecting the idea of an abstract universal perspective (sometimes seen as characteristically 'male') in favour of an idea that knowledge is always positional, and that the marginalized are often better able to view matters 'objectively', precisely because they lack the biases that holding power tends to foster. (See also Hekman 1997, and replies from Collins, Harding, Hartsock and Smith in the same issue of *Signs*; McLaughlin 2003: 47–69; Stanley and Wise 2000.)

The idea of a distinctive 'third wave' of feminism beginning in the 1980s is less clearly defined. Although there are considerable continuities, the 'third wave' has featured a call for a less essentialized and more diversified concept of women and their problems, particularly from the perspectives of racial and ethnic minorities, working classes, and women in the developing world. It has also shown regard to more fluid conceptions of gender and sexuality, often signalled by the term 'queer' (Butler 2000; Sedgwick 1990). The fact that the 'second wave' tended to be led by middle class white women from the most affluent countries in the world, especially the US, eventually led to an internal critique, problematizing the idea that all women were unified by a common identity and condition of oppression. Black feminist, bell hooks (1984) argued that minority and working class women had been treated as second class citizens within the feminist movement, echoing the original complaints of second wave feminists that, in the radical politics of the 1960s, men had treated women as secondary adjuncts to their political projects. To women stuck in multiple insecure and low-paying jobs while also trying to raise a family, the goal of rejecting housewife-hood and pursuing a career seemed more of a luxury than a confrontation with actual conditions. Moreover, there were vexing questions about how gender solidarities are crosscut by those of class, race, ethnicity, religion and sexuality (Moraga and Anzaldua 1983), leading to the idea of 'intersectionality' (Crenshaw 1991), that social inequality is compli-cated by the fact that groups, sub-groups and individuals will experience their positions as arising out of the intersection of multiple social structures and dimensions of identity and hierarchy that are not reducible to single factors. These arguments obviously raise problems for the 'standpoint' approach (see Collins 1991; Haraway 1991).

The feminist movement as a whole has focused attention on how we un-derstand the scope of power relations, the significance of social positioning for theorizing and the difficulty in defining unified identities in regard to power struggles. However, these are questions that ultimately reach beyond matters of gender, pertaining to all kinds of collective political mobilization, and how individuals relate to these. I explore these issues further in the next chapter on personhood and identity, and the vexed question of identity, as both a basis for, and effect of, power struggles.

## Conclusion

This chapter has argued three things. First, a long, historical and cross-cultural perspective is needed to adequately pose and investigate basic questions about the nature and origins of male domination. No simple answers are available, but patterns and clues are discernable. Secondly, I have argued that among the most valuable analytical tools for understanding patriarchy is the concept of the public/private distinction. Again, this needs to be viewed historically, as an evolving social pattern which is especially associated not just with capitalism or modernity but state formation, both ancient and modern. Finally, I have tried to suggest that feminist theorizing needs to be understood as conditioned by both academic traditions and practice, and the wider social movement from which it emerges. It brings into focus particular issues that arise when the subjective experience of the theorist is also part of the object of inquiry, when attempts to understand domination, arise out of the condition of being dominated.

# CHAPTER 10

# Identity and Personhood

## Introduction

A passage from Chinua Achebe's *Home and Exile* (2000), offering reflections on his youth as a student in pre-independence Nigeria, evokes many of our main themes in this chapter.

> The intention of my English professors to introduce us to such an out-standing novel written about a place and people we would be familiar with and therefore easily able to appreciate, was quite unexceptionable. But things did not turn out the way they should have. One of my classmates stood up and told an astounded teacher point-blank that the only moment he had enjoyed in the entire book was when the Nigerian hero, Johnson, was shot to death by his British master, Mr. Rudbeck. The rest of us, now astounded too, offered a medley of noises in reaction. My own judgment was that our colleague, and the rest of us perhaps, still had a lot to learn on how to express adverse literary opinion; but beyond that we all shared our colleague's exasperation at this bumbling idiot of a character whom Joyce Cary and our teacher were so assiduously passing off as a poet when he was nothing but an embarrassing nitwit! Now this incident, as I came to recognize later, was more than just an interesting episode in a colonial classroom. It was a landmark rebellion. Here was a whole class of young Nigerian students, among the brightest of their generation, united in their view of a book of English fiction in complete opposition to their English teacher, who was moreover backed by the authority of metropolitan critical judgment. The issue was not so much who was right as why there was that absolute divide. For it was not my experience that Nigerians, young or old, were much inclined to be unanimous on anything, not even on the greatest issue of the day – the timing of their independence from British rule (Achebe 2000: 22–3).

In this vignette the white teacher offers the young colonial subjects a sup-posedly sympathetic portrayal of their identity, only to be rebuffed by the response – that's not us, that's not someone with whom we want to identify. An uneasy dialogue is set up between the students, the teacher, the author and his character, in which literary 'generosity' is revealed as just domination in another form. And these sets of relations, especially those between students and teacher in that moment, become focused instantiations of the much larger context of colonial rule that shapes them. Questions of identity always involve complex linkages between more immediate problems of personhood, and more encompassing questions of power.

I will approach the subject from three main angles. First, an overview of how and why our talk about identity has changed since the 1960s, paying attention to questions of how identity structures power relations, as routinely understood. Identities can be both the bases for, and outcomes of, the pursuit of power. They can be both mobilizing and empowering, and labelling and dominating. The relationship is double-edged. Second, I will consider how the subject of identity once again invokes what I have called 'epistemological approaches' in Chapter 5. In particular I consider a strain of recent ideas about identity that has stressed the shifting, indeterminate, and even illusory, nature of identity. Here, identification becomes an unstable process that threatens to dominate us by essentializing who we are, and from which we can seek escape and liberation. Finally, I offer an alternative 'ecological model' of identity that, unsurprisingly, harks back to the 'evolutionary approaches' discussed in Chapter 6. I argue that we need to distinguish sharply between identity in the sense of unique embodied persons or selves and in the sense of socially recognized categories with which we talk about the world. To say useful things about power and identity we need to distinguish between these senses, and theorize their relationship. Moreover, that relationship turns out to be heavily conditioned and mediated by various forms of social organization that are not themselves 'identities', but are often the lenses through which the relationship between the two senses are refracted.

## Shifting discourses of power and social identity

The sheer scale and scope of writing and theorizing about identity is readily evident in any general review of literature, and well represented by various current readers and collections on the topic (see Alcoff and Mendieta 2003; Calhoun 1994; Du Gay *et al.* 2000; Hall and Du Gay 1996). In 1968 Dennis Wrong published a short piece entitled 'Identity: Problem and Catchword' in *Dissent* (Wrong 1968), and although the theoretical language of identity has exploded and diversified since then, his view that this is an idea with which both social scientists and people more generally are peculiarly preoccupied continues to hold true (Brubaker and Cooper 2000: 3–4).

Wrong's article focused particularly on the influential work of Erik H. Erikson who is credited with coining the term 'identity crisis' (1968). Influenced by Anna Freud, Erikson was a psychoanalyst and social psychologist who was interested in psychosocial development, and particularly sensitive to the impact of cultural and historical context on psychological processes. He is probably best remembered for his eight-stage model of human development from birth to the end of life. We can leave aside the details, but the essential proposal of the model is that personal and social development pose different problems for the individual at different stages, problems that are overcome by acquiring characteristic strengths: hopefulness, self-control, diligence, the capacity for intimacy, a sense of purpose in life and so on (1965: 239–66). Correspondingly, he saw failure to grapple successfully with these hurdles as disabling and inhibiting psychological and emotional development. The model may strike many as rather formulaic today, but the basic insights are enduring and relevant for the present discussion, because it fundamentally links identity to a personal sense of power and efficacy in the individual's life, while recognizing that identity formation is shaped by various external factors. Because his ideas are oriented to a notion of the healthy, well-adjusted individual, it may seem that Erikson's approach is fundamentally functionalist and conservative, supporting the given *status quo*. However, there is nothing about Erikson's model that really prescribes conformism or political quietism. His psychobiographical study of the young Martin Luther treated Luther's rebellion against the authority of the Catholic Church as a part of his resolution of his personal identity crisis, not as a symptom of maladjustment (1958).

Another key social psychological approach to social identity has been that of Henri Tajfel (1978, 1982) and his followers, known as 'self-categorization theory'. A Polish Jew, prisoner of war and survivor of the holocaust, Tajfel was deeply motivated to understand the causes of prejudice and stereotyping. The approach distinguishes between 'personal' and 'social' identities, and focuses on the latter, understood as the process by which ideas of distinct social groups and one's membership of them are formed. Central are the ideas that we get a sense of who we are by how we categorize ourselves, and that this involves forming notions of in-groups to which we belong and out-groups from which we are excluded. Moreover, there is a strong tendency to concretize these categories through intergroup comparisons that reflect positively on the in-group and negatively on the out-group, and to exaggerate similarity within the in-group and differences between the in-group and out-groups. Group membership provides both a sense of social location, and a basis for self-esteem. Thus the theory sees a powerful tendency to view social identity in terms of 'we' versus 'they', and tends to treat the self as the sum total of in-group identifications and their oppositions to various out-groups that compose the individual. The theory was developed through experiments that formed arbitrary groups out of sets of individuals, and observed how, without any further bases, subjects so organized tended to engage in the differentiating processes just described, suggesting that these are primary, underlying social and cognitive processes. It has been suggested that these artificial conditions may in fact be misleading, and that real world intergroup dynamics are much more mediated by overlapping interests and accommodations (Jenkins 2004: 88–91).

Tajfel's emphasis on group formation and dynamics contrasts sharply with Erikson's emphasis on individual development, but this is a difference in focus, not necessarily an incompatibility in their perspectives. Each in their own way have things to say about power: Tajfel about why groups come into conflict and may aim to denigrate or dominate each other, and Erikson about how persons manage or fail to develop robust psychologies that support them through life. Clearly there are many questions about how these two dimensions of identity interact.

In the 1970s and into the 1980s, the term 'identity politics' became prominent in the social sciences (see Heyes 2009). To examine why this happened, we need to distinguish between changes in objective patterns of political mobilization and arguments about the very basis of political action. In other words, is identity a matter of *how* politics is organized or *what* it is about in the first instance? The term has conventionally come to cover political mobilization around an array of bases for identification, most prominently race, ethnicity, gender and sexuality, but also such bases as religion and disability, and potentially many others. Interestingly, politics based on urban or regional issues, while often involving a dimension of identification, are rarely regarded as 'identity politics', and usually subsumed under the rubric of 'interests'. As an idea, the heartland of identity politics has been the US, and more widely the other Anglophone liberal democracies, especially Canada, Australia and the UK. It arises out of the civil rights movements that developed in the US in the 1960s, first in regard to African-Americans, and then ramifying out into various protests against oppression and inequality in regard to the positions of women (as we saw in the previous chapter), Native Americans, Chicanas/Chicanos, Gays and others. Whereas previously politics had tended to be conceived either along liberal lines as a matter of contention among multiple, diverse and changing interest groups, built up out of aggregated individual interests, or along more marxian lines as a matter of confrontation between certain fundamental, economically-based classes, the civil rights movements brought a new kind of politics. Disconcertingly for some, this new style of politics combined the pluralism of classical liberal politics, with a sense of socially structured exploitation and oppression more akin to Marxism and socialism. On the liberal side this has elicited fears of social fragmentation and the erosion of core shared values in the face of 'multiculturalism'. On the socialist left it has often been seen as a distraction from the more fundamental concerns of class conflict, one version of this being feminist debates about the relationship and/or priority between capitalism and patriarchy as social structures of domination. Regardless of these objections, identity politics is a manifest historical reality, now a basic part of how politics is done. Indeed one might simply view it as the normalization and routinization of the civil rights movements in liberal democratic contexts.

The term 'identity politics' suggests perhaps too strongly that there are other kinds of politics in which identity is not an important feature. But, as Marx famously argued, the key problem for proletarian revolution was to transform the brute fact of class structure, 'class in-itself', into conscious mobilization of workers as such, on that basis, into 'class for-itself' (Marx in

Tucker 1978: 608). In other words, the aim is to augment a structural position of the class as a group with an active identity. So the rise of 'identity politics' is not so much a matter of the replacement of class by identity as a principle of organization, as a shift from one main socially structured identity (class) to multiple socially structured identities at play in the political process. (Although such things as the deeper history of waves of feminist movements should make us cautious about even this characterization of the 'shift'.) And of course any political mobilization, such as a neighbourhood attempting to block the building of a polluting plant in its midst, entails some degree of identification with the community and cause, and will succeed or fail partly on how well an (at least temporary) identity is achieved. So there is a sense in which all politics is identity politics, and all identity politics has structural underpinnings, sets of conditions that unify the interests of the identifying group.

Identity politics of course has correlates in many kinds of indigenous politics taking place beyond the core countries of the 'west'. A prime example of an effort to explore this point is the Subaltern Studies Group formed in the early 1980s, under the mentorship of Ranajit Guha, to bring together Indian historians and historians of India in a project to critique and reform Indian historiography (Chatterjee 1995; Guha 1997, 1998; Guha and Spivak 1988). The core criticism was that up until that point the history of India had been told largely in a top down fashion. By emphasizing how first the British colonizers and then the Indian elites that dominated the struggle for independence in 1947 had set the terms of politics and provided the key political agency, they had, in effect, made Indian history. The aim of subaltern studies, much like the earlier movement of marxian social history in the UK, was to retell the story from below, to recover forgotten 'insurgencies' and reclaim the historical role of those previously excluded from national history. The term 'subaltern' was adopted from Gramsci (see Chapter 3), a key theoretical influence, who had used it as a general term for diverse groups dominated by a ruling elite, for example both rural peasants and urban workers in nineteenth century Italy. The term allowed subaltern studies to deal with the social complexity of excluded groups in Indian society, based on caste, gender, religious communities, livelihoods and so forth, without erasing important analytical differences under the general heading of 'class'. Moreover, there was a critique of the whole nation-building project, and a belief that this had misguidedly modelled itself on an homogenizing western liberal democracy in a way that could not take account of India's multi-ethnic, multi-religious complexity. And so Gramsci's critique of the failure of the Italian Risorgimento to create a true unified country and his hope for a further socialist revolution that would do so was also, in a sense, theoretically transposed to India (see Guha 1988: 41–3).

Let me move this discussion to a more general level. We can think of identities, in the sense of social categories formed and available in the public discourse, as being either claimed by people, imposed on people or as situations people are fatefully landed in due to circumstances beyond anyone's control.

Whichever is the case, there are implications for the dynamics of power. Discussions of identity politics tend to emphasize claiming, the assertion of an identity by individuals and groups. Occasionally, as with the politicization of the concept of queerness, understood as a claim to the freedom to be relatively open and indeterminate in one's sexuality, there is a sense of a new category of social identity being forged. Usually, as with much of the feminist movement, it is not so much a matter of creating new identities out of whole cloth as one of bringing into focus and reinterpreting the problems, issues and concerns that define the identity. And sometimes this process involves a strategic revalorization of a socially stigmatized identity, as notably summed up in such political mottos as 'black is beautiful' or 'it's OK to be gay'. The key point is that in regard to identity politics, we tend to have foremost in mind the situation of social groups laying claim to their identities, how they are defined, understood, valued and portrayed. Such identity claiming is an unavoidable part of doing politics and struggling over power between individuals and groups.

Richard Jenkins has argued that none of this should allow us to forget another side of identification – categorization as a process of domination and control – the imposition of identities on groups, regardless of their views about it (1994, 2000, 2004: 79–93). He counsels against an overly romantic view of identification. On the one hand, the claims made within a group to its own definition of its identity are normally bound up with acts of categorizing others, especially those others who are seen as the enemies or oppressors of the group in question. Women and men, black and white, gay and straight, Muslim and Christian, young and old, are defined against one another through exaggerated contrasts. Sometimes there is a pitched battle between relatively balanced forces, but often there is an asymmetry, a dominant voice against which another is struggling to be heard. On the other hand, as in classic labelling theories of deviance (Becker 1963), some find themselves primarily on the receiving end of identity-making, as prosecuted by the powerful. As we saw in Chapter 5, the power of categorization, as the imposition of truth, was a central aspect of Foucault's (1980) conception of how power is embedded in knowledge. As Jenkins also notes, control through categorization isn't always a matter of public contests over identity. Numerous powerful agencies, corporations and bureaucracies are involved in scientifically gathering information about people and classifying them, as types of consumers, insurance risks, swing voters and so on, in ways that are largely beyond the awareness of those being classified (cf. Hacking 1990). These are not cases of self-identification, but 'identity in the eye of the beholder'. Although we need to distinguish clearly between categorization in this sense, and identification, we need to appreciate that the latter is bound up with the former. It is difficult to build identities without categorizing, and categorization can provoke acts of identification where they didn't exist previously.

Amid this language of actively claiming and imposing identities, we need to remember that people are always born into a social landscape of categories and identities, which are encountered in the first instance as just given. A great deal of identifying goes on in commonsensical and uncontested ways. This is not to turn away from one of the main themes of this book – that social relations always involve power. But whether, when and why those power relations and the social identities in which they are encoded lead to social conflict and contestation is an open question. The language of identity politics can become overheated, suggesting that the process of identification itself is intrinsically and quintessentially a point of conflict and struggle, when this manifestly isn't true. Leaving aside moral questions about whether certain patterns of identity ought to be contested, the key empirical question is why contestation arises in some periods and contexts, and not in others. Given that we will inevitably live with and through some set of power relations mediated by social categories and identities, when and why do these 'heat up', and 'cool down'?

## A problem of knowledge?

For reasons already broached, the theorization of identity is particularly susceptible to what I have called 'epistemological approaches' to power in Chapter 5. While I have tried to suggest so far that social identities, both claimed and imposed, usually arise out of sets of structural and institutional conditions shaping distributions of power, it is also possible that more purely ideological and/or psychological processes are the primary locus of identity generation. It is possible that power relations have their genesis in how we think. I want to look now at some perspectives that suggest precisely this, to an increasing degree as I work through them.

There is a longstanding strain of theoretical reflection on the nature of 'race' and race relations, concerned both with historical origins in imperialism, colonialism and world capitalism, but also more specifically with the power-laden dynamics of racial identification in the US and UK, especially between blacks and whites. Successive generations of black scholars have sought to articulate the experience of subjectivity for black peoples, and their relationships to whites, with an emphasis on problems of consciousness, recognition and representation. As the American sociologist and historian W.E.B. Du Bois (1868–1963) famously expressed it in 1903:

> It is a peculiar sensation, this double-consciousness, this sense of always looking at one's self through the eyes of others, of measuring one's soul by the tape of a world that looks on in amused contempt and pity. One ever feels his twoness – an American, a Negro; two souls, two thoughts, two unreconciled strivings; two warring ideals in one dark body, whose dogged strength alone keeps it from being torn asunder (2005: 14).

Du Bois grappled with the chronic elision of 'American' and 'white', at the same time looking forward to a time when there would be no seeming contradiction between 'American' and 'black'. Perhaps Frantz Fanon (1925–1961), the Martinique-born psychiatrist and Algerian revolutionary, put it most succinctly: 'not only must the black man be black, he must be black in relation to the white man' (2003: 62). Both Du Bois and Fanon had sophisti-cated understandings of the concrete history of power relations that underlay these dilemmas of consciousness and identity, but it is their articulations of the psychological condition that has been the most enduringly influential.

In recent years, from the field of cultural studies, Stuart Hall and Paul Gil-roy have extended this line of argument. Both have emphasized that 'race' is not so much a biological category as a discursive one which, while shaped by economic and political processes, nonetheless has its own logic and dynam-ics (Gilroy 1987: 38–40). Thus for Hall, 'representation', in the sense of how people's collective identities are imagined and portrayed by themselves and others in various acts of popular discourse and cultural expression, is central to politics and contestation around race and ethnicity (2003). Gilroy, seeking to move beyond the frame of analysis of black–white relations in national contexts, posits the idea of a Black Atlantic diasporic culture by tracing a trans-Atlantic intellectual history of blacks/Africans (1993). Thus he recasts Du Bois' 'double consciousness' as one between this hybrid, slave-descended macro-culture and its European and New World 'others'.

This work in the area of cultural studies and race dovetails with the field of postcolonial studies, concerned with the continuing ramifications of colonial-ism in culture and politics after formal colonialism has ended (see McLeod 2000, Nayar 2010). Edward Said's (1978) thesis of 'orientalism' has been very influential in studies of postcolonialism and beyond. Said reinterpreted a term that had been used to designate the representation of 'eastern' themes by 'western' occidental artists and writers, giving it a new, politicized edge. Born in a well-to-do Palestinian Christian family and educated in the US, he was particularly concerned with the western representation of the Arab-Islamic world. Influenced by the ideas of Foucault and Gramsci, he argued that, beyond the obvious stereotyping and exoticizing tendencies in orientalist art and literature, orientalism in his terms involved a power-suffused view of east by west. This image replaced the real cultural diversity of the 'east' with homogenizing representations, characterizing non-western cultures as inher-ently weak, irrational and often feminized, and thus justifying the imperial power of the west. Critics have argued that Said's historical scholarship is at times slipshod, that his polemics distort his account, and that he himself reifies a monolithic 'west' to construct his argument (Lewis 1993; Proudman 2005; Varisco 2007). For the present discussion the main point is that Said tends to reduce power to symbolic representation. While he clearly appreciated the economic and geopolitical underpinnings of imperialism, evidenced in his ad-vocacy of the Palestinian cause, as a literary theorist his attention fell largely on the realm of representations, on the misperception and misrepresentation of the Arab world by the west, as constitutive of patterns of domination.

Gayatri Chakravorty Spivak (1999) is another key figure in the field of postcolonial studies, connected to the Subaltern Studies Group discussed above. Trained in English literature and literary theory, and a translator of

Derrida (see below), she has been particularly concerned with the problem of representing postcolonial peoples, particularly women. In a much-cited essay she posed the question: 'can the subaltern speak?' (1988), in other words, do western systems of knowledge and theory inevitably exclude the non-western, subaltern experiences of those in the postcolonial world, or misrepresent them through incorporation into an alien system of knowledge. Are they silenced by how they are known? She has used the term 'epistemic violence' (1987), reminiscent of Bourdieu's 'symbolic violence', to describe this problem of domination of postcolonial subjects by western knowledge. As with Said, while Spivak clearly grasps that there are complex economic and political processes at work in the disempowerment of postcolonial peoples, as a theorist, she addresses the problem as primarily one of epistemological domination.

In the previous chapter we noted feminist debates about whether theoretical knowledge can be legitimated by the theorist's privileged standpoint, for example, women potentially having a better understanding of patriarchy than men. Here I would simply observe that this same question arises repeatedly in regard to these other subaltern subject positions just discussed, with the same problems of essentializing any given standpoint and erasing differences within the category. However, another strain of theorizing has tended to avoid this dilemma precisely by treating the search for a firm foundation for identity as the problem. It is not treated just as an unrealizable goal, but as a source of domination in the first place. Two particular touchstones for this perspective have been the work of the French psychoanalyst, Jacques Lacan (2000), and the French philosopher Jacques Derrida (2000). I offer only the barest sketch of their often controversial approaches here, enough to suggest their implications for some theorizing about identity. Lacan is best known for his theory of the 'mirror-stage' of infant development of identity. Treating the child's initial delighted reaction to its own image in a mirror as a powerful metaphor, Lacan argued that there is at the core of identity development a kind of 'lie', in that the whole, mirror-image of the self nonetheless lacks any depth, and fails to correspond to the child's actual uncoordinated welter of experience and feeling. Thus for Lacan, the self is in a sense an illusion cobbled together out of perceptions of the external world, an attempt to anchor and define something that is ultimately inchoate and indeterminate (Elliot 2001: 53–60). Notoriously difficult to define, Derrida's philosophy, or method, of 'deconstruction' seeks to take what is posited – a text, an idea, a philosophical system – and disarticulate it into its elements, understanding the object proper as lacking an independent existence, but rather constituted through its relations with that which lies beyond it. Thus, when analyzed, the 'text' as an object disperses into its 'context'. Derrida stressed his idea of '*différance*' in this process, that is, that whatever is 'present' (concept, text and so on) is constituted through and destabilized by non-presence, by what it is not. The objects of philosophical scrutiny are understood as radically incomplete and susceptible to limitless (re)interpretation, because their contexts can never be finalized. Thus the completion of understanding is endlessly deferred. In both Lacan and Derrida, identity, whether of persons or texts, is understood through an analogy to language and its indeterminate and generative qualities.

Two places where this approach strongly intersects with discussions of identity are in the work of the philosophers Judith Butler (1990, 2004) and Slavoj Žižek (1989). Drawing on the ideas of Foucault and Lacan among others, and arguing against essentializing tendencies in feminist theories of identity, Butler maintains that identity is radically performative. Selves are fictions, inferred to make sense of the various actions and utterances – performances – that proceed according to culturally defined scripts of behaviour, or 'regulative discourses' in Foucauldian terms. Our identities, whether in terms of gender or other categories, are discursive effects of external power relations, projections of our performances onto the blank and indeterminate surface of the self. On this basis Butler calls for pluralism and liberation through performative transgression of the discursive categories and dichotomies (male/female, homosexual/heterosexual) that bind us, for instance by playing with gender roles, exploring 'perversity' and so on. The self becomes not the thing to be discovered and promoted, but the trap from which we must restlessly escape through performative experimentation. The Slovenian Žižek takes a more specifically Lacanian psychoanalytic approach, mixed with Hegelianism and Marxism, to the analysis of social issues. In keeping with Lacan's image, Žižek treats the self as a traumatic absence or lack, caught up in a desperate search for compensation in the form of fantasized identities projected onto the external world. He sees the major identities mobilized in politics (nations, races, ethnicities, genders) as chimerical attempts to stabilize un-fixable self-identity. Thus the politicization of identity tends toward the extreme, such as casting the Jews as a dangerous and unassimilable 'other' in relation to an Aryan purity, which is in fact a projection of the terrifying irresolvable nature of self-identity onto the German politics of the 1930s (Elliott 2001: 75–7; Parker 2004).

It is notable that we have been discussing the influential ideas mostly of philosophers, psychoanalysts, literary and cultural theorists, and these are fields in which the analysis of language *per se* tends to be the primary method through which the world is engaged. While the social sciences (such as sociology, psychology, politics, economics, anthropology) often emphasize the linguistic dimension of human existence, this is also more counterbalanced by other modes of inquiry and explanation. My main contention in regard to the perspectives we have just been considering, especially with Said, Spivak, Butler and Žižek, is that they tend to seriously over-generalize language as an explanatory metaphor. From the obvious fact that language is an extremely important aspect of what defines us as a species, there is a slide to the view that a theory of language can provide an exhaustive basis for understanding human beings. But it is truer to say that we are animals *with* language, not *made by* language. It is the interaction of language and symbolic processes with our non-linguistic, organic, animal natures that makes us the complex creatures we are (although our minds are understandably highly attuned to our meaning-creating dimension) (cf. Porpora 1997). The results of such approaches can be rather like a version of Zeno's paradox. A classic example: before I can walk from one end of the room to the other, I must first walk half-way, and before I can walk half-way, I must walk half of that, and so on *ad infinitim*. The paradox suggests that logically I can never get anywhere. This is a problem of the descriptive mismatch between an abstract logic of infinitely divisible space and actual finite space. Similarly, treating language-using creatures as though they were, in fact, simply language itself can generate beguiling arguments that nonetheless disengage from human experience.

## An ecological model of identity

This last section lays out the way I have generally come to view questions of power and identity. It owes much to various approaches we have examined above, but perhaps puts them together in a somewhat different way. It also stoutly rejects exaggerated scepticism about the reality and importance of individual, personal selves. My aim is simply to provide a heuristic model for thinking about identity processes that I have found, and hopefully others will find, useful. I contend that to talk effectively about identity we need to view it as involving a complex, interactive 'ecology' among three very distinct processes: (1) the formation and maintenance of selves, (2) the generation of, and change in, social categories of thought, and (3) the role of social organization, both formal and informal, in generating, fostering, using and mediating myriad notions of identity in diverse ways. Much talk about identity tends unhelpfully to collapse and fuse these three aspects into a single image, of a somewhat indeterminate self, possessed of a multiplicity of identities that it draws on situationally, in effect playing different roles according to the social context. In my view this doesn't really describe how people experience and engage with identity. In what follows I am attempting to disarticulate this image, addressing these three specified aspects of identity and identification in turn (cf. Layder 2006: 271–301).

### Selves

As we have just seen, and argued against, one extreme position is to cast doubt on the very idea of the self, to treat it as illusory, as pure negation. But even among more moderate theories of identity, there can be a certain hesitancy to commit to the idea of an 'inner self', fearing that this always invites a misplaced essentialism, a reification of the individual, and neglect of our social natures. Richard Jenkins, for instance, argues for a conception of identity as the dialectical interaction of the internal and the external, as in some sense neither 'in' nor 'out of' the person. As he puts it: 'in identification, the *collective* and the *individual* occupy the same space' (2004: 24, emphasis in original; cf. Mead 1934). While I understand his reticence, I believe that putting the matter this way obscures necessary analytic distinctions between different processes of individual psychology and social interaction. Others, such as Anthony Elliott, whose work is grounded in a certain acceptance of a distinct realm of intra-psychic processes, call for a clearer distinction between 'social identity' and 'the self', and recognition of the tensions between them (2001: 30, 155–6).

I agree with Erikson (1965) that the self needs to be understood as a distinctive locus of emotion, motivation and agency which has developed through a particular history of experiences, bodily anchored in time and space. At times the experience of self may be shifting and inchoate, but just as often, if not more so, the self is experienced as a set of tendencies in one's dispositions, a narrative trajectory through life, a grappling with an inner nature. No doubt our capacity to tell ourselves stories about ourselves allows us to narratively 'clean up' our messy biographies (Bourdieu 2000). But our actual historical specificity as beings, the way our pasts causally shape and constrain our presents and futures, also contributes to that narrative coherence and tension. Very often a core challenge of life is not the self's indeterminacy, but precisely its fateful determination, so difficult to divert in its course. And our personal histories, manifestly a part of the wider human web of histories, nonetheless are experienced as inwardly anchored, and shape our behaviour in those terms. In the context of this book, the point to be emphasized is that the self is fundamentally experienced as a locus of power. Human mental well-being depends on a sense of power over one's life and circumstances, adequate to one's basic needs. Too little power cripples and too much deranges the human psyche. Derek Layder has been particularly attentive to the self's need for power, particularly in regard to interpersonal interaction and intimacy (2004a, 2004b, 2009). He explores how human relationships depend not on the absence of power, but on the negotiation of power relations. Thus he coins concepts such as 'benign control' to talk about how power is involved in the capacity to care for others, and argues that mutually caring relationships will involve a shifting yet framed balance of power between the individuals (2004a: 104–14). Layder also discusses the fact that interpersonal power relationships can become pathological and destructive. But his underlying insight is that this is not the intrusion of power into the relationship, but one direction that power, inevitably a part of all relationships, can take. I ask the reader to keep this conception of the self and power in mind as the discussion proceeds, because the sphere of the self and its interpersonal relations, though definable, is never neatly bound off from the much wider and larger dynamics of power in society. We must assume an interaction. Thus, for example, the very large structures of patriarchal gender relations and the brutalities of domestic violence against women are clearly in a mutually reinforcing relationship. In such instances, micro and macro come violently together. In many and often less direct ways, our small local universes of power are influenced by, and influence, power at large.

## Categorization

Humans manage their relationships to their world through categorization, by constructing taxonomies (a system of mutually defining categories) that help organize the relevant world (Sturtevant 1964). And this of course involves achieving control over, and power in, both physical and social worlds. Taxonomies are generalizing abstractions that tend to develop for utilitarian, often power-laden, reasons. The categories we use to classify people are simply one variant on this larger taxonomic tendency. However, there is the crucial existential difference: we are often obliged, compelled or motivated to locate ourselves and others within these social taxonomies. Moreover, categorization is not static. Taxonomies evolve and change, rise and fall, according to what differences are salient and relevant to processes of control. In societies regulated by kinship categories, lineage groups and their relations will provide a core social taxonomy, while in later industrial societies notions of race and ethnicity, aligned with a stratified labour market, have provided more salient social categories. In the wake of nineteenth century immigration from southern and eastern Europe, American anthropologists of the early twentieth century often developed highly complex classifications of European 'races' based on such things as skull shape (Coon 1939, Ripley 1899). But these categories never took much hold in the popular imagination, while the division between 'white' and 'black', so central to social stratification and power, came to define 'race' as a system of social classification.

Social taxonomies also move from being relatively implicit and taken for granted to much more explicit and contested, according to the political conditions of their use. Frequently the redesign of national censuses involves considerable public contestation over census categories as different groups either seek proper recognition and categorization or to evade the confines of inappropriate categorization. As the data gathered informs social policy, these are matters of serious political import. The language of identity politics tends to direct our attention towards social categories that are often regarded as 'natural' and somehow obligatory. Whatever one would prefer, it can be all but impossible to refuse social classification according to such things as sex and race because of the outward bodily signs that are by convention taken to represent them. Ethnicity, when not tightly connected to notions of race and understood more in terms of cultural practices, can be less rigidly prescribed. Similarly, class operates as a more fluid category because there is an idea that individuals can move between classes according to their economic fortunes. Even if in fact there is limited mobility between classes, the idea that in principle there can be movement tends to weaken the category. Moreover, there can be contending interests in an ideology of class divisions. In the early days of industrial capitalism, ruling elites often had a strong interest in the preservation and naturalization of class boundaries, and were inclined to defend the status of 'old money' against the pretensions of 'new money'. But as such societies became more dependent on a manifestly expanding middle class and the ideological demonstration of 'open access' to the wealthiest ranks of society, principled support of class boundaries, even among economic elites, weakened. There are also other, more 'voluntarist', social categories which nonetheless function as parts of major social taxonomies, such as those around religion and formal public politics. Religion provides particularly complex systems of taxonomic levels: atheists and the religious, within the latter, major world religions, and within those, various sects and confessions and so on. In politics, people identify both with broad political stances – conservative, socialist, feminist, green and so on – and with more specific institutional traditions, such as the Labour Party. With both of these, especially religion, there is a tendency for people to 'inherit' their position from their parents, even though they can in principle, at least in more liberal forms of society, 'switch' or 'opt out'. I am trying to acknowledge the important differences between these various types of social taxonomies and the ways they anchor and elicit identification. But the point is that they can come into greater and lesser degrees of alignment, and that can have implications for the overall tenor of identification and its political implications. For instance, in Scotland, because of patterns of industrialization and nineteenth century immigration, there have been strong associations in the twentieth century between being of Irish descent, being Catholic, being 'working class' and being a supporter of the Labour Party. Recent decline in Labour Party power in Scotland is partly attributable to a weakening of these alignments. The lesson is that a careful analysis of identity processes will generally require us to look into these gradated bases for identification and their relationships, and cannot simply stop at a symbolic analysis of the major categories.

Selves are born into a universe of categories with a particular enduring history. Whether they want to or not, people are usually obliged to situate and make sense of themselves in terms of those categories they are 'thrown' into. As we noted in the last chapter in regard to the idea of 'intersectionality' (Crenshaw 1991) social taxonomies don't just align but also crosscut one another, creating subcategories and sometimes forcing those so situated to make difficult decisions about how they relate to and prioritize their various 'identities'. Moreover, people are highly variable in how they invest themselves into social categories. Some embrace, some resist, and some just go along. Some are attracted to a single overriding basis of identification, others prefer a more loose and diversified relationship with the social categories presented to them. Some find that with time and experience their categorical identities become uncomfortable, and need to be reconsidered. This involves not just reflections on the self, but also reflections about who we want to be grouped with and how. And there are often political – either 'big P' or 'little p' – motivations and effects associated with these decisions. Individual biography, the personal history of the self, will play a role in these decisions. Personal experiences of power will have implications for how persons situate themselves in regard to larger processes of power and identification. This is not to say that larger sociological patterns of identification cannot be discerned and fruitfully analyzed regardless of the personal dimension. But it does suggest that one part of the causal process is being taken for granted when we do this, and that when there are exceptions to the rule and we want explanations, we may need to turn our attention to the level of personal biography and motive.

## Organization

Processes of relating selves to social categories are heavily mediated by various forms of social organization. Indeed, the three are mutually defining. On the one hand, there is organization in the larger, social structural sense. In general, the politics of identity do not arise as an alternative to struggles over social stratification and inequality, but rather as its substantiation. In the US, gender, race, ethnicity and sexuality have become the foci of political conflict because they are associated with various maldistributions of power and forms of discrimination. These are complex, involving distributions of wealth and resources, fair access to opportunities, equal treatment before the law and other factors. But they have hardly taken place in a realm of pure identification. And such maldistributions tend to be compounded by the spatial organization of community, the concentration of identity groups in particular neighbourhoods, regions, employment sectors and so on. Moreover, these aspects of social organization obviously tend to align with those of kinship and family, reinforced by tendencies toward group endogamy. (And once again, the way that gender as a category cuts across all boundaries of kinship and community is something that makes it both central to, and problematic for, the analysis of social power.)

It is not just organization in the social structural sense, but also the more focused formal sense, that is consequential for identification. Most obviously, there are organizations explicitly concerned with the interests and identities of major groups, such as the National Association for the Advancement of Colored People (NAACP) or the National Organization of Women (NOW) in the US. Such groups are both products and generators of group politicization. But, just as social identities, under the right conditions, will call forth organizations to articulate and serve group interests, any organization will tend to generate a degree of corresponding identity. To the degree that an organization is sufficiently formalized that one can be defined as a member or constituent in some sense, it will act as a basis for identification. In their efforts to cultivate support and loyalty all manner of organizations – employers, charities, recreational associations and so on – will be identified with to some degree. This may be in a narrow, shallow and compartmentalized way, with little implication for wider power dynamics in society. But these organization-specific modes of identification can become articulated with larger patterns of social identity. Again drawing on Scotland, there is an association between Protestantism and Catholicism and the two major football clubs, Rangers and Celtic respectively, even amid a marked decline in religiosity. And my own fieldwork in 2001–2002 in the Bank of Scotland, as it merged with the English bank Halifax to form HBOS, revealed that the ostensibly non-political Bank of Scotland nonetheless encoded notions of Scottish identity, and that culturally embedded tensions between Scottish and English identities became contextually salient, a part of local organizational politics amid the strains of merger (Hearn 2007, 2009b).

There are also formal organizations that sit somewhat mid-range between the two types just outlined. For instance, churches, political parties and alumni associations are clearly required to cultivate identification by their very purpose. These are identities linked to the organization itself, not 'free-standing' in the wider social structure. Nonetheless these kinds of organizations often forge connections between the organization-specific identity of allegiance and membership, and the larger social categories with which they are aligned: African-Americans with the Baptist Church, US elites with Yale University, British industrial workers with the Labour Party. Again we get a complex layering and aligning of bases of identification.

The preceding has tried to outline a broad social ecology of identity processes, emphasizing the interactions between selves, categorization and organization. I use the analogy to ecology to suggest that what we call 'social identity' isn't really a single thing with a primary locus. Just as a natural ecology, a relatively stable but evolving system, emerges out of the balance of forces between various elements (plants, animals, microbes, soil, rainfall and so on), I am describing identity as an emergent balance of forces. In the latter case, the balance is between self-making, social systems of categorization and diverse forms of social organization, each with its own distinctive power dimension, but tending to combine into a larger whole. The term 'ecology', however, can have somewhat rosy connotations, of a 'happy balance'. My use of the term does not intend any normative judgment in the first instance. Systems of domination, exploitation and oppression of which we may disapprove can be, in fact usually are, part of an ecology of identity processes. The point is to recognize social identity as an emergent complex, a system in flux, not ultimately centred in any one of these three aspects.

Having said this, paradigmatically, we think of identity, or at least identity politics, as involving the confluence of these three factors, as individuals collectively converge on a project of investing themselves in particular categories, redefining them and organizing around them, in a range of formal and informal ways. This is identity as the empowerment of individuals through the empowerment of the groups to which they belong. But there isn't always congruence. Because these are relatively autonomous power processes, they can also develop more separately. People can develop a sense of personal empowerment through other means, such as using their consumer power to satisfy their desires or pursuing projects of self-discipline, mastery and improvement in their professions, through the development of artistic or athletic skills and so on. These will often also involve social categories (for instance 'musicians') and enabling organizations, but usually in more voluntaristic and less politicized ways. Similarly, like language as a whole, systems of social categorization evolve and change according to their salience, utility and general acceptance. For instance, older and more elaborate systems of reckoning kin relations have generally become more attenuated as societies have gone through the disruptions and transformations of industrialization. And in the early days of the Spanish Empire in the New World, there were elaborate legal rules for racial classification by degrees, called 'castas', of those of mixed Iberian and Indian heritage. But in time these became too complex and dissolved into a simpler trichotomy of Spanish, Indian and Mestizo. These are power-laden categories, but they function in regard to society-wide patterns of social hierarchy with their own dynamic, distinct from individual biographies. Although social categorization may be fostered by powerful organizations, especially states, ultimately they tend to be carried along by natural linguistic processes not fully under the control of any state or group. Finally, organizations too have their own distinct power dynamics, concerning such things as recruitment, membership, resources capture and such. In some contexts they are able to make strong claims on people's identities, such as the role of the Catholic Church in Quebec prior to the 'quiet revolution' of the 1960s that loosened the Church's grip on francophone society. In other contexts, for instance where there are a number of competing organizations of the same type, loyalties may perforce be weaker and memberships more fluid, and organizations more beholden to their members as people are able to exercise options of 'voice' and 'exit' (Hirschman 1970). Each of these three identity factors poses its own characteristic power-problems, which may or may not combine with the others.

Two examples will help to further illustrate the complexity of the relationship between selves and social identities. The anthropologist Saba Mahmood (2001) has sought to problematize certain feminist assumptions about the nature of liberation, empowerment and agency in her study of Egyptian Muslim women participating in Islamic pedagogy through the Mosque movement. This is an option that was not available to women before the 1960s. The women she encountered sought, through the study of the Quran and Islamic doctrine, to become 'virtuosos of piety' (2001: 212), to learn through religious reflection and discipline how to better confront life's hardships, including those of living in a patriarchal society. While not offering an endorsement of the social circumstances these women find themselves in, Mahmood calls for recognition that these women are not simply subjugated and suffering from 'false consciousness'. Instead, they are exercising what she calls 'docile agency', that is, agency that involves the willing submission to a path of discipline (as found in all kinds of social practices that cultivate craft, skill, and ability). This leads her to take issue with Judith Butler's notion of agency as the performative resistance to social norms; as subversion, but never submission (2001: 211). In effect Mahmood is arguing, against a paradigm of liberal progressivism, that 'power over' and 'power to' are not logically opposed. Submission to a particular conception of Islamic religious discipline involving intellectual engagement with texts and doctrines is empowering for these women within the culturally given context, helping them to address their own lives.

The journalist Christoph Reuter offers a nuanced study of the motivations and social forces behind suicide bombing in *My Life is a Weapon* (2004). Considering a wide variety of cases, he rejects conventional explanations of ideological fervour and belief overriding normal rationality and self-preservation. Moreover, while in some of the more sect-like movements intensive indoctrination (something like 'brain-washing') may be a factor, in many cases the positive valuation of suicide bombing becomes a wider societal norm. In these contexts, among the key factors he identifies are: (1) individuals with relatively high levels of education, but also with frustrated expectations about their ability to achieve and maintain a corresponding social status; (2) a social setting in which martyrdom (an exalted status) is highly valued among family and personal acquaintances; and (3) an ideological environment intensively promoting the ideal of martyrdom through suicide attacks, and linking this to a liberation struggle. Thus there is a fateful convergence of matters of personal biography (which may involve propensities to suicide in the first place), of a categorical social identity and icon, the religious martyr, and various reinforcing organizations, from religious institutions to families and social networks. In such cases, Reuter suggests, individuals find a fatal solution to personal experiences of disempowerment through a single, devastating act of power that promises that the suicide bomber will be remembered and venerated. In overcoming the fear of death, one overcomes one of the most fundamental means of domination as well, transforming death into an act of empowerment. Reuter's point is not to justify or condone, but to direct our attention to the complex interaction of self and social identity, of disempowerment and the basic human need and search for power, involved in suicide bombing. Here 'power over' and 'power to' fuse in one ultimate and final act.

## Conclusion

I have argued in earlier chapters that power cannot be reduced to knowledge, and I have argued here that neither can identity be reduced to knowledge. It is power understood broadly, not problems of epistemology, that most helps us to understand processes of identification. Against recent approaches that regard the relatively stable and coherent self as an impossibility, a chimera, I have argued that a sense of unique, personal history of experience is real and constitutive of who we are. These are existential conditions to be confronted and built upon, not illusions to escape from. And I have argued that this sense of self needs to be understood in relation to, in an ecology with, a wider environment of shifting social categorization and diverse forms of both dominating and enabling social organization. But they also need to be clearly distinguished. When we talk about identity we are usually talking about some interaction among these elements.

On the one hand I have tried to suggest not only that matters of power at the individual level are central to understanding the formation of personal identity, but also that these will get their salience from their wider social context and, under the right conditions, the personal will be experienced as reverberating with the social, even the global (cf. Mills 1959). On the other hand, we cannot deduce from the larger social power struggles the resonances they will have for people. Nor can we infer from the trials of individual personhood how these might add up to larger social issues, conflicts and struggles about power. Precisely because there are relatively autonomous processes involved, we have to make separate investigations into these different dimensions of power and identity, and bring them together in an analytic interpretation. There are good reasons to always assume an interactive relationship, but what forms it will take is without exception an historically particular matter that cannot be read off from theoretical premises. But I also mean to suggest that each of us has, as a part of our constitution, a sort of barometer of power, a capacity to gain insight into these connections, because we are always subject to them ourselves. A good student of power will reflect on their own experiences of power and powerlessness, how these relate to their wider environment, and take lessons from this about how others might be doing the same thing, under different circumstances.

CHAPTER 11

# Conclusion: To and Over, Is and Ought

## Introduction

The time has come to pull together and briefly review themes that run through the previous chapters. I do this in three ways. First, I return to the basic question of the conceptualization of power, central to Part I. Then, I consider the narratives we compose about our evolving understandings of power, including my own comprehension that underlies Part II. And finally I engage once more with the question of 'is' and 'ought', more specifically, the question of whether we can extract any moral guidance from a particular assessment of what power is.

## A useful concept

Probably all or most concepts in the social sciences have a metaphorical aspect, using simplifying images to get a handle on complex reality (Boyd 1993; Kövecses 2002). I doubt we can avoid this, so the best strategy is to be mindful of metaphor, to pay discerning attention to how metaphors inevitably steer our thinking. But, unlike literary metaphor, the ultimate test of a social science concept is not its beauty or arresting comparisons, but rather its utility – does it help us identify and make sense of a distinct range of phenomena, in all their variability? And one of the surest, though by no means failsafe, indicators of usefulness, is the way a concept 'beds down' into ordinary language, becoming a part of common sense. While common sense definitely needs to be examined and challenged at points, we should not lightly abandon normal everyday conceptions, of power for instance, because these will encode the practical experience of myriad speakers, whose collective wisdom deserves respect, though not reverence. In what follows I champion garden-variety concepts of power, as opposed to the exotic.

We have encountered a range of approaches to the concept of power. At one extreme we have seen Bruno Latour's suggestion that the idea of power is a chimera, that we should abandon the concept altogether. If Latour is right, then this entire book is irrelevant. But assuming for the sake of argument that he is wrong, and that there are good, practical reasons for the diverse attempts at conceptualizing power that we have encountered, let us sum up some of these, and compare. Foucault's notion of power treats it not as a property or propensity of particular entities, but rather as a diffuse, uncentred aspect of social relations. He emphasizes its micro-manifestations, describing it as 'capillary'. This in itself is a curious metaphorical choice because, while it appears to place power throughout a system at its fine ends, it also implies a cardiovascular system in which capillaries are linked to veins, arteries and a heart, in other words, a highly centralized system. The metaphor of capillary makes little sense apart from this. As noted before, language itself, as a relatively spontaneous but structuring social process, seems to provide a key metaphor for power in Foucault's thinking. But how useful is this? Is the way language undoubtedly guides, usually implicitly, our thoughts, feelings and actions the most helpful paradigm for thinking and talking about power in all its operations? This conception leaves us ill-equipped to talk about and analyze clashes of wills and intentions, deliberate bids at domination, contests over authority and legitimacy. Foucault also emphasizes that power is positive, not just forbidding, which is a salutary point, but not an insight as unique to Foucault as is often suggested. Not even Hobbes in his *Leviathan* conceives of power as strictly a matter of negation (see Chapter 4). I would argue that the general concept of power that emerges from Foucault's writings is chronically vague, and not his best contribution to social theory. Rather, it seems to me, that his greatest insights arose out of his specific contemplation of modern, liberal power, mostly under the heading of 'governmentality', in which he grappled closely with the paradox of controlling through enabling, of 'action upon action'. I feel that his attempts to grapple with the historical particularity of power in contemporary liberal society, and to grasp its genealogy, generates a specific set of ideas about power, that then seep back into a general, ahistorical conception of power, scattered across his writings.

Another predominant image of power is the one I have summed up with the term 'cryptic domination', exemplified by Lukes and to a degree by Bourdieu. Here it is not so much a matter of diffuseness as obscurity. Although he uses a language of 'faces' and 'dimensions', it is difficult not to read Lukes' analysis of power as describing three 'layers', in which a surface of explicit power contests covers, first, a substrate of agenda setting and, more deeply, a core of value constitution, the third and most important face of power. Perhaps this is unfair to Lukes, in that his purpose in formulating the third dimension of power was more corrective, to rebalance the skewed conception arising out of the pluralist/behaviourist tradition of Dahl and others. However the thrust of his arguments tends to present the first and second dimensions of power as misleading, as failing to get to the heart of the matter in the way that his third dimension does. The pluralist conception of power is often unfortunately anodyne, and embedded in a normative defence of American democracy in ways that impairs its generalizability. I question the utility of concepts in which our understanding of power is made to hinge either on its clear manifestation or its obscurity. Power can be either obvious or hidden, but I don't think it makes sense to make these aspects of how we encounter it internal to our conception of it.

Turning to the more 'evolutionary' approaches we explored in Chapter 6, I would highlight two conceptual tendencies. On the one hand there is the social holism of Wolf's approach, picking up on aspects of Marx's concept of modes of production. Here power appears as a general analytic principle, binding together diverse dimensions of social life – material, ideational, organizational, institutional – in a particular sociohistorical setting. Such settings are not understood as social isolates, causally detached from wider human relations. Rather, they are heuristically defined by the concentration of power processes under investigation. To impose a sharper metaphor, Wolf's concept of power is something like a 'gravitational field', pulling together, orienting and propelling complex social arrangement, and also sometimes failing, sending systems into crisis and fragmentation. This contrasts with some of the other approaches examined in the same chapter. Mann, Poggi, Gellner and Hall, all more indebted to Weber, tend to rely more on analytic, multi-part models, dividing power up into its main institutional manifestations: ideological, political, economic (and military for Mann), tending to treat these as distinct macro-variables interacting with one another in ways that can be compared across historical cases. The metaphor here is more anatomical, but I would emphasize that in all these 'evolutionary' approaches, there is a strong sense of nominalism, that concepts of power are analytic strategies for getting a handle on a diverse and messy reality. There is minimal concern with what power 'really is', and instead more emphasis on the utility of certain conceptions for facilitating an integrated comparative perspective on human social life.

Let me return to the contrasting pairs of terms we began with in Chapter 1. There I argued that, while it is true that we should not model our concept of social power on crude analogies to physical power, this should not blind us to the complex interactions of physical and social power. There is a close connection between being powerful and consuming and deploying energy, as the work of Richard Adams (Chapter 6), but also many others we have encountered, attests. I also argued that power, by its nature, cannot be conceived as uniformly dispersed, but must be concentrated in various centres: persons, offices, organizations, states and so on. It may be relatively balanced or unequal between various centres, these may form alliances and become embedded in hierarchies, and the strength of each may wax and wane through time. But without this initial variability and changeability in distributions, it is difficult to imagine why we would have any use for a concept of power at all. Flattening power out, like background radiation from the 'big bang', is of little use. The dialectic of agency and structure also seems indispensable. But this needs to be understood in terms of a gradation, from the paradigmatic agency of the individual acting on intentions, through various aggregations of individuals in organizations, up to large social patterns that affect capacities for agency but are not themselves direct products of intention. Power is not a matter of agency *versus* structure, but of agencies *in* structures, which is part of the account of its variable distribution. Again, without some notion of human agency and the vagaries of its structural realization or frustration, it is difficult to see why we would take an interest in social power in the first place. And indeed, this is the upshot of Latour's scepticism about the usefulness of the power concept. At several points I have affirmed Morriss' claim that power is a 'dispositional concept', and I do so one last time. When we ascribe power to someone or something, we are making broad suppositions, in regard to particular objects, about possible future states based on our knowledge and experience of past states. We are not identifying some mysterious property contained within the object. Here I think Morriss simply formalizes our common sense understandings. Most of us are not as misled by reified notions of power as some social theorists seem to think we are. Rather, we are attentive to potentialities in our environments that matter practically.

I have repeatedly stressed the interdependence of 'power to' and 'power over'. Indeed, this point may be seen as driving the whole book. The entire trajectory of human history, which we saw sketched several times in Chapter 6, is a story of the mutual maximization of power 'to' and 'over.' Complex but flexible hierarchy is crucial to the prosecution of organizational interests in this world. My interest in the general composition of power in liberal society, pursued in Chapter 7, is based on this idea. It is the historical form of macrosocial organization that currently excels at maximizing the combination of 'to' and 'over', precisely by both dispersing power through such elements as market dynamics, civil society, rights to private domain, and individualized opportunities to compete and 'get ahead', while also integrating and orienting such localized power around a larger, albeit sometimes vague, societal project. We might see Foucault's late conception of power as 'action upon action', for which I have more sympathy, as a particular phrasing of this general point: that power is most effective when it channels diverse agents, governs while also realizing subordinate liberties.

## Stories about power

Several narrative threads have helped to structure our argument from Chapter 3 on. Picking up on the previous point, one has been the long-term evolution of the interdependent 'to' and 'over' aspects of power. Thus in the early modern period we saw Machiavelli and Hobbes wrestling with contexts in which the power to achieve ends was largely embedded in princes, their courts and feudal hierarchies, and occasionally in republican city-states. The strength of these historical institutional forms was bound up with how effectively they ruled over populations. As we moved on to the modern period, represented by Marx, Durkheim and Weber, the twinned growth of capitalism and the bureaucratic state, combined with colonial conquest, expanded and intensified power to – to seize resources, produce and trade goods, prosecute large scale war, manage populations and so on. And corresponding expansions of power over, particularly of the burgeoning state, are increasingly justified by recourse to the idea of demos, of the people gaining power over themselves. For all three of our representative moderns, in different ways, there is a strong sense of estrangement from these new, dwarfing forms of systemic power.

By the late nineteenth and into the twentieth century, democracy and the demos itself, as means of achieving power over the new modern political economy, become key objects of scrutiny. As we saw in regard to the Italian theorists of elitism, one response was sceptical, a profound doubt about the capacity of masses, the demos, to rule itself apart from through strong elite leadership, and suspicion toward the promises of revolutionary socialism. Even the counter-arguments of Gramsci operated within the same horizon, advancing the idea of the Revolutionary Party as at once the ideal prince who leads and also the very embodiment of the people. These same debates and concerns carry through to the social science of the post-Second World War US, in which the status of democracy, the existence and role of elites, are key terms in assessing whether the massive political and economic power of that particular state were sufficiently under public control. C. Wright Mills exemplified the view that burgeoning power to was shrinking the people's power over and, in its stead, empowering a new elite, while Dahl offered the more sanguine argument that the balance between to and over was about right, as good as could be expected, and best not unhinged by a severe crisis of faith in the system. By this point, the complex relationship of power to/over has been fully recast, from being a problem for princes to being a problem for peoples.

Running parallel to this narrative thread of 'to and over' is the other I have emphasized – the narrative of the historical distancing of 'is' from 'ought'. At the end of Chapter 2 we introduced Gellner's thesis that modernity involves a growing rupture between referential and moral knowledge; the capacity to ideologically ground moral authority and social order in a natural order is permanently weakened. This thesis has reappeared at various points along the way. With Machiavelli the idea of God persists, but as a distant director of events, separate from the practical assessments of good leadership that preoccupied the Florentine. With Hobbes, writing amid violent conflict over which faction enjoyed God's approval, the solution is to philosophically hard-wire divine authority to *de facto* rulership (within limits), in order to place claims to divine sanction beyond the bounds of public debate. From the time of the moderns on, religion no longer has a monopoly on the grounding of ought, but there are other candidates: the emancipatory logic of history (Marx), the inner logic of society itself (Durkheim). Weber is admirably ambivalent on this question. Increasingly moral authority is lodged in the demos itself, leading to understandable preoccupations with the health of democracy. But this move cannot resolve the question of why the demos should be the locus of moral authority, or what to do when the demos is divided in its moral norms. Wrestling with these questions has been the bread and butter of normative political theorists for the last 150 years or so. Chapter 7 was also about how liberal societies achieve a degree of legitimacy in the absence of a strong, widely recognized or prescribed locus of moral authority (apart from 'the people'). Ideas of civil society and the public/private divide help to provide the 'good fences' that make 'good neighbours', facilitating the creation of sub-communities of the morally like-minded and terms of tolerance toward other such communities. Highly ritualized competition provides a deeply socially embedded procedure, which is imbued with a certain moral authority for achieving outcomes, in its own right. This can of course be challenged, but sheer ubiquity and habituation makes this difficult.

I also approached this question from another angle in Chapter 8. There I argued that a modern tendency in secularized society to compartmentalize, to apportion matters of power to political and economic institutions, and matters of morality and meaning to a more privatized and optional religious sphere, obscures the deeper connections between religion and the contemplation of power. This compromise is itself a manifestation of the same rupture. But if I am right, that the wellsprings of religion lie in the irreducible human need for power, more so than the search for morals and meaning, then this is destined to be an uneasy compromise, largely dependent on the wider principles of compromise and tolerance found in liberal forms of society.

In terms of academic discussions of power, the situation we find ourselves in today is the general polarization or at least bifurcation of theories outlined in Chapters 5 and 6. I have told a story about how discourses on power gradually become domesticated, shifting from the reflections of intellectuals variously involved with politics and under the patronage of the powerful, to the current, institutionally embedded discourses of professional intellectuals serving the educational needs of mass society. I have emphasized how, within this context, two distinct strains of power discourse have developed: the one, perhaps more novel, tending to assimilate problems of power to problems of knowledge; the other, more continuous with a deeper discursive tradition, tending to treat power as a question of evolving social forms. Each of these strains tends to bring with it its own narrative thrust. Evolutionary approaches tell a story of the growing institutional concentration of power, to and over, in organizations and networks defined by various activities (political, economic, ideological, military), and in complex combinations of these (modes of production). Although hardly unidirectional, there is an overall direction of travel. The epistemological approaches on the other hand, in part seem to tell the same story, with the modern state and economy developing ever greater powers of administration and surveillance, while at the same time often aiming to debunk the story of power increasingly concentrated in centres, treating this as a myth which hides the actually dispersed, de-centred, and even illusory, nature of power. The image of the Leviathan is rejected in favour of discourses and actor networks.

Both these perspectives echo longstanding narrative tensions in the western Enlightenment tradition. On the one hand, there is the idea of the gradual emancipation of humanity from being the passive subject of nature, to becoming the self-determining master of its own fate. On the other, there is the narrative associated with Rousseau, of humanity's primitive condition of liberty declining to our modern state of social subordination. Both evolutionary and epistemological approaches preserve, however bracketed off, a certain concern with human emancipation as a moral ideal. However, the very problem of grounding has been driven down into the question of 'is' itself by epistemological approaches. The problem becomes not 'how do we derive ought from is?', but 'how do we derive is from is?', if all claims about 'what is' are saturated with further claims to power and authority, especially when they are about power and authority. I have staked my position at the more naturalistic, evolutionary end of the spectrum, seeing the alternative as leading to recursive circularity. I brashly predict that the older, more mundane tradition of power analysis will show more endurance, while intensely epistemological approaches will exhaust themselves. I think the tortoise will ultimately outlast the hare.

## A qualified 'ought'

The idea of rupture between is and ought can be overdone. I strongly agree with Andrew Sayer (2011) when he argues that we have no deep crisis or deficit of morality, which is quite natural to us and robust. The similarities in moral sentiments among all peoples are more striking than their differences. People everywhere generally approve of benevolence, kindness and honesty, and abhor selfishness, brutality and dishonesty. The 'golden rule' of 'doing unto others as you would have them do unto you' is widely recognized. There are of course deep conflicts over some values, conceptions of 'the good' and methods of moral instruction; and values are often confused with instrumental self-interest. But these conflicts do not go 'all the way down'. Like Sayer, and such figures as David Hume and Adam Smith of the Scottish Enlightenment, I believe that much of morality arises naturally in the first instance, out of the basic dynamics of human interaction. Our very organic need for care and concern from others tends to teach us to reciprocate, as long as we develop in a reasonably caring environment. But as Sayer also observes (2011: 28–30), much social science and analytic philosophy proceeds as though all moral values are simply arbitrary historical, cultural and linguistic constructs, with no necessary relationship to human nature. In social science language the is/ought rupture is often phrased as being between 'facts' and 'values', it being impossible to derive the latter from the former. With Sayer, I reject this extreme position.

However, taking my lead from Hume and Gellner, the problem I have been trying to highlight is not about whether morality has grounding in reality, but rather about the grounding of authority, which, while often central to enforcing morality, is not the same thing as morality. Authority helps to put the moral obligation into the moral inclinations which Sayer and I are confident are quite real and general. What is at issue is not so much the content of an ought utterance as the capacity to make such utterances authoritatively. As the modern, scientific worldview takes hold, the natural world becomes de-coupled from authority, offering only truths about morally indifferent causal determination. From this perspective the natural world ceases to be a source of signs about the wills and moral injunctions of spirits and gods. Instead, ei-ther supernatural moral messages must present themselves inwardly, privately, intuitively, or morality must become a matter of social consensus, underwrit-ten by the collective, sometimes democratic, authority of social groups. Of course, as I have argued, supernatural reasoning is far from being banished by science, but it is hemmed in by it. Often there is a combination of both these principles operating in modern society, where private beliefs, whether supernaturally, ideologically or philosophically anchored, inform, but are usu-ally subordinated to, collective public authority. Be that as it may, the overall effect is a sense of uncertainty about the foundations of authority, at once located both in public convention and private conviction, and a product of endless compromise. In the context of modern liberal society, in which power over oneself is highly valued, but social complexity necessitates coordination with and subordination to a wider society on every front, there is a sharp dis-sonance and ambivalence. And the stories we tell ourselves about power often reflect this, agonizing about the reduction of individual to collective identity, searching for the cryptic sources of our domination that belie and undermine our autonomy.

It has been observed that, while statements about what one ought to do, in the strong sense of moral obligation, cannot be logically derived from state-ments about how the world is, if certain premises about desired outcomes are accepted at the outset, then one can reason one's way to what one should do to secure those outcomes (Black 1969). This is a qualified sense of 'ought', a practical ought derived from more fundamental oughts, that are just given. Let me conclude with a few thoughts about power, arrived at in this manner. If we accept, as a point of departure, that we find ourselves in a world in which the human capacities for both 'power to' and 'power over' are extreme, and there are both profound benefits and dangers in this situation, how should we proceed? If we want to preserve this collective potential, while also protecting against its capacity to abuse those subordinated by it (almost all of us in one way or another), what should we do?

First, we should not rest easy with Lenski's claim, presented at the begin-ning of Chapter 6, that inequality has reduced in the modern world, compared to the highly stratified agrarian societies that preceded it. There is no guar-antee that this situation will persist rather than evolve into some new form of extreme global stratification. Indeed there are some signs that the latter might be happening. This suggests to me that we should aim as best we can at two goals. The first is to encourage a world populated by diverse, relatively balanced and countervailing powers, both between states and within civil societies. Multi-centred arenas of power provide the surest check on over-weening power in any one centre, especially when some overarching community of interest can be established among powers. A notion of power that has no centres is debilitating from this perspective. Secondly, the reduction of inequality, both globally and within state societies, is also imperative. In recent years in the advanced capitalist economies we have seen the argument that as long as a country is prospering, and standards of living are generally rising, it does not matter that some are accruing wealth and power much more rapidly, that relative inequality is increasing. This position should be regarded with great suspicion. When great disparity develops in the capacities of individuals and social groups to command their own fates, then in effect the very conditions of common society break down. When power is more widely distributed, binding people's fates to one another, interdependence and common interest is cultivated. We should be worried by the polarization of basic power in many contemporary liberal societies, characteristically into an inter-generationally underemployed and marginalized working class, a relatively stagnant middle class, and a stratospherically wealthy and relatively autonomous upper class. The powerlessness and over-mighty power at either extreme tend to detach both of these groups, in different ways, from the necessary conditions for moral obligation to society as whole.

Finally, humanity must live with the extreme levels of power that we have today, and probably even greater levels in the future. To cope with that situation, we must on some level reconcile ourselves to it. As just suggested in regard to problems of power distribution and inequality, this does not mean that we have to acquiesce, or take no stance in regard to power. But it does mean that we have to let go of dreams of ultimately transcending, resolving or outwitting the burdens of power. We cannot theorize our way out. We must be powerful, and we must learn better how to do it.

# Glossary

This glossary provides brief definitions of terms and concepts used in this book. Inevitably there is divergence in how many of these terms are defined and understood. I aim for something close to a 'general meaning' but with some emphasis on how I have used these terms in this book.

*Actor-Network Theory (ANT)*
Emerging from the sociology of science, ANT takes the main object of social scientific study to be interacting 'networks' of 'actors' in which actors can be both human and non-human, animate and inanimate, natural and artificial entities (e.g. as combined in a laboratory). In this view, causal processes should be attributed to these networks rather than narrowly to human actors.

*Agency*
Minimally, agency is the capacity for action. Conventionally this implies conscious, willed action, but some social theorists use it more generally to mean any action or cause, regardless of awareness or intent. It is frequently opposed to 'structure' in the sense of rules, institutions and organizations that guide and constrain action.

*Authority*
The power to make commands and have them obeyed, which is seen as legitimate by those subject to those commands.

*Capitalism*
Narrowly, an economic system based on the pursuit of profit through the investment of privately owned wealth (capital), and characterized by extensive and relatively open and competitive markets in commodities, land, financial assets and human labour. More broadly, a form of society based on these principles, both practically and ideologically. Capitalism is a system, but also a regionally varied historical process in which different aspects have been sequentially prominent, e.g. commercial trade in commodities (especially agricultural), the industrial organization of work and production, and more recently trade and speculative investment in financial assets.

*Civil society*
Refers to the range of association, organization and mobilization in society that lies outside of and between the direct purviews of the state and kinship ties. It is normally viewed as particularly characteristic of modern, liberal, democratic and capitalist forms of society. There tends to be a tension

between conceptions that emphasize market freedom and those relating to political association in the definition of civil society. Either way civil society is normally understood as a social good.

## Class
A class is a general structural position in the economy and labour markets held by groups of people. Taken together, classes form a general system of social stratification. Attempts to operationalize class for purposes of research may either define a few major classes (e.g. peasants, workers and capitalists) or many more finely grained distinctions (e.g. professionals, skilled and un-skilled workers, etc.). Used especially to refer to roles in the modern capitalist economy, it nonetheless shades into other forms of social stratification determined by such things as social prestige, heritable status, capture in war and so on.

## Communitarianism
This refers to a normative position in philosophy and social theory that emphasizes the human predisposition to need and form communities, and the view that norms and values have their basis in historically specific communal contexts, not in any transcendent ground.

## Constitutional state
Emphasizes that aspect of the modern state that involves the formalization of the functions and domains of political institutions, and the coordination of the political system through the rule of law.

## Culture
Conventionally used in the social sciences to refer to a system of symbols, ideas and beliefs that coordinate social behaviour and understandings of reality. Older anthropological uses were less narrowly focused on processes of ideation, and tended to also suggest the more general coordination of livelihoods and ways of life through organizations, institutions, and material conditions.

## Cultural studies
A branch of social research developing since the 1980s in which the analysis of culture, in the more narrow ideational sense, is made central to social analysis. Cultural studies tends to draw on linguistic and literary theory for its analytic equipment, and to focus on major symbolic forms found in 'high' and 'popular' culture.

## Discourse
Made popular particularly through the work of Foucault, this term can be taken in the more narrow sense of modes of spoken and written linguistic expression, but is now commonly used in an extended sense to refer to any large, meaning-laden, human creations that govern social interaction, such

as sciences, notions of race or gender. Discourse can also be encoded in such things as architecture, manners and sports. It tends to serve as an alternative to the concept of ideology.

## Division of labour
In the writings of Adam Smith this referred to the practice of dividing up phases in the process of production into specialized tasks done by different workers, thereby increasing productivity and efficiency. Under Emile Durkheim the meaning was extended to refer to the general increasing complexity and functional differentiation of modern society into interdependent institutional and organizational parts (e.g. government with its various subdivisions, economy, religion, education and so on) and social groups and classes.

## Domination
A relationship in which an agent exercises relatively stable, ongoing control over the actions of other agents ('agents' taken broadly to mean anything from individual persons, to social groups, to organizations and institutions). Domination is not episodic. Relations of domination are, by definition, firmly established, and often naturalized and taken for granted.

## Elite
Often used very loosely to suggest a small, hidden, and self-reproducing social group with a monopoly of power. More precisely it can be used to define relatively stable positions of organizational power and the shifting occupants of those positions and their relative ability to control access to those positions. In this more specific sense, elites are a given aspect of complex forms of social organization.

## Epistemology
In philosophy, the study of what knowledge is, and what can be known. In the social sciences the term has tended to become generalized to mean something like 'a system of knowing', and thus there can be various 'epistemologies'. This sense begins to converge with notions of ideology and culture.

## Feudalism
A largely agrarian social system particularly characteristic of medieval Europe in which power is hierarchically distributed through a system of nobility led by a monarch, and regulated by the allocation of control of land, its produce, and populations living on those lands to lower levels of the nobility. In turn, nobles had to deliver various forms of tribute to the monarch.

## Hegemony
As developed by Antonio Gramsci, a kind of domination achieved by intellectual and moral leadership, persuasion and consent, and distinctly contrasted with domination by force.

## Hermeneutics

The study of the principles of interpretation. Originating in problems of biblical and historical exegesis, in the social sciences it has come to mean approaches that see social research as defined by problems of interpretation, as in the study of literature, and by this token less closely tied to the scientific and experimental methods of the physical sciences.

## Identity

In regard to the study of social groups 'identity' refers to the attribution of commonality and temporal continuity by a group to its members, and the corresponding differentiation between groups according to these principles. However, societies also generate taxonomic systems of social identities, with their own dynamics, into which people are categorized regardless of self-attribution. There is a distinct meaning of identity in regard to individual persons, where this refers to an individual's sense of unique and evolving historical being within a specific social context.

## Ideology

A system of ideas and beliefs about the world, including moral evaluations. More narrowly this refers to an explicit set of political and moral tenets (liberalism, socialism, conservatism), but the term also gets used in a broader sense to suggest a general understanding of reality. Terms such as worldview, culture, and discourse can be close cognates.

## Institutions

Conventionally used to refer to large and important organizations, the social scientific meaning refers more to deeply and widely established practices in society. Thus, while there can be educational institutions, such things as marriage, money and Christmas are also social institutions. In this sense institution carries connotations of tradition, custom, convention and ritual.

## Legitimacy

The condition of power, in the form of authority, being regarded as justified according to rules or principles, by those subject to that power/authority. In practice, legitimacy shades into habituated acceptance.

## Liberalism

A moral and political philosophy or ideology that emphasizes the inherent value of the individual and their relative autonomy, freedom and capacity to make choices. Liberalism tends to also value rationality and to see markets, democracy and the rule of law as key means for realizing these ideals.

## Liberal society

A descriptive and analytic term I use to refer to the general historical formation of societies characterized by the combination of liberal values (as defined under 'liberalism'), capitalist economic organization and democratic political structures. These three dimensions are seen as having a functional affinity, and are augmented by well-developed civil society, public/private distinctions and the deep institutionalization of competition.

## Mercantilism
Associated with a period of European colonial and commercial expansion, a theory and system of political economy that promoted the national accumulation of wealth by acquiring precious metals and achieving favourable balances of trade with other countries.

## Modernity/Modernization
When exactly modernity begins is debated, and depends on what criteria are emphasized. Broadly it is the last 200 to 500 years, characterized by pronounced expansion of such things as an extensive market-based economy, large bureaucratic states, science and literacy, accelerating technological innovation, industrialization, faster and more extensive modes of communication, and more normatively, an accompanying attitude that positively values change, innovation and newness, and is optimistic about their effects. Modernization is the process of these changes coming about.

## Nation-state
A modern form of territorial political organization in which the legitimacy of the state and those who control it is based on the consent and support of a distinctive 'people' (nation) who are seen as the state's reason for being. These peoples are variable, and can be relatively homogeneous or heterogeneous in terms of such traits as ethnicity, language, religion or political creed, although a minimum of shared culture is generally necessary.

## Naturalism
Usually, the idea that social science should model itself as much as possible on the natural sciences. However, within philosophy and social science, it can also indicate a concern with understanding human nature, and humans as a part of the natural world, regardless of questions of scientific method.

## Natural law
An attempt to derive law and ideas of right from fundamental principles of nature, rather than directly from divine instruction, but also opposed to treating law as merely social convention. Natural law theory was closely associated with social contract theory, developing particularly in the seventeenth and eighteenth centuries.

## Nominalism
Used in this book to indicate the loose and inexact relationship between language and the reality it is used to represent. This implies that we must

scrutinize and seek to improve that representational relationship, but also be aware of its imperfectability.

## Objectivism
The premise that there is a reality substantially separate from the observer, which is nonetheless cognitively accessible. More broadly an approach to social science based on this assumption.

## Organization
In social science, the integration of people, resources and practices into ongoing patterns of action. This can happen in very large scale and diffuse ways, such as the way languages and markets coordinate human interaction, or in more bounded ways by more formal organizations, such as states, corporations, NGOs or even families. The capacity to generate myriad forms of social organization is one of the most basic aspects of human society, and is fundamental to the formation of power.

## Patriarchy
A system of gender relations characterized by men's domination of women.

## Patronage
An ongoing relationship between a patron and a client or set of clients. The patron is the dominant partner in such relationships, commanding greater resources, and normally providing protection and aid to clients in exchange for various kinds of service.

## Phenomenology/Phenomenological
In philosophy, phenomenology is the close analysis of what is immediately present to the human mind (appearances), leaving aside questions of objective or subjective causes of those appearances. In the social sciences a phenomenological approach is one that sees the social world as constituted through a web of mutual perceptions, thus attempting to by-pass analytic problems posed by positing a distinction between objective and subjective realities.

## Postcolonialism
A field of interdisciplinary study focusing on the enduring effects of colonialism on colonized peoples after formal colonialism has ended. Although there are various theoretical approaches, the influence of literary and linguistic theory has been strong in this field.

## Power
The capacity of agents (broadly defined, see 'domination') to achieve intended and foreseen effects. These effects can be on other agents, or the world more generally.

## Public/private dichotomy

The pronounced distinction between public and private spheres of power and action, especially characteristic of liberal society. On the one hand this serves as a mechanism for distributing and regulating social power at various levels – of the individual, the household, civil society, the state. On the other hand, the boundary between domains of public and private is the locus of multiple and recurrent power struggles in liberal society.

## Realism

The assumption that an objective reality exists beyond our experience, about which we can have valid knowledge, however imperfect. More generally, the premise that this is a necessary starting point for social research.

## Reformation

The long movement in European Christianity, centred on the sixteenth century, which called for a more direct relationship between the faithful and their God, through access to the bible in the vernacular, and reform of the mediating role of the church. The result was the proliferation of Protestant sects, often in conflict with one another, and the nationalization of many new Protestant churches (e.g. Episcopalian, Lutheran, Presbyterian), especially in northern Europe.

## Renaissance

A cultural movement beginning in the fourteenth century in the Italian city-states, and spreading through European elite culture up to the seventeenth century. Shaped by the rise of modern printing and expanding literacy, the movement was stimulated by the recovery and study of ancient Greek and Roman texts, and argued the value of studying humankind and the natural world as such, apart from traditions of religious and philosophical scholarship. The movement stimulated a general florescence of the arts and sciences.

## Republicanism

The belief in a political order in which a people governs itself through its own state, without a class of inheriting rulers such as monarchs. It was a feature of ancient Rome in some periods and of the Italian city-states for parts of the Renaissance period. Most modern nation-states are either constitutional or *de facto* republics.

## Social contract

The idea that the nature of society and social and political obligation can be illuminated by the metaphor of a contract between society's members, i.e. a binding agreement to live under a common system of law and authority. Originating in the early modern period with such figures as Hobbes and Locke, the idea continues to figure in political theory to this day.

## Social evolution
Not to be confused with biological evolution, theories of social evolution propose that the long-term historical developments in human society can best be explained through basic principles of social adaptation to environments, often under conditions of scarcity and competition. However, the entities doing the adapting (societies, states, organizations, institutions and so on), and the mechanisms of adaptation (culture, knowledge, tradition, innovation and so on) are diverse and difficult to specify precisely.

## Social structure
Relatively stable and pervasive (but also evolving) patterns of social relations, often bolstered by, or even constituted through, more specific social organizations, institutions and norms. Prime examples would be class structures, systems of patriarchy, the general division of labour (see 'labour') in society, and in my analysis of liberal society, the public/private divide.

## Society
A relatively large scale, complex and integrated web of social relations, characterized by a certain density and frequency of social interaction. Despite the bounding effects of states that often roughly correspond to them, societies intersect and are porous at the margins, with people sometimes situated between more than one society.

## Subaltern
Originating in the work of Antonio Gramsci and often used in postcolonial studies, this is a general, covering term for various kinds of groups under the domination of a ruling group. Thus class, race, ethnicity, gender and so on can all provide bases for relations of domination, constituting subaltern groups.

## Subjectivism
The premise that knowledge and experience are inherently personal and constituted through individual being. More broadly an approach to social science based on this assumption.

## World system
A conceptualization of global history that emphasizes economic interactions and interdependencies among societies, through markets, trade and, in the modern era, capitalism. World systems theories, often with Marxist underpinnings, treat the maximal sphere of economic interactions, rather than separate societies, polities, economies, states and so on, as the most basic unit of analysis.

# References

Achebe, C. (2000) *Home and Exile* (New York: Anchor Books).

Adams, R.N. (1975) *Energy and Structure: A Theory of Social Power* (Austin and London: University of Texas Press).

Adams, R.N. (1988) *The Eighth Day: Social Evolution as the Self-Organization of Energy* (Austin: University of Texas Press).

Aiken, M. and P.E. Mott (eds) (1970), *The Structure of Community Power* (New York: Random House).

Albertoni, E.A. (1987) *Mosca and the Theory of Elitism*, P. Goodrick (trans.) (London: Basil Blackwell).

Alcoff, L.M. and E. Mendieta (eds) (2003) *Identities: Race, Class, Gender and Nationality* (Oxford: Blackwell).

Aleksov, B. (2004) 'Marian Apparitions and the Yugoslav Crisis', *Southeast European Politics* 5(1): 1–23.

Allen, D. and E.O. Springsted (2007) *Philosophy for Understanding Theology*, 2nd edn (Louisville and London: Westminster John Knox Press).

Allen, L. (2001) *The Global Financial System, 1750–2000* (London: Reaktion Books).

Althusser, L. (2000) 'Ideology Interpellates Individuals as Subjects', in P. du Gay, J. Evans and P. Redman (eds) *Identity: A Reader* (London: Sage).

Anderson, B. (1990) *Language and Power: Exploring Political Cultures in Indonesia* (Ithaca and London: Cornell University Press).

Andreski, S. (1971) *Military Organization and Society* (Berkeley: University of California Press).

Arendt, H. (1969) *On Violence* (London: Penguin).

Arendt, H. (2002) 'From On Violence', in M. Haugaard (ed.) *Power: A Reader* (Manchester: Manchester University Press).

Aristotle (1988) *The Politics*, S. Everson (ed.) (Cambridge: Cambridge University Press).

Aron, R. (1968) *Main Currents in Sociological Thought, Vol. 1: Montesquieu, Comte, Marx and Tocqueville*, R. Howard and H. Weaver (trans.) (Garden City, NY: Anchor Books).

Aron, R. (1970) *Main Currents in Sociological Thought, Vol. 2: Durkheim, Pareto, Weber*, R. Howard and H. Weaver (trans.) (Garden City, NY: Anchor Books).

Arrighi, G. (1994) *The Long Twentieth Century: Money, Power, and the Origins of Our Times* (London: Verso).

Asad, T. (1983) 'Anthropological Conceptions of Religion: Reflections on Geertz', *Man*, new series, 18(2): 237–59.

Asad, T. (1993) *Genealogies of Religion: Discipline and Reasons of Power in Christianity and Islam* (Baltimore, MD: Johns Hopkins University Press).

Asad, T. (2003) *Formations of the Secular: Christianity, Islam, Modernity* (Stanford, CA: Stanford University Press).

Ashcraft, R. (1971) 'Hobbes's Natural Man: A Study in Ideology Formation', *The Journal of Politics* 33(4): 1076–117.

Bachrach, P. and M.S. Baratz (1962) 'The Two Faces of Power', *American Political Science Review* 56(4): 941-52.

Bachrach , P. and M.S. Baratz (1963) 'Decisions and Nondecisions: An Analytic Framework', *American Political Science Review* 57(3): 632–42.

Bacon, F. (2000) *The New Organon*, L. Jardine and M. Silverthorne (eds) (Cambridge: Cambridge University Press).

Bailyn, B. (1992) *The Ideological Origins of the American Revolution*, enlarged edn (Harvard, CT: Harvard University Press).

Ball, T. (1993) 'Power', in R. Goodin and P. Pettit (eds) *A Companion to Contemporary Political Philosophy* (Oxford: Blackwell).

Barnes, B. (1977) *Interests and the Growth of Knowledge* (London: Routledge & Kegan Paul).

Barnes, B. (1986) 'On Authority and Its Relationship to Power', in J. Law (ed.) *Power, Action and Belief: A New Sociology of Knowledge?* (London: Routledge & Kegan Paul).

Barnes, B. (1988) *The Nature of Power* (Chicago: University of Illinois Press).

Barnes, B. (1993) 'Power', in R. Bellamy (ed.) *Theories and Concepts of Politics: An Introduction* (Manchester: Manchester University Press).

Barnes, B. (2003) 'The Macro/Micro Problem and the Problem of Structure and Agency', in G. Ritzer and B. Smart (eds) *Handbook of Social Theory* (London: Sage).

Barnes, S.T. (1990) 'Women, Property, and Power', in P.R. Sanday and R.G. Goodenough (eds) *Beyond the Second Sex: New Directions in the Anthropology of Gender* (Philadelphia: University of Pennsylvania Press).

Bax, M. (1987) 'Religious Regime and State-Formation: Towards a Research Perspective', *Anthropological Quarterly* 60(1): 1–11.

Bax, M. (1991) 'Marian Apparitions in Medjugorje: Rivalling Religious Regimes and State-Formation in Yugoslavia', in E.R. Wolf (ed.) *Religious Regimes and State-Formation: Perspectives from European Ethnology* (Albany, NY: State University of New York Press)

Bax, M. (2000) 'Warlords, Priests and the Politics of Ethnic Cleansing: A Case Study from Rural Bosnia Hercegovina', *Ethnic and Racial Studies* 23(1): 16–36.

Becker, H. (1963) *Outsiders: Studies in the Sociology of Deviance* (New York: Free Press).

Beetham, D. (1991) *The Legitimation of Power* (Basingstoke: Palgrave Macmillan).

Bellah, R.N. (1964) 'Religious Evolution', *American Sociological Review* 29(3): 358–74.

Bellah, R.N. (1979) 'New Religious Consciousness and the Crisis in Modernity', in P. Rabinow and W.M. Sullivan (eds) *Interpretive Social Science: A Reader* (Berkeley: University of California Press).

Bellamy, R. (1994) 'Introduction', in A. Gramsci, *Pre-Prison Writings*, R. Bellamy (ed.) V. Cox (trans.) (Cambridge: Cambridge University Press).

Bendix, R. (1960) *Max Weber: An Intellectual Portrait* (London: Heinemann).

Bendix, R. (1978) *Kings or People: Power and the Mandate to Rule* (Berkeley: University of California Press).

Benn, S.I. and G.F. Gaus (eds) (1983) *Public and Private in Social Life* (London: Croom Helm).

Benton, T. (1981) '"Objective" Interests and the Sociology of Power', *Sociology* 15: 161–84.

Berlin, I. (1969) *Four Essays on Liberty* (Oxford: Oxford University Press).

Black, M. (1969) 'The Gap Between "Is" and "Ought"', in W.D. Hudson (ed.) *The Is/Ought Question* (New York: St Martin's Press).

Bloor, D. (1976) *Knowledge and Social Imagery* (London: Routledge & Kegan Paul).

Bobbio, N. (1989) *Democracy and Dictatorship* (Minneapolis: University of Minnesota Press).

Bohman, J. (1999) 'Practical Reason and Cultural Constraint: Agency in Bourdieu's Theory of Practice', in R. Shusterman (ed.) *Bourdieu: A Critical Reader* (Oxford: Blackwell).

Bottomore, T.B. (1966) *Elites and Society* (Harmondsworth: Penguin).

Bottomore, T.B. (1983) 'Class', in T. Bottomore (ed.) *A Dictionary of Marxist Thought* (Cambridge, MA: Harvard University Press).

Bourdieu, P. (1979[1963]) *Algeria 1960* (Cambridge: Cambridge University Press).

Bourdieu, P. (1984) *Distinction: A Critique of the Judgment of Taste*. R. Nice (trans.) (London: Routledge & Kegan Paul).

Bourdieu, P. (1989) 'Social Space and Symbolic Power', *Sociological Theory* 7(1): 14–25.

Bourdieu, P. (1990) *The Logic of Practice* (Cambridge: Polity Press).

Bourdieu, P. (1991) *Language and Symbolic Power* (Cambridge: Polity Press).

Bourdieu, P. (1994) 'Structures, Habitus, Power: Basis of a Theory of Symbolic Power', in N.B. Dirks *et al.* (eds) *Culture/Power/History: A Reader in Contemporary Social Theory* (Princeton, NJ: Princeton University Press).

Bourdieu, P. (1996) *The State Nobility: Elite Schools in the Field of Power*, with the collaboration of M. de Saint Martin, L.C. Clough (trans.) (Cambridge: Polity).

Bourdieu, P. (2000) 'The Biographical Illusion', in P. Du Gay *et al.* (eds) *Identity: A Reader* (London: Sage).

Bourdieu, P. *et al.* (1999) *The Weight of the World: Social Suffering in Contemporary Society*, P.P. Ferguson (trans.) (Cambridge: Polity).

Boyd, R. (1993) 'Metaphor and Theory Change: What is "Metaphor" a Metaphor for?', in A. Ortony (ed.) *Metaphor and Thought*, 2nd edn (Cambridge: Cambridge University Press).

Bowles, S. and Gintis, H. (1987) *Democracy and Capitalism: Property, Community, and the Contradictions of Modern Social Thought* (New York: Basic Books).

Braudel, F. (1973) *Capitalism and Material Life 1400–1800* (New York: Harper & Row).

Brownmiller, S. (1976) *Against Our Will: Men, Women and Rape* (Harmondsworth: Penguin).

Brubaker, R. and Cooper, F. (2000) 'Beyond "Identity"', *Theory and Society* 29(1): 1–47.

Bruce, S. (1993) 'Religion and Rational Choice: A Critique of Economic Explanations of Religious Behavior', *Sociology of Religion* 54(2): 193–205.

Bruce, S. (2002) *God is Dead: Secularization in the West* (Oxford: Blackwell).

Bryant, J. (2006) 'Grand, yet Grounded: Ontology, Theory, and Method in Michael Mann's Historical Sociology', in J.A. Hall and R. Schroeder (eds) *An Anatomy of Power: The Social Theory of Michael Mann* (Cambridge: Cambridge University Press).

Burdick, J. (1993) *Looking for God in Brazil* (Berkeley: University of California Press).

Burke, P. (2005) *History and Social Theory*, 2nd edn (Cambridge: Polity).

Burton, M.G. and J. Higley (1987) 'Invitation to Elite Theory: The Basic Contentions Reconsidered', in G.W. Domhoff and T.R. Dye (eds) *Power Elites and Organizations* (London: Sage).

Butler, J. (1990) *Gender Trouble: Feminism and the Subversion of Identity* (New York: Routledge).

Butler, J. (1999) 'Performativity's Social Magic', in R. Shusterman (ed.) *Bourdieu: A Critical Reader* (Oxford: Blackwell).

Butler, J. (2000) 'Critically Queer', in P. Du Gay *et al* (eds) *Identity: A Reader* (London: Sage).

Butler, J. (2004) *Undoing Gender* (New York: Routledge).

Calhoun, C. (ed.) (1994) *Social Theory and the Politics of Identity* (Oxford: Blackwell).

Callon, M. (1986) 'Some Elements in a Sociology of Translation: Domestication of the Scallops and the Fishermen of St Brieuc Bay', in J. Law (ed.) *Power, Action and Belief: A New Sociology of Knowledge?* (London: Routledge & Kegan Paul).

Callon, M. (1991) 'Techno-economic Networks and Irreversibility', in J. Law (ed.) *A Sociology of Monsters: Essays on Power, Technology and Domination* (London: Routledge).

Canguilhem, G. (2003) 'The Death of Man, or Exhaustion of the Cogito?', in G. Gutting (ed.) *The Cambridge Companion to Foucault*, 2nd edn (Cambridge: Cambridge University Press).

Carr, E.H. (1939) *The Twenty Years' Crisis, 1919–1939: An Introduction to the Study of International Relations* (London: Macmillan).

Chagnon, N.A. (1968) *Yanomamo: The Fierce People* (New York: Holt, Rinehart & Winston).

Chatterjee, P. (ed.) (1995) *Texts of Power: Emerging Disciplines in Colonial Bengal* (Minneapolis: University of Minnesota Press).

Chimombo, M.P.F. and R.L. Roseberry (1998) *The Power of Discourse: An Introduction to Discourse Analysis* (London and Mahwah, NJ: Lawrence Erlbaum Associates).

Chodorow, N. (1978) *The Reproduction of Mothering: Psychoanalysis and the Reproduction of Gender* (Berkeley: University of California Press).

Clegg, S.R. (1989) *Frameworks of Power* (London: Sage).

Coady, C.A.J. (1993) 'Politics and the Problem of Dirty Hands', in P. Singer (ed.) *A Companion to Ethics* (Oxford: Blackwell).

Coleman, J. (1995) 'Machiavelli's *Via Moderna*: Medieval and Renaissance Attitudes to History', in M. Coyle (ed.) *Niccolo Machiavelli's The Prince: New Interdisciplinary Essays* (Manchester and New York: Manchester University Press).

Colish, M.L. (1999) 'Republicanism, Religion and Machiavelli's Savonarolan Moment', *Journal of the History of Ideas* 60(4): 597–616.

Collins, P.H. (1991) *Black Feminist Thought: Knowledge, Consciousness and the Politics of Empowerment* (London: Routledge).

Collins, R. (1994) *Four Sociological Traditions* (New York and Oxford: Oxford University Press).

Collins, R. (2004) 'Lenski's Power Theory of Economic Inequality: A Central Neglected Question in Stratification Research', *Sociological Theory* 22(2): 219–28. [Special issue: 'Religion, Stratification and Evolution in Human Societies: Essays in Honor of Gerhard E. Lenski'].

Connell, R.W. (1983) *Which Way Is Up?: Essays on Sex, Class and Culture* (London: Allen & Unwin).

Connell, R.W. (1987) *Gender and Power* (Cambridge: Polity Press).

Connell, R.W. (2005) *Masculinities*, 2nd edn (Berkeley: University of California Press).

Connolly, W.E. (1983) *The Terms of Political Discourse*, 2nd edn (Princeton, NJ: Princeton University Press).

Connolly, W.E. (1993) *The Terms of Political Discourse*, 3rd edn (Oxford: Blackwell).

Coon, C. (1939) *The Races of Europe* (New York: Macmillan).

Cornell, D. (1998) *At the Heart of Freedom: Feminism, Sex and Equality*, (Princeton, NJ: Princeton University Press).

Crawford, C.S. (2004) 'Actor Network Theory', in G. Ritzer (ed.) *Encyclopedia of Social Theory*, 2 vols (Thousand Oaks, CA: Sage).

Crenshaw K.W. (1991) 'Mapping the Margins: Intersectionality, Identity Politics, and Violence against Women of Color', *Stanford Law Review* 43(6): 1241–99.

Crenson, M.A. (1971) *The Un-Politics of Air Pollution: A Study of Non-decisionmaking in the Cities* (Balitmore, MD: Johns Hopkins Press).

Crouch, C. (2004) *Post-Democracy* (Cambridge: Polity).

Crouch, C. (2011) *The Strange Non-Death of Neoliberalism* (Cambridge: Polity).

Curley, E. (1994) 'Introduction to Hobbes' *Leviathan*', in T. Hobbes, *Leviathan, with selected variants from the Latin edition of 1668*, E. Curley (ed.) (Indianapolis and Cambridge: Hackett Publishing Company, Inc).

Dahl, R.A. (1957) 'The Concept of Power', *Behavioral Science* 2(3): 201–15.

Dahl, R.A. (1958) 'A Critique of the Ruling Elite Model', *American Political Science Review* 52(2): 463–9.

Dahl, R.A. (1961) *Who Governs: Democracy and Power in an American City* (New Haven: Yale University Press).

Dahl, R.A. (1963) *Modern Political Analysis* (Englewood Cliffs, NJ: Prentice Hall).

Dahl, R.A. (1966) 'Further Reflections on "The Elitist Theory of Democracy"', *American Political Science Review* 60(2): 296–305.

Dahl, R.A. (1968) 'Power', in D.L. Sills (ed.) *International Encyclopedia of the Social Sciences*, vol. 12 (New York and London: Collier & Macmillan).

Dahl, R. (1971) *Polyarchy: Participation and Opposition* (New Haven: Yale University Press).

Dahl, R.A. (2000) *On Democracy* (New Haven and London: Yale University Press).

Daly, M. (1978) *Gyn/Ecology: The Metaethics of Radical Feminism* (London: Women's Press).

Davidson, A.I. (2003) 'Ethics as Aesthetics: Foucault, the History of Ethics, and Ancient Thought', in G. Gutting (ed.) *The Cambridge Companion to Foucault*, 2nd edn (Cambridge: Cambridge University Press).

Davie, G. (1990) 'Believing without Belonging: Is This the Future of Religion in Britain?', *Social Compass* 37(4): 455–69.

Davis, K. (1988) *Power Under the Microscope: Toward a Grounded Theory of Gender Relations in Medical Encounters* (Dordrecht: Foris Publications).

Davis, K. *et al.* (eds) (1991) *The Gender of Power* (New York: Sage).

Dawkins, R. (1989) *The Selfish Gene* (Oxford: Oxford University Press).

de Beauvoir, S. (1953) *The Second Sex*, H.M. Parshley (trans.) (London: Jonathan Cape).

De Graaf, N.D. and M. Te Grotenhuis (2008) 'Traditional Christian Belief and Belief in the Supernatural: Diverging Trends in the Netherlands between 1979 and 2005', *Journal for the Scientific Study of Religion* 47(4): 585–98.

Delphy, C. (1984) *Close to Home: A Materialist Analysis of Women's Oppression* (Amherst: University of Massachusetts Press).

Derrida, J. (2000) '*Différance*', in P. Du Gay, *et al.* (eds) *Identity: A Reader* (London: Sage).

Dewey, J. (1927) *The Public and its Problems* (New York: Holt).

Dirks, N.B., G. Eley and S.B. Ortner (eds) (1994) *A Reader in Contemporary Social Theory* (Princeton, NJ: Princeton University Press).

Domhoff, G.W. (1967) *Who Rules America?* (Englewood Cliffs, NJ: Prentice-Hall).

Domhoff, G.W. (1978) *Who Really Rules? New Haven and Community Power Reexamined* (New Brunswick, NJ: Transaction Books).

Domhoff, G.W. (1983) *Who Rules America Now?* (New York: Simon & Schuster).

Domhoff, G.W. (2005a) 'Who Really Ruled in Dahl's New Haven?', at Domhoff's website: http://sociology.ucsc.edu/whorulesamerica/local/new_haven.html, date accessed 10 June 2011.

Domhoff, G.W. (2005b) 'Basics of Studying Power', at Domhoff's website: http://sociology.ucsc.edu/whorulesamerica/methods/studying_power.html, date accessed 10 June 2011.

Domhoff, G.W. (2006) 'Mills's *The Power Elite* 50 Years Later', *Contemporary Sociology* 35: 547-50. Also at Domhoff's website: http://sociology.ucsc.edu/whorulesamerica/, date accessed 10 June 2011.

Domhoff, G.W. (2007) 'C. Wright Mills, Floyd Hunter, and 50 Years of Power Structure Research', in-text citation from document downloaded at website: http://sociology.ucsc.edu/whorulesamerica/methods/studying_power.html, date accessed 10 June 2011. Also available at *Michigan Sociological Review* 21: 1–54.

Douglas, M. (1986) 'The Social Preconditions of Radcial Scepticism', in J. Law (ed.) *Power, Action and Belief: A New Sociology of Knowledge?* (London: Routledge & Kegan Paul).

Dreyfus, H. and P. Rabinow (1999) 'Can There Be a Science of Existential Structure and Social Meaning?', in R. Shusterman (ed.) *Bourdieu: A Critical Reader* (Oxford: Blackwell).

Du Bois, W.E.B. (2005) *The Illustrated Souls of Black Folk*, E.F. Provenzo Jr (ed.) (Boulder, CO and London: Paradigm Publishers).

Du Gay, P. *et al.* (eds) (2000) *Identity: A Reader* (London: Sage).

Dunn, J. (2006) *Setting the People Free: The Story of Democracy* (London: Atlantic Books).

Dupré, L. (2004) *The Enlightenment and the Intellectual Foundations of Modern Culture* (New Haven and London: Yale University Press).

During, S. (ed.) (1999) *The Cultural Studies Reader*, 2nd edn (London and New York: Routledge).

Durkheim, E. (1964[1892]) *The Division of Labor in Society* (New York: Free Press).

Durkheim, E. (1965[1912]) *The Elementary Forms of Religious Life* (New York: Free Press).

Durkheim, E. (1992) *Professional Ethics and Civic Morals*, C. Brookfield (trans.) (London and New York: Routledge).

Eagleton, T. (1991) *Ideology: An Introduction* (London: Verso).

Earle, T.K. (1987) 'Chiefdoms in Archaeological and Ethnohistorical Perspective', *Annual Review of Anthropology* 16: 279–308.

Elliott, A. (2001) *Concepts of the Self* (Cambridge: Polity).

Ember, C. (1983) 'The Relative Decline in Women's Contribution to Agriculture with Intensification', *American Anthropologist* 85: 285–304.

Erikson, E. (1958) *Young Man Luther* (New York: Norton).

Erikson, E. (1965) *Childhood and Society*, revised edn (Harmondsworth: Penguin).

Erikson, E. (1968) *Identity: Youth and Crisis* (London: Faber & Faber).

Etienne, M. and E. Leacock (eds) (1980) *Women and Colonization: Anthropological Perspectives* (New York: Praeger).

Evans-Pritchard, E.E. (1965) *Theories of Primitive Religion* (Oxford: Oxford University Press).

Fairclough, N. (1993) 'Critical Discourse Analysis and the Marketization of Public Discourse: The Universities', *Discourse and Society* 4(2): 133–168.

Fairclough, N. (2001) *Language and Power*, 2nd edn (Harlow: Longman).

Fanon, F. (2003) 'The Fact of Blackness', in L.M. Alcoff and E. Mendieta (eds) *Identities: Race, Class, Gender and Nationality* (Oxford: Blackwell).

Farfán, J.A.F. and A. Holzscheiter (2011) 'The Power of Discourse and Discourse of Power', in R. Wodak, B. Johnstone and P. Kerswill (eds), *The Sage Handbook of Sociolinguistics* (London: Sage).

Faulkner, W. (2001) 'The Technology Question in Feminism: A View from Feminist Technology Studies', *Women's Studies International Forum* 24(1): 79–95.

Ferguson, A. (1966[1767]) *An Essay on the History of Civil Society*, D. Forbes (ed.) (Edinburgh: Edinburgh University Press).

Finke, R. and R. Stark (1992) *The Churching of America, 1776–1990: Winners and Losers in our Religious Economy* (New Brunswick, NJ: Rutgers University Press).

Finke, R. and R. Stark (1998) 'Religious Choice and Competition', *American Sociological Review* 63(5): 761–6.

Firestone, S. and A. Koedt (1970) *Notes from the Second Year: Women's Liberation* (New York: Radical Feminism).

Flammang, J.A. (1983) 'Feminist Theory: The Question of Power', *Current Perspectives in Social Theory* 4: 37–83.

Fligstein, N. (1996) 'Markets as Politics: A Political-Cultural Approach to Market Institutions', *American Sociological Review* 61: 656–73.

Flynn, T. (2003) 'Foucault's Mapping of History', ', in G. Gutting (ed.) *The Cambridge Companion to Foucault*, 2nd edn (Cambridge: Cambridge University Press).

Flyvbjerg, B. (1998a) *Rationality and Power: Democracy in Practice* (Chicago: University of Chicago Press).

Flyvbjerg, B. (1998b) 'Habermas and Foucault: Thinkers for Civil Society', *British Journal of Sociology* 49(2): 210–33.

Flyvbjerg, B., N. Bruzelius and W. Rothengatter (2003) *Megaprojects and Risk: An Anatomy of Ambition* (Cambridge: Cambridge University Press).

Flyvbjerg, B. (2005) 'Machiavellian Megaprojects', *Antipode* 37(1): 18-22.

Fontana, B. (1993) *Hegemony and Power: On the Relation Between Gramsci and Machiavelli* (Minneapolis and London: University of Minnesota Press).

Forgacs, D. (1989) 'Gramsci and Marxism in Britain', *New Left Review* I/176: 70–88.

Foucault, M. (1965) *Madness and Civilization: A History of Insanity in the Age of Reason*, R. Howard (trans.) (London: Tavistock).

Foucault, M. (1970) *The Order of Things: An Archaeology of the Human Sciences*, A. Sheridan-Smith (trans.) (New York: Random House).

Foucault, M. (1973) *The Birth of the Clinic: An Archaeology of Medical Perception*, A.M. Sheridan-Smith (trans.) (London: Tavistock).

Foucault, M. (1979) *Discipline and Punish: The Birth of the Prison*, A. Sheridan (trans.) (New York: Random House).

Foucault, M. (1980) *Power/Knowledge: Selected Interviews and Other Writings, 1972–1977*, C. Gordon (ed.) (New York: Pantheon).

Foucault, M. (1988) *The Care of the Self: The History of Sexuality, Vol. 3*, R. Hurley (trans.) (New York: Random House).

Foucault, M. (1990) *The History of Sexuality: An Introduction, Vol. 1*, R. Hurley (trans.) (New York: Random House).

Foucault, M. (2000) *Power, Essential Works of Michel Foucault, 1854–1984*, J.D. Faubion (ed.), R. Hurley *et al.* (trans.) (New York: The New Press).

Foucault, M. (2008) *The Birth of Biopolitics: Lectures at the Collège de France, 1978–1979*, N. Senellart (ed.), G. Burchell (trans.) (Basingstoke: Palgrave Macmillan).

Frank, A.G. (1978) *World Accumulation 1492–1789* (New York: Monthly Review Press).

Fraser, N. (1985) 'Michel Foucault: A "Young Conservative"?, *Ethics* 96: 165–84.

Freeden, M. (2003) *Ideology: A Very Short Introduction* (Oxford: Oxford University Press).

Fried, M.H. (1967) *The Evolution of Political Society: An Essay in Political Anthropology* (New York: Random House).

Friedan, B. (1965) *The Feminine Mystique* (Harmondsworth: Penguin).

Friedl, E. (1975) *Women and Men: An Anthropologist's View* (New York: Holt, Rinehart and Winston).

Gallie, W.B. (1955–56) 'Essentially Contested Concepts', *Proceedings of the Aristotelian Society* 56: 167–214.

Gardiner, J.K. (2002) *Masculinity Studies and Feminist Theory: New Directions* (New York: Columbia University Press).

Geertz, C. (1973) *The Interpretation of Cultures* (New York: Basic Books).

Gellner, E. (1983) *Nations and Nationalism* (Ithica, NY: Cornell University Press).

Gellner, E. (1991) *Plough, Sword and Book: the Structure of Human History* (London: Paladin).

Gellner, E. (1996) *Conditions of Liberty: Civil Society and Its Rivals* (London: Penguin).

Gerth, H. and C.W. Mills (1958) 'Introduction: the Man and His Work', in H. Gerth and C.W. Mills (eds) *From Max Weber: Essays in Sociology*, (New York: Free Press).

Gibson, M. (2007) *Culture and Power: A History of Cultural Studies* (Oxford and New York: Berg).

Giddens, A. (1971) *Capitalism and Modern Social Theory* (Cambridge: Cambridge University Press).

Giddens, A. (1981) *A Contemporary Critique of Historical Materialism: Vol. I, Power, Property and the State* (London: Macmillan).

Giddens, A. (1984) *The Constitution of Society* (Berkeley: University of California Press).

Giddens, A. (1987) *The Nation-State and Violence: Vol. II of A Contemporary Critique of Historical Materialism* (Berkeley: University of California Press).

Giddens, A. (1994[1968]) '"Power" in the Recent Writings of Talcott Parsons', in J. Scott (ed.) *Power: Critical Concepts, Vol. I* (London: Routledge) (Original in *Sociology* 2: 257–72, 1968).

Gilbert, F. (1939) 'The Humanist Concept of the Prince and the Prince of Machiavelli', *The Journal of Modern History* 11(4): 449–83.

Gilbert, F. (1965) *Machiavelli and Guicciardini: Politics and History in Sixteenth Century Florence* (Princeton, NJ: Princeton University Press).

Gilroy, P. (1987) *There Ain't No Black in the Union Jack* (London: Routledge).

Gilroy, P. (1993) *The Black Atlantic: Modernity and Double Consciousness* (London and New York: Verso).

Glendinning, T. (2006) 'Religious Involvement, Conventional Christian, and Unconventional Nonmaterialist Beliefs', *Journal for the Scientific Study of Religion* 45(4): 585–95.

Glendinning, T. and S. Bruce (2006) 'New Ways of Believing or Belonging: Is Religion Giving way to Spirituality?', *The British Journal of Sociology* 57(3): 399–414.

Gluckman, M. (1954) *Rituals of Rebellion in South-East Africa* (Manchester: Manchester University Press).

Gobetti, D. (1997) 'Humankind as System: Private and Public Agency at the Origins of Modern Liberalism', in J. Weintraub and K. Kumar (eds) *Public and Private in Thought and Practice: Perspectives on a Grand Dichotomy* (Chicago: University of Chicago Press).

Goldstone, J. (2002) 'Efflorescence and Economic Growth in World History: Rethinking the "Rise of the West" and the Industrial Revolution', *Journal of World History* 13(2): 323–89.

Goody, J. (2004) *Capitalism and Modernity: the Great Debate* (Cambridge: Polity).

Gordon, C. (2000) 'Introduction', in M. Foucault, *Power*, J.D. Faubion (ed.) (New York: The New Press).

Gorski, P.S. (2006) 'Mann's Theory of Ideological Power: Sources, Applications and Elaborations', in J.A. Hall and R. Schroeder (eds) *An Anatomy of Power: The Social Theory of Michael Mann* (Cambridge: Cambridge University Press).

Gramsci, A. (1971) *Selections from the Prison Notebooks of Antonio Gramsci*, Q. Hoare and G.N. Smiths (eds and trans) (New York: International Publishers).

Gramsci, A. (1994) *Pre-Prison Writings*, R. Bellamy (ed.), V. Cox (trans.) (Cambridge: Cambridge University Press).

Greer, G. (1971) *The Female Eunuch* (London: Paladin).

Guha, R. (1988) 'On Some Aspects of the Historiography of Colonial India', in R. Guha and G.C. Spivak (eds) *Selected Subaltern Studies* (Oxford: Oxford University Press).

Guha, R. (ed.) (1997) *A Subaltern Studies Reader, 1986–1995* (Minneapolis: University of Minnesota Press).

Guha, R. (1998) *Dominance Without Hegemony: History and Power in Colonial India* (Delhi: Oxford University Press).

Guha, R. and G.C. Spivak (eds) (1988) *Selected Subaltern Studies* (Oxford: Oxford University Press).

Guthrie, S. (1993) *Faces in the Clouds: A New Theory of Religion* (Oxford: Oxford University Press).

Gutting, G. (ed.) (2003) *The Cambridge Companion to Foucault*, 2nd edn (Cambridge: Cambridge University Press).

Habermas, J. (1974) 'The Public Sphere: An Encyclopedia Article (1964)', S. Lennox and F. Lennox (trans.) *New German Critique* 3: 49–55 (Autumn 1974).

Hacking, I. (1990) *The Taming of Chance* (Cambridge: Cambridge University Press).

Hale, J.R. (2001) *Florence and the Medici: The Pattern of Control* (London Phoenix Press).

Halford, S. and P. Leonard (2001) *Gender, Power and Organizations* (Basingstoke: Palgrave Macmillan).

Hall, J.A. (1986) *Powers and Liberties: The Causes and Consequences of the Rise of the West* (Berkeley: University of California Press).

Hall, J.A. (1988) *Liberalism* (London: Paladin).

Hall, J.A. (1995) 'In Search of Civil Society', in J.A. Hall (ed.) *Civil Society: Theory, History, Comparison* (Cambridge: Polity Press).

Hall, J.A. (2010) *Ernest Gellner: An Intellectual Biography* (London: Verso).

Hall, J.A. and F. Trentmann (2005) *Civil Society: A Reader in History, Theory and Global Politics* (Basingstoke: Palgrave Macmillan).

Hall, S. (1980) 'Cultural Studies: Two Paradigms', *Media Culture and Society* 2: 57–82.

Hall, S. (2003) 'New Ethnicities', in L.M. Alcoff and E. Mendieta (eds) *Identities: Race, Class, Gender and Nationality* (Oxford: Blackwell).

Hall, S. and P. Du Gay (eds) (1996) *Questions of Cultural Identity* (London: Sage).

Hanisch, C. (2009) 'The Personal is Political: The Women's Liberation Movement classic with a new explanatory introduction', at: http://www. carolhanisch.org/CHwritings/PIP.html, date accessed 10 June 2011.

Hann, C.M. (ed.) (1998) *Property Relations: Renewing the Anthropological Tradition* (Cambridge: Cambridge University Press).

Haraway, D. (1991) *Simians, Cyborgs and Women: The Reinvention of Nature* (New York: Routledge).

Harding, N. (1986) *Feminism and Methodology* (Bloomington: Indiana University Press).

Hartmann, H.I. (1979) 'Capitalism, Patriarchy and Job Segregation by Sex', in Z.R. Eisenstein (ed.) *Capitalist Patriarchy* (New York: Monthly Review Press).

Hartsock, N. (1983) 'The Feminist Standpoint: Developing the Ground for a Specifically Feminist Historical Materialism', in S. Harding and N.B. Hintikka (eds) *Discovering Reality: Feminist Perspectives on Epistemology, Metaphysics, Methodology, and Philosophy of Science* (Dordrecht: D. Reidel).

Hartsock, N. (1990) 'Foucault on Power: A Theory for Women?', in L. Nicholson (ed.) *Feminism/Postmodernism* (London: Routledge).

Hartsock, N. (1998) *The Feminist Standpoint Revisited and Other Essays* (Boulder, CO: Westview).

Haugaard, M. (1997) *The Constitution of Power: A Theoretical Analysis of Power, Knowledge and Structure* (Manchester and New York: Manchester University Press).

Haugaard, M. (2002) 'Arendt', in M. Haugaard (ed.) *Power: A Reader* (Manchester: Manchester University Press).

Hawley, W. and J. Svara (1972) *The Study of Community Power: A Bibliographic Review* (Santa Barbara, CA: American Bibliographic Center, Clio Press).

Hay, C. (1997) 'Divided by a Common Language: Political Theory and the Concept of Power', *Politics* 17(1): 45–52.

Hearn, J. (2000) *Claiming Scotland: National Identity and Liberal Culture* (Edinburgh: University of Edinburgh Press).

Hearn, J. (2002) 'Identity, Class and Civil Society in Scotland's Neo-nationalism', *Nations and Nationalism* 8(1): 15–30.

Hearn, J. (2006) *Rethinking Nationalism: A Critical Introduction* (Basingstoke: Palgrave Macmillan).

Hearn, J. (2007) 'National Identity: Banal, Personal, and Embedded', *Nations and Nationalism* 13(4): 657–74,

Hearn, J. (2008) 'What's Wrong with Domination?', *Journal of Power* 1(1): 37–49.

Hearn, J. (2009a) 'The Origins of Modern Nationalism in the North Atlantic Interaction Sphere', *Sociological Research Online* 14:5.

Hearn, J. (2009b) 'Small Fortunes: Nationalism, Capitalism and Changing Identities', in F. Bechhofer and D. McCrone (eds) *National Identity, Nationalism and Constitutional Change* (Basingstoke: Palgrave Macmillan).

Hearn, J. (2011a) 'Domination', in K. Dowding (ed.) *Sage Encyclopedia of Power* (London: Sage).

Hearn, J. (2011b) 'Global Crisis, National Blame', in D. Halikiopoulou and S. Vasilopoulou (eds) *Nations and Globalisation: Conflicting or Complementary?* (London: Routledge).

Heelas, P. and L. Woodhead (2004) *The Spiritual Revolution: Why Religion is Giving Way to Spirituality* (Oxford: Blackwell).

Hegel, G.W.F. (1977[1807]) *Phenomenology of Spirit* (Oxford: Oxford University Press).

Hekman, S. (1997) 'Truth and Method: Feminist Standpoint Theory Revisited', *Signs* 22(2): 341–65.

Helle, H.J. (2008) 'Soziolofie Der Konkurrenz—Sociology of Competition by Georg Simmel', *Canadian Journal of Sociology*, 33(4): 945–78.

Heyes, C. (2009) 'Identity Politics', in E.N. Zalta (ed.) *Stanford Encyclopedia of Philosophy*, Spring 2009 edn, at http://plato.stanford.edu/entries/identity-politics/, date accessed 10 June 2011.

Hill, J.P. and D.V.A. Olson (2009) 'Market Share and Religious Competition: Do Small Market Share Congregations and Their Leaders Try Harder?', *Journal for the Scientific Study of Religion* 48(4): 629–49.

Hindness, B. (1996) *Discourses of Power* (Oxford: Blackwell).

Hirschman, A.O. (1970) *Exit, Voice and Loyalty: Responses to Decline in Firms, Organizations and States* (Cambridge, MA: Harvard University Press).

Hirschman, A.O. (2002) *Shifting Involvements: Private Interest and Public Action*, new edn with foreword by R.H. Frank (Princeton: Princeton University Press).

Hobbes, T. (1994) *Leviathan, with selected variants from the Latin edition of 1668*, E. Curley (ed.) (Indianapolis and Cambridge: Hackett Publishing Company, Inc).

Hobson, J.M. (2004) *The Eastern Origins of Western Civilization* (Cambridge: Cambridge University Press).

Hobson, J.M. (2006) 'Mann, the State and War', in J.A. Hall and R. Schroeder (eds), *An Anatomy of Power: The Social Theory of Michael Mann* (Cambridge: Cambridge University Press).

Hodgson, G.M. (2005) 'Generalizing Darwinism to Social Evolution: Some Early Attempts', *Journal of Economic Issues* 39(4): 899–914.

Hodgson, G.M. and T. Knudsen (2006) 'Why we need a Generalized Darwinism, and why Generalized Darwinism is not Enough', *Journal of Economic Behavior and Organization* 61: 1–19.

Holton, R.J. (2003) 'Talcott Parsons: Conservative Apologist or Irreplaceable Icon?', in G. Ritzer and B. Smart (eds) *Handbook of Social Theory* (London: Sage).

hooks, b. (1984) *Feminist Theory: From Margin to Center* (Boston: South End Press).

Horton, R. (1967) 'African Traditional Thought in Western Science', *Africa* 37: 50–71, 155–87.

Hughes, H.S. (1965) 'Gaetano Mosca and the Political Lessons of History', in J.H. Meisle (ed.) *Pareto and Mosca* (Englewood Cliffs, NJ: Prentice-Hall, Inc.).

Hume, D. (1978) *A Treatise of Human Nature*, 2nd edn, L.A. Selby-Bigge and P.H. Nidditch (eds) (Oxford: Clarendon).

Hunter, F. (1953) *Community Power Structure: A Study of Decision Makers* (Chapel Hill: University of North Carolina Press).

Ingham, G. (2004) *The Nature of Money* (Cambridge: Polity).

Ingham, G. (2008) *Capitalism* (Cambridge: Polity).

Jaggar, A.M. (1983) *Feminist Politics and Human Nature* (Brighton, UK: Harvester Press).

Jenkins, R. (1994) 'Rethinking Ethnicity: Identity, Categorization and Power', *Ethnic and Racial Studies* 17(2): 197–223.

Jenkins, R. (2000) 'Categorization: Identity, Social Process and Epistemology', *Current Sociology* 48(3): 7–25.

Jenkins, R. (2002) *Pierre Bourdieu*, 2nd edn (London: Routledge).

Jenkins, R. (2004) *Social Identity*, 2nd edn (London: Routledge).

Kaufman, S.J. et al. (eds) (2007) *The Balance of Power in World History*, (Basingstoke: Palgrave Macmillan).

Kehoe, A.B. (2006) *The Ghost Dance: Ethnohistory and Revitalization* (Long Grove, IL: Waveland Press).

Kelly, M. (ed.) (1994) *Critique and Power: Recasting the Foucault/Habermas Debate* (Cambridge, MA: MIT Press).

Klein, L.F. (2004) *Women and Men in World Cultures* (New York: McGraw-Hill).

Kolegar, F. (1967) 'The Elite and the Ruling Class: Pareto and Mosca Re-Examined' *The Review of Politics* 29(3): 354–69.

Komter, A. (1991) 'Gender, Power and Feminist Theory', in K. Davis *et al.* (eds) *The Gender of Power* (London: Sage).

Kövecses, Z. (2002) *Metaphor: A Practical Introduction* (Oxford and New York: Oxford University Press)

Lacan, J. (2000) 'The Mirror Stage', in P. Du Gay *et al.* (eds), *Identity: A Reader* (London: Sage).

Lakoff, G. (1995) 'Metaphor, Morality, and Politics, Or, Why Conservatives Have Left Liberals In the Dust', *Social Research* 62(2): 177–213.

Lakoff, G. (2002) *Moral Politics: How Liberals and Conservatives Think*, 2nd edn (Chicago and London: University of Chicago Press)

Lakoff, G. and M. Johnson (1980) *Metaphors We Live By* (Chicago and London: University of Chicago Press).

Landes, J.B. (ed) (1998) *Feminism, The Public and the Private* (Oxford: Oxford University Press).

Lansing, J.S. (2003) 'Complex Adaptive Systems', *Annual Review of Anthropology* 32: 183–204.

Latour, B. (1986), 'The Powers of Association', in J. Law (ed.) *Power, Action and Belief: A New Sociology of Knowledge?* (London: Routledge & Kegan Paul).

Latour, B. (1987) *Science in Action: How to Follow Scientists and Engineers through Society* (Cambridge, MA: Harvard University Press).

Latour, B. (1993) *We Have Never Been Modern*, C. Porter (trans.) (Cambridge, MA: Harvard University Press).

Latour, B. (2000) 'When Things Strike Back: A Possible Contribution of "Science Studies" to the Social Sciences', *British Journal of Sociology* 51(1): 107–23.

Law, J. (1991) 'Power, discretion and strategy', in J. Law (ed.) *A Sociology of Monsters: Essays on Power, Technology and Domination* (London: Routledge).

Law, J. (1992) 'Notes on the Theory of the Actor Network: Ordering, Strategy and Heterogeneity', paper published by the Centre for Science Studies, Lancaster University, Lancaster LA1 4YN.

Layder, D. (1985) 'Power, Structure and Agency', *Journal for the Theory of Social Behaviour* 15: 131–49.

Layder, D. (2004a) *Emotion in Social Life: the Lost Heart of Society* (London: Sage).

Layder, D. (2004b) *Social and Personal Identity: Understanding Yourself* (London: Sage).

Layder, D. (2006) *Understanding Social Theory*, 2nd edn (London: Sage).

Layder, D. (2009) *Intimacy and Power: the Dynamics of Personal Relationships in Modern Society* (Basingstoke: Palgrave Macmillan).

Leacock, E.B. (1972) 'Introduction', in F. Engels, *The Origin of the Family, Private Property and the State*, E.B. Leacock (ed.) (New York: International Publishers).

Ledbetter, J. (2011) *Unwarranted Influence: Dwight D. Eisenhower and the Military–Industrial Complex* (New Haven and London: Yale University Press).

Lenski, G. (1952) 'American Social Classes: Statistical Strata or Social Groups?' *American Journal of Sociology* 58: 139–49.

Lenski, G. (1954) 'Status Crystallization: A Non-Vertical Dimension of Social Status', *American Sociological Review* 19: 405–13.

Lenski, G. (1966) *Power and Privilege: A Theory of Social Stratification* (New York: McGraw-Hill).

Lewis, B. (1993) *Islam and the West* (Oxford: Oxford University Press).

Lipset, S.M. (1968) 'Introduction', in R. Michels, *Political Parties*, 2nd edn, E. Paul and C. Paul (trans.) (New York: Free Press).

Lukes, S. (1973a) *Emile Durkheim, His Life and Work: A Historical and Critical Study* (London: Allen Lane).

Lukes, S. (1973b) *Individualism* (Oxford: Basil Blackwell).

Lukes, S. (1974) *Power: A Radical View* (Basingstoke: Macmillan)

Lukes, S. (2005) *Power: A Radical View*, 2nd edn (Basingstoke: Palgrave Macmillan).

Lukes, S. and L. Haglund (2005) 'Power and Luck', *Archive European Sociologie* 46(1): 45–66.

MacCormack, C. and M. Strathern (eds) (1980) *Nature, Culture and Gender* (Cambridge: Cambridge University Press).

Machiavelli, N. (1970) *The Discourses*, B. Crick (ed.) (Harmondsworth: Penguin).

Machiavelli, N. (1985) *The Prince*, H.C. Mansfield Jr (trans.) (Chicago: University of Chicago Press).

MacInnes, J. (1998) *The End of Masculinity* (Buckingham and Philadelphia: Open University Press).

MacKinnon, C. (1987) *Feminism Unmodified: Discourses on Life and Law* (Cambridge, MA: University of Harvard Press).

Mahmood, S. (2001) 'Feminist Theory, Embodiment, and the Docile Agent: Some Reflections on the Egyptian Islamic Revival', *Cultural Anthropology* 16(2): 202–36.

Malesevic, S. and M. Haugaard (eds) (2007) *Ernest Gellner and Contemporary Social Thought* (Cambridge; Cambridge University Press).

Malinowski, B. (1979) 'The Role of Magic and Religion', in W.A. Lessa and E.Z. Vogt (eds) *Reader in Comparative Religion: An Anthropological Approach*, 4th edn (New York: Harper & Row).

Mann, M. (1986) *The Sources of Social Power, Volume I: A History of Power from the Beginning to A.D. 1760* (Cambridge: Cambridge University Press).

Mann, M. (1988) *States, War and Capitalism* (Oxford and Cambridge, MA: Blackwell).

Mann, M. (1993) *The Sources of Social Power, Volume II: The Rise of Classes and Nation-States, 1760–1914* (Cambridge: Cambridge University Press).

Mann, M. (1995) 'Sources of Variation in Working-Class Movements in Twentieth-Century Europe', *New Left Review*, July–August 1995, I/212: 14–54.

Mann, M. (2004) *Fascists* (Cambridge: Cambridge University Press).

Mann, M. (2005) *The Dark Side of Democracy: Explaining Ethnic Cleansing* (Cambridge: Cambridge University Press).

Mann, M. (2006) 'The Sources of Social Power Revisited: A Response to Criticism', in J.A. Hall and R. Schroeder (eds), *An Anatomy of Power: The Social Theory of Michael Mann* (Cambridge: Cambridge University Press).

Mannheim, K. (1936) *Ideology and Utopia*, L. Wirth and E. Shils (trans.) (New York: Harcourt, Brace & World, Inc.).

Martin, J.P. and B. Voorhies (1975) *Female of the Species* (New York: Columbia University Press).

McLaughlin, J. (2003) *Feminist Social and Political Theory: Contemporary Debates and Dialogues* (Basingstoke: Palgrave Macmillan).

McLellan, D. (1995) *Ideology*, 2nd edn (Minneapolis: University of Minnesota Press).

McLeod, J. (2000) *Beginning Postcolonialism* (Manchester: Manchester University Press).

McNay, L. (1994) *Foucault: A Critical Introduction* (Cambridge: Polity Press).

McNeill, W.H. (1982) *The Pursuit of Power* (Chicago: University of Chicago Press).

Mead, G.H. (1934) *Mind, Self and Society from the Standpoint of a Social Behaviorist*, C.W. Morris (ed.) (Chicago: University of Chicago Press).

Meisle, J.H. (ed.) (1965a) *Pareto and Mosca* (Englewood Cliffs, NJ: Prentice-Hall, Inc.).

Meisle, J.H. (1965b) 'Introduction: Pareto and Mosca', in J.H. Meisle (ed.) *Pareto and Mosca* (Englewood Cliffs, NJ: Prentice-Hall, Inc.).

Meyer, J. (1991) 'Power and Love: Conflicting Conceptual Schemata', in K. Davis *et al.* (eds) *The Gender of Power* (London: Sage).

Michels, R. (1968[1911]) *Political Parties*, E. Paul and C. Paul (trans.) (New York: Free Press).

Miller, D.C. (1958), 'Industry and Community Power Structure: A Comparative Study of an American and an English City', *American Sociological Review* 23: 9–15.

Mills, C.W. (1956) *The Power Elite* (New York: Oxford University Press).

Mills, C.W. (1958) 'The Structure of Power in American Society', *British Journal of Sociology* 9(1): 29–41.

Mills, C.W. (1959) *The Sociological Imagination* (Oxford: Oxford University Press).

Mills, C.W. (1962) *The Marxists* (New York: Dell).

Molotch, H. (1976) 'The City as Growth Machine', *American Journal of Sociology* 82: 309–30.

Moore, B. Jr (1984) *Privacy: Studies in Social and Cultural History* (London: M.E. Sharpe, Inc.).

Moraga, C. and F. Anzaldua (eds) (1983) *This Bridge Called My Back: Writings by Radical Women of Color* (New York: Kitchen Table Press).

Morris, B. (1987) *Anthropological Studies of Religion: An Introductory Text* (Cambridge: Cambridge University Press).

Morriss, P. (2002) *Power: A Philosophical Analysis*, 2nd edn (Manchester: Manchester University Press).

Mosca, G. (1939) *The Ruling Class, Elementi di Scienza Politica*, A. Livingston (ed.), H.D. Kahn (trans.) (New York: McGraw-Hill).

Mounce, H.O. (1999) *Hume's Naturalism* (London: Routledge).

Mouzelis, N.P. (2008) *Modern and Postmodern Social Theorizing: Bridging the Divide* (Cambridge: Cambridge University Press).

Mueller-Vollmer, K. (ed.) (1988) *The Hermeneutics Reader: Texts of the German Tradition from the Enlightenment to the Present* (New York: Contimuum).

Mukhopadhyay, C. and P. Higgins (1988) 'Anthropological Studies of Women's Status Revisited: 1977–1987', *Annual Review of Anthropology* 17: 461–95.

Najemy, J.M. (1999) 'Papirius and the Chickens, or Machiavelli on the Necessity of Interpreting Religion', *Journal of the History of Ideas* 60(4): 659–81.

Nayar, P.K. (2010) *Postcolonialism: A Guide for the Perplexed* (London and New York: Continuum)

Nederman, C.J. (1999) 'Amazing Grace: Fortune, God and Free Will in Machiavelli's Thought', *Journal of the History of Ideas* 60(4): 617–38.

Neihardt, J.G. (1979) *Black Elk Speaks: Being the Life Story of a Holy Man of the Oglala Sioux*, revised edn (Lincoln and London: University of Nebraska Press).

Niebuhr, R. (1938) *Beyond Tragedy: Essays on the Christian Interpretation of History* (London: Nisbet).

Nolan, P. and G. Lenski (2006) *Human Societies: An Introduction to Macrosociology*, 10th edn (Boulder, CO and London: Paradigm Publishers).

Nussbaum, M. (1999) *Sex and Justice* (New York: Oxford University Press).

Okin, S.M. (1991) 'Gender, the Public and the Private', in D. Held (ed.) *Political Theory Today* (Stanford: Stanford University Press).

Ollman, B. (1976) *Alienation: Marx's Conception of Man in Capitalist Society*, 2nd edn (Cambridge: Cambridge University Press).

Olsen, M.E. (ed.) (1970) *Power in Societies* (New York: Macmillan).

Olson, D.V.A. (2002) 'Competing Notions of Religious Competition and Conflict in Theories of Religious Economies', in T. Jelen (ed.) *Sacred Canopies, Sacred Markets: Essays on Religious Markets and Religious Pluralism* (Lanham, MD: Rowman & Littlefield).

O'Neill, J. (1987) 'The Disciplinary Society: from Weber to Foucault', *British Journal of Sociology* 37: 42–60.

Ortner, S. (1974) 'Is Female to Male as Nature is to Culture?', in M.Z. Rosaldo and L. Lamphere (eds) *Women, Culture and Society* (Stanford: Stanford University Press).

*Oxford Dictionaries Online* (2011a) 'Authority', in Oxford Dictionaries Online at http://oxforddictionaries.com/definition/authority, date accessed 10 June 2011.

*Oxford Dictionaries Online* (2011b) 'Competition', in Oxford Dictionaries Online at http://oxforddictionaries.com/definition/competition#m_en_ gb0168020, date accessed 10 June 2011.

*Oxford Dictionaries Online* (2011c) 'Legitimate', in Oxford Dictionaries Online at http://oxforddictionaries.com/definition/legitimate, date accessed 10 June 2011.

Palmer, R.E. (1969) *Hermeneutics: Interpretation Theory in Schleiermacher, Dilthey, Heidegger, and Gadamer* (Evanston, IL: Northwestern University Press).

Pareto, V. (1963[1916]) *Treatise on General Sociology* (New York: Dover).

Pareto, V. (1968[1901]) *The Rise and Fall of the Elites: An Application of Theoretical Sociology* (Totowa, NJ: Bedminster Press).

Pareto, V. (1984[1920]) *The Transformation of Democracy*, C.H. Powers (ed.) R. Girola (trans.) (London: Transaction Books).

Parker, I. (2004) *Slavoj Žižek: A Critical Introduction* (London: Pluto Press).

Parsons, T. (1977) *The Evolution of Societies*, J. Toby (ed.) (Englewood Cliffs, NJ: Prentice-Hall).

Parsons, T. (1979) 'Religious Perspectives in Sociology and Social Psychology', in W.A. Lessa and E.Z. Vogt (eds), *Reader in Comparative Religion: An Anthropological Approach*, 4th edn (New York: Harper & Row)

Parsons, T. (1994[1957]) 'The Distribution of Power in American Society', in J. Scott (ed.) *Power: Critical Concepts, Vol. III* (London: Routledge).

Parsons, T. (2002[1963]) 'On the Concept of Political Power', in M. Haugaard (ed.) *Power: A Reader* (Manchester: Manchester University Press).

Pateman, C. (1989) *The Disorder of Women: Democracy, Feminism and Political Theory* (Stanford: Stanford University Press).

Pateman, C. (1998) 'The Patriarchal Welfare State', in J.B. Landes (ed), *Feminism, The Public and the Private* (Oxford: Oxford University Press).

Pellegrin, R.J. and C.H. Coates (1956) 'Absentee-Owned Corporations and Community Power Structure', *American Journal of Sociology* 61: 413–19.

Percy, W. (1954) *The Message in the Bottle: How Queer Man Is, How Queer Language Is, and What One Has to Do with the Other* (New York: Farrar, Strauss and Giroux).

Pew Forum (2008) *U.S. Religious Landscape Survey: Religious Affiliations: Diverse and Dynamic* (Washington DC: Pew Forum on Religion and Public Life).

Pierson, C. (1991) *Beyond The Welfare State* (University Park, PA: Pennsylvania State University Press).

Pinto, L. (1999) 'Theory in Practice', in R. Shusterman (ed.) *Bourdieu: A Critical Reader* (Oxford: Blackwell).

Plamenatz, J. (1970) *Ideology* (London: Pall Mall Press).

Plamenatz, J. (1992) *Man and Society: Political and Social Theories from Machiavelli to Marx, Vol. 1*, revised edn, M.E. Plamenatz and R. Wokler (eds) (London and New York: Longman).

Poggi, G. (1978) *The Development of the Modern State: A Sociological Introduction* (Stanford, CA: Stanford University Press).

Poggi, G. (1990) *The State: Its Nature, Development and Prospects* (Stanford, CA: Stanford University Press).

Poggi, G. (2000) *Durkheim* (Oxford: Oxford University Press).

Poggi, G. (2001) *Forms of Power* (Cambridge: Polity).

Poggi, G. (2006) 'Political Power Un-Manned: A Defence of the Holy Trinity from Mann's Military Attack', in J.A. Hall and R. Schroeder (eds) *An Anatomy of Power: The Social Theory of Michael Mann* (Cambridge: Cambridge University Press).

Polanyi, K. (1957) *The Great Transformation: The Political and Economic Origins of our Time* (Boston: Beacon Press).

Polanyi, K. (1971) 'The Economy as Instituted Process', in G. Dalton (ed.) *Primitive, Archaic and Modern Economies: Essays of Karl Polanyi* (Boston, MA: Beacon Press).

Polsby, N.W. (1960) 'How to Study Community Power: The Pluralist Alternative', *Journal of Politics* 22(3): 474–84.

Polsby, N.W. (1963) *Community Power and Political Theory* (New Haven: Yale University Press).

Pomeranz, K. (2000) *The Great Divergence: China, Europe and the Making of the Modern World Economy* (Princeton, NJ: Princeton University Press).

Porpora, D. V. (1997) 'The Caterpillar's Question: Contesting Anti-Humanism's Contestations', *Journal for the Theory of Social Behaviour* 27(2/3): 243-63.

Pounds, N.J.G. (1990) *An Historical Geography of Europe* (Cambridge: Cambridge University Press).

Powers, C.H. (1984) 'Introduction: The Life and Times of Vilfredo Pareto', in V. Pareto, *The Transformation of Democracy*, C.H. Powers (ed.) R. Girola (trans.) (London: Transaction Books).

Powers, C.H. (1987) *Vilfredo Pareto* (London: Sage).

Proudman, M.F. (2005) 'Disraeli as an Orientalist: The Polemical Errors of Edward Said', *Journal of the Historical Society*, 5(4): 547–68.

Quinn, N. (1977) 'Anthropological Studies on Women's Status', *Annual Review of Anthropology* 6: 181–225.

Rabinow, P. (ed.) (1984) *The Foucault Reader* (New York: Pantheon Books).

Rabinow, P. and W.M. Sullivan (eds) (1979) *Interpretive Social Science: A Reader* (Berkeley: University of California Press).

Reeve, A. (1995) 'Property', in R.E. Goodin and P. Pettit (eds), *A Companion to Contemporary Political Philosophy* (Oxford: Blackwell).

Reich, R. (2008) *Supercapitalism: The Battle for Democracy in an Age of Big Business* (Cambridge: Icon Books).

Reiter, R.R. (1975) 'Men and Women in the South of France: Public and Private Domains', in R.R. Reiter (ed.) *Toward an Anthropology of Women*, (New York: Monthly Review Press).

Reus-Smit, C. (2002) 'The Idea of History and History with Ideas', in S. Hobden and J.M. Hobson (eds) *Historical Sociology of International Relations* (Cambridge: Cambridge University Press).

Reuter, C. (2004) *My Life Is a Weapon: A Modern History of Suicide Bombing* (Princeton, NJ: Princeton University Press).

Ripley, W. Z. (1899) *The Races of Europe: A Sociological Study* (New York: D. Appleton & Co.).

Rosa, E.A. *et al.* (1988) 'Energy and Society', *Annual Review of Sociology* 14: 149–72.

Rosaldo, M. Z. (1974) 'Women, Culture and Society: A Theoretical Overview', in M.Z. Rosaldo and L. Lamphere (eds) *Women, Culture and Society* (Stanford: Stanford University Press).

Rosaldo, M.Z. (1980) 'The Use and Abuse of Anthropology: Reflections of Feminism and Cross Cultural Understanding', *Signs* 5(3): 389–417.

Rosinski, H. (1965) *Power and Human Destiny*, R.P. Stebbins (ed.) (London: Pall Mall Press).

Rossi, P.H. (1960) 'Power and Community Structure', *Midwest Journal of Political Science* 4(4): 390–401.

Rouse, J. (2003) 'Power/Knowledge', in G. Gutting (ed.) *The Cambridge Companion to Foucault*, 2nd edn (Cambridge: Cambridge University Press).

Russell, B. (2004) *Power: A New Social Analysis* (Basingstoke: Palgrave Macmillan).

Sacks, K. (1975) 'Engels Revisited: Women, the Organization of Production, and Private Property', in R.R. Reiter (ed.) *Toward and Anthropology of Women* (New York: Monthly Review Press).

Said, E. (1978) *Orientalism* (New York: Vintage Books).

Sanday, P.R. (1973) 'Toward a Theory of the Status of Women', *American Anthropologist* 75: 1682–1700.

Sanday, P.R. (1981) *Female Power and Male Dominance: On the Origins of Sexual Inequality* (Cambridge: Cambridge University Press).

Sawicki, J. (2003) 'Queering Foucault and the Subject of Feminism', in G. Gutting (ed.) *The Cambridge Companion to Foucault*, 2nd edn (Cambridge: Cambridge University Press).

Sayer, A. (2011) *Why Things Matter to People: Social Science, Values and Ethical Life* (Cambridge: Cambridge University Press)

Schattschneider, E.E. (1960) *The Semisovereign People: A Realist's View of Democracy in America* (New York: Holt, Rinehart & Winston).

Schlegel, A. (1972) *Male Dominance and Female Autonomy: Domestic Authority in Matrilineal Societies* (New Haven: Human Relations Area Files).

Schneider, J. (1991) 'Spirits and the Spirit of Capitalism', in E.R. Wolf (ed.) *Religious Regimes and State-Formation: Perspectives from European Ethnology* (Albany, NY: State University of New York Press).

Schneider, J. and R. Rapp (eds) (1995) *Articulating Hidden Histories: Exploring the Influence of Eric R. Wolf* (Berkeley: University of California Press).

Schulze, R.O. (1958) 'The Role of Economic Dominants in Community Power Structure', *American Sociological Review* 23(1): 3–9.

Schumpeter, J.A. (1976[1943]) *Capitalism, Socialism and Democracy* (London: George Allen & Unwin).

Scoble, H.M. (1964) 'Book Review: Community Power and Political Theory', *Administrative Science Quarterly* 9(3): 313–15.

Scott, J. (ed.) (1994) *Power: Critical Concepts*, 3 vols (London: Routledge).

Scott, J. (1996) *Stratification and Power: Structures of Class, Status and Command* (Cambridge: Polity Press).

Scott, J. (1997) *Corporate Businesses and Capitalist Classes*, 3rd edn (Oxford: Oxford University Press).

Scott, J. (2001) *Power* (Cambridge: Polity).

Sedgwick, E.K. (1990) *Epistemology of the Closet* (Berkeley: University of California Press).

Seligman, A. (1992) *The Idea of Civil Society* (New York: Free Press).

Selka, S. (2010) 'Morality in the Religious Marketplace: Evangelical Christianity, Candomblé, and the Struggle for Moral Distinction in Brazil', *American Ethnologist* 37(2): 291–307.

Sewell, W.H. Jr (1992) 'A Theory of Structure: Duality, Agency and Transformation', *American Journal of Sociology* 98(1): 1–29.

Shapin, S. and S. Schaffer (1985) *Leviathan and the Air Pump* (Princeton: Princeton University Press).

Shapiro, M. (ed.) (1984) *Language and Politics* (New York: New York University Press).

Shusterman, R. (ed.) (1999a) *Bourdieu: A Critical Reader* (Oxford: Blackwell).

Shusterman, R. (1999b) 'Bourdieu and Anglo-American Philosophy', in R. Shusterman (ed.) *Bourdieu: A Critical Reader* (Oxford: Blackwell).

Silverblatt, I. (1980) '"The Universe has Turned Inside Out... There is No Justice for Us Here": Andean Women Under Spanish Rule', in M. Etienne and E. Leacock (eds) *Women and Colonization: Anthropological Perspectives* (New York: Praeger).

Silverblatt, I. (1987) *Moon, Sun, and Witches: Gender Ideologies and Class in Inca and Colonial Peru* (Princeton, NJ: Princeton University Press).

Simmel, G. (1964) *Conflict and the Web of Group-Affiliations*, K.H. Wolff and R. Bendix (trans) (New York: Free Press).

Skinner, Q. (2000) *Machiavelli: A Very Short Introduction* (Oxford: Oxford University Press).

Smart, B. (1982) 'Foucault, Sociology and the Problem of Human Agency', *Theory and Society* 11(2): 121–41.

Smith, D. (1987) *The Everyday World as Problematic: A Feminist Sociology* (Milton Keynes: Open University Press).

Smith, O. (1984) *The Politics of Language, 1791–1819* (Oxford: Clarendon Press).

Smooha, S. and T. Hanf (1992) 'The Diverse Modes of Conflict Resolution in Deeply Divided Societies', *International Journal of Comparative Sociology* 33(1/2): 2647.

Spencer, H. (1880[1862]) *First Principles* (New York: A.L. Burt).

Spivak, G.C. (1987) *Other Worlds: Essays in Cultural Politics* (London: Methuen).

Spivak, G.C. (1988) 'Can the Subaltern Speak?', in C. Nelson and L. Grossberg (eds) *Marxism and the Interpretation of Culture* (London: Macmillan).

Spivak, G.C. (1999) *A Critique of Postcolonial Reason: Towards a History of the Vanishing Present* (Cambridge, MA: Harvard University Press)

Springborg, P. (1975) 'Leviathan and the Problem of Ecclesiastical Authority', *Political Theory* 3(3): 289–303.

Stanley, L. and S. Wise (2000) 'But the Empress has No Clothes!: Some Awkward Questions about the "Missing Revolution" in Feminist Theory', *Feminist Theory* 1: 261–88.

Sturtevant, W.C. (1964) 'Studies in Ethnoscience', *American Anthropologist* 66(3): 99–131.

Swanson, G. (1960) *The Birth of the Gods: The Origin of Primitive Beliefs* (Ann Arbor: University of Michigan Press).

Swanson, G. (1967) *Religion and Regime: A Sociological Account of the Reformation* (Ann Arbor: University of Michigan Press).

Swedberg, R. (2005) *The Max Weber Dictionary: Key Words and Central Concepts* (Stanford, CA: Stanford University Press).

Tajfel, H. (ed.) (1978) *Differentiation Between Social Groups: Studies in the Social Psychology of Intergroup Relations* (London: Academic Press).

Tajfel, H. (ed.) (1982) *Social Identity and Intergroup Relations* (Cambridge: Cambridge University Press).

Taylor, C. (1986) 'Foucault on Freedom and Truth', in D. Hoy (ed.) *Foucualt: A Critical Reader* (Oxford: Blackwell).

Tilly, C. (ed.) (1975) *The Formation of National States in Western Europe* (Princeton: Princeton University Press).

Tomasello, M. (1999) 'The Human Adaptation for Culture', *Annual Review of Anthropology* 28: 509–29.

Tong, R. (1989) *Feminist Thought: A Comprehensive Introduction* (London: Routledge).

Toolan, M. (ed.) (2002) *Critical Discourse Analysis, Critical Concepts in Linguistics: Volume II, Leading Advocates* (London and New York: Routledge).

Trejo, G. (2009) 'Religious Competition and Ethnic Mobilization in Latin America: Why the Catholic Church Promotes Indigenous Movements in Mexico', *American Political Science Review* 103(3): 323–42.

Tuck, R. (1989) *Hobbes* (Oxford and New York: Oxford University Press).

Tucker, R.C. (ed.) (1978) *The Marx-Engels Reader*, 2nd edn (New York and London: W.W. Norton & Company).

United Nations (2010) *The World's Women 2010: Trends and Statistics*, prepared by the United Nations Statistics Division (New York: United Nations).

van Dijk, T. (1993) *Elite Discourse and Racism* (London: Sage).

Varisco, D.M. (2007) *Reading Orientalism: Said and the Unsaid* (Seattle: University of Washington Press).

Viroli, M. (1998) *Machiavelli* (Oxford: Oxford University Press).

Wajcman, J. (2000) 'Reflections of Gender and Technology Studies: In What State is the Art?' *Social Studies of Science* 30(3): 447–64.

Walby, S. (1990) *Theorizing Patriarchy* (Oxford: Basil Blackwell).

Wallerstein, I. (1974) *The Modern World-System: Capitalist Agriculture and the Origins of the European World-Economy in the Sixteenth Century* (New York: Academic Press).

Walker, J.L. (1966) 'A Critique of the Elitist Theory of Democracy', *American Political Science Review* 60(2): 285–95.

Wallace, A.F.C. (1956) 'Revitalization Movements', *American Anthropologist* 58: 264–81.

Walters, M. (2005) *Feminism: A Very Short Introduction* (Oxford: Oxford University Press).

Weber, M. (1927) *General Economic History* (London: Allen & Unwin).

Weber, M. (1958) *From Max Weber: Essays in Sociology*, H. Gerth and C.W. Mills (eds) (New York: Oxford University Press).

Weber, M. (1964) *The Sociology of Religion*, E. Fischoff (trans.) (Boston: Beacon Press).

Weber, M. (1978) *Economy and Society, Vols 1 & 2*, G. Roth and C. Wittich (eds) (Berkeley: University of California Press).

Weintraub, J. (1997) 'The Theory and Politics of the Public/Private Distinction', in J. Weintraub, and K. Kumar (eds) *Public and Private in Thought and Practice: Perspectives on a Grand Dichotomy* (Chicago: University of Chicago Press).

Weintraub, J. and K. Kumar (1997) *Public and Private in Thought and Practice: Perspectives on a Grand Dichotomy* (Chicago: University of Chicago Press).

Weiss, L. (2006) 'Infrastructural Power, Economic Transformation, and Globalzation', in J.A. Hall and R. Schroeder (eds) *An Anatomy of Power: The Social Theory of Michael Mann* (Cambridge: Cambridge University Press).

Wenke, R.J. and D.I. Olszewski (2007) *Patterns in Prehistory: Humankind's First Three Million Years*, 5th edn (New York and Oxford: Oxford University Press).

White, L.A. (1949) *The Science of Culture* (New York: Grove Press, Inc.).

White, L. Jr. (1967) 'The Historical Roots of our Ecological Crisis', *Science*, new series 155(3767): 1203–07.

White, M.K. (1978) *The Status of Women in Preindustrial Societies* (Princeton, NJ: Princeton University Press).

Wiesner-Hanks, M.E. (2011) *Gender in History: Global Perspectives*, 2nd edn (Oxford: Wiley-Blackwell).

Williams, R. (1958) *Culture and Society 1780–1950* (London: Chatto & Windus).

Williams, R. (1977) *Marxism and Literature* (Oxford and New York: Oxford University Press).

Williams, R. (1983) *Keywords: A Vocabulary of Culture and Society*, revised edn (New York: Oxford University Press).

Wodak, R. (1997) 'Critical Discourse Analysis and the Study of Doctor–Patient Interaction', in B.L. Gunnarsson, P. Linell and B. Nordberg (eds), *The Construction of Professional Discourses* (London: Longman).

Wodak, R., R. de Cillia, M. Reisigl and K. Liebhart (1999) *The Discursive Construction of National Identity*, A. Hirsch and R. Mitten (trans) (Edinburgh: Edinburgh University Press)

Wodak, R., B. Johnstone and P. Kerswill (eds) (2011) *The Sage Handbook of Sociolinguistics* (London: Sage).

Wodak, R. and B. Matouschek (1993) 'We Are Dealing with People Whose Origins One Can Clearly Tell Just by Looking: Critical Discourse Analysis and the Study of Neo-Racism in Contemporary Austria', *Discourse and Society* 4(2): 225–48.

Wolf, E.R. (1982) *Europe and the People Without History* (Berkeley: University of California Press).

Wolf, E.R. (ed.) (1991) *Religious Regimes and State-Formation: Perspectives from European Ethnology* (Albany, NY: State University of New York Press).

Wolf, E.R. (1999) *Envisioning Power: Ideologies of Dominance and Crisis* (Berkeley: University of California Press).

Wolf, E.R. (2001a) 'Ideas and Power', in *Pathways of Power: Building and Anthropology of the Modern World* (Berkeley: University of California Press).

Wolf, E.R. (2001b) 'Facing Power—Old Insights, New Questions', in *Pathways of Power: Building and Anthropology of the Modern World* (Berkeley: University of California Press).

Wolf, E.R. (2001c) 'The Mills of Inequality: A Marxian Approach', in *Pathways of Power: Building and Anthropology of the Modern World* (Berkeley: University of California Press).

Wolf, N. (1991) *The Beauty Myth* (New York: Doubleday).

Wrong, D. (1956) 'Power in America', *Commentary* 22: 272–80.

Wrong, D. (1961) 'The Oversocialized Conception of Man in Modern Sociology', *American Sociological Review* 26: 183–93.

Wrong, D. (1968) 'Identity: Problem and Catchword', *Dissent* 15: 427–35.

Wrong, D. (1996) 'Discourses of Power: From Hobbes to Foucault' [book review], *American Journal of Sociology* 102(3): 869–72.

Wrong, D. (2002) *Power: Its Forms, Bases and Uses*, 3rd edn (London: Transaction).

Wuthnow, R. (1987). *Meaning and Moral Order: Explorations in Cultural Analysis* (Berkeley: University of California Press).

Young, I. (1981) 'Beyond the Unhappy Marriage: A Critique of Dual Systems Theory', in L. Sargent (ed.) *Women and Revolution: The Unhappy Marriage of Marxism and Feminism* (London: Pluto Press).

Žižek, S. (1989) *The Sublime Object of Ideology* (London: Verso).

# Index

Page numbers in *italic* refer to definitions in the Glossary.

Aalborg (Denmark)   95–6
Achebe, Chinua   190
actor-network theory (ANT)   39 (fig.),
    86, 92–5, 103, 105, 187, *218*
Adams, Robert N.   39 (fig.), 107, 108,
    112–13, 114, 121, 211
administration   68, 90, 110, 139, 157,
    181, 182, 214
affluence   12, 116
African-Americans   24, 193, 196–7, 205
agency   9–13, 16, 20, 43, 45, 79–81, 86,
    90, 93, 95, 100, 111, 131, 171, 194,
    201, 206, 211–12, *218*
Agraria   114, 117, 173
agrarian societies/states   30, 33–4, 110,
    114, 115, 116, 118, 119, 122, 130,
    156, 161–2, 174, 177, 178, 216
Agta   175
alienation   49, 51, 54, 64, 70
Althusser, Louis   85–6, 87
America   *see* United States
American Revolution   24
Anderson, Benedict   15
animism   161–2, 171,
'anticipatory influence'   74
Arendt, Hannah   166–7
Asad, Talal   163–4
Austin, J.L.   97
authority   1, 6, 8, 9, 18, 22–35, 41,
    45–8, 52–7, 60, 76–8, 79, 84, 97,
    98, 100, 102, 103–5, 110, 111,
    117, 118, 122–5, 131, 133, 136–7,
    139, 141–4, 146–8, 153, 154, 157,
    159–61, 165, 167, 170–1, 175, 181,
    182, 187, 190, 192, 210, 213–16,
    *218, 221, 224*
Aztecs   124

Bachrach, Peter   39 (fig.), 74, 78
Bacon, Francis   46, 83–84
banking and credit crisis   25, 168
banks/banking   25, 42, 50, 66, 68, 116,
    137–9, 168, 204–5
Baratz, Morton S.   39 (fig.), 74, 78

Barnes, Barry   27, 32, 39 (fig.), 86–7, 92,
    94, 103
Barth, Karl   165
Bax, Mart   159–61
Beauvoir, Simone de   186
behaviorists   71, 80
Bellah, Robert   165
Bendix, Reinhard   34–5, 64
'benign control'   201
bio-power   89–90
Bourdieu, Pierre   19, 20–1, 28, 32, 33,
    37, 39 (fig.), 81, 84, 97–100, 102,
    103, 104, 108, 131, 198, 210
Britain/UK   15, 24, 25, 48, 49, 57, 61,
    138, 145, 152, 168, 183, 184, 185,
    186, 193, 194, 196
Buddhism   118
Bultmann, Rudolf   165
bureaucracy   13, 56, 61, 70, 77, 91, 115,
    119, 120, 136, 177
Butler, Judith   199

Callon, Michel   39 (fig.), 93–4
capitalism   41, 42, 48–52, 64, 67, 70, 86,
    118–20, 122, 123, 128, 129, 135,
    137–9, 140, 148, 161–2, 169, 173,
    184, 186, 188, 189, 196, 202, 212,
    *218, 225*
'capstone state'   119
castas   206
Catholic Church   115, 160, 192, 206
Catholicism   204
censuses   181, 202
charisma   29–30, 55–6, 61, 64, 160, 165
chiefdoms   123, 175
China   6, 120, 123, 180
Christianity   67, 118–20, 160, 161,
    163–5, 182, *224*
city-state   41–5, 137, 175, 212
civil rights movement   24, 76, 145, 185,
    193
civil society   32, 47, 61–2, 81, 120, 133,
    135, 139–42, 145, 150, 151, 159,
    212, 214, *218–19, 222, 224*

class   9, 11, 12, 20, 24, 33, 34, 48,
    49–51, 52, 54, 55–6, 57, 59, 60, 61,
    62, 64, 69, 70, 72, 73, 76, 80, 84,
    85, 97–100, 101, 104, 107, 109,
    110, 116, 122, 125, 128, 130, 146,
    150, 157, 158, 163, 174, 182, 184,
    185, 186, 188, 193, 194, 202, 203,
    217, *219*, *225*
coercion   23, 26, 27, 78, 114, 116–17,
    122, 125, 146, 147, 176
cognition (social)   33, 114, 117, 131,
    150
colonialism   129, 173, 181, 182, 196,
    197, *223*
commands   23, 27–9, 31, 55, 71, 86,
    125, 127, 128, 131, 139, 180, 181,
    217, *218*
common sense   x, 10, 11, 20, 28, 45, 98,
    136, 142, 155, 209, 212
communitarianism   140
community power studies   39 (fig.),
    68–70, 81
competition   6, 8, 31, 51, 56, 58, 64,
    69, 75, 99, 108, 111, 112, 116,
    120, 123, 129, 133, 135, 137, 138,
    147–50, 151, 158, 159, 178, 214,
    222, *225*
Confucianism   118, 119
Connolly, William   169
conservative   6–7, 16, 41, 57, 61, 76, 80,
    82, 102, 192, 203
constitutional state   41, 42, 128, 130,
    181
corporations   11, 76, 81, 94, 126, 137–9,
    143, 168, 179, 195, *223*
'creative intellectuals'   125–6
critical discourse analysis (CDA)   101
criticism   170, 187
Croce, Benedetto   62
culture   x, 15–16, 62, 63, 89, 91, 98,
    100–3, 107, 109, 119, 122, 123,
    149, 155, 165, 177–8, 197, *219*,
    *220*, *221*, *222*, *224*, *225*
cultural studies   102–3, 197, *219*

Dahl, Robert   39 (fig.), 71–6, 78–82, 91,
    121, 210, 213
Darwin, Charles   108
deconstruction   198
democracy   32, 42, 57–60, 63, 67, 70–6,
    82, 95, 110, 117, 120, 126, 135,
    148, 194, 120, 213, *221*
demos   7, 181, 213
Derrida, Jaques   198

deviance   195
Dewey, John   141
dirty hands, problem of   44, 168
discipline   28–9, 31, 43, 87, 89, 163,
    186, 205, 206–7
discourse   18, 30, 37, 41, 47, 58, 70, 84,
    88–91, 101–2, 103, 104, 117, 163,
    164, 168, 185, 186, 191, 194, 197,
    199, 214, *219–20*, *221*
division of labour   9, 34, 52–3, 77, 110,
    116, 157, 171, 175, *220*, *225*
Domhoff, G. William   70, 74–5, 82
domination   1, 6, 18–22, 23, 24, 25, 27,
    28–31, 32, 35, 43, 53, 55–6, 62, 67,
    77, 79, 87, 97–8, 103–4, 118, 125,
    128, 131, 133, 135–6, 140, 142,
    144–7, 158, 163, 164, 169–71, 186,
    190, 193, 195, 197–8, 205, 207,
    *220*, *225*
    cryptic   21–2, 25, 27–9, 32, 35, 100,
        187, 210, 216
    male   145, 172–3, 176, 178, 180, 184,
        189, *223*
Douglas, Mary   104
doxa   20, 22
Du Bois, W.E.B.   196–7
Durkheim, Emile   38, 39 (fig.), 41, 51–4,
    57, 64, 77, 82, 100, 116, 153–4,
    156, 159, 165, 212, 213

economy   12, 20, 25, 26, 49, 52, 53,
    57, 66, 76, 111, 112, 115, 119,
    126, 133, 135–42, 144–51, 158,
    173, 174, 213, 214, *219*, *220*,
    222
Egypt   177, 206
Eisenhower, Dwight D.   67
elites   15, 37, 41, 57–61, 63–4, 67–76,
    81, 84, 99, 109–12, 119, 120, 122,
    125, 131, 145, 146, 148, 150, 153,
    181–3, 194, 202–3, 205, 213, *220*
    circulation of   59, 75
Elliot, Anthony   201
energy   3, 4–6, 52, 94, 107–9, 112–13,
    118, 122, 167, 211
Enlightenment, The   34, 63, 214, 215
epistemes   84, 88, 91, 103, 117
epistemology/epistemological   37–8,
    39 (fig.), 81, 83–105, 106–7, 151,
    187–8, 191, 196, 198, 207, 214–15,
    *220*
Equal Rights Amendment   186
equality   24, 184,
Erikson, Erik H.   191–3, 201

ethics of the self   90
ethnicity   7, 158, 188, 193, 197, 202,
   204, 222, *225*
Europe   6, 34, 41–65, 66, 67, 88,
   114–15, 118–20, 122–4, 128–9,
   137–9, 144, 146, 148, 152, 158,
   161–2, 179, 202
European Union   32, 112
evolution   52, 63, 77, 106–31, 146, 147,
   150, 212, *225*
   biological versus social   107–8
   human   7, 107, 154
existentialism   88, 164


Fanon, Frantz   196–7
feminism   172, 184, 185–9
feudalism   42, 115, 122–3
Feurerbach, Ludwig   51, 54
First World War   7, 56, 66, 124,
Flyvbjerg, Bent   39 (fig.), 95–6, 103
football (soccer)   149, 204
foraging societies   109–10, 114, 122,
   161, 173, 175, 176, 179
*fortuna*   45
Foucault, Michel   5, 19, 20, 21, 28,
   32, 22, 39 (fig.), 81, 83–4, 87–92,
   94, 95, 96, 97, 101, 102, 103–5,
   117–18, 121, 131, 151, 163, 187,
   195, 197, 195, 210, 212
France   xi, 19, 24, 42, 46, 52, 58, 93,
   100, 185
Franciscan Fathers   160–1
Freud, Anna   191
Freud, Sigmund   153
Fried, Morton   130
Friedan, Betty   186


Geertz, Clifford   154–5, 163–5
Gellner, Ernest   33–4, 39 (fig.), 106–7,
   114–18, 120, 131, 150, 173, 211,
   213, 215
gender   xi, 9, 20, 102, 133, 143, 172–89,
   193, 194, 199, 201, 204
   nature/culture dichotomy and   177–8
   sex versus   172
'Ghost Dance'   162–3
Giddens, Anthony   10, 78, 130–1
Gilroy, Paul   197
Gouges, Olympe de   185
governmentality   89–90, 151, 210
Gramsci, Antonio   39 (fig.), 41, 61–3, 64,
   84, 140, 194, 197, 213
Greer, Germaine   186

'growth coalition'   69
Guha, Ranjit   194
Guthrie, Stewart   153–5


Habermas, Jürgen   96, 141,
habitus   20, 84, 98–100, 103, 104
Hall, John A.   39 (fig.), 107, 114, 118–20
Hall, Stuart   197
Hanisch, Carol   187
Hegel, G.W.F.   49, 51, 140, 164, 199
hegemony   61–3, 81, 84, *220*
Heidegger, Martin   164
hermeneutics   165, *221*
*Herrschaft*   28–30, 55, 77, 125
Hinduism   118–20
Hirschman, Albert O.   145–6
Hobbes, Thomas   33, 39 (fig.), 41, 45–8,
   54, 55, 58, 64, 109, 210, 212, 213,
   *224*
hooks, bell   188
horticultural society   110, 11, 161,
   173–7
Horton, Robin   154
humanism   41, 45, 88
Hume, David   4, 14, 34, 117, 153, 215
Hunter, Floyd   39 (fig.), 68–9, 71, 72


identity   xi, 19, 55, 101, 104, 112,
   188–9, 190–208, 216, *221*
   categorization and   195, 202–4
   ecological model of   200–7
   organization and   204–5
   selves and   200–1
   social psychology and   191–3
identity politics   193–6, 202, 205
ideology   19, 60, 62, 77, 78, 81, 84–6,
   100, 107, 124, 129, 131, 150–1,
   152, 161–2, 202, *220, 221*
IEMP model   127–8
IMF (International Monetary Fund)   146
Inca Empire   181–3, 185
Industria   114, 117, 173
industrial society   53, 110, 112, 117, 154
inequality   110, 173, 177, 189, 193, 204,
   216–17
institutions   ix, 8, 11, 20, 24, 32, 34–5,
   55, 56, 64, 76, 77, 80, 87, 89, 99,
   100, 108, 110–15, 119–20, 125,
   128, 131, 133, 135, 137, 139,
   141–2, 145, 147, 148, 150, 151,
   152–3, 159–60, 163, 170–1, 184,
   187, 207, 214, *218, 219, 220, 221,*
   *225*

intention 9–12, 16, 20, 38, 87, 89, 92–3, 107–8, 154, 156, 168, 171, 210, 211
intersectionality 189, 203
Inuit 174
'iron law of oligarchy', 60, 112
Iroquois Nations 174
is/ought 34, 56, 61, 64, 155, 168, 209, 213, 215–17
Islam 118–20, 161, 206–7
Italy 42, 57–63, 137, 194

Jenkins, Richard 99, 195, 200
Jouvenel, Bertrand de 8

Kierkegaard, Soren 164
kinship 11, 122, 140, 150, 175, 183, 202, 204, 218
!Kung San 174
Kwakiutl 123–4

Labour Party 203, 205
Lacan, Jaques 198–9
Lakoff, George 102
language x, 10, 15–16, 80, 88, 92, 98, 100–2, 107, 126, 142, 143, 144, 148, 165, 187, 198–200, 206, 209, 210, 222
Latour, Bruno 5, 39 (fig.), 94, 209
Layder, Derek 12–13, 201
Lenski, Gerhard 39 (fig.), 108, 109–11, 112, 114, 173,
liberalism 57, 58, 61, 67, 77, 90–1, 118, 120, 135, 140, 166, 186, 221, 222
liberal society xi, 18, 120, 135–51, 159, 186, 187, 210, 212, 216, 221, 224, 225
legitimacy 1, 15, 18, 22–32, 35, 43, 47, 55, 56, 94, 100, 104–5, 110, 125–6, 131, 133, 135–7, 139, 141, 142, 143, 147, 148, 170, 187, 210, 214, 221, 222
legitimate 9, 22–3, 26, 28–31, 33, 44, 48, 60, 76, 78, 98, 133, 149, 157, 183, 218
legitimation 15, 23, 26, 31, 41, 115, 119, 125, 139, 143, 147–50, 173
*Leviathan* 46–8, 88, 210, 214
Lotka's Principle 113
Lukes, Steven 10, 19, 21, 28, 32, 39 (fig.), 68, 78–81, 82, 91, 121, 169–70, 210,
Luther, Martin 192

Machiavelli, Niccolo 33, 37, 39 (fig.), 41, 42–5, 48, 58, 60, 61–2, 64, 90, 96, 212, 213
*Macht* 28, 55, 125
Mahmood, Saba 206–7
'male breadwinner' 183
Malinowski, Bronislaw 153
Mann, Michael 37, 39 (fig.), 107, 114, 126–30, 150, 151, 211
Mannheim, Karl 85
market exchange 111–12, 127 (tab.)
Marx, Karl 38, 39 (fig.), 41, 49–51, 52, 53, 54, 57, 59, 64, 70, 84, 95, 99, 106, 121–3, 126, 130, 137, 153, 193, 211, 212, 213
Marxism 32–3, 37, 61, 63, 70, 80, 85, 87, 97, 102, 118, 121, 123–4, 166, 185, 186, 188, 193, 194, 199, 211, 225
masculinity 29, 173
matriarchal societies 173
Mbuti pygmies 173, 175
meaning 15, 16, 46, 88, 98, 101, 113, 128, 129, 131, 153, 155, 163–6, 200, 214, 219
Medici 42–3, 125, 137
Medjugorje apparition 160–1
megaprojects 95–6
'memorable alliance' 137, 148, 150
mercantilism 122, 137, 222
metaphor 5, 8, 15, 101–2, 148, 198, 199, 209–11, 224
methods/methodology 13, 33, 43, 46, 69, 71, 75, 83, 84, 89, 92–5, 97, 101, 103, 106, 121, 154, 198, 199, 221, 222
Michels, Robert 60–1, 63, 112
micro and macro 12, 32, 131, 133, 149, 187, 201
military–industrial complex 67
militias 42–3
Mills, C. Wright 39 (fig.), 69–71, 72, 76–8, 82, 84, 85, 187, 213
mirror stage 198
mode of production 49–50, 122–3
modernity/modernization 17, 32–5, 37, 41, 42, 48–57, 64, 77, 117, 124, 128, 148, 152–3, 189, 213, 222
morality xi, 34, 43, 52–3, 83, 102, 152–3, 163–4, 166–70, 214, 215–16
Morriss, Peter 10, 14–15, 73, 80, 169–70, 212

Mosca, Gaetano 39 (fig.), 41, 59–61, 63, 64, 70, 109
mosque movement 206–7

nation-building 64, 194
nation-state 5, 45, 57, 65, 70, 115, 116, 124, 129, 135, 151, 222
National Association for the Advancement of Colored People (NAACP) 204
National Organization of Women (NOW) 186, 204
nationalism 101, 160
natural law 143, 222
naturalism ix, x, 222
Navajo 174
New Haven 71–2, 74
Niebuhr, Reinhold 165, 166
Nigeria 177, 190
nominalism ix, x–xi, 211, 222

objectivism 97, 223
Ollman, Bertell 51
'operating units' 112–13, 121
'organic state' 120
organization (social) 7, 13, 16, 23, 26, 50, 55–6, 57, 60, 64, 71, 77, 82, 86, 103, 107, 109, 111–13, 114, 119, 122, 127–30, 138, 142, 149, 151, 156, 158–9, 170, 175, 181, 186, 191, 194, 200, 204–5, 207, 212, 218, 220, 222, 223
'organizational materialism' 118
Ortner, Sherry B. 177–8

Papagoes 174
Parsons, Talcott 8, 10, 26–7, 32, 39 (fig.), 68, 76–8, 79, 82, 86, 91, 165
Pareto, Vilfredo 39 (fig.), 41, 58–60, 63, 64, 75, 109
pastoral societies 119, 120, 173–4
Pateman, Carol 183–4
patriarchy xi, 133, 172–89, 193, 198, 223
patronage 42, 125, 160, 214, 223
peasants 34, 48, 50, 57, 61, 62, 115, 120, 160, 161, 171, 182, 194, 219
'personal is political, the' 187
personhood xi, 27, 133, 189, 191–208
phenomenology/phenomenological 88, 95, 167, 223
philosophic history 106, 114
pluralists 71–6, 79, 80, 210

Poggi, Gianfranco 39 (fig.), 107, 124–6, 128, 130, 150, 159, 160, 211
Polanyi, Karl 111
'political formula' 60, 84
political parties 7, 11, 32, 51, 55–6, 64, 108, 125, 141, 205
Polsby, Nelson 39 (fig.), 72, 74, 78, 80
postcolonialism 197–8, 223, 225
power
    actual versus potential 1, 4, 13–15, 78, 82, 91, 171, 212
    asymmetrical versus symmetrical (balanced, countervailing) 1, 4, 7–9, 13, 16, 70, 82, 116, 125, 129, 131, 137, 147, 171, 195, 211, 216–17
    definitions of 3, 10, 13, 16, 26, 28, 54–5, 73, 79, 81, 86, 88, 126–7, 167, 209–11, 223
    dispositional concept 14–16, 73, 75, 212
    epistemological approaches 37, 38, 83–105, 106–7, 187, 191, 196, 214–15
    evolutionary approaches 37, 84, 103, 106–31, 148, 151, 187, 191, 211, 214
    exercise fallacy 14
    forms of 100, 124–5, 130, 159, 170
    Javanese concept 15
    narratives of 212–15
    physical 1, 4–6, 13, 16, 27, 49, 108, 112–13, 114, 116, 167, 171, 176, 180, 211
    'power over' 1, 6–7, 14–15, 17, 20, 47, 51, 76–7, 79, 82, 86, 109, 113, 114, 118, 121, 125, 127, 140, 151, 168, 171, 206–7, 212–13, 214, 216
    'power to' 1, 4, 6–7, 8, 10, 12, 13–14, 16–17, 20, 47, 51, 76, 82, 86, 109, 114, 118, 121, 127, 140, 151, 168, 171, 206–7, 212–13, 214, 216
    responsibility, and 12, 35, 168–70
    social (versus physical) 4–6
    sources of 96, 126–9, 152, 170, 178
    symbolic 20, 98
    three dimensions (Lukes) 21, 121, 78–9, 210–11
    vehicle fallacy 14
    zero-sum conception 8, 76, 110, 147
'power-stand-off' 120
*Prince, The* 44, 62, 63, 90

Protestant ethic thesis 115
Protestantism 119, 158, 204
Prussia 49
public, the 25, 70, 79, 84, 141, 143,
public sphere 141, 145, 178
public/private dichotomy 133, 135,
       142–7, 150, 214, 222, 224, 225
    civil society and 145–6
    gender and 178–85, 189
    history of distinction 143–4
    households and 144–5
    individuals and 144
    state and 146

Quebec 24, 206
'quiet revolution' 206

race 188, 193, 196–7, 202, 204, 220,
       225
racism 24, 101
radical(ism) 6–7, 17, 49, 57, 69, 76–7,
       78–9, 81, 82, 91, 106, 169, 186,
       188
realism ix–x, 224
*realrationalität* 95–6
reciprocity 111, 161–2
redistribution 111, 116, 123–4
Reformation 41, 45, 62, 115, 158,
       161–2, 224
religion xi, 7, 20, 34, 45, 47–8, 51, 54,
       64, 119–20, 129, 133, 143, 144,
       152–71, 184, 185, 188, 193, 203,
       213, 214, 220, 222
    definition of 152
    economies of 158–9
    meaning, and 163–6
    medium of power struggles 159–63
    reflection of power structures 156–9
    salvationism 161–2
    secularization 152–3
    theories of 153–6
Renaissance 41, 45, 62, 88, 224
Republicanism 41–3, 52, 96, 224
reputational method, 69, 75
Reuter, Christoph 207
revitalization movements 124, 163
'rise of the west' 118, 120
*Risorgimento* 57, 194
Roman Empire 42, 120,
Rosinski, Herbert 19
ruling class 59–60, 122, 182
Russell, Bertrand 3, 10

Said, Edward 197–9
St Brieuc Bay (France) 93–4
Sanday, Peggy Reeves 178
Savonarola 45
Sayer, Andrew 215–16
Schneider, Jane 161–2
science 45, 58, 60, 83, 85, 86, 92, 95,
       104, 113, 148, 153, 154, 155,
       164–5, 166, 171, 179, 216, 218,
       222
Scotland 25, 46, 203, 204–5
Scottish devolution 25
second law of thermodynamics 113
Second World War 37, 66, 69, 121, 160
secularism 163–4
self-categorization theory 192
Semang 174
sexuality 87, 89, 145, 184, 188, 193,
       195, 204
Silverblatt, Irene 181–3
Smith, Adam 215, 220
Smith, Olivia 15
social change 3, 19, 24–5, 34, 41, 58,
       78, 105, 111, 116, 117, 131, 184,
       187
social contract 47, 143, 222, 224
social control 21
social evolution 52, 77, 106–31, 225
social labour 49–51, 52, 57, 121–2
social order 6, 19, 29, 33, 34, 43, 50,
       77–8, 80, 85, 86, 100, 105, 116,
       117, 128, 142, 150, 165, 213
social science ix–xi, 3, 23, 96, 130, 133,
       152–3, 164–5, 209, 213, 215, 222,
       223, 225
social structure 1, 9, 11–3, 34, 80, 82,
       85, 95, 97, 156–9, 160, 171, 189,
       193, 205, 225
society (general conceptions of) 10, 11,
       21–2, 32, 35, 52–3, 76–7, 90, 94,
       117, 127
sovereignty 9, 46, 88–9, 92, 143–5, 147,
       180
Soviet Union 67, 120
Sparta 175
Spencer, Herbert 108
Spivak, Gayatri Chakravorty 197–8, 199
standpoint theory 187–9, 198
state, the 9, 33, 45, 48, 51, 53, 57, 62,
       64, 72, 112, 124–5, 128, 129, 150,
       185, 218, 222, 224
    civil society and 140–2
    economy and 135–9

gender and 174–5, 177, 180–1, 183–5
public/private dichotomy and 143–7
religion and 159–60
state of nature 47–8
Stein, Getrude 16
stratification (social) 55, 72, 109, 112, 115, 157, 173, 175, 185, 202, 204, 219
subaltern 194, 198, 225
Subaltern Studies Group 194, 197
subject, the 20, 85, 87–91, 98
subjectivism 88–9, 97, 225
suicide bombing 207
surplus 50, 110–12, 114, 116, 123
Swanson, Guy 156–60

Tajfel, Henri 192–3
taxonomies 202–3, 221
Tea Party movement 70–1, 76
technology 92, 104, 108, 110, 112, 127, 175
Third Reich (Germany) 124
Tillich, Paul 165
Tomasello, Michael 107, 154
truth 20, 22, 62, 83, 91, 117–18, 128, 195, 216
Tswana 174
Tylor, Edward B. 154

United States (of America) 24–5, 37, 61, 63, 66–82, 102, 109, 120, 138, 145, 152, 158, 162–3, 168, 179, 183, 185–6, 188, 193, 196, 197, 204, 205, 213
utility (of concepts) x, 1, 12, 21, 91–2, 105, 117, 131, 164, 206, 209–11

violence 50, 94, 109, 125, 126, 128, 129, 146, 166–8
against women 176, 179–80, 184, 201
symbolic/epistemic 98–100, 104, 198
Viroli, Maurizio 43
*virtù* 45

Walby, Sylvia 184, 186
Walker, Jack L. 75–6
Wallace, Anthony 163
Weber, Max 18, 28–30, 31, 34, 38, 39 (fig.), 41, 54–7, 60, 64, 70, 77, 91, 106, 115, 130, 131, 137, 119, 125, 139, 165, 211, 212, 213
welfare state 146, 183,
White, Leslie 109, 112
Williams, Raymond 102
witchcraft (demonization of) 161–2, 182
Wittgenstein, Ludwig 97
Wolf, Eric R. ix, 39 (fig.), 107, 121–4, 125, 128, 130, 151, 211
Wolf, Naomi 186
Wollstonecraft, Mary 185
world system 121, 225
Wounded Knee massacre 162
Wrong, Dennis R. 7, 10, 16, 27–8, 29, 70, 74, 191

Yanamamo 174
Yoruba 177

Zeno's paradox 200
Žižek, Slavoj 199